THE
TROJANS

A Story of Southern California Football

Contents

Foreword
Shades Of Cardinal And Gold

1. Wild Mustard, Cockleburrs, And Football 13
2. A Team Is Born 17
3. Death And Reincarnation 22
4. Fight On For Old S. C. 26
5. A Swan Emerges 31
6. Hold That Tiger 40
7. On To Pomona 50
8. Rugby, Anyone? 57
9. The Last Of The Chariots 65
10. Time Out: "Gloomy Gus" Henderson 78
11. Time Out: Leo Calland 85
12. Bury My Wounded Pride At Berkeley 89
13. A Rose Bowl And Thorns 100
14. Time Out: Chet Dolley 108
15. The Trojans Go To War 113
16. Time Out: Howard Jones 122
17. Time Out: Morley Drury 133
18. The Sound Of Thunder 139
19. That Championship Season 150

20.	Time Out: Nate Barragar	159
21.	Time Out: John Wayne	166
22.	Ernie And The Boys	175
23.	The Game	187
24.	Hail The Conquering Heroes	196
25.	Time Out: Ernie Smith	208
26.	The Whispering Herd	216
27.	Decline And Fall	225
28.	Time Out: Nick Pappas	235
29.	Frank Merriwell Arrives	243
30.	A $120,000 Kiss For Your Sister	254
31.	War And Pieces	263
32.	Time Out: Jeff Cravath	271
33.	A Bunch Of Roses	279
34.	Time Out: John Ferraro	289
35.	Thrown To The Wolverines	294
36.	Earthquakes	303
37.	Time Out: Jess Hill	309
38.	California, Here We Come	321
39.	Time Out: Jim Sears	326
40.	Daring Young Men	331
41.	Time Out: Jon Arnett	339
42.	Time Out: C. R. Roberts	348
43.	Scandal	354
44.	Time Out: Don Clark	360
45.	Byrd's Last Game	366
46.	The McKeever Incident	370
47.	Time Out: John McKay	374
48.	Hooray For Hollywood	387
49.	The Old 84-Z	396
50.	Time Out: Mike Garrett	402
51.	Where Have You Gone, Mike Garrett?	411
52.	Time Out: O. J. Simpson	416
53.	The Tunnel Of Love	427
54.	More Important Than Life Or Death	437
55.	The Simpson Bowls	445
56.	Goodbye O. J., Hello J. J.	454
57.	Going Home	466
58.	1973 A. D.	480
	Appendix	491

To My Mother And Father,
With Deep Love And Admiration

Copyright 1974
By Ken Rappoport
All Rights In This Book
Reserved Including The Right
To Reproduce This Book Or Parts
Thereof In Any Form — Printed In U.S.A.
Library Of Congress Catalog Number 74-81346
Standard Book Number 87397-033-0

THE
TROJANS

A Story of Southern California Football

by
Ken Rappoport

THE STRODE PUBLISHERS
HUNTSVILLE, ALABAMA 35802

Foreword

Not even Notre Dame, nor Yale, nor Harvard, nor Princeton, among other collegiate football giants, have enjoyed a more glorious past than have the Trojans of the University of Southern California.

With a meager beginning in 1888, and for many years thereafter, the Trojans rose to high stature during the Elmer "Gloomy Gus" Henderson coaching era, in the early twenties. For their might upon the gridiron they were paraphrased as the "Thundering Herd."

Then came the never to be forgotten sixteen-year Howard Jones coaching regime, sprinkled plentifully with intersectional and Rose Bowl victories, National Championships, and all-Americans.

Troy, the bailiwick of Trojan football in Los Angeles, continued to celebrate eventful seasons in following years under the leadership of coaches Sam Barry, Jeff Cravath, Jess Hill, and Don Clark. There were more Rose Bowl victories, and all-Americans.

John McKay took over the Trojan reins in 1960 and has prospered with exceptional success. With the mounting honors came Heisman Trophy winners.

Along the line, however, as is the way with collegiate football, Southern California has endured some lean years. Perhaps these may have been the most dramatic Trojan seasons.

In any event, Ken Rappoport, a very able, veteran journalist, already a talented author, has wrapped the Southern

California football story into one exciting volume—it could have been twenty. As it is, it is packed with a myriad of narratives which unfold the Trojans' triumphs, glories, and, as well, disappointments and heartaches. It is geared for fast reading, comparable to watching a movie thriller.

Rappoport, although one with Eastern environment, has been unequivocally enraptured by the spirit of Troy, "Fight On!," alas. If one did not know otherwise, one would suspect that Ken has Cardinal and Gold flowing through his veins.

A graduate of Rider College, in Trenton, New Jersey, Ken Rappoport began his journalistic career in 1960. He owns eleven-year credentials with the Associated Press, with service in Philadelphia and now New York City. In recent years his coverage has been varied, but chiefly so on football, baseball, and basketball.

One of Ken's early assignments for the Doylestown, Pennsylvania, *Intelligencer* was that of authoring a newspaper supplement on the Civil War which tempered him properly for recording, in flourishing manner, the spirited USC-UCLA gridiron duels, of Civil War kind, which is one of the features of *The Trojans*.

Other features, of course, dwell heavily upon the traditional USC-Notre Dame engagements, and Rose Bowl skirmishes, and, not to forget, special references to Morley Drury, Ernie Pinckert, Doyle Nave, Mike Garrett, O. J. Simpson, and their immortal likes.

For Pennsylvania State, Ken authored *The Nittany Lions*, published in 1973.

The Trojans, as Rappoport has blended his writings with intersectional flavor, should capture the fancy of collegiate football followers all over the nation. Additionally so because of the fact that Southern California has claimed as many as five national championship crowns, all adeptly reviewed. This, alone, brings *The Trojans* into national perspective.

W. R. Bill Schroeder,
Managing Director
Citizens Savings Athletic
Foundation

Shades Of Cardinal And Gold

A rich panoply unfolded on the field of the Los Angeles Coliseum.

It was the Battle of Los Angeles, the War of the Roses, and the Holy Grail of college football all socked into one game.

UCLA was winning the big one 20-14 before an audience larger than most American cities. The noise was stupefying, but players do not hear crowds at such peak moments.

Into this colorful setting stepped O. J. Simpson, the cardinal and gold blur of Southern Cal. Quarterback Toby Page called O. J.'s play at the line after a change of plans: "Twenty-three blast."

As Simpson lined up deep behind the line of scrimmage, Page set the "twenty-three blast" in motion. The best college halfback in football went between guard and tackle on the left side and somebody threw a heck of a block.

"He's free," voices screamed on the Trojan sidelines.

Simpson flashed down the left side of the field, picked up a phalanx of bodyguards, and made a 90-degree cut to the center. Everyone of the 90,780 people in the place knew where he was going—the Promised Land.

In one stunning burst, the most famous long run in college football during the season of 1967, Simpson carried the ball 64 yards over the UCLA goal line.

It gave Southern Cal a Hollywood-like 21-20 victory, the Pacific-8 title, a berth in the Rose Bowl, and eventually, the country's mythical football championship.

Southern Cal historians put that one right up there with the most dramatic of Trojan victories.

There have been other such theatrical productions at Southern Cal. Ever since football began, it seems, never has a school won more important games by fewer points. Close ones are a Trojan trademark.

A series of Great Escapes punctuate the length and breadth of Southern Cal's gold-plated football history.

The greatest of these, perhaps, the one that they still talk about, happened 43 years ago at Notre Dame. A Johnny Baker field goal in the last minute gave Southern Cal a tingling 16-14 victory over the Fighting Irish, one of the headiest moments in Trojan folklore.

The Game has been replayed in bars and kitchens over the years and honored so that even John McKay grows weary of it. The present coach points out, and perhaps rightly so, that HIS teams have produced moments as golden. John will tell you that the aforementioned victory over UCLA was not too bad. And what about Rod Sherman's touchdown catch in the last two minutes that beat Notre Dame 20-17 in 1964? Or Ron Ayala's 17-yard field goal in the last second to give the Trojans a 26-24 victory over Stanford in 1969?

Of course McKay is liable to get some disagreements from other people of other eras. You could argue that the 1951 California game was exciting. Remember, Leon Sellers won it 21-14 for Southern Cal with a whirling dive over the goal line in the final second.

And what about that 1944 game with the San Diego Navy team, when Jim Hardy's daring passes secured a 28-21 thriller in the last five minutes?

A student of the 1930s would also have a strong case, if McKay cared for a debate. Not only could he use as ammunition the famous Notre Dame game of 1931, but the contests with California and Duke as well. In 1933, when McKay was just a youngster, Cotton Warburton ripped off a 59-yard touchdown run in the fourth period to beat Cal 6-3. In the January 2, 1939, Rose Bowl, when McKay was in his formative school years, Doyle Nave came off the bench in the last two minutes to throw a touchdown pass that defeated Duke 7-3.

Such Hollywood endings are believable if it is Southern Cal. Any school that boasts magical names such as John Wayne and O. J. Simpson, sits in the lap of the movie capitol, and has regurgitated as many pro players as anyone in our cosmos, has to be believed.

It is not entirely true that the Trojans will ALWAYS win the close ones. But when they do, which is a lot of the time, the reason is eloquently simple. Explains Steve Sogge, quarterback on the national championship team of 1967:

"Southern Cal players have always been taught tough discipline. That—and the heritage—usually carries them through in close games. I know we always felt that we were going to win, no matter the circumstances. It was a psychological factor that we had over the other guys. We were a great team under pressure. McKay instilled some pressure in practices, so that when you got into a game, you could handle it."

From humble beginnings in 1880, when Methodists founded the college that "had outrun the railway and established itself before the connecting link was made between the Mississippi and Southern California coast," the years have been good to Southern Cal.

And football, of course, has been a palpable force in a wide spectrum of intellectual and athletic successes. So here is the Southern Cal football story.

Wild Mustard, Cockleburrs, And Football

Somewhere between the exploding wild mustard and cockleburrs, a group of leonine youths with handlebar mustaches and padded vests began playing football on the campus of Southern California. This was the 1880s, not long after the cornerstone was first laid at the tiny Methodist college. You would not have recognized the game.

Football at this time was a free-form exercise combining soccer, rugby, and mass murder. It inspired this poem for the "weaker sex" who watched with delicious glee from the sidelines:

"Football As Girls See It"
I took the gentle Annabel
To see a football game,
And thus unto a friend of hers
Did she describe the same.
"Oh, May, you should have seen them play,
'Twas such a lovely sight!
And though the first game I had seen,
I understood it quite.
First came one team, all dressed in blue,
Then the other came in red,
One fellow yelled, the rest all tried
To jump upon his head.
And then one fellow stopped and stooped

> And all the rest got round;
> And every fellow stopped and stooped
> And looked hard at the ground.
> And then another fellow yelled,
> And each man where he stood,
> Just hit and struck and knocked and kicked
> At everyone he could.
> And then one fell upon his neck,
> And all the others ran,
> And on his prone and prostrate form
> Leaped every blessed man.
> And then the ambulance drove on,
> And loading up with men
> With twisted necks and broken lungs
> Went driving off again.
> Oh, football's just the cutest game!
> It cannot be surpassed;
> But yet it really is a shame
> to use men up so fast!"

If these gladiatorial bouts sparked such humorous literature, it was not funny to the men who played the game. It was serious stuff, this bloody football business.

"Perhaps it was the invigorating country air of the lane known as University Avenue, or maybe it was just the rugged stock of those pioneer students," writes onetime Southern Cal sports publicist Al Wesson. "At any rate, the desire to win athletic championships along with scholastic honors was revealed early in the history of the University of Southern California students. Within a few years after the founding of the university (1880), eleven sturdy young men sporting handlebar mustaches and padded vests drew lines on a vacant lot, erected wobbly goalposts, and challenged all comers to contest in that 'new-fangled push-and-tug' business called football.

"Competition was informal at first with the team sponsored by the Los Angeles YMCA and a group of former eastern players who organized an eleven in Pasadena offering themselves up as S.C.'s first gridiron victim. It was not until 1889 that intercollegiate competition was begun, and then St. Vincent's College, forerunner of Loyola University, bravely accepted the University Avenue challenge and was rewarded with a 40-0 beating."

Rooted and flowering in the East, football had finally come to a place called "The Garden of Paradise."

Los Angeles was obviously named for its cozy, warm weather and gaudy, exotic scenery. Thick-walled adobes with large, enclosed patios laced the town. Wild mustard and cockleburrs lingered in the California sun, not to mention flaming orange groves and pleasant grape vineyards, walnut, almond, and fruit orchards, and thick, rich vegetable and flower gardens.

Football first reached California's golden slope from England. A version of it started up north in San Francisco.

"Pacific Coast football was originally imported from Britain," wrote Alexander Weyand in his book: *The Saga of American Football*. "About 1880, former British citizens residing in the San Francisco Bay area organized rugby clubs. On December 2, 1882, one of these clubs, the Phoenix, played the University of California, where the students had been playing intramural soccer since 1877. The game was played on the old recreation grounds in San Francisco with 15 on a side, and the clubmen won, 1 goal—2 touchdowns.

"A few weeks after the game, on Christmas 1882, a team from Colorado College, captained by Frank E. Johnson, defeated the Sigafus Hose Company of Colorado Springs, 10 touchdowns—8 touchdowns. This, too, was rugby, but it was the American brand with 11 on a side. Previously, the same teams had played under soccer rules. On April 11, 1885, the first intercollegiate football game in the Far West was played; Colorado College defeated Denver, 12-0.

"About this time, American football gained a foothold west of the mountains (the Rockies). In 1885, Oscar S. Howard, who had won a football letter at Harvard, returned to his native California and plunged into a one-man crusade to convert the San Francisco region to the American game. On January 16, 1886, the first game of American football was played on the Pacific Coast, on the (California) University athletic field, before a crowd of three hundred. California, captained by Fred Turner, defeated the Wasps, 20-4."

Gwynn Wilson, a onetime student manager of the Southern Cal football team, remembered the incubation period at his school.

"From 1881 to 1887, there was hardly any football played in Southern California and at the university most of the activity was confined to class affairs and that in the field of baseball rather than football," he wrote in an article for the *Pigskin Review*, the Trojans' football program. "There was practically no competition possible in the South during this period and the young men who wanted a college education and some football thrown in generally found it by attending either Stanford or the University of California at Berkeley.

"There were several other colleges in the South at this time but all were going through the period of financial stress that always can be depended on during the first years of any educational undertaking."

Money—or lack of it—was Southern Cal's problem, too. Recalled one oldtimer: "It was back in 1881 when Los Angeles was still in the bloom of fandangoes and chili sauce that a pigskin was first rolled out on a Trojan field. But financial difficulties and lack of enthusiasm put the period 1881-1887 in all of Southern California in a very pale light. The gridiron game was left to mold on the shelf along with plenty of husky boys who had the possibilities of attracting the eye of even Walter Camp (the noted football authority)."

But you did not need a big cash outlay for a ball and bat, nor a pair of spiked shoes, and thus the sports of baseball and track grew like the California Sequoias.

About these sports, Wilson recalled: "Gradually the University of Southern California gathered strength with numbers and growing interest on the part of the local public. Pomona and St. Vincent's then suggested that the colleges meet in the various lines of sport and baseball games with field days resulted."

About football: "But football was considered a greater undertaking and for still a longer period, nothing was done with the war of the gridiron."

Nothing, that is, until 1888.

A Team Is Born

There were no jaunty hats, no fashionable high-neck shirts with a team name splashed in front, no britches, no smart, high-top, cleated shoes and worst of all, no protection. Southern Cal's first football team was a sight for sore eyes, recalled T. N. Carver.

"We had no uniforms in those days," said Carver, an original member of the first official football team at Southern Cal. "Each individual played in the oldest clothes he had. Consequently we looked rather ringstreaked and piebald in comparison with the other teams."

The campus beat of the late 1880s was recorded in a letter Carver once wrote to the school.

"I entered USC in the fall of 1888," he said in his letter. "There was already a well-organized football team which had been playing for a year or two before that. I do not know just how long. In the fall of 1888 when I entered, Will Whitcomb from Glendora, California, was the captain of the team. He played fullback. A fellow named Bailey (I have forgotten his initials) from Julian, was one of the halfbacks. I am uncertain as to who the other one was.

"E. A. Reed was center. Ed Young, who lived with his parents at Figueroa Street, one block south of Washington Street, was right guard. Unless my memory fails me, Lloyd Christie of Phoenix, Arizona, was one of the tackles. I have forgotten who the other one was. A fellow who was called "Shorty" Carroll was quarterback. The personnel of the team shifted a good deal and it has been a long time ago. This makes it rather difficult for me to supply the names of all the players..."

An old gentleman looking back in time can be forgiven for a slip or two. Actually, the school's yearbook listed the original team as follows: Captain Will Whitcomb, Elger A. Reed, Tommy Robinson, T. N. Carver, Ed Young, C. C. Carpenter, Frank Lapham, John Norton, Frank Suffel, Elmer Hall, Harvey Bailey, Arthur "Shorty" Carroll, Henry Lillie, F. E. Davis, and a "sub" named Haemon. Suffel and Henry H. Goddard were co-coaches of the team, although there was no salary for such luxury at the time.

"There were no other colleges in Southern California with football teams," said Carver. "Men did not travel long distances in those days to play football. Stanford was not yet in existence and we did not play with the state university (presumably California). Consequently, there were no games with other colleges that year..."

However, there WAS a game. Two, actually. On November 14, 1888, the Southern California "Methodists" (the nickname "Trojans" was a future consideration) played against a local athletic club composed of a "group of downtown youths." It was no contest. USC beat the Alliance Athletic Club, 16-0. In the second game of the "season" with Alliance, January 19, 1889, USC won again, this time by a 4-0 score.

The campus spirit of the day was contagious, reported the school yearbook, the *El Rodeo*:

"In January, 1888, the Class of '90 organized and adopted a class badge, color, and motto. Its members have been among the first in the classroom; in the literary societies, on the football field, and in Hallow-E'en pranks. The Class of '90 took an active part in the infusion of more class spirit in the separate classes and was always represented in the (football) scrimmages resulting from the same."

The class colors, purple and gold, were the forerunner of today's rich cardinal-and-gold combination.

By 1889 Southern Cal was ready to play intercollegiate football. Gwynn Wilson, a onetime graduate manager of the team, remembered the history-making circumstances.

"In 1889, the Southern (California) University had

*Southern California's First
Official Football Team, 1888*

Standing, left to right: John Norton, Harvey Bailey, Will Whitcomb, Ed Young, Coach Frank Suffel, Elmer Hall. Seated, left to right: Henry Lillie, Elger Reed, C. C. Carpenter, F. E. Davis, Arthur Carroll, Frank N. Lapham. (Tommy Robinson, T. N. Carver, and a sub named Haemon, three other original members of the first team, were not available for this photograph.)

attained a certain degree of strength in all lines, while at the same time St. Vincent's College, now Loyola, was also showing signs of athletic unrest," Wilson said. "During the spring of 1889, considerable attention was given football because of the big interest that was being taken in the game among the students of California. These two universities (Southern Cal and St. Vincent's) began by making the first spring campaign on record in the west for the fall semester's work. A great deal was written and said about this, and the rest was a challenge being issued by the athletic powers at St. Vincent's to those of the

University of Southern California for a game to be played the following fall, just before Thanksgiving.

"The challenge was accepted. All through the summer months of vacation the two institutions labored to gather material and knowledge. When college opened in the fall, the whole city was agog with excitement. The contest was spoken of as the big game. Suits were bought and footballs obtained by popular subscriptions, and the work of selecting a team began. No eligibility rules were thought of at this time; it was to be a fair battle with no quarter given and no quarter asked. After weeks of unrelenting toil, the team was chosen, more or less through that time-honored test of the survival of the fit."

Southern Cal's "fit" turned out to be: A. E. Jones and Captain Tommy Robinson, ends; George Christy and George L. Brown, tackles; A. B. Embree and Charles Smith, guards; Lee Youngworth, center; Paul Arnold (formerly a Southern Cal professor), quarterback; Jon A. Grey and J. E. Young, halfbacks; and T. N. Carver, fullback.

Putting perhaps an exaggerated value on the situation, Wilson recalled that there was "a million dollars worth of secret practice" by the teams before the game. Probably not exaggerating though, Wilson remembered that the teams spent "long hours with the rule book and the official football guide." The game was still somewhat of a mystery in California.

After all this preparation, "the team (Southern Cal) was declared ready and was exhibited on several occasions in signal practice," Wilson said.

"In the meantime," Wilson added, "the reports from the rival host were none too cheering."

The "Methodists" need not have worried, however. They overturned the odds and trounced St. Vincent's, 40-0.

"It will never be forgotten by members of the 'old guard,'" Wilson reported. "The USC eleven was considered the short ender because the St. Vincent men were supposed to have had more actual experience. But they had not figured on the active brains of Arnold and Carver. This pair figured out a set of dazzling plays and signals that proved too much for the doughty Saints.

"The game went the regular time limit, but after the first fifteen minutes of play, it was easily seen that the men from the university had the 'class.' Most of the scoring was done in the second half, after Arnold had worn out the Saints by putting them on a strenuous defense. The final score was 40-0 in favor of the University of Southern California—a terrible upsetting of the dope which nearly caused a riot in college circles."

There were awed officials from neighboring schools in the crowd that day.

"Pomona, Chafee, and Occidental had been interested spectators," recalled Wilson, "but decided not to challenge until better prepared to meet the mighty men of the university."

However, a team from Pasadena was willing to take on the "mighty men" of Southern Cal. Carver had "some very vivid recollections of that game."

"The Pasadena team was largely made up of players from eastern colleges," Carver said. "We had just heard rumors from the Far East (New York, not Tokyo) of the famous Yale Wedge. I remember with what trepidation we watched the formation. However, we succeeded in breaking it up the first time it was tried, and that gave us plenty of courage. They were a fine lot of athletes individually, but had not much time to practice team work. We had our signals and our team work pretty well mastered, and the game was a very clear demonstration of the superiority of teamwork over individual prowess. We had an easy victory (26-0)."

The Yale Wedge of which Carver spoke was a play of brute power whereby the ball-carrier was sandwiched for protection between two burly lines of teammates. There were no subleties to this play. It was just meant to run over the opposition.

At any rate the next time the Southern Cal players saw Pasadena's dreaded "Wedge" it was from underneath, looking up.

"The last game we played with them they beat us 12-2, our only score being made on a safety," recalled Carver. "They had time to learn their signals and to perfect their teamwork."

Death And Reincarnation

The Athletic Association at Southern Cal died a quick, painless death along with the football team. It was whimsically portrayed in an exaggerated "obituary" in *The Sibyl*, a student handbook.

"It is with profound sorrow that we note the death of our beloved Athletic Association," the self-styled obit began.

On top of the article was an amusing sketch of a jackass with a man's face. The face, wearing glasses and a beard, stared blankly at the reader as if to say, "What hit me?" Underneath the sketch was an identifying phrase, "The Athletic Ass."

To tell the truth, the poor thing had been hit by student apathy. Lack of financial support had killed the "Athletic Ass." and, concurrently, the football team. Therefore there was no football at Southern Cal in 1890.

"Strange as it may seem, one of our most important college organizations is having great difficulty in obtaining the support that it should have from our students," complained *The Rostrum*, the school newspaper.

While football was king east of the Rockies, it had certainly not taken off right away in Southern California. Students found other things more palatable.

"Eating contests are becoming quite fashionable," said *The Rostrum* in a front-page story.

Years before they loaded into telephone booths, students tried to eat themselves silly. It was a fad of the times, and obviously more easily digested on the Southern Cal campus than football in the early 1890s.

The Rostrum described the following episode:

"The two senior lasses indulged in one last week. The older of the senoritas proved the victor by several pounds of meat, vegetables, loaves of bread, and other small things too numerous to mention." The prize? "A swell supper given by the vanquished to the victor."

But these fringe entertainments did not inhibit *The Rostrum* from carrying on a full-scale campaign for football support. In a scathing editorial one week, *The Rostrum* chastised Southern Cal students for bad spirit.

"It seems that many persons who have enjoyed and are enjoying the privileges of the school will manifest no interest in anything which does not benefit directly their own, little selves," *The Rostrum* said. "They care for nothing which is not a source of very immediate enjoyment or profit to themselves. So far from helping any laudable and important student movement, they do all in their power, by groundless and bitter criticism and fault-finding, to defeat every effort that is made to advance the honor of the school."

Outraged, *The Rostrum* asked: "Why cannot all our students, even if it should involve a little self-sacrifice, do something to show their interest in the welfare of the college?"

The editorial concluded: "The immediate cause for this article is the attitude of the students toward the Athletic Association. This organization, in the hope of getting the body of the students interested in its work, has placed its initiation fee and dues at an almost ridiculously low figure. Yet from a majority of the students, it has received no encouragement or support."

While Harvard, Princeton, and Yale were pulling in crowds of 50,000, Southern Cal did not even field a football team. In 1891, when Southern Cal did resume an abbreviated schedule with the likes of the Olive Club, the Southern California Academy, and St. Vincent's (Loyola), there was little interest. Up north Stanford and California were making more noise. Stanford was born in 1891 and a year later scheduled a football game with California. A crowd of 9,500 turned out to see the game on the baseball grounds at Haight and Stenyan Streets in San Francisco. For the second game of the Stanford-California series, a rousing crowd of 18,753 was on hand.

Southern Cal was not only not playing much, it was not playing well. In 1891 when football weakly fluttered to life, the "Methodists" lost to the Olive Club 16-12 and St. Vincent's 10-2. They beat the Southern California Academy 34-0.

The season of 1891 was more notable for USC's first yell. For the few who wanted to chant it, it went:

"Rah! Rah! Rah! Rah!
U! S! C! Ah!
Boom! Rah! Boom! Rah!
Rah! Rah! Rah! Rah!"

As yells went, it was about average. Certainly it did not compare to this one from nearby Throop Academy of Pasadena:

"Whoop! Throop!
Baby's Got the Croup.
Zip! Boom! Ta-ra-ra!
Land 'em in the soup!
Whoop!"

It appeared for a while that USC's blasé cheer would not be aired in 1892. It was well into November and a football team had not yet been reestablished. But a small article under "Athletics" in *The Rostrum* announced that something was brewing.

"There is a rumor in the air that a Foot Ball Club is about to be organized," said the student newspaper in its November 26 issue. "We hope it is true, as we most assuredly need one."

A long-suffering campaigner, *The Rostrum* was rewarded with a team later in the year.

"Relations were reopened with St. Vincent's and practically the same team (as 1889) was lined up for this battle and the one scheduled with the YMCA of San Diego," recalled onetime student manager Gwynn Wilson. "However, Paul Arnold and T. N. Carver were not on the team and their absence was keenly felt. In the game with St. Vincent's, the Saints managed to get revenge (for their 1889 beating) by defeating the university 14 to 2. But the university went south and defeated the YMCA by the score of 20 to 0."

People still were not sure that football was all that important, however. A local newspaper felt that it should be put in its proper perspective in college life.

"Now, while this struggle of brawn and scientific practice is a most excellent thing, and match games good advertisements for the respective colleges, still there seems to be a tendency to overdo the thing at present," the newspaper said. "Some students seem to devote more time to athletics than study, and an expert player at football or baseball generally receives more attention and honor than a cum laude graduate."

But football was in the air, and in 1893 some definitive things began to happen at Southern Cal.

The things that began to happen to Southern Cal in 1893 led to this "formidable" 1895 team that faced the "Flying Wedge." Front row, from left: A. P. Thomson, J. S. Pitman, Jesse Tucker, Dwight Funk, F. C. Wright, and Ben Smith. Back row: Sid Quin, Pat Newman, C. E. Carver, Arville Phillips, H. L. Martin, A. Yerja, and J. A. Gray.

Fight On For Old S.C.

Long before the Southern Cal fight song became the rage, it was fashionable to "fight on for old S. C." Literally. Players did not need any musical accompaniment, nor an excuse for that matter, to punch a guy in the nose during a football game.

"Thanksgiving week was one tremendous scene of football carnage," wrote *The Rostrum* in a typical story of the early 1890s.

Pomona and Southern Cal, starting their great, early rivalry in 1894, staged some beautiful battles. They also got some football in.

"That annual tussle with the Sagehens from Pomona called for as many good prize fighters as it did for finished half-backs," recalled one oldtimer.

The style of the game, of course, was to blame for all this nonsensical violence. Loose rules permitted such mayhem, and it took more than a decade before an American football revolution changed all that.

In one respect, though, the brawling was a sign of good times for Southern Cal. It meant that the school was playing a lot of football, something it had not been doing in previous years. Southern Cal was obviously not a national power, nor even a threat to California or Stanford on the West Coast. But in its own backyard, it was not doing too badly.

In 1893 the first Southern Intercollegiate Conference was formed. Southern Cal was invited and happily accepted to join Pomona, Throop Polytechnic, and Chaffey College in the cozy group. Southern Cal's step into higher football circles was mirrored in *Rostrum* articles.

"Football is now as popular as baseball and the interest in it is spreading rapidly," said one story.

"Although we are handicapped by no athletic grounds and by poor facilities for training, our boys can find places and opportunities for training," said another.

That year, the executive committee of Southern Cal's Athletic Association (it was breathing again) held a closed contest to decide on the members of the "College Athletic Team."

"Every student that has a particle of athletic ability should get to work in practice," said *The Rostrum*, exhorting Southern Cal's players on to bigger and better things.

Football in particular and athletics in general in the Southern California area got even more of a push with the organization of the Intercollegiate Athletic Association. Its members were Southern Cal, Pomona, Chaffey, and Occidental, and its purpose was "to arrange for intercollegiate sports such as football, baseball, tennis, and track..."

Out of these new associations, and some others, Southern Cal could stock its schedule the year round with football games. The team actually played from January to December in those days.

Although Pomona forfeited a game with USC in 1893, Southern Cal played Throop, St. Vincent's, Chaffey, the Chaw-Sir Club, and Cal Tech twice.

The Chaw-Sir game, which opened the season in mid-January, was won 14-2 by Southern Cal. *The Rostrum*, of course, had a man on the scene.

Related the student reporter: "RAH! FOR THE RED RIBBON. The university team defeated the Chaw-Sir club team at football last Saturday afternoon by a score of 14 to 2. The yellow ribbons (Chaw-Sir) have almost turned blue in consequence of their inglorious defeat. It was a great game and well repaid the 200 or more spectators who were on the grounds shouting or waving decorated parsols and sticks whenever their team was ahead or some one made a good play. The Chaw-Sir club had a four-foot horn with a basso profundo voice, which greatly added to the melody of the occasion."

The contest was an artistic, pastel painting in dirt.

"The opening play was one of the prettiest in the game," the article noted. "The Chaw-Sirs formed in a line behind the ball, rushed forward, then off at an angle, running so close together, that the tacklers could not get through at the full back, until he had made 25 yards. This rattled the reds for a while, but they faught (his spelling) stubbornly, and it was twenty minutes before a point was scored, when the yellows made a safety."

Unable to score in the first half, Southern Cal "seemed to get warmed up (in the second half), and Garton scored a touch down in fifteen minutes."

The "reds" turned the game into a rout later on when a fellow named J. H. Rogers blocked a kick by the Chaw-Sirs' Elmer Hall.

"As the yellows were getting desperate, Hall kicked the ball and it would have sailed well into the opponents' field had not Rogers reached forth his upper extremities in an imploring attitude and caused the ball of unclean extraction to flee back again to the yellows. Every yellow thought this a most foul proceeding, and when (Percy) Thomson picked up the shattered remains of the innocent 'bone of contention' and rushed down the field and over the yellows' line, no one gainsayed him nay, but let him go in peace. A long and hot debate, very tiresome to the spectators, followed but the touch down was granted for the reds and Gray kicked a goal."

Along with Rogers, a guard, and Thomson, a quarterback, the starting lineup for Southern Cal that day included: fullback, John Gray; a halfback named Bray and another, George Cook; center, A. B. Embree; a guard named Wilkins; a tackle named Charnock and another, Will Sawyer; and two ends, Grelly Bently and Val Brown.

Throop was a 64-0 victim to Southern Cal, St. Vincent's fell 22-4, and Cal Tech was beaten 22-12 and 14-4. Before the end of the season, though, was the big game with Chaffey.

"Chaffey College is anxious to meet our school in a round about at football," said *The Rostrum* in an article heralding the important contest. "Well, we are ready for them and the day has been set for December 17. Now, boys, let's block solid and beat them. This means practice, for they average 170 lbs. in weight and are in good trim. If we organize and practice up we will stand some show."

Apparently they did not practice enough, for Southern Cal's players were beaten badly, 32-6.

In 1894 Southern Cal played Pomona for the first time, and the game resulted in a 0-0 tie that was called "one of the hardest fought games ever played in the west." The first of Southern Cal's bonafide stars emerged that season—the aforementioned Thomson.

"It was during 1894 that little A. P. Thomson, the famous 110-pound quarterback, came into prominence," said an article assessing the players of that era. "He was very fast and developed a system of end runs and off tackle bucks that proved very effective."

Just how good Thomson was in comparison to players in the rest of the land was academic, of course. There was no national standard of excellence in those days. And because of the comparative isolation of Pacific Coast teams due to logistical difficulties, there were few chances to judge the quality of East versus West.

The first chance anyone in the West had to see "eastern" football was in 1894, when Amos Alonzo Stagg brought his Chicago team to California. In a Christmas Day game in warm weather, Chicago crushed Stanford, 24-4. Before anyone east of the Rockies had a chance to say "I told you so," Stanford turned around and won their next meeting at Los Angeles, 12-0. Stanford, by the way, was acknowledged champion of the Pacific Coast at the time. Chicago also lost to the Reliance Athletic Club, and on the way home routed the Salt Lake City YMCA 52-0.

Occidental joined the Southern Intercollegiate Conference in 1895 and immediately mastered Southern Cal 10-4 despite inferior material. The reason for that beating, explained a writer, was due to the work of a Professor Goodell:

"(This) graduate of Amherst coached and played on the team with the result that Occidental developed some brand, new plays that proved too much for the rather cut and dried style that had hitherto been in vogue."

It was really unfair in a way. Southern Cal was coachless—actually had been since Frank Suffel and Henry

Goddard's one-year term in 1888.

Because of the circumstances, some players were forced by necessity to develop leadership qualities. One such fellow was Leroy Bradley, a standout player for Southern Cal in that loss to Chaffey two years before. The brawny fullback captained Southern Cal's 1895 team and along with Thomson was one of the "name" players of the early and mid-1890s.

Bradley stood tall in a laborious game of tough guys—an era of swaggering brutes with quick fists and tempers to match.

"Football was a game of brute strength, bulk, weight, and hammering force," a player once recalled. "It was a football game of giants."

Robert Edgren, a player in Bradley's time, remembered the pleasure, but mostly pain, of oldtime football in an article in the *Los Angeles Herald*. One of the favorite plays of the day was the "Flying Wedge," a formation which was later prohibited because "its crushing force caused many injuries and deaths on the gridiron."

Edgren gave a first-hand account of the virulent formation:

"In the Flying Wedge, the attacking team fell into a wedge formation as the ball was put into play, the man with the ball slipping into a protected position within the entering point of the wedge. The whole wedge then swept forward on the run, the men locked together, crushing down and trampling over all opposition. I won't forget the sensation of being ground down under the Flying Wedge. It cost me two dislocated shoulders and a dislocated knee."

A Swan Emerges

Lewis Freeman and the shower stalls arrived just about at the same time on the Southern Cal campus.

There was perhaps something dramatically symbolic in the addition of a sparkling, new athletic room equipped, as the school yearbook described it, "with shower baths and lockers."

There was, however, nothing symbolic about Freeman—a brief but palpable force in Southern Cal's early football history. He coached only one year, 1897, but it was enough to help the team reverse its field.

"Long, hard training, with the able instructions of Lewis R. Freeman of Stanford, placed in the field a team that defied southern California and came well nigh being invincible," reported the *El Rodeo,* the school year book.

Winning five out of six games may not seem like a huge success. But life is relative with a loser, which Southern Cal had been for a few years.

Losing, in fact, had developed the character of the present team. The *El Rodeo* pointed out:

"Probably one of the aids to our success was the fact of the defeats we have received during the previous years. Most of the '97 team had played the year before and against teams that were far superior to our own, but this served only as an experience to aid in overcoming past records. Another point that aided vitally in the results of the season was the addition of several strong new men, of whom Robert Jones of Whittier and O. D. Walker of DePauw are worthy of mention."

*The Southern California Football Team of 1897
Included in the group are: Coach Lewis Freeman, C. J. Hinman, Charles Holland, Bob James, Ralph Avery, Austin O. Martin, William F. Lloyd, Foster C. Wright, Carl Williams, Purnell Pratt, Charles Christy, Orrin D. Walker, and two players named Decker and Thompson.*

The record was as fancy as ever made by a Southern Cal team. Freeman's appearance had signaled an expansion, and a strengthening, of the athletic program.

Along with the "commodious and well-lighted" athletic room, which gave the football scene a small touch of class, the athletes wore fancy, new uniforms with "USC" emblazoned in white across the fronts of the high-neck shirts. Baseball-style caps could be tilted swaggeringly over the eye, if one wished. The knee-length britches were the latest thing in football fashion and so were the high stockings and ankle-high shoes.

"Under the able management of C. J. Hinman and the efficient labors of Captain A. O. Martin, we succeeded in placing in the field the best equipped team that had graced the

USC gridiron for many years," said the *El Rodeo*.

The ugly duckling had turned into a swan. Even the Athletic Association, that black sheep of the campus not many years before, was going strong.

"Prominent among the institutions of USC is the Athletic Association," announced the *El Rodeo*. "Believing in the development of the body as well as the mind, the students of USC loyally support this organization."

There were more students than ever, to be sure. From that first cornerstone ceremony in September 4, 1880, when the privately-owned university was born in a riotous plain of wild mustard, Southern Cal's campus population had exploded from 150. Interest was high in all activities and the "bright and newsy" *University Courier*, the student newspaper, sold plenty of one-year subscriptions for one dollar.

In 1898 Freeman was gone from the scene, but the material he had nurtured was proclaimed champion of Southern

Harvey Holmes (middle, rear) and his well-to-do 1904 Southern California football team. "His successes were nothing to be sneezed at," noted the Pigskin Review.

California colleges. The "Methodists" beat everybody that year but Los Angeles High School, a brawny, pugilistic team of teenagers that had little respect for university men. Southern Cal victories were recorded over the Pasadena Athletic Club, Pomona, the 7th Regiment (an Army unit in the Southern California area), the Phoenix Indians, and the Santa Barbara Athletic Club. There was a scoreless tie and a 6-0 loss to Los Angeles High School mixed into the seven-game schedule, the biggest until that point.

Marshall Stinson remembered the pulse of the day. They marched to a different beat then, he recalled.

"We played forty-five minute halves," said Stinson, who played for Southern Cal in 1898. "There was no halt unless a player was hurt so that he couldn't get up. No player who was taken out of a game could reenter the game. Almost every player went through the entire game. The game was played in a much more snappy fashion and called for greater endurance.

"The team which had the ball put it in play as soon as its men were on side, as opposing players who were off side could not take part in the play. That made both teams leap into position. The players also had to have enough brains to work out the complicated system of signals in a flash instead of wasting time in huddles.

"I took part in one of the famous games of the period, between Los Angeles High School and USC, on a muddy field in December. The high school had beaten all its other opponents, high school and college, and held the university to a scoreless tie. For many years Los Angeles High School played USC and on two occasions, defeated it."

Stinson was among several, bright new faces at Southern Cal in the period of the late 1890s and early 1900s.

"After 1898 the schedule fell off in number of games played, there being but one annual intercollegiate contest each season with Pomona," recalled a historian. "However, some very good players came to the university during this time: Robert Jones and Tossie Wright, both of whom later became prominent lawyers in Los Angeles and members of the city council; Charles Broderson, who came in during the season of 1898; and Captain H. D. Ryus, who later was one of the leading auto merchants in the state. Ryus returned from his campaign in Cuba, during the Spanish-American War, and was elected captain and acting coach."

In 1901 during a loss to arch-rival Pomona, Tully Knoles came into his own under the guidance of Coach Clair S. Tappaan.

"Knoles, later a professor in the university, started here and later developed into a wonderful quarterback," said the historian.

In 1902 it was the Caley brothers—Elwin and Dan. They starred at the halfback positions. Elwin Caley brightened the season with a 107-yard punt return against Pomona. Pomona was hard to beat in those days, though. Oriented to the Ivy League schools, Pomona had taken a page from those early football powers and dominated all those around it. Recalled Pomona historian Frank Brackett:

"By the year 1900 football had come into its own again with Blount as coach. Seven successive victories had brought Pomona the championship of Southern California, the telling scores being 17-0 with Occidental and 10-0 with USC. The following year, with Seaborn Wharton as graduate coach, Pomona held first place, winning from Occidental 6-0 and from USC 6-0. The season of 1902 was not so successful... However, 1903 found Pomona once more in possession of a championship team which played an undefeated season."

While the schools in Southern California were beating each other's heads in, the schools in Northern California were getting the recognition. Noting the improvement in Far West football, Walter Camp gave all-America honorable mention to California fullback Lawrence Kaarsberg in 1889. In 1900 he similarly rewarded Frank Slaker, a Stanford halfback.

How much Far West football had improved, though, was suspect. The Rose Bowl had its first game in 1902, and Stanford was selected to represent the West against Eastern power Michigan. The Wolverines routed Stanford 49-0 in the Pasadena special, and this so embarrassed the bowl's founding fathers that they sent no further invitations east for 14 years. In fact chariot races took over for football in that time.

In 1903 when John Walker took over as Southern Cal football coach for one year, Charles Parsons, the famous sprinter, joined the team. A decided upheaval gripped the

A football player from the old school, Ray Tufs. He played on the 1904 Trojan team.

school in 1904 with the arrival of Harvey Holmes. Under Holmes, the first football coach to be hired under salary, Southern Cal had its best season to date—six victories and one loss. Holmes, who came to Southern California from Wisconsin University, developed a number of good players including, John DeLappe, Frank Acker, John White, Oliver Best, Carl Elliott, and Reed Miller.

The 17-0 loss to the Sherman Indians that year was "considered very complimentary," according to one writer, because Sherman had been tied 6-6 by a great eastern power, Carlisle.

"Holmes rolled around on the Trojan campus with some new ideas on how to play this game," reported the *Pigskin Review*, Southern Cal's football magazine. "His successes were nothing to be sneezed at, including one over Los Angeles High School—a 34-4 victory. This was just about the period that these six-foot lads from the prep school on the hill were breaking the back of California's Golden Bears as well as a number of universities and colleges which tramped across their path."

Holmes went for bigger game in 1905, playing Stanford for the first time on an expanded, 10-game schedule. To be sure there were some breathers along the way. The Southern Cal players beat Whittier Reform 75-0 and an Alumni team 63-0 in a year of 6 victories, 3 losses, and 1 tie. They could not do the same to Stanford, though. In the first meeting of their long and illustrious rivalry, Southern Cal journeyed north to take a 16-0 beating.

A national football revolution took place during Holmes' tenure at Southern Cal. During the 1905 season the White House declared war on football because of its virulent brutality. Enraged by the photograph of a bloodied player, President Theodore Roosevelt issued an ultimatum to football authorities to eliminate rough play immediately or have the game abolished.

An official of California University saw Stanford brutalize his team in one game and wired officials in Chicago: "The game of football must be entirely made over—or made to go." When there was no satisfactory action, Cal and Stanford joined a growing legion of teams who dropped football in 1906. They

The 1906 team used Harvey Holmes' "Sausage Grinder" to go undefeated in four games.

The 1907 Southern California team dropped out of the cramped Southern Conference and searched for bigger game.

abandoned the American sport in favor of British rugby.

The 1905 casualty list across America read: 18 dead, 159 seriously injured.

Out of this football renaissance period came important, new rules that drastically changed the face of the game: legalization of the forward pass; lengthening the required yardage for a first down from 5 to 10 yards; shortening the game from 70 to 60 minutes; addition of an official; creation of a neutral zone between opposing lines; and strengthening of the rules against foul play.

The situation affected USC, of course, forcing a dropoff in competition. Only four games were played in 1906, and the inventive Holmes developed a new play for the "modern" game—the Sausage Grinder. It only sounded bloody, though.

"Occidental was defeated 22-0 due to this play invented by Holmes," related a magazine writer. "Merrill of Occidental was working on an open game due to the change of rule at this time and opened up his defense and attack. Holmes planned a play something like the evolving wedge in its start but which ended with a cross-tackle buck upon the opposite side to that taken at the start. It was good for nearly all the scores made in the first half. Pomona was defeated by the same method, 14 to 0, but Sherman managed to hold the plunging university backs, 0 to 0."

Undefeated in four games Southern Cal became an intercollegiate champion once again in its own area. A Southern Conference title pleased Holmes, to be sure, but he obviously felt cramped in the tiny league because in 1907 the team dropped out and went independent.

"Southern California was already looking forward to some sort of union with the larger universities up state," reported a magazine.

In his last year, 1907, Holmes went out with a flourish—winning 5 of 6 games. His presence had been strongly felt. Southern Cal's first bona fide coach posted a 4-year record of 19 victories, 5 defeats, and 3 ties.

Hold That Tiger

"A panting young man, his solid set shoulders encased in a soaked sweater, his face so covered with dust and perspiration that his own family would scarcely have recognized him, and his tattered uniform heavily coated with the grime of battle was lifted upon the shoulders of the Cardinal rooters and carried in triumph from Bovard Field at the finish of yesterday's desperate engagement between those two old rivals, USC and Occidental..."

Here was a not-unusual newspaper account of a bitter struggle between two friendly enemies, Southern Cal and the Occidental Tigers. These teams, along with Pomona, formed a triumverate of rivals that was unmatched in early Southern California football history. The combat was staged on a smaller scale than, say today's games with Notre Dame and UCLA, but it was no less intense.

Both Pomona and Occidental had joined the Southern Cal schedule in the 1890s, and by 1909 the competitive fires were roaring. A 3-3 tie with Occidental and a scoreless tie with Pomona that year were indicative of their fierce engagements. One newspaperman called the game with Occidental "one of the most spectacular ever played in the South."

A newspaper account of the pre-game rally verifies the climate:

"It might have been taken for a fire, or an anarchists' indignation meeting, or just a plain case of murder, from the noise which came from the University of Southern California's football campus last evening; but it was none of these; it was the student body's annual 'jolly up' before the big Occidental-USC football game. A huge bonfire in the middle of the field, around which students waved in the serpentine dance, lighted up the scene, where for more than an hour prophecies were made as to the outcome of this afternoon's game.

"The festivities opened with the burning of Occidental. An effigy, marked 'Oxy', was first paraded back and forth before the bleachers and then dragged to the fire and thrown in amid wild cheers from the crowd. Then came the cheering and singing while the school's rival burned. A band made up of students added to the tumult..."

The game was more spirited and spectacular than the rally, if that was possible. Chester Lawrence, a Los Angeles sportswriter, witnessed "one of the greatest gridiron struggles ever seen in Southern California." It finished in total darkness and in controversy, not unusual for a Southern Cal-Occidental game.

"Occidental sent a man over the line after the stars had been twinkling down on a field filled with thousands of spectators who could not see across the gridiron," Lawrence reported. "The conference officials will decide the point which is contended (by Southern Cal) that the time-keeper's whistle blew before the play was made. No law of conference or sportsmanship could ever rule that the game was anything but a tie, because no official alive could state truthfully that he could see the ball except rarely through the dusk during the last ten minutes of play, when the game should have been called."

A crowd of 3,500 saw the game at Occidental's Baer Field. Included was President Baer of Occidental, who fainted in the arms of bystanders once when his son George had been dropped by a terrific tackle. He enjoyed the rest of the game, though, along with the other "thrilled spectators."

"Never did those crowds see a finer, cleaner, faster game," wrote Lawrence. "It was the apothesis of Southern California's greatest amateur sport."

The crowds arrived early and stayed late. Said Lawrence in his drama-filled story:

"Those who filled Baer Field with its greatest crowd started early for the game. They arrived by the car load, by autos and afoot. The hosts of the University of Southern

The Occidental Tiger straddles a fence here, but there was no fence-straddling when it came to playing Southern California. Fierce loyalties persisted on both sides when their football battles raged.

California must have depopulated the west side of Los Angeles, so great was their number, so tremendous their cheering... The vast stands were filled to overflowing, and the entire field seemed choked with old age, youth and all that goes between...they rocked the stands with roaring cheers...Here was a spectacle that will never leave the memories of the throng that witnessed it."

The game was a highlight during Dean Cromwell's first year. The famous track master had taken over as coach of the Southern Cal football team in 1909 after Bill Traeger's one-year term in 1908. Cromwell had walked into tenuous times, in the role of peacemaker. The circumstances would have taxed Henry Kissinger, for Southern Cal was belabored by many off-the-field pressures.

"The football team was being accused by the *Los Angeles Times* of certain 'irregularities' in technical features of the game and criticized by Pomona College for not meeting eligibility requirements," said coauthors Manuel P. Servin and Iris Higbie Wilson in their book, *Southern California And Its University*. "Then the *University Advocate* reported that a check for $25 had been made out to the football team captain, Dan Calley, for 'services rendered.'"

The school newspaper responded to this charge rhetorically, asking: "Has professionalism been present in our school and no one the wiser?"

"A student resolution censured and condemned the team manager and captain," wrote Servin and Wilson. "The students further resolved that the Athletic Board of Control be commended for discovering the payment and placing its 'absolute condemnation upon professionalism in its first appearance.'"

Hoping to hold that Tiger, Southern California students hold a goat before the big game with Occidental. The symbolism is clear.

The 1908 Southern California team "played a battering game" against Occidental. The Trojans won 14-0, causing a demon-

Not only was money used to pay a star athlete on occasion, it was also used to build facilities. Southern Cal forked out $3,500 to erect a gymnasium and have its playing fields enclosed.

The competition with Occidental and Pomona flourished through the first decade of the 1900s, but this three-cornered rivalry also had painful side effects. In 1908 battles flared off as well as on the football field as Southern Cal was accused of loose eligibility requirements for its athletes.

"The present embroglio between the three institutions

strative celebration by students through overwhelmed Los Angeles.

rests on the contention of Occidental and Pomona that the (Southern Cal) university limit the candidates for athletic teams to bona fide students of the College of Liberal Arts," explained a newspaper. "The (Southern Cal) university, as an association of several colleges, claims justification in maintaining the institution as a whole in athletics, and whether the Methodists will risk eliminating students of the professional schools from participating in the southern intercollegiate contests is the bone of dispute."

Perhaps this war of words made the football games even

more fierce, victories more delicious, and defeats more bitter. After a 14-0 Southern Cal victory over Occidental in 1908, a Los Angeles newspaper reported that "the teams showed little class, but both elevens played a battering game."

"Battered and disappointed, the Occidental players walked from the field, but the Presbyterian rooters continued to yell and wave their pennants, refusing to acknowledge the defeat," said the newspaper story. "The USC students swarmed on the field and held a dance, after which the college band, accompanied by a crowd of rooters, paraded the downtown streets. Few USC supporters expected their team to run up a big score and the players were overwhelmed by congratulations."

The demonstrative celebration erupted through Los Angeles—and 150 rooters from Southern Cal were stopped by police for marching without a permit.

"Officer H. V. Henderson detained the noisy enthusiasts until (Southern California) President Bovard secured a pass from police headquarters," said a reporter.

Then Bovard and Southern Cal yell leader Sam Dick jumped into a car and, singing the school victory song to the accompaniment of a brass band, reestablished the parade through Los Angeles streets.

It was a shining hour for Southern Cal. The "Methodists" were not supposed to win that one.

"Occidental brought to the contest a veteran team supremely confident of victory," said Southern Cal's yearbook, the *El Rodeo*. "Even the non-partisan laymen admitted little chance for our varsity."

But, it turned out, Southern Cal had more character that day. Reported the *El Rodeo*:

"Before the game had progressed five minutes the visitors realized their weakness. On the seventh play, Hal Paulin electrified the rooters by successfully trying a place kick from the 35-yard line. Pandemonium broke loose. Oxy was surprised but still confident. The collegians jumped into the struggle with even greater fierceness. It was then that Southern California, backed by the rooters, put up the most remarkable game ever seen on a local gridiron. Out-weighed five pounds to the man, it was the Methodist spirit that pushed back the strong attack of the Black and Gold."

Paulin kicked two field goals that day, and Captain Stan Burek scored a touchdown, leading Coach Traeger to say: "Class counts—and USC outplayed Occidental at every stage of the game."

The Occidental coach, by the way, did not help his team any by drawing a penalty.

"Coach Gorton of Occidental was the only person on the sidelines caught in the act of coaching the players and the penalty, which was inflicted, was the direct cause of the Methodists' only touchdown," reported a newspaper. "USC had the ball on the Presbyterians' 20-yard line in the second half when Field Judge Wilson made the decision, and the ball was moved up to Occidental's 5-yard line. On the next play, Burek went through a hole between center and right guard for the only touchdown of the game."

Few new plays were exhibited. It was a game of good, old-fashioned power football without frills. But considering the times, and the location, it was unusual. Football played in those parts was usually considerably more wide-open than the stuff back east, or in the north for that matter.

"The game in the south (of California) is the fast one found formerly at Michigan and Chicago, while in the north, the close formation of Dartmouth and Harvard is tenaciously clung to despite the fact that their backs are very fast," said Spaulding's *Football Guide*. "In southern California, end runs double and triple passes, punts, and trick plays abound."

The face of Pacific Coast football had been altered in these times. Stanford and California, owing to America's football revolution, were now playing the English game of rugby. This left the polarization of football on the Coast to the Great Northwest and Southern California. Way up north Washington's Huskies began a reign of terror in their territory in 1908, eventually going through nine straight years of undefeated seasons. In the south Southern Cal fought for football dominance in the state with Occidental, Pomona, and St. Vincent's—and sometimes came out on top of the "Big Four."

With players like Paulin, a halfback; Burek, a fullback; and quarterback Sid Ickes, Traeger's 1908 Southern Cal team played plenty of power football.

"He turned out a good, fast team, depending on a

stonewall defense to bring home the money," recalled a sportswriter.

In 1909 a new Athletic Board of Control was established at Southern Cal. That completed the transition from student to faculty control of intercollegiate athletics. One of the members of the first board was Dean Cromwell, the new track and football coach. Although more renowned for his work in track and field, Cromwell turned out some pretty good football teams, too. In 1909 Southern Cal won three games, lost but one, and tied two. In 1910 the team went undefeated in eight games. There was a memorable 9-9 tie with Pomona on the season's last day.

How Cromwell accomplished this under extreme pressure was unimaginable. Not only was Southern Cal in a constant battle with Occidental and Pomona over athletic eligibility requirements, Cromwell also had to deal with dissension among his players.

Aggressive fraternity brothers had caught hold of the Southern Cal ship, and their demoralizing cliques threatened to sink it. Explained a newspaper:

"Cromwell is dissatisfied with athletic conditions at USC, particularly the domineering influence of fraternities in all student activities on Bovard Field. Members of the football squad rebelled openly during the season just closed (1909) and the 'frat' boss spirit has also caused dissatisfaction among the players of the basketball team. If the 'frat' influence is manifested in the track season, Cromwell will very likely seek shelter in the Tigers' lair."

The last sentence referred to speculation that Cromwell would return to his alma mater, Occidental, rather than put up with the small-minded fraternity nonsense at Southern Cal.

"Demoralizing to consistent training and team spirit, so essential to athletic success, is the influence of the clique spirit on the athletic squads," said Cromwell. "I have had all kinds of troubles with certain players on the football team, and I could not at first discover the reason for the dissatisfaction until I found out the players giving the most trouble were members of the college fraternities.

"Members of the team became peeved when I ordered them out of a game for wretched playing, or relegated them to the second team for the same reasons. These players seemed to think their standing in the fraternities gave them greater prestige and a right to greater consideration when a question of their ability was considered. At the training table, which was inaugurated for the purpose of team spirit as much as for physical benefits, I soon found the 'frat' men bolting out of the front door as soon as the meal was over. Their sympathies were not so 'common' as to mix with the 'barbs' and they were called away to the frat houses, where their freedom was not restricted by training regulations. The sudden departure of 'frat' players, of course, broke up any opportunity for good relationship between the players."

If team spirit was lacking, good food was not. Cromwell's training table—first in Southern Cal's history—was a caloric delight.

"Several interesting facts could be related of the life at the training quarters, for instance the amazing capacity of certain young freshmen for milk," reported the *El Rodeo*.

Among those enjoying training table food that year was Hal Paulin, "a captain who kept the spirit of the team at high water...a consistent player behind the line and possessing a knack of kicking field goals." Court Decius was another star of the team. Said the *El Rodeo*: "He excelled in all departments of the game. His splendid tackling and running with the ball never ceased to be commented upon. He was picked for halfback on the All Southern team." There was also Sid Ickes, "our handsome quarterback, whose fine generalship and superior work in running in punts won him the position of quarterback on the All Southern team." And Walt Hall, "the all-around member of the team, (who) can play any position from end to fullback...a man who works hard and is to be depended upon at all times."

In 1910 some of these players would find the training table even more delicious. Southern Cal was in for its best football season in history until that point.

On To Pomona

The day of the big game dawned bright and clear. Skies were outrageously blue, the clouds white cotton candy. Excitement gripped the Southern Cal campus. The long-awaited match with Pomona was at hand.

A football "special" put out by the campus newspaper outlined the drama of the day in a bold, red headline proclaiming: "On To Pomona." In smaller letters, the newspaper said: "We Did It To Occidental, We Can Do It At Claremont."

What Southern Cal did to Occidental was beat the Tigers, which is what the Methodists had been doing to everyone else in the 1910 season. Coach Dean Cromwell had overcome internal problems among his players and external sniping from competing schools to fashion an excellent record of seven straight victories.

Victimized along the way was giant-killer Long Beach High School, Chaffey High School, Cal Tech, San Diego High School, Redlands, Occidental, and Whittier. Pomona was the last game on the schedule and the most meaningful. A battle of unbeatens, it was for the championship of the Southern California Intercollegiate Conference, which Southern Cal had recently rejoined.

The game took on more glitter, since football had indeed polarized in the Southern California area. Pointed out Spaulding's *Football Guide*:

"Although Stanford and the University of California

played the English game of rugby and caused practically all the football activity to be confined to the southern part of the state, this season has undoubtably been the most successful the Pacific Southwest has seen for several years. The new rules are an unqualified success. The style of play was open, fast and spectacular. The teams were evenly matched and their rivalry was intensely keen. There were no fatalities and slight injuries were reported."

The Southern California Intercollegiate Conference flourished with five members—Southern Cal, Pomona, Occidental, Whittier, and Redlands.

"The Pomona team, then the University of Southern California together with Occidental, drew immense crowds," reported Spaulding's *Guide*. "Intercollegiate football placed Los Angeles in the foreground as a center for football interest in the state. Five colleges and principal high schools placed first-class elevens in the field and the public expressed their favor for the intercollegiate games by attending all games in large numbers."

A crowd of 5,000 attended the game between Southern Cal and Occidental at Bovard Field, and everyone got his money's worth. A newspaper account recorded the upbeat tempo:

"A full hour before the game's first whistle, the big bleachers and grand stands began to fill up. Occidental's rooters were early on the stands. They occupied the east end of the stands. It was 3 o'clock, however, before the late comers had reached the field. The (Southern Cal) university enthusiasts filled the west section and by the time the game was called the crowd welled over onto the field on both sides of the stands. About 2,000 persons filled the stands. Another 500 rooters crowded for vantage points on the sides of the stands."

Many more people sat in cars and squeezed into open spaces ringing the field.

"Parked along the north side of the field scores of autos poked their hoods close to the sidelines," reported the newspaper. "Two university tallyhos, each alive with gaily-dressed coeds, sought admission to the west gate. The low top bar of the gate would not allow the rigs to carry the eager spectators onto the field. The girls scrambled down, and gaining their seats within the grounds, were dashed away to the reserve parking.

"Before the teams appeared the rooters were quiet. The (Southern Cal) university eleven trotted out first and was greeted with round after round of yelling. Scarcely a minute later the Tigers, resplendent in new black and orange jerseys, came filing from the training quarters. It was the signal for tremendous cheering. The (Southern Cal) university rooters wore new tobaggan caps, the hood of deep cardinal, the topnot of gold tassle."

The newest Southern California cheer rolled down from the stands:

    Rackety Hackety! Wah! Who! Wah!
    Rackety Hackety! Wah! Who! Wah!
     Zip Boom Bah! Zip Boom Bah!
     U! S! C! and a Rah! Rah! Rah!

With this lively exhortation ringing in the air, Southern California's players inched the ball against Occidental's mar-

"Rackety Hackety! Wah! Who! Wah! U! S! C! and a Rah! Rah! Rah!" It was not classic poetry, but the yell leaders got their point across during football games.

They came out to Bovard Field not only to watch the traditional battles between Southern California and Pomona but also to watch the yell leaders. Here one frantic fellow (far right) has the crowd's rapt attention.

velous defensive team.

"The game little Tiger band stood up like a stone wall against the killing assaults of (Coach Dean) Cromwell's warriors," reported sportswriter H. M. Walker. "During the first few minutes, USC had the ball at Oxy's three-yard line. Two ineffectual attempts to buck the line gave the Cardinal their first glimpse of the Tigers' defensive strength. It was at this early period that (Hal) Paulin and his place-kick came into prominence. Instead of trying for the third gain, the ball was snapped back to Cohan on the fifteen yard line, who held it in position for Paulin. A graceful movement of Hal's leg, a thud and the ball swished through the goal posts."

The crowd reaction was typically animated.

"The 'Noise Demons,' or yell leaders, were working overtime," reported Walker. "In an unmusical chant, the Tiger rooters were inquiring: 'What's the matter with Oxy?' To which query the USC boosters gave more than one sarcastic answer."

There was only one in the place that was not too enthused, and that was "Spareribs," Southern Cal's mascot. The dog had wandered out of the clubhouse to see what all the noise was about and apparently did not think much of it. He found a nice warm spot in the sun and rolled over for his afternoon nap.

Paulin later kicked a 20-yard field goal to give Southern Cal a 6-0 victory, prompting this newspaper reflection: "New and open football triumphed over the old, close formations Saturday afternoon at Bovard Field. The game was close and hard fought all the way and the superiority of the open game as played by Cromwell's Puritans (there was another Southern Cal nickname for the times) was manifest at every stage of the contest. The ball was in the Occidental territory nearly all of the first three-quarters of the play."

After beating Occidental, Southern California defeated another conference colleague, Whittier, 11-3, and set up a dramatic meeting with Pomona for the Southern Conference title.

For ten cents students read this front page story in the *USC Football Special* on Thursday, November 17, 1910:

"The undefeated varsity eleven of our own university will meet the hitherto victorious pigskin artists of Pomona College in the 'deadly shock battle' on the latter's field, Saturday afternoon at 2:00 o'clock. This will be by all odds the battle royal of the present football season. The tide of feeling is running high at both institutions."

Fair skies were expected for the important game.

"Barring a weather fluke," said the football special, "this will be the great battle of 1910. The university eleven started out last September to win the football championship. Step by step we have approached this ideal. The 'Podunk' aggregation remains as the last stronghold to be taken."

Fans echoed the intense feeling. Florence Parmelee wrote in the student newspaper: "We co-eds are just as much a part of the institution as Jack Malcomb, Hal Paulin or Frank Burleson and the conflict Saturday means just as much to us as to our football men or the most enthusiastic rooters. The men know we are there and when the girls on the bleachers stand up as the team comes on the field the men feel that they would fight with their last drop of blood rather than suffer defeat before the loyal co-eds who have come all the way to see them."

Southern Cal was an underdog because of comparative scores with Occidental. While USC had only beaten the Tigers by 6 points, Pomona had won 28-0.

"That 28 to 0 at Occidental haunts me pretty close," confessed Southern Cal Coach Dean Cromwell. "I hate to concede them (Pomona) a touchdown but on the surface it looks like we have to do it. I am counting strong on the fact that Pomona has played their best game and are on the downhill so far as form and training. My men will be in the best shape Saturday and should play the best game of the season by all odds. Looks like we ought to win."

He was only half right. Southern Cal did not win, but neither did Pomona. The game resulted in a 9-9 tie and proved to be "the hardest fought gridiron contest staged in this vicinity in several seasons," reported Spaulding's *Football Guide*.

"USC's line was invincible and Pomona failed to cross her goal line but was saved by Clary's third field goal which was scored from the 35-yard line, in the last minute of play," said the *Guide*. "Pomona's interference was nothing less than wonderful and on defense she fought desperately but well. But USC succeeded in crossing her line. Paulin scored one beautiful field goal. The play by both teams was spectacular. One minute the Blue and White would run away with the Cardinal; the next minute USC would tear great holes in Pomona's defense. Both teams were aggressive throughout the game. The attack presented a variety of kicks and forward passes..."

The tie was not exactly like kissing your sister, as the saying goes. Southern Cal and Pomona were awarded a piece of the Southern Conference championship for their efforts. Along with the accomplishment of a co-championship in 1910, Southern Cal placed several men on the all-State Team: end Arthur Hill, center Roy Allan, tackle Bryon Stookey, guard Stewart Kellar, and halfback Hal Paulin.

Diagnosing Hill and Allan, a writer said: "Hill was the best end on the gridiron in these parts in playing a game in point of speed and knowledge. As a center, Allan was in a class by himself and was declared the greatest man at his position both in speed and strength, while his judgement in passing was exceptional."

The best season until that point in Southern Cal history was a landmark year in more ways than one. American football was kicked out after 1910 in favor of rugby, the English game that was catching hold in northern California. Southern Cal's split from the Southern Conference was a prestige move, the university unabashedly stated.

"We hope for a foothold on the athletic ladder that will carry us to a level of competition more to the proportion of our ambitious, restless, growing young institution," announced the school.

While the Southern Conference fell apart, Southern Cal turned north and entered into rugby relations with Stanford and California. It turned out to be a disastrous move.

Rugby, Anyone?

"The game of American football, whether justly or not, is doomed to go down and out, and it's the wise rat that leaves the sinking ship before it's too late."

Rugby star Mowat M. Mitchell used an unfortunate choice of words in describing the new state of affairs on California's golden slope. If anyone was a "rat," thought Pomona and Occidental, it was Southern Cal for breaking up that old football gang of theirs.

But Southern Cal was not at the time especially interested in nobility, merely mobility. The "Methodists" were attempting to keep up with the Joneses of the rugby world and in effect snubbed several Southern California neighbors to do it.

Breaking away (and breaking up) the Southern California Intercollegiate Conference, Southern Cal joined rugby forces with Stanford and California, among others, in an attempt to reach a higher level of competition. It was a sad mistake, for USC was outclassed by schools of richer rugby tradition in the games from 1911 through 1913. The school not only suffered on the field, but in the box office as well.

"The results were severe financial losses during this three-year venture," reported Manuel P. Servin and Iris Higbie Wilson in their book, *Southern California And Its University*.

Perhaps if they knew what they were in for, Southern Cal's administrators would not have taken the step. It was a step backwards, to be sure, despite Mitchell's beliefs.

Billed as "Southern California's great football star (football was used interchangeably with rugby)," Mitchell wrote in a Los Angeles newspaper: "The adoption of rugby by the University of Southern California is a great step in the development of the game in America."

But Mowat was wrong. The appearance of rugby lightened attendance in both the new English game and the old American game.

"It often happened that both forms of the pastime were staged in the same city on the same day and both games suffered," reported Spaulding's *Football Guide*.

There were isolated pockets of interest, of course. Rugby had an appeal to the bloodthirsty. It was, in many ways, more violent than football. Players wore no protection, only skimpy shirts, shorts, and high socks, much like today's soccer uniforms. Yet they tackled as hard.

"Players sometimes taped their ears to their heads to keep them from being torn off," said a coach, reflecting on the "good, old days."

Rugby was continuous movement and concentrated mayhem.

"It was a wild scramble, much rougher than football in many cases because of the tackling without pads," said the coach. "The rugby players usually laughed at American football players, because they thought they were sissies."

Into this exotic scene stepped Pat Higgins, the first rugby coach at Southern Cal. He was at once confident that he could field a representative team.

"I never did think the Northerners were so far ahead of us," he said. "Rugby is merely a man-to-man game. The Stanford and California men have the experience; we will have when we meet them. When my players get confidence, I'll spring a few things that will have the Northern teams guessing.

"The situation looks good. I have had the aspirants out for three days, and have given them some stiff workouts. But I shall be careful at over-training, for I do not want them to run stale. I shall have them so that in the big games they will have every bit of stamina and vitality on tap."

A newspaper preview of the 1911 season cited "Smoke" Adamson and Mike Brown as "the giants of the bunch, both tipping the beam at 220.

"Smoke" Adamson captained the 1912 Southern California rugby team. He did not throw his 220-pound weight around too well, though, because the Trojans lost every game.

"Harry Huntington is light, but he fights every minute and is an 'oldhead' at the game so that he will in all probability end on the team selected by Higgins to represent the university. Roy Malcolm, Frank Pitcher, Mike Kaprillian, Fred Teschke, and Raymond McGrew—they call him 'Minute'—complete the register of promising material out for the pack."

These fellows were in for an education, explained Mitchell. Rugby in style and climate was vastly different from American football.

"The American system...has developed into a matter of strict discipline and rigorous training and has become the greatest importance and the prime object in life to the university athlete," said Mitchell. "This is totally at variance with the Englishman's idea of sport. He truly believes in sport for sport's sake and plays the game for the sake of the game, and not primarily for winning."

If that was the case, then Southern Cal had not completely caught the full spirit of the thing. Tied together rather loosely by Higgins, Southern Cal's rugby team did manage to win a few games in its first season—even if some of the victories were over high schools, athletic clubs, and college freshmen. And some of the players almost got into a fight with the Olympic Club of San Francisco, which was terribly un-English of them.

"The unsportsmanlike attitude of some of the Northern players spoiled the game for many of the bleachers," reported the *El Rodeo*. "Much time was wasted in disputing decisions, and some of the Northerners even tried to support their arguments with their fists. Our men stood up well under the trying circumstances."

There was more excitement on that trip north. Coach Higgins had his hands full of animated players on the train, and many refused to follow curfew rules.

"The poor coach had to give the porter orders to hit (Fred) Teschke over the head," reported a student manager. "It was the only way to get him to sleep."

The fidgety youngsters also lifted magazines and towels for keepsakes.

"Magazines, side lights, and towels are souvenirs put around the train by the kind porter for people to take (only college boys know this)," noted the student manager.

There was also full-scale shoplifting at their hotel. Higgins simmered slowly.

"The proprietor of the Hotel Arlington used to be a colleger himself so he made good with the boys to such an extent that they only took small articles for souvenirs," said the student manager. "I can vouch for the fact that every bed and dresser remained in its proper place."

When playing teams like Stanford, of course, Southern California was overmatched. This, however, did not diminish some of that old, college spirit. Higgins' gallants fought the stronger northern team to a scoreless tie at the half before succumbing 6-0. The game was closer than a lot of people expected, reported Owen R. Bird, the sports editor of the *Los Angeles Times*. He told about the feverish halftime activities.

"The USC bleachers went wild, and a fair coed got on the yell leaders' stand and led the songs for a while," Bird said in his game story. "Excitement was rife. Gloom had settled over the Stanford followers as the two teams were rushed to their respective quarters. Before the game started, many were saying the score should be 40 to 0.

Southern California played rugby in 1911, but not very well. The team lost games—and money, to boot.

"In the USC gym, Higgins was pleading with his men to keep up the pace while the battle-scarred heroes were being rubbed down. In the Stanford quarters, Coach Presley was calling down the wrath of the gods on the devoted heads of his slaves. He ripped them up first one way, then another during the whole time between the halves. Stanford was on the field first for the second half and was greeted by a few scattering cheers. When the USC team came on the scene of battle, the bleachers rose to a man and one of the greatest ovations ever accorded a team in the south was given the gritty USC fighters."

Predictably, Southern Cal fell apart in the second half.

"The pace began to tell," said Bird, gloomily.

Truck Manning had no better luck with Southern Cal's rugby players in 1912. The team did not win a game, leading the *El Rodeo* to tactfully sum up a season of "courage" thusly: "While the varsity lost badly this year, they have gained a reputation of hard fighters, good losers, and gentlemen. They were against unequal odds in every match, but they played with every ounce of strength in them and they played clean ball. What more can be said?"

Whether losing 41-0 to the Waratah Team of Australia or taking a more civilized beating from the California Freshman, 23-3, Southern Cal was noble in defeat. Indeed it was an indomitable spirit in the face of big odds in both rugby and track competition that eventually led to the nickname, "Trojans."

Bird, a prejudiced viewer of Southern Cal athletics in the growing-up years, told the story of the christening:

"The birth of the name 'Trojan' came about in the early spring of 1912. At this time the University of Southern California was called the Methodists, Wesleyans, and many other nicknames, which were not looked upon with favor by the powers then in control at the university. At this time Warren Bovard was directing the athletic destinies of the university and told me that his father, Dr. George F. Bovard, then president, was very much disgusted with the appellations applied to the university by the newspaper men and that he suggested I pick an appropriate name to take the place of the numerous names then in use, a name that would stick and one that would really mean something.

Southern California's first rugby captain: "Truck" Manning. He and his companions were overmatched. Manning played in 1911 and coached in 1912.

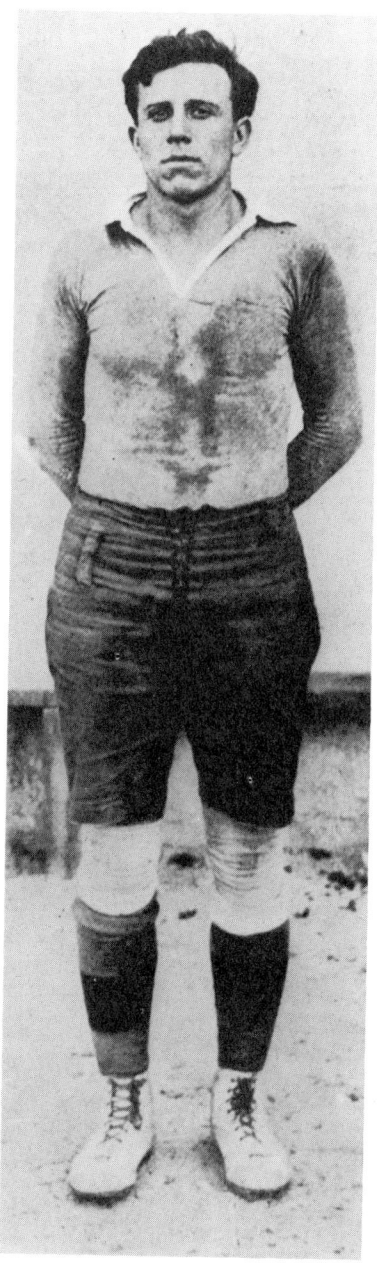

"In my capacity as sporting editor of the *Times*, at this particular period, I had a great deal to do with the activities at Southern California and was very closely associated with Dr. Warren Bovard. It was about at this period that Mr. Bovard and others decided to break out of the small college class and strive for the big league, as it were. Owing to this particular decision, or adoption of policy, it became more than ever necessary to hit upon a name for the varsity teams that would be catchy, mean something, and be acceptable at the same time to the sporting world at large.

"Owing to the terrific handicaps, under which the athletes, coaches, and managers of the university were laboring at this time and at the same time appreciating their splendid fighting spirit and ability of the teams to go down under overwhelming odds of bigger and better equipped teams with their colors gloriously nailed to the mast, it seemed to me that the name 'Trojan' fitted their case; so on February 28, 1912, prior to the dual Inter-Collegiate (track) meet between Stanford and Southern California, I came out with an article in the sporting section of the *Times*, calling attention to the fighting spirit of the Trojans and naming them 'Trojans' because of their ability and spirit. This was the first public announcement of the term."

The nickname was again used in a *Times* headline a few days later—and from then on at every possible opportunity in the newspaper. Bird's contemporaries picked it up, and in a couple of years it was universally adopted by society.

"Fundamentally, the term 'Trojan' as applied to Southern California means, in my mind, that no matter what the situation, what the odds, or what the conditions, the battle must be carried on to the end, and those who strive must give them all they have and never be weary in well doing, never be weary in giving," said Bird, defining his intimate love for a school.

Higgins returned to coach the rugby team in 1913, and the newly-annointed "Trojans" continued to "strive" and improve. But financial pressures squeezed Southern California's rugby world—and this was harder to beat than any team.

After a long struggle between contending factions representing the English game and the American game, football won.

Rugby was out, and football back in, at Southern Cal.

The Last Of The Chariots

Rich memories linger long after the game, locked forever in one's psyche. Going back in time is sweet, says Chet Dolley. He thinks of Dean Cromwell often.

"Cromwell was a fine gentleman and particularly kind," remembers Dolley, who played football for Southern Cal in the 1920s and knew the Trojans' popular coach of all seasons.

Cromwell was a father image to his athletes, a gentle patriarch who treated each of his "sons" with tender, loving care. A common scene was Cromwell with an arm draped around one of his athletes, instilling self-confidence.

"He was always talking to the boys and getting them to do better than their best," says Dolley. "He could talk to kids and get them to do well. He'd say, 'Come on, champ, you can do it,' to all of his boys."

Dolley recalls meeting Cromwell for the first time: "It was before I went to USC. My dad took me to a ballgame at old Bovard Field and introduced me to him. He was a gentleman all the way."

Coaching track was his nirvana. Cromwell was almost an afterthought in Southern Cal's football program. He was thrown into the game as a quick replacement, since no one else was readily available. He did all right, considering that it was not his forte. Cromwell coached football in 1909 and 1910, before the rugby renaissance, then came back for the 1916, 1917, and 1918 seasons. His football teams won 21, lost 6, and had 8 ties, one of them a significant scoreless game with California in

Dean Cromwell "conned everyone into thinking they were great." A coach for all seasons, Cromwell succeeded mostly at track but also gave football a spin.

1917.

"We had some good teams when we were playing Occidental and Cal in those days," Dolley recalls. "Cromwell had Charlie Paddock, who was billed as 'the world's fastest human;' Fred Kelly, an Olympic high hurdles champ; and Bud Howser. It was an all-around team, a good, running team."

Kelly was still heroic after his college days. He later became a pilot and the first one to fly air mail in the United States from Salt Lake City to the West Coast.

It was not surprising that Cromwell developed people of character.

"Cromwell was an excellent coach, but his main idea was to make you feel as if no one could beat you," says Al Wesson, a longtime sports information director at Southern Cal who knew Cromwell in his student days. "He conned everyone into thinking that they were great. Some people thought he was a con artist. I don't know about that. He built everyone up...of course, he was more famous in track than football."

Cromwell first drew attention as a football player, though.

"He will be remembered by the oldtimers as one of the headiest backs that ever carried a ball across a southern goal," recalled a contemporary. "He acquired his initial knowledge at Occidental when that school was noted for its good teams, and (he) was regularly picked on all-star teams."

He coached at Willamette University in Oregon for a while before coming to Southern Cal, unheralded, in 1909. His first team won the Southern Conference meet over Pomona, Occidental, and Whittier, and Cromwell thus laid the foundation for a track dynasty. In 40 years Cromwell became a national byword in the sport. He spawned at least one Olympic champion in every meet from 1912 through 1948, when he retired. His teams won 8 Pacific Coast Conference track championships in 11 years of PCC competition and 12 national titles in 19 attempts. (His teams finished second in NCAA competition 5 times, as well.) When he retired from Southern Cal, Cromwell was an obvious choice to coach the United States Olympic track and field team.

"He was a genial leader in all athletic competition," recalled Southern California's *Pigskin Review*. "Dean injected a new life into the boys."

When Cromwell came back into football in 1916, the sport had become a West Coast passion. Two years before, rugby had died at Southern Cal, giving way to the "good, old intercollegiate game."

Rugby was kicked out of Southern Cal in one, swift boot—dropped as easily as it was picked up. The Trojans returned to American football in 1914 and humbly put together the pieces with some old "friends," Occidental and Pomona.

It was not so much a question of choice between the two styles of football, explained the *El Rodeo*. It was rather a question of "greater advantages to be derived by the university as a whole from games with her natural rivals, the colleges of the south."

It was, perhaps, more a question of finances. Road trips to the northern end of the state were exceedingly expensive. The *El Rodeo* explained, "while the gate receipts were good, at least one-half had to be used to defray traveling expenses."

The return of the American game to the Trojan campus made a lot of people happy, including the folks who published the annual Spaulding *Football Guide*.

"The American game of football made 1913 a powerful year in California," the *Guide* reported. "The sport-loving public rallied to its support in a convincing manner showing they favored intercollegiate football to rugby. The brilliant and spectacular exhibitions put up by Pomona, Occidental, and Whittier checked the invasion of the English game, and gave the American game its first decisive victory since the introduction of rugby in America by Stanford and California. Southern Cal is convinced the sport is for American colleges and has decided to return to the good, old intercollegiate game."

The transition presented immediate obstacles for Southern Cal. The Trojans reestablished a Southern Conference relationship with Occidental and Pomona—but also reestablished the old saw about eligibility requirements. Pomona battled Southern Cal off the field about freshman participation in football and finally knocked the Trojans down in this matter. Although Southern Cal disputed it, a conference agreement was finally signed with Pomona and Occidental: no freshmen. This new ruling, plus the formation of a "green team" under Coach Ralph Glaze, had painful after-effects in the Trojans' season of

Warm rapport between two coaching greats—Amos Alonzo Stagg and Southern California's Dean Cromwell.

1914. They were beaten by both Occidental and Pomona in the reincarnation of their fierce rivalries.

While all this drama was taking place in Southern California, the northern California theater was preparing to stage a new play, too. The University of California made plans to resume football in 1915. The inexperienced Bears took a 72-0 beating that year from a powerful Washington team, the rage of the Northwest. However, California progressed so quickly and so well that in 1917 the Bears defeated the Huskies 27-0 to break their famous string of 63 undefeated games.

In 1915 the Pacific Coast Intercollegiate Athletic Conference (the PCC) came to life. On December 2, 1915, members met in the Oregon Hotel in Portland to draw up the league's first constitution. Present were representatives of California, the University of Oregon, Oregon State, and the University of Washington. Stanford became a member in 1916, although continuing to play rugby through 1917. Washington State also applied for membership in 1916 and was accepted.

The period was a landmark for the West Coast in another way. After featuring several years of Roman circus-like chariot races, the Tournament of Roses officials decided to change to a football game for the celebration on January 1, 1916. This marked the real beginning of the Rose Bowl game and helped deliver the final knockdown blow to rugby. Football was really the only game in town now, and Washington State polished the image of the West with a 14-0 victory over Brown, the East's representative. Because of bad weather, attendance was held down to 8,000, and the Tournament of Roses committee lost $11,000. But despite that the committee decided to try again on New Year's Day in 1917, and the result was an unqualified success. A crowd of 25,000 attended the game, and thousands more were turned away. Oregon defeated Penn 14-0, giving Western football another shot in the arm and Eastern football a kick in the pants.

The victories by Western teams had a definite effect on the Eastern establishment. In 1917 the *New York Sun* took note that there was, indeed, a West by placing Washington State No. 7 in its national Top Ten. But it was not until Andy Smith's "Wonder Team" at California in 1920 that Western football became truly golden. Smith, a former Pennsylvania fullback and

When Southern California said goodbye to rugby and hello to football in 1914, Tommy Davis, left, was the Trojan captain. At right is Leonard Livernash, captain of the 1915 Trojans.

later coach at his alma mater and Purdue, took over at California in 1916 and in four years raised the level of West Coast prestige to the highest in the land.

Southern Cal luckily caught California at its low-water mark in 1915, when the Golden Bears just resumed playing football, and won a 28-10 decision in one of two games that year. California won the other meeting, 23-21, and it would be 1926 before the Bears would lose another game to the Trojans.

The 1915 season was also significant for Southern Cal in that the school once again broke away from the inhibiting bonds of the Southern Conference. The Trojans yearned for big-time football and scheduled, along with California, teams like St. Mary's, Oregon, and Utah. They wound up losing more games than they won that year, but it was not because they were not trying.

"Coach Glaze tackled a difficult task as any man has ever tackled," said a writer. "His material was worse than inexperience because he had to pound out of the heads of the players all the rugby they had learned and teach them the fundamentals of American football."

Glaze, a former Dartmouth star, was not wholly without talent, though, and tutored superb athletes such as end George James, center Fred Teschke, halfback Fred Kelly, and tackle Eugene Bayley. And while they were not winning as many games as they would have liked, the Trojans were certainly winning fans. A record crowd of 8,000 showed up for the second California game in 1915. The previous high was 3,000. While making more money, Southern Cal was spending more, too. It cost the university approximately $1,800 to field a football team in those days, and plans were afoot to spruce up old Bovard Field.

"A perfectly arranged field is promised, with new buildings, commodious bleachers and modern equipment," said the *El Rodeo*.

If they did not win every game in 1915, the Trojans did expand their horizons. They made a trip to Salt Lake City to play Utah, a journey of negative and positive implications.

On the negative side the Trojans were beaten 20-13 on an intercepted pass, Frank Malette was knocked cold three times, and the trip was a "long, hard one," according to the *El Rodeo*.

On the positive side the "scenery" was nice and the hosts were hospitable.

"Probably the most notable thing on the calendar of events was the royal welcome which the many pretty coeds extended to our boys," said Teschke. "Without the slightest warning, our fellows burst in on an entertainment given by them on Friday afternoon, and were shown a good time for the rest of the day. I fear that a few more days of their hospitality would have meant the loss of a few of our star performers."

The Southern Cal player also commended the Utah people for good fellowship.

"Special mention should be made of the fact that the management of Utah did all they could to satisfy our every want," Teschke said. "They even went so far as to have Mr. Smith come from Colorado to act as referee at our suggestion.

CALIFORNIA OR BUST—Southern California students pile into a jalopy, circa 1915, for the California game. Note, "Where Is Cal?" scrawled in chalk on the side of the car.

This entailed an expense of about $80, but they bore the expense with their ever-present spirit of fair play."

There was an indication that Southern Cal would have won the game, had Malette not made a crucial error. Apparently, because of a case of mistaken identity, he neglected to make a key tackle.

"Utah outplayed us in the line smashes, but we more than evened up with our modern football and had not Malette mistaken (through the fact that both teams wore crimson jerseys) one of their men for our halfback Murray the score would have been in our favor at the end of the game."

The 23-21 loss to California that year was literally a dark day. Beaten by a field goal at the end, the Trojans battled the last 10 minutes in darkness. The conditions were definitely not in their favor, according to the student newspaper.

"The (Los Angeles) *Times* suggests that the local players are not used to being out after dark," said the *Trojan*. "Be this as it may, the score was reversed after it was too dark to see the ball."

With Cromwell's reappearance in 1916 came a training table, the reconstruction of Bovard Field, and a winning team.

"Consistent hard work by Coach Cromwell brought this team from a weak team at the beginning of the season to one of the most highly rated teams on the West Coast at the end," said Spaulding's *Football Guide*. "This team was barely able to beat a good high school team at the beginning."

Included among five victories in eight games were successes over Sherman Institute and Arizona, two of the newest additions to Southern Cal's exotic schedules. The season of 1917 was an artistic as well as financial success with four victories and an imposing tie with California in seven games. Cromwell produced several good players that year and several good nicknames as well. There was "Rabbit" Malette, "Tank" Campbell, "Turk" Hunter, and "Duck" Miller. Sans nickname, but just as colorful, was Dan McMillan.

Malette, a quarterback, was aptly described as "the greatest backfield man the University of Southern California ever produced" until that point. Assessing the players of that era, a writer said that Malette's last season was a "grand series of spectacular and brilliant playing...his open-field running, his

Herb Jones was the Trojan captain in 1916, when Dean Cromwell reappeared along with a training table, a refurbished Bovard Field, and a winning team.

Frank Malette, "the greatest backfield man produced at Southern California" in his time, captained the artistic 1917 team.

remarkable footwork, his ability as a dodger stamp him as the greatest. He was always to be relied upon to run a punt back fifteen or twenty yards and was as slippery as an eel."

The writer praised Campbell for consistency and self-improvement, the marks of a true champion: "From a mediocre player, Jim advanced and continued to improve throughout the season, until the California game on Thanksgiving Day, when the big boy, alone and unaided, staved back the onward march of the Norsemen, and in the last few minutes of play broke through the opposing line and threw the California men back for an eight-yard loss. He was even more valuable on the offensive than the defensive. Time and again when yards counted most, Jim was always to be relied upon for a hole large enough to push a wagon through."

Hunter, a 19-year-old, 180-pound fullback, was "unexcelled as a line-plunger," according to the writer. "The harder the game and the closer the score, the harder that handsome young man hit the line. He was going his best at the Saint Mary's game and was good for from three to six yards each time he carried the ball."

Miller was a halfback as hard to stop "as a tank...he hit the line like a steam roller. He played a clean, hard game and seemingly the harder the knocks the more he enjoyed the game."

McMillan played at tackle and earned all-state honors. Ironically, after World War I, he transferred to California University and made Walter Camp's all-America team.

The war interrupted a lot of careers in intercollegiate football, as in all walks of life. It caused, among other things, an abbreviated schedule in 1918.

But by 1919, when Johnny came marching home, there was a different drummer at Southern Cal. Under "Gloomy Gus" Henderson, the Trojans moved to a new beat.

Time Out: "Gloomy Gus" Henderson

Gus Henderson was a man of rare achievement, illogically given to lingering pessimism before or after triumph. They did not call him "Gloomy Gus" for nothing. Once asked about his first game as coach of Southern Cal's football team, Henderson replied: "Pomona will mop up on us." Southern Cal won, 6-0.

Another time after a preseason exhibition victory over Poly High School in Los Angeles, Henderson turned to the opposing coach and asked: "Did you ever see a rottener college outfit than that one of mine?"

"Nope, it isn't possible," replied the opposing coach, tongue in cheek.

"Therein lies the secret of Gus's freak nickname—as well as its fallacy," explains Leo Calland, who played for Henderson in the 1920s. "Whenever the newspapermen approached Henderson concerning the ability of his team, he told them the truth. But the gods of fate were unkind, and invariably 'Gloomy's' trick squad came through by winning the game and giving the newspapermen a chance to prove Henderson's pessimism."

Named for a well-known cartoon character of the day, Henderson was anything but a joke at Southern Cal despite his laughable pessimism. He brought the Trojans out of the Dark Ages and opened bright, new horizons in big-time football. From 1919 through 1924, while playing an expanded major league schedule, Henderson's team twice won 10 games in a season, including a Rose Bowl game, and he compiled a lofty record of 45 victories and 7 losses. The winning percentage of

.880 was the best in Southern Cal's history.

"I thought Henderson was ahead of his time," says Calland, a star lineman for Southern Cal from 1920 through 1922 who also played earlier for Henderson at Seattle's Broadway High School. "In high school we had various spread formations and T-formations similar to what the pros use today."

Born in the college town of Oberlin, Ohio, Henderson was a precocious football child. It was said that he could play the game better at the age of five than boys ten years his senior. The Oberlin High School coach, Doc Spiers, first noticed this phenom playing football on a back lot, a tubby little fellow running around in shorts.

"In 1904, Oberlin High gained the first of its string of star performers from the house of Henderson," remembers Calland. "As the babies in Oberlin were raised on footballs, father Henderson's first ambition was to see his oldest son on the high school eleven. This ambition was fulfilled, and with a vengeance, as Elmer made his letter in five sports for four years."

The seed for Henderson's famed pessimism was perhaps planted at Oberlin College, Calland explains.

"The college team at the time carried a trainer by the name of Bill Chambers," says Calland. "Bill was noted for his pessimistic outlook on life in general and the team in particular. Every time the varsity would trot out he would moan, 'Ah, it's a crime, you bo's is shure gwine to be slaughtered. You don't know nothin' about football, you is sure gwine to get beat.'"

After playing out a glittering college career, Henderson coached at the Chamberlain Academy in New York and in 1914 joined Broadway High School on the West Coast. In four years there his teams lost only two games and tied one in 24, outscoring the opposition 586 to 84 in what was known as a "balanced" high school league.

After a Navy commission in 1918, when he directed athletics at the training station in Seattle, Henderson was picked for the Southern Cal job. The story goes that a Los Angeles sportswriter, Harry Grayson of the *Express*, was largely responsible for bringing Henderson to the Trojan campus. Working together with Sports Editor Mark Kelly of the *Los Angeles Examiner*, the two campaigned fiercely to bring big-time

"Gloomy Gus" Henderson coached Southern California for six pessimistic years. Despite his well-known crying towel he brought the Trojans out of the dark ages.

football to Southern Cal. Their reasoning was that Los Angeles was doomed to civic failure unless represented by a nationally-recognized college football team.

Of course, university officials were receptive to their plans, and Grayson was given the green light to approach Henderson. Grayson recognized the abundance of football talent in his native Pacific Northwest, where they had been playing the American game longer than in any sector on the West Coast. When he telephoned Henderson and offered him the job at Southern Cal, the stipulation was that he bring his players south with him.

The conversation went something like this:

Grayson: "How many members of your team can you bring down here to Los Angeles?"

Henderson: "All of them."

Grayson: "Line up your boys, because I'm giving you the job."

Henderson's "boys" did all right once he assembled them on a Southern California football field. The 1919 season started the Trojans' ball rolling toward national prominence. Southern Cal beat Stanford by two touchdowns that season and lost by only one point to formidable California, a longtime bully over the Trojans. In 1920 Henderson gave Southern Cal its first perfect season with victories over Cal Tech, Stanford, Occidental, Pomona, Nevada, and Oregon. The Trojans were beaten only once in eleven games in 1921 and that by a California team considered as good as any in America. An identical 10-1 season followed in 1922, including a 14-3 victory over Penn State in the first Rose Bowl game played at the present Pasadena site.

The Trojans' sudden emergence from mediocrity fanned the fires of jealousy on the West Coast. Soon both Stanford and California were charging Southern Cal with under-the-table dealings in getting top football talent. Actually Henderson was just an able and aggressive recruiter.

"He was a good recruiter," remembers Chet Dolley, who played for Henderson from 1922 through 1924. "He got the best boys from local high schools. He also got his players to recruit. One of my 'assignments' was to bring Morely Drury to the school."

(Drury became one of the biggest stars in the 1920s and

later was immortalized as "The noblest Trojan of them all.")

"Henderson had more rapport with the players than most coaches," recalls Calland. "He went out and got a lot of the boys himself, and as a result we kept getting better material at Southern Cal."

While earning the respect of other teams, Henderson also had the respect of his own.

"Henderson was one of the greatest men who ever lived—clean, good principled, treated you like a man, and respected you," says Calland. "As a result you treated him the same way. He was very fair and a very easy man to talk to as well."

When recruiting the best high school prospects in the Los Angeles area, Henderson was sure to attract players with a flair. That was his style. Recalls Calland:

"Henderson was wide open when he had to be. He set up his passes by establishing his running and kicking game—just like what the pros are doing now. He wasn't a guy who threw passes right off the bat, but he could throw it down your throat."

Southern Cal's successes under "Gloomy Gus" soon became so exasperating to Stanford and California that they broke off relations with the Trojans in 1924. Stanford's inability to beat Henderson teams, in fact, was one of the main reasons that a frustrated and beleaguered "Pop" Warner relinquished his coaching job there and headed east.

But, ironically, Henderson in turn could not beat California and—conversely—that was the beginning of the end for him at Southern Cal in 1924. In his last season he scheduled a far-reaching schedule and beat the boys from Syracuse, Missouri, Idaho, Oregon State, Nevada, and Arizona among nine victories. But among two defeats was one by Andy Smith's California "Wonder Team."

"That was the reason Henderson lost out at Southern Cal," says Calland. "He kept losing to California."

Calland recalls an ironic sidelight to the bitter situation when Henderson was finally "paid off" by Southern Cal officials.

"One time Notre Dame came out to play Stanford and beat the Indians," says Calland, "and Knute Rockne, the Fighting Irish coach, said in jest, 'I'll have to come out and

Gus Henderson, "a very fair and a very easy man to talk to as well." Henderson even befriended dogs.

coach USC to show them how to beat the California team.' Well, Southern Cal officials took that as a come-on by Rockne and thought that he was shooting for a job as the Trojan coach."

On that off-hand remark Southern Cal officials got rid of Henderson and expected to sign Rockne, says Calland. Naturally, it did not happen.

"Were the USC faces red when they found out that Rockne was just kidding!" says Calland.

As a result Southern Cal officials had to settle for "second best." They got Howard Jones, whose Iowa team had beaten the great Rockne back in the Midwest. Jones, of course, became an extravagantly successful coach at Southern Cal in the next 16 years, as near legend as man can be. But it was Henderson who laid the groundwork for Jones' famous "Thundering Herd" teams. Jones reaped the benefits of Henderson's recruiting work with such players as Brice Taylor and Mort Kaer, Southern Cal's first all-Americans.

From Southern Cal, Henderson went to Tulsa, a team that had won only three games in the two previous years. Overnight "Gloomy Gus" changed the Golden Tornado into a Southwest power. He coached for eleven years there before returning to California to take charge of the Los Angeles Bulldogs. With the use of Henderson's wide-open style of spread formations (the forerunner of today's game), the professional team became a big winner in the old National Football League. Henderson later moved to the Detroit Lions and then went back to college coaching at Occidental until the Second World War. After the war he ran a boys camp on Catalina Island until his death in 1965.

Henderson is eulogized on a football plaque among Southern Cal's memorabilia as "A courageous competitor who inspired his men to fight like Trojans."

Calland recalls the more personal side.

"He was a thoroughly principled and clean man," says Calland.

"I loved him."

Time Out: Leo Calland

The dance rage was the "Black Bottom," Charlie Chaplin was in his tragicomic glory, the catch-phrase of the day was "Twenty-Three Skidoo," and a car, if you were lucky enough to own one, was called a "flivver."

This was the Roaring 20s, a romantic fragment of Americana. But Leo Calland had little time for such sweet luxuries as dancing, movie-going, and Sunday driving. He was a football player.

"We didn't have weights in those days, so we had to work in places like mining camps to tone up our bodies," recalls Calland. "We had to have muscles to play football."

Of course, football was exacting, torturous labor, too.

"We shoved and sweated," says Calland, a star lineman for Southern Cal from 1920 through 1922. "We were like fighters going to the finish. We came out throwing leather, so to speak. We had to play a whole game usually, and it was more like a boxing bout to the finish."

Calland could more than hold his own, though. Sportswriter Paul Lowry once wrote in the *Los Angeles Times*: "A big powerful fellow of 200 pounds, Calland was a riot the minute he stepped on a Southern California football field."

One of the finest guards who ever played on the West Coast, Calland was lured to Southern Cal on the premise that he would play for his high school coach, "Gloomy Gus" Henderson. They were both at Broadway High School in Seattle, Washington, and in fact drove south together in Henderson's rusty old car in 1919.

"Henderson was offered the job on a proposal that he take some of his high school players with him to Southern Cal," remembers Calland. "Henderson was the sole reason I wanted to go."

As a freshman, Calland could only watch the varsity play. As a sophomore, he WAS the varsity.

"I played everyplace," he says, chuckling. "In my sophomore year we didn't have a center, so I played center. In my junior year I played running guard, and in my senior year I played tight end and sometimes defensive center. I played every spot on the line, and later in the Navy I was a quarterback on the service team. There wasn't any reason why I shouldn't have been knowledgeable about football. I knew the signals for every position."

Calland's glory in the trenches was exemplified by his extraordinary ability to smash open holes for Southern Cal's fine stable of running backs. He also was a fierce pass protector. He had to be—because of the Trojans' wide-open style.

"We passed as much as anybody in those days," Calland says. "Henderson used a spread formation and worked a lot of interesting plays from it. We also used the Single Wing, but whenever we got stopped on the Single Wing we'd go to a more diversified offense."

As Calland remembers, only about 26 players showed up for Henderson's first practice in 1919. By the time Calland was in the starting lineup in 1920, there were not many more out for the team. But what Henderson had was quality rather than quantity.

"Henderson was a very wonderful man," says Calland, "and he got the best out of his players. And because of Henderson, we kept getting better material as the years went by."

As a sophomore, Calland played on the first undefeated team at Southern Cal. As a senior, he played on the school's first Rose Bowl team. The Trojans defeated Penn State 14-3 on January 1, 1923, and completed a second straight glittering season of 10 victories in 11 games. Calland, not incidentally, was named player of the game in the Rose Bowl.

"There were no lights and we finished in the dark," says

Calland, recalling his last hurrah as a Trojan. "It was my most satisfying game because it was a lifelong dream of mine to play in a Rose Bowl.

"I remember, Penn State was a tough club. They had this Harry Wilson, a helluva back, and he was running through us like crazy in the early part of the game. Well, we stopped him the rest of the game with a seven-man line. And because we stopped him, we stopped Penn State completely. He was their best runner. I don't think they made over two first downs the rest of the game after that first quarter."

An enormous crowd for the time, "about 43,000," watched the first game ever played in the present Pasadena Rose Bowl site. But the noise was in another world, as far as Calland was concerned. No butterflies here.

"We didn't give a damn about the crowd," he says. "We just wanted the honor of playing in the Rose Bowl. When we played, I didn't even know the crowd was there. I concentrated on the ballgame."

Southern Cal gathered spinoffs from a Rose Bowl victory.

"After the Rose Bowl we had our choice of all the boys in Southern California," recalls Calland. "About 100 turned out for the freshman team the following year."

Calland had the good fortune to associate not only with Henderson, but with Howard Jones as well. After graduating in 1922, Calland was a line coach when Jones was building national champions at Southern Cal.

"They were two entirely different personalities," says Calland. "Henderson had more rapport with his players than Jones. Howard was a big god up at the top. Nobody on the staff ever called him Howard. He was very withdrawn and cold. A wonderful coach...but not any better than Henderson. Both were fine coaches, though."

Calland, who stayed on at Southern Cal with Henderson, left when "Gloomy Gus" disappeared from the Trojan scene in 1924. Calland coached football, basketball, and baseball at Whittier before returning to his alma mater in the late 1920s.

"When I came back to USC, I got the biggest surprise of my life," Calland remembers. "Jones told me I would coach the freshman team. I was his freshman coach, and that was that."

Calland was more pleasantly surprised when he looked at

the material he had. It was one of the best freshman teams ever produced at Southern Cal, harboring Gus Shaver, Jim Musick, Johnny Baker, Ernie Smith, and Ernie Pinckert. This team went on to win the national championship for Southern Cal in 1931.

Calland later coached at Idaho and then declined a chance to coach at San Diego State because "I got tired of beating my brains out against California." So he moved south again and helped form the forerunner of the State College Conference in California. Then along came World War II—and that was the end of his serious football activity. A seaman second class in World War I, Calland eventually rose to commander in the Navy and upon his retirement from the service was park and recreation director for the city of San Diego until 1960.

At the age of 73—a lively 73, that is—Calland serves as managing director of the San Diego Hall of Fame, an honorary institution that reveres San Diego-developed athletes. In his spare time he and his wife Sarah visit with their nine grandchildren and three great-grandchildren, and he renews treasured friendships.

"When I got together recently with the other fellows for our 50th anniversary celebration of the Rose Bowl team, it was quite touching," says Calland, a smile in his voice. "They were all fine men and went on to other successes. We didn't have a rotten egg in the whole bunch. A lot of them became teachers, coaches, and administrators."

One important face was missing from the party, though—Henderson. "Gloomy Gus" had since passed away.

"He was a good teacher and a good coach," says Calland of the man who influenced his life more than any other. "I'll always be grateful."

Bury My Wounded Pride At Berkeley

Prior to a football game between Southern Cal and California in the early 1920s, a newspaper sonneteer was inspired to these modest poetic heights:

"Oh, there he goes! Oh, there he goes!
Tiernan dressed up in his football clothes;
He's fast as the deuce and he goes up there
To twist the tail of the Golden Bear."

This bard may have known something about iambic pentameter but nothing about football. In those days the Trojans had their hands full with the Golden Bears, and a trip to Berkeley usually proved to be a lost weekend. In fact Gus Henderson's inability to beat Andy Smith's teams from 1919 through 1924 caused great concern at Southern Cal and eventually cost "Gloomy Gus" his job.

It was unfortunate that Southern Cal's arrival into big-time football in 1919 coincided with California's most golden era under Smith, an honored and revered coach. A 7-0 loss in 1919 to Washington was the last one in a while for the Golden Bears, whose victory margins in the next few years included scores like 127-0 and 79-7. One year they compiled a staggering 510 points to a trifling 14 for their opponents.

California raised the level of West Coast football to unprecedented heights by beating a powerful Ohio State team 28-0 in the January 1, 1921, Rose Bowl. This loss to a Western opponent so embarrassed the Big Ten Conference that its officials reportedly prevented teams from returning to the Rose

Bowl classic for many years. No Big Ten team came back to Pasadena until 1947, when Illinois beat UCLA 45-14.

Henderson's sour luck with California began in his first season, when he lost a 14-13 thriller. The 1919 game was a premonition of things to come. Southern Cal had the early lead when Charley Dean "scooped up a California fumble and sped 60 yards to pay dirt," but the Golden Bears staged a dramatic, disheartening rally in the second half to pull it out.

"Gloomy Gus," so named for his pessimism, had every right to feel funereal where California was concerned in the next few years. Though not playing the Golden Bears in 1920, Southern Cal was beaten by California 38-7 in 1921, 12-0 in 1922, 13-7 in 1923, and 7-0 in 1924. It took two more years and a Howard Jones team to wipe out the Golden Bears.

While California was Henderson's Waterloo, he had uncommon success with the other schools that Southern California played. His six-year record was nonpareil in the Trojans' rich history.

Henderson's arrival at Southern Cal came in the flush of varied school refinements, both physical and aesthetic. In 1919 the cornerstone was laid for a new administration building, to cost $500,000 and to be built in the early Italian-Romanesque style. Physical education was made compulsory for all underclassmen. The students drafted and adopted a new constitution for the student body. And Spooks and Spokes, an honorary women's society, was organized.

In terms of football the school was growing, too. Officials thought in terms of national status and began promoting future games and larger schedules for the Trojans. Only five games were played in 1919, and six in 1920, but a far-ranging schedule soon grew to eleven games in Henderson's time. Henderson's popularity dilated immediately with his first glorious season.

"Successful beyond all hopes, the University of Southern California football season of 1919 ended with the Trojan eleven conceded to be one of the strongest teams on the Pacific Coast," trumpeted the *El Rodeo*.

Besides the one-point loss to arch-enemy California, Henderson's first team had victories over Pomona, Occidental, Utah, and Stanford. A terrified witness of the Pomona game recalls a mass of Trojan "monsters."

"Papa wheeled my plush perambulator through the Bovard Field gates, and soon after our entry Gus Henderson's juggernaut began grinding out a 6-0 victory over game—but unlucky—Pomona college," once wrote *Los Angeles Times* sports editor Braven Dyer, Sr., recalling his college days.

"I was a freshman at the time, one of the youngest ever admitted to Pomona, but well remember USC's men of might and the way they picked on our outmanned squad of scrawny teenagers. In subsequent seasons I learned from painful personal encounter how well "Gloomy Gus" started the Trojans on the way to national prominence. If you care to drop by some evening at cocktail time, I'll show you the bruises."

Dyer pointed out that USC "had its share of football giants in those long-ago days."

"Johnny Leadingham, a truly great punter, was the star of that 1919 win over Pomona," Dyer reminisced in an issue of Southern Cal's *Pigskin Review*. "Some of his spirals didn't come down until last week. Charley Dean, the fierce fullback, hit as hard as any back I ever saw. There were fine linemen like Swede Evans, Andy Toolen, Ken Townsend, John Fox, Deacon Beale, Jimmy Smith, Lowell Lindley, Eddie Simpson, Orrie Hester, and Bill Isenhouer. There was a young back named Dan McMillan who came out of Manual Arts and later transferred to California at Berkeley where he became an all-American tackle.

These players were trailblazers for the 1922 team which won USC's first Rose Bowl engagement, 14-3, over Penn State on New Year's Day.

Because of the scarcity of playing dates in Henderson's first season the opening day was on October 25—a distinct difference from today's jumble of over-lapping sports schedules. The Trojans sold 850 season tickets that year, a figure which "delighted" Henry W. Bruce, the football team's graduate manager. He was even more delighted when a record crowd of 9,000 showed up for the California game. The people who bought the tickets in 1919 got their money's worth, for the Trojans were a "most agreeable surprise," according to a 1920 football guide.

"Under the able leadership of Elmer Henderson, the team had a very successful season," the guide said. "The Trojans were hard to figure out at the start of the season as no one had been allowed to see them work out. (But) the results exceeded all expectations. Henderson built up a defense which was superb, all the Trojans' opponents having a hard time trying to penetrate it."

The Trojans were seriously considered for a Rose Bowl bid, but that prestigious assignment eventually went to Oregon. (Harvard beat the Ducks 7-6 in the 1919 classic.) Southern Cal did gain some attention, though, by placing several players on all-star teams—Eddie Simpson ("probably the best center seen in this vicinity for years," according to *El Rodeo*); Swede Evans ("who featured the games by his brilliant work at tackle and his high-class booting"); guard John Fox, the team captain; end Jimmy Smith; halfback Charley Dean; and fullback Johnny Leadingham.

The Trojans had an even more impressive season in 1920, winning all six games for their first perfect record in the "modern" era. But still it was not enough to overshadow awesome California. The Golden Bears were considered the best of the West, and as a result the "Wonder Team" got the Rose Bowl berth and beat Ohio State soundly before 42,000 people.

But Southern Cal's 1920 season was more than respectable, recalls Leo Calland.

"I remembered from my freshman year that Oregon played Harvard in the Rose Bowl in 1919, and the Ducks had almost the same team in 1920," says Calland, a star lineman for Southern Cal in the 1920s. "We were higher than a kite for Oregon, and we beat them 21-0. That was one of the games that made us."

That impeccable season the Trojans also beat Cal Tech 46-7, Stanford 10-0, Occidental 48-7, Pomona 7-0, and Nevada 38-7.

"We were getting better material," Calland recalls, pointing to Henderson's recruiting talents and the fact that there was a growing tendency on the part of star high school athletes to remain in the Southern California area. "We were growing."

A singular motivation stirred Southern Cal to greater accomplishments, according to Calland.

"We were trying to get into the Pacific Coast Conference," he remembers. "We wanted badly to get into the PCC."

It was not until 1922 that the Trojans were accepted into

John Fox, captain of the 1919 team, Gus Henderson's first at Southern California.

that prominent brotherhood. By then they had established themselves with an impressive 10-1 record in 1921. The undefeated team of 1920 started them toward their goal.

Henderson's passion for wide-open football confounded opponents. Sportswriters wrote flowery, lyrical leads such as the following in praise of the Trojans:

"At a late hour last night, Dr. Spivens, popular and well-known veterinary surgeon, announced that the Occidental Tiger would live but there was little hope that it will ever look the same. Dr. Spivens reports a complete warping of the Tiger's stripes, a heavy droop in the tail and a serious crossing of the eyes brought on by trying to watch USC's cross-bucks."

After Southern Cal's third straight victory over Stanford, a writer reported: "Though the score reads USC 10, Stanford 0, the true status of the beating is not at all revealed by the figures...the score (could) have read more like a city census than a respectable ball game. Never was the Trojan goal in any danger and but twice in the game was the ball in Trojan territory in the hands of the enemy."

However, a pedestrian, straightforward approach was best when a monarchy was decided. Reported the *Los Angeles Times* in a dispatch from Claremont:

"USC won the football championship of Southern California today by defeating Pomona College, 7 to 0, in one of the most desperate and hotly contested games ever played on Alumni Field.

"The only score of the hectic conflict resulted from a blocked punt toward the close of the first quarter. Paul Beale, the tall, rangy chap who does his bit as left tackle for USC, rumbled through the line and stuck his body in front of one of Covington's boots. The pill bounced back like a rubber ball and hopped gaily toward the Pomona goal line with Beale in hot pursuit.

"Overtaking the pigskin on the 1-yard line he fell on it, several Pomona players thereupon falling upon Mr. Beale. (Clarence) Butterfield tried to smash through the Sagehen line, but was stopped with no gain. Jimmy Woodward rose to the occasion and slipped through an orifice on the next play. Swede Evans kicked the goal and the score was 7 to 0, where it remained to the bitter end."

Southern California's Andy Toolen flies through the air with the greatest of ease and picks up yardage against Occidental in this 1921 game.

    The first football program surfaced in 1920 at Bovard Field. Entitled quite simply *Souvenir Football Program*, it had 20 pages and a buff cover with a stylized "SC" in maroon in the center and sold for 25 cents. It had a distinction that would not be repeated in the subsequent years when it became the *Pigskin Review*. The editors of the first program were starters on the football team, quarterback Jimmie Woodward and end Paul V. Greene.

    The booklet presented an offer that would surely cause irrepressible traffic jams in today's merry-go-round world. Earl A. Maginnis, a distributor of Jordan cars, promised "every Jordan automobile owner one-half hour SERVICE WITHOUT CHARGE each day, as long as he has a Jordan, for the purpose of adjustment and inspection."

    By 1921 the Trojans had become kings of football in the southern half of California. There remained, however, the omnipresent force of California, stirring mightily to the north.

    Victories over seven opponents by a composite score of 306 to 7 inspired disquieting confidence in the Trojans. Some believed that the team at last had attained equality with the Golden Bears. But some others emphasized that four of Southern Cal's victories, all lopsided shutouts, were fashioned against weak service teams.

Pomona, an ancient college rival, was the only one to score a touchdown against Southern Cal in the first seven games. The Trojans beat Pomona 35-7 despite three key fumbles by fullback Charley Dean. The mistakes so agitated Coach Henderson that Dean received an unusual punishment. Handing Dean an inflated football, the coach ordered him in front of the entire team to carry it with him everywhere for a week.

"Take it with you to your classrooms, to training quarters, to your meals and take it home with you at night," Henderson said. "Everywhere you go, that football must be under your arm. Maybe you'll learn to hold it by the time we play California."

Accepting the punishment gracefully, Dean remarked: "I have no excuse for my fumbles. The coach has plenty of reasons to be sore."

While punishing him for his mistakes, however, Henderson neglected to pat his star runner on the back for his achievements. He had ripped off a dazzling 80-yard touchdown run during the day's activities.

Perhaps you could excuse Henderson's slight injustice, though. Dean's fumbles came at a most inopportune time—one week before the crucial game with California. Henderson's season, and as it turned out later, his career, was at stake in the game at Berkeley. "Gloomy Gus" was never more pessimistic, never more perturbed.

"If I could smear Dean's arm with glue maybe that might help," he said. "Or maybe I might persuade California to let my backfield men carry the ball in a sack. I'll have to invent something to stop that fumbling."

Since both teams were undefeated and the weighty game would decide the state championship, intense hoopla preceeded the struggle. Bet the bank roll on California, said Golden Bear Coach Andy Smith. Conversely, Henderson hotly denied charges that he had placed a $2,500 bet on his team.

Rumors of the big bet were spread by California supporters to "bait me," said the Southern Cal coach. "I would not make the bet for two reasons. First, I firmly believe my team will lose by three touchdowns. Secondly, I haven't that much money."

Henderson added, characteristically: "No, I'm not betting a dime on my team to win, and I sincerely hope all Southern California will take my advice and keep their money at home."

The pessimistic Henderson, however, could not quash the spirit of the Southern California campus. Pre-game interest ran high. Reported the school newspaper, the *Trojan*:

"With every deck in shining readiness and with a passenger list of hundreds of University of Southern California students and alumni, bound for the battlefield at Berkeley, the good ship Yale will sail into the deep blue waters of the Pacific Friday afternoon. As the big steamer breaks away from the locks, the thirty-piece band carried by the students will play, 'Three Cheers for S. C.', and the 'Alma Mater,' the battle songs of the campus."

For only the second time in its history California Field was filled to its 26,000 capacity. The sky broke clear and blue for the passionate customers. Scalpers were still outside the stadium, getting $10 and $15 for the few tickets that had fallen into their hands.

"This he-man's battle in the lee of the Berkeley hills has created a terrific volume of excitement," wrote Paul Lowry in his *Los Angeles Times* story.

"I expect California to play a punting game," said Henderson. "Smith orders his men to punt, punt, punt."

However, on that November day, they passed, passed, passed. And, it turned out, Southern Cal supporters had overestimated their team against a California squad that had double the number of reserves, and perhaps twice the amount of good football players. California won overwhelmingly 38-7 and left no doubt as to which team was the best on the Pacific Coast that year.

"Perfect forward passing let California beat Southern California, although USC made many more yards than U. C. in line plays," reported a newspaper writer. "Andy Smith's chief scoring strategy was a forward pass on a fake end run play, which brought the ball down to within scoring distance repeatedly."

If the game was dull in one respect, it was colorful in another.

"It was more of a spectacle than a contest," said another sportswriter. "Everything was done on a scale that reminded one of a picture production. The colorful formations of the California rooting section will never be forgotten.

"There were 5,000 strong, and each equipped with two hats, one gold and one blue. Before the game, they represented a huge checkerboard with blue and yellow squares. At a signal, they formed a yellow 'C' with a blue background. Almost instantly, it was changed to a blue letter, with a yellow setting."

The spectacle would have had more color—blood red—but Henderson stopped a possible free-for-all by acting as a peacemaker. A newspaper reported:

"Elmer Henderson's quick wit saved many a fist fight Saturday afternoon. When he recalled Dean to the bench, the USC captain passed Stephens (a California player) as he ran across the field. Several times, Dean had been accused of rough work during the game, and Stephens thought to show he had overlooked the incidents by offering his hand as the Trojan captain passed him. Dean waved it away. The spectators, surprised, booed indignantly.

"A California supporter near the USC bench leaped forward and hurled a lemon at Dean. One of the Trojan water carriers was on him like a flash. Several northerners leaped to the rescue of Dean's assailant. Flying fists filled the air for several minutes, but police finally separated the contestants. Meanwhile Henderson cooled Dean's temper, and the big halfback raced out on the field and shook hands with the Californian. If he hadn't, Southern Californians may have had to fight their way out of the park."

California went to the Rose Bowl that season, and Southern Cal went home. The Trojans' significant loss, however, was later tempered by an invitation into the Pacific Coast Conference. A long sought-after goal, Southern Cal joined the PCC along with Idaho for the 1922 season and took equal footing with the status-conscious teams of the North—California, Stanford, Washington, Oregon, Oregon State, and Washington State.

Entrance into the PCC was a prestige triumph for Southern

Cal and Henderson.

"He took a small Methodist college and put it into a strong Pacific Coast Conference," recalls Calland. "It was quite an achievement."

It was only the beginning. Next came the Rose Bowl.

A Rose Bowl And Thorns

The January 1, 1923, Rose Bowl game was scheduled to start at 2:15 p.m., but Penn State had not made an appearance on the field by 2:30. A crowd of 43,000 and the Southern California football team fidgeted in the blazing sun.

"Gloomy Gus" Henderson, the Southern California coach, was one of the most agitated. "Where can they be?" he asked rhetorically while pacing nervously up and down the field.

After what seemed like an interminable wait, Penn State Coach Hugo Bezdek appeared. Henderson rushed to confront him.

"Where've you been?" Henderson asked Bezdek.

"We got caught in a traffic jam trying to get here," said Bezdek.

Henderson would not buy that, however. He told Bezdek that he tried to stall "so we would get itchy." Furthermore, Henderson stated, "you wanted the sun to lower, believing you'd have a better chance when it's cool."

"You're a lot of bunk," snapped Bezdek.

"You're a liar," shouted Henderson.

"Remove your glasses," screamed Bezdek.

But Henderson felt that discretion was the better part of valor.

"I had just climbed out of bed with the flu and could hardly stand up," he explained afterwards. "Also, I knew Bezdek had earned his way through the University of Chicago fighting as a pro under an assumed name, so I decided it would be wiser if the two teams decided the issue."

This bizarre, midfield scene in full view of the audience preceded the first Rose Bowl game played in the present Pasadena site in an area called the Arroyo Seco.

The wild argument was a fitting exclamation point to a year studded with controversies and battles. The West Coast football society had painful familial problems in the 1922 season.

This was obvious when a Seattle newspaper accused California, Stanford, and Southern Cal of "unethical conduct" in recruiting players. The newspaper urged that the three California schools be kicked out of the Pacific Coast Conference.

"Let us restore the conference to the northern part of the Pacific Coast and let (the state of) California shift for itself in the future," said the newspaper.

Sportswriters felt that the northerners were jealous of success by California schools. The University of California won PCC titles in 1920, 1921, and 1922.

"Washington hasn't taken any too kindly to California's domination of what Washington believes its own," wrote Mark Kelly of the *Los Angeles Examiner*. "The entrance of Southern California was another eyesore to both Oregon and Washington. The best proof of this is in a recent article appearing in a Seattle newspaper in which California, Stanford, and Southern Cal were accused of steen dozen different brands of unethical conduct. The fact that Washington State was trimmed here last year while California beat Washington University has more than a little to do with the comment."

Meanwhile, the PCC started another controversy when it attempted to pull the Rose Bowl out of the Southern California area and transplant it further north in Palo Alto, Stanford's home. But the conference was foiled because Stanford had scheduled a game with Pittsburgh on December 30.

"The conference then 'kindly' decided to play the game at Pasadena," said Kelly. "For the love of Swiss cheese, what else could they do? But it is to be noted that they tried FIRST for the Palo Alto Stadium and had it firmly set that they would pass up Pasadena. Now Pasadena gets the game and has to give almost one-third less to the coast competing team than it voluntarily offered two months ago. It's a good laugh, and doubtless the Tournament of Roses folks are enjoying it."

The 1922 season was also shaken by a uniform numbering controversy, a gloomy proclamation by Southern Cal President Rufus Von KleinSmid that football was doomed by commercialism, a California snub of the Rose Bowl, and a stormy student revolt over ticket prices in the Pasadena classic.

After California and Southern Cal christened the Rose Bowl Stadium in the middle of the 1922 season, sportswriters were outraged by the uniform numbering system. They claimed that the numbers were too small and that players could not be properly identified.

"The new Pasadena Stadium brought the shortcoming home vividly," wrote Kelly after California defeated Southern Cal 12-0. "The Trojans and the Bears both wore numbers too small to be identified in that vast field. Saturday, Idaho and USC meet there again. They'll wear the small number again. That's a lot of booting for the management. The public is paying $2 to see the game. The public is entitled to the same consideration that baseball gives 'em."

The problem of player-spotting became excessively worse for writers—and fans—that year. Said Kelly after a 6-0 Southern Cal victory over Stanford: "No one could tell who made USC's touchdown until two hours after the game, and then we had to ask members of the team. One San Francisco paper, in its play by play reports, had names of four men who never did appear on the field, and three of which DIDN'T EVEN BELONG ON THE SQUAD."

The officials made it doubly hard for the reporters and the fans in that game. The Trojans took the field in white vests which completely covered their already inadequate numbers.

"It was not the fault of USC, but the fault of officials who forced the Trojans to wear vests so they could distinguish them from the Stanford men," remarked an annoyed Kelly. "Stanford, mind you, was wearing a crimson jersey; USC, a striped maroon. Yet 15,000 spectators and 100 newspaper folks were overriden in an arbitrary ruling in behalf of FOUR MEN."

Von KleinSmid, one of the most reknowned and beloved of Southern California presidents, interrupted the season with a disquieting pronouncement that football would soon be buried in its own gold.

"Football is a legitimate college game, but I find that the public is beginning to look with great suspicion upon the tremendous gate receipts," he said. "There is a feeling the game is becoming too greatly tainted with commercialism."

That was a professional condition that poisoned the morality of amateur sports, said Von KleinSmid after a tour of Eastern and Northwestern schools. He sounded the trumpets of doom with his prediction: "The day is coming when football must be abandoned, despite its great good."

Von KleinSmid's death warning was unfounded. As time progressed, football only established itself more firmly.

"Football's hold upon the public is increasing tremendously," reported a Los Angeles sportswriter. "At the Southern Cal-Arizona game, the university athletic officials had planned on a crowd of 7,500. More than 12,000 squeezed inside the enclosure and packed the place. That marks the end of Bovard Field's usefulness as a home for the Trojans. They've outgrown football's short trousers."

At the end of the golden season came the Rose Bowl—a rich prize for the most successful West Coast team. California was invited, but the Bears stunned the PCC monarchy by turning down the offer.

"The University of California, twice defender of the honor of the West Coast, has by the action of the Associated Students in caucus, definitely refused to meet Penn State and act as representative of the West," reported the *Los Angeles Times*.

The newspaper could guess at the real California motives, although the students said they wished to give their football players a Christmas vacation after two straight Rose Bowl games.

Said the *Times*: "In all probability the chief reason for the retirement of the Bears is the result largely of the muddle regarding the New Year's Day game which resulted in a belated choice of an Eastern representative last year, the demand for an enormous financial "cut" by the California management, the loss in popularity of the California team, the turning over of the New Year's Day game to the Pacific Coast Conference and latest, the somewhat surprising choice of Penn State as the Eastern representative."

Southern Cal thus was the Rose Bowl choice of the PCC after a glossy season of ten victories and one defeat.

"In selecting Southern California, the conference made a wise decision," wrote Kelly. "It will be a home team for a change, instead of an importation from the far north. It will give the home folks considerably more to chirp about. And from where we click these lines off, it appears as though a lot of cheering would be needed for USC. Our private opinion is that Coach "Gloomy Gus" Henderson will win this tilt by ten points on a dry field. A soggy turf will handicap Henderson."

Tickets went on sale for the big event, but Southern Cal students balked at the prices.

"The Trojan undergrads are up in arms over the report that they must pay $5.50 for seats at the New Year's game," said the *Los Angeles Examiner*. "No provision for student tickets has been made by the Tournament of Roses committee. University authorities demand that the rate be cut in half."

The students' screams brought action after several days. President J. J. Mitchell of the Tournament of Roses committee agreed to a price reduction. He promised that a block of 2,500 seats in the $5.50 section would be reserved for Southern Cal students at $2.75 a ticket.

All of this peripheral drama, however, was just an appetizer for the real meat of the hour—the intense spectacle of Rose Bowl day.

Pasadena, a city growing up in its 50th year, bulged with passionate spectators. The crowd viewing the pre-game Rose Bowl parade was the size of a metropolitan city—300,000. An official of the Pacific Electric Railway announced, "We brought in 100,000 people ourselves."

May McAvoy, a popular film star of the era with gigantic eyes and cupid's bow lips, was a dazzling Rose Bowl queen. She carried an enormous bunch of roses in her lap and an endearing smile on her face.

Neither football coach was there for such frivolity, however. Bezdek put his players through strenuous, secretive practice sessions. The abrasive Nittany Lions coach was surly to newspapermen and made it plain that he did not like them watching his preparations.

"I'll let you in the first few minutes of each practice, but no pictures," he told photographers, suspecting that they might pass some vital information along to Southern Cal.

Bucking the surly Bezdek, a *Los Angeles Examiner* photographer placed his camera on the ground near his foot and stood with his hands in his pockets. Each time the Penn State team came near, he tripped the shutter with his right foot. Those pictures were all over the *Examiner*'s sports pages the following day.

Henderson was no less agitated about the game. Concerned over ferocious Penn State workouts, the Southern California coach flew to Palo Alto to get advice from Pop Warner, whose Pitt team was playing Stanford.

The Trojans were favored but the odds vanished on the day of the game because of Penn State's fiercely dedicated preparations. "Since the Nittany Lions have been working out here, the impression that was so general before their arrival— that the easterners were merely a setup for the coast team—has disappeared almost completely," said a newspaper. "Now, the Bezdek machine is looked upon as a more powerful outfit, likely to more than hold its own against Southern California."

All roads led to the Arroyo Seco, an area where once upon a time Spanish sportsmen had staged bullfights and hunted wildcat and boar in a panorama of rocks and gravel. The crowds came to the newly-opened playground, nestled in picturesque foothills, and filled the horseshoe-shaped stands. The roads jammed quickly. It was a good day for football, if a little on the warm side.

After opening ceremonies at the $272,000 stadium, they presented the first Rose Bowl game in the Arroyo Seco after eight years in Pasadena's Tournament Park. But not before Penn State's embarrassing late arrival and that explosive scene between Bezdek and Henderson on the bright, green field.

Despite Bezdek's protests that his team had gotten locked into a Rose Bowl parade traffic jam, a Pittsburgh sports columnist thought differently. Chester L. Smith, an intimate of the angry Penn State coach, said: "Bezdek had held up the game because it was a warm day and he wanted to wait until the sun started to drop behind the Sierra Madre."

Be that as it may, nothing could help Penn State that day after the game started at 3:05. The Nittany Lions scored first on a 20-yard field goal by Mike Palm after several long gains by Harry "Lighthorse" Wilson, but that was their offense for the afternoon. Leo Calland, Southern Cal's brutish lineman, structured the defense differently to shut off Wilson the rest of the game.

"This early score prompted us to change our defense," says Calland, the Trojan captain. "Immediately after that scoring drive, I pulled our tackles and ends in and drifted wide myself from my center position. We found that Penn State's main power was inside from a shift either way. So we switched from a seven-man diamond defense to a six-man line with me playing a sliding center. I filled when a hole opened or drifted with the wide stuff."

Before the game's rhythm changed for Southern Cal, however, the Trojans survived a bizarre play. Fullback Gordon Campbell and halfback Roy "Bullet" Baker had penetrated steadily through Penn State and took the ball to the one-yard line. But the Trojans lost the easy scoring opportunity when the center's snap went awry.

Henderson explained later: "Lowell Lindley, our center, ordinarily snaps the ball directly back of him. This time the play called for a sideways pass-back to our back who was crouched close to the line of scrimmage near the end of the line. Lindley snapped the ball in the correct direction, but as our line heaved forward, the pigskin hit someone's heel and shot over the Penn State line."

To everyone's surprise the ball sailed over the goal line, and a Penn State defender fell on it for a touchback. The Nittany Lions saw little of the ball afterwards, though. Baker and Campbell saw to that.

Southern Cal's fine running combination carried the ball to the Penn State 10-yard line in the second quarter. Harold Galloway flew through the air to make a gorgeous catch of a Baker pass on the two. The receiver skidded on his back and was knocked out in the play but miraculously managed to hold onto the ball. On fourth down Campbell went over from the one on a delayed buck for a 7-3 Southern Cal lead. Campbell and Baker did the legwork for the Trojans in the third period, too. Baker scored Southern Cal's second touchdown on a one-yard run, and the Trojans took a 14-3 decision as the game

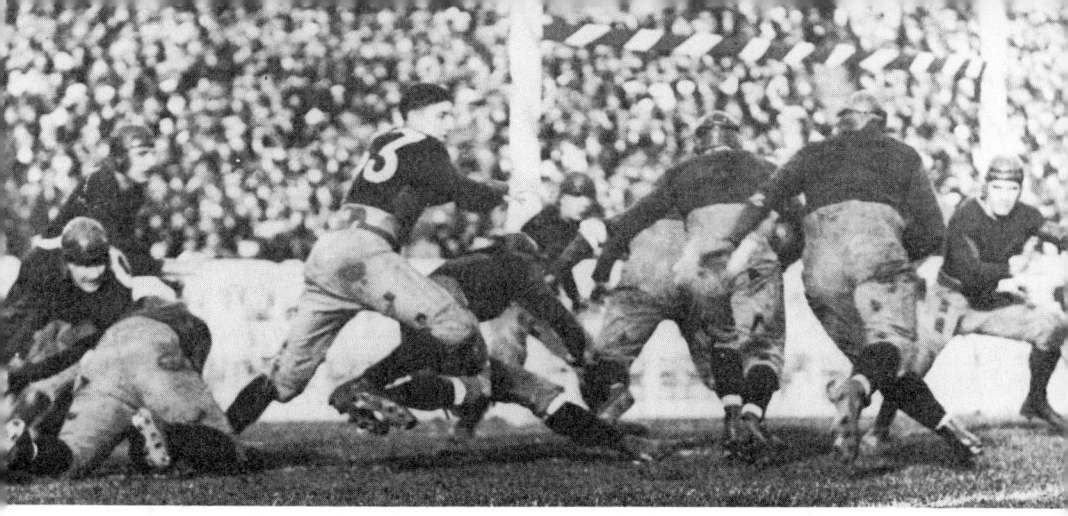

Southern California's Roy Baker (No. 33) follows the blocking of Gordon Campbell (No. 3) in the 1923 Rose Bowl game against Penn State. Baker carried the ball to the Nittany Lions' one-yard line on this play.

ended in the dark. Sportswriters were forced to light matches to complete their stories.

The bitter pre-game feelings carried over afterwards as both coaches barred writers from the dressing rooms.

Henderson was quoted as saying: "The best team won. Good coaching, like the effect of cigarettes, always tells in the long run. We should have won by four more touchdowns. Thank God for the guy who made it a criminal offense to hit a man wearing glasses. Hugo Bezdek is no gentleman."

Bezdek was just as boorish in his comments, if they were really true.

"The best team lost," Bezdek was supposed to have said in his half of the repartee. "The best team and the best coaching in the world couldn't have won against the luck that USC had today. When at its best, my team could beat USC by 40 points. My only regret is that Elmer Henderson had left his glasses on."

Later, a composed Bezdek really said: "Southern California was too fast for us, they played better football. They said the climate was a big factor in our downfall. I don't think it had anything to do with the outcome of the game. Their line was stronger and faster than ours, and their backfield men were exceedingly fast."

Time Out: Chet Dolley

Chet Dolley's home is a big-game Valhalla. The busy walls are inhabited with gargantuan conquests. Mounted game stare insouciantly at a visitor, artifacts from safari hunting in Africa.

Dolley tells you that he is particularly proud of some of the collection, "elephant tusks weighing 94 and 98 pounds—the biggest I ever shot."

"And," he says, "I also shot the widest skulled lion ever recorded—10 and 7/8 inches."

From big-time football player to big-game hunter, Dolley's life has been filled with passion and excitement. It is not that much of a step from tackling people to tackling elephants, says Dolley.

"Of course elephants are a little tougher," says Dolley, a star for the Southern California football team in the days of "Gloomy Gus" Henderson.

Dolley played quarterback ("essentially a blocking back in the Single Wing—I called signals") and helped Trojan teams win 25 games and lose only 5 from 1922 through 1924. The Rose Bowl beckoned Southern Cal for the first time and Dolley was there.

"Yes, I remember the Rose Bowl," says Dolley, talking about the January 1, 1923, game with Penn State. "Harold Galloway's catch of a pass was a beautiful thing. There was a big crowd. But you don't know the crowd's there once you start playing."

With the aid of the Galloway catch, Southern Cal defeated

Penn State 14-3 in the first Rose Bowl game played at the present Pasadena site in an area called the "Arroyo Seco" (dry gulch). Earlier that season, Dolley recalls, he helped christen the place with a game against California. Dolley also had another "first" at Southern Cal. He played in the kickoff game of the Los Angeles Coliseum, when the Trojans hosted Pomona College on October 6, 1923, before 12,863 people.

He remembers the Rose Bowl game most vividly, though, because of its significance.

"There must have been 60,000 people in the stadium, everyone of them hollering," says Dolley.

Romanced by Southern Cal players, Dolley came from Long Beach to join the burgeoning football program in 1922. He was not disappointed.

"The good teams started at this time," says Dolley. "Henderson had some fine players, and he actually built the nucleus that Howard Jones inherited. Jones later came in and had national champions with the material that Henderson left him."

Dolley reveres Henderson as a man of soul and conscience as well as a football coach.

"Henderson not only turned out good football players," says Dolley, "but he turned out people who would be a credit to the university. He not only recruited good players, but good yell leaders and good students as well."

Dolley saw his first college football game "about 1917 or 1918." He played in his first one in 1922, as a sophomore at Southern Cal. That was probably MORE demanding than shooting overgrown elephants, he says.

"It was Single Wing in those days," says Dolley. "We had a fatter football, and it was harder to pass because you couldn't hold the ball so well. The substitution rule was tough, too. You were only allowed to come out of the half once. Another thing, an incoming player wasn't allowed to bring in information like he does today. And, of course, you weren't allowed to coach from the sidelines—like they do today. I don't ever recall Henderson being penalized for coaching from the sidelines. It probably is a little bit easier for the players today. The game's improved so much."

Road trips were exciting, but formidable.

Chet Dolley, captain of the 1923 Trojan team, played in Southern California's first Rose Bowl game.

"We caught a train for our trips out of town," recalls Dolley. "We didn't play any Eastern schools, but a trip to the state of Washington was really an event. It was quite a lot for us kids."

Some of the most significant—and passionate—games were played with Stanford and California. But in 1924 the northern schools got "jealous" of Southern Cal's sudden rise and broke off relations for a year. Dolley remembers the picture, sharply.

"There were strained relations with Stanford and Cal when they canceled games because they were jealous of our good teams," says Dolley. "They always used to beat USC, and the Trojans came back and started to beat them. They charged under-the-table dealings, said we must have been subsidizing athletes. But we couldn't do it—we were too poor.

"In those days, players didn't get anything. Kids didn't even own cars. It was a different life. And when we worked we worked for 40 cents an hour. Heck, even the football looked like a basketball before we could get a new one. By the time we got through kicking it around, it really got tattered on the ends and just ballooned out of proportion."

Dolley himself was one of those people he earlier referred to—"a credit to the university." His football status was enhanced by his academic accomplishments. He studied law and was student body president of Southern Cal's Law School.

After graduation he "worked like hell practicing law for 15-18 years and then started in the oil business."

Dolley struck black gold in California and became the quarterback of the Atlantic Oil Company, a large, oil-drilling network in the state. At present he has 11 scattered drilling rigs digging for the stuff.

Leisurely, Dolley hunts wild African game. But he has also humanely devoted part of his life to keeping certain other creatures alive. Dolley is the catalyst of Ducks Unlimited, a conservation group founded to perpetuate water fowl in the North American continent.

"We've raised a lot of money for that, better than five million dollars, and I'm proud," says Dolley. "We help build dams and help the farmers with their crops, particularly in Canada. The ducks and geese just have to have water and food. If there's a drought, all the offspring will die."

Dolley enlisted movie star John Wayne to help in this humanitarian movement. Wayne graciously narrated a documentary film for the group, and contributed money as well.

"He did a terrific job. He went over the script again and again to make sure that he would get it right," says Dolley. "I asked him to be a sponsor—and he sent me a check for three times the normal amount."

Dolley's big-game passion flowered relatively late in life. He was magnetized by hunting books, particularly ones written by former President Theodore Roosevelt.

"A friend of mine asked me once if I wanted to go hunting with him to Africa," says Dolley. "That was 1960—and I've been going ever since."

High adventure excites Dolley. He goes after seven-ton elephants and has "60 to 70" game of various ilk mounted in his California home.

"You go hunting for trophy heads, not just to shoot anything that moves," explains Dolley. "You go out into the bush country where there's no track at all. You run into pigmies. It's like in the movies."

At an age when most men would retire to a farm, the 72-year-old Dolley seeks new vistas. He recently has been slowed by an eye operation, but vows that his free spirit has not been broken.

"I guess I'm just an adventurer at heart," he says.

The Trojans Go To War

In 1923 a cream-colored colossus dominated the edge of the Southern California campus. The Los Angeles Coliseum could be seen—and heard—from the lanes of student travel.

Inhibited by the bonds of Bovard Field, Southern California acknowledged the passionate popularity of football with an enormous, new arena to feed the appetite of the crowds and fill its own coffers.

"Games at Bovard Field were handicapped from the standpoint of moneymaking by the inadequate seating facilities," wrote sportswriter Mark Kelly in the *Los Angeles Examiner*. "The Nevada and Arizona games packed Bovard Field (in 1922) but packing Bovard Field isn't so much of a much."

The Trojans christened their swanky place by beating Pomona 23-7 on October 6, 1923. The game was witnessed by 12,863 people, a microscopic figure considering the population for the rest of the 1923 season. Helped by the sizeable hometown crowds, the Trojans played before their largest season attendance to that juncture—259,000.

"From a standpoint of attendance, never before was football so well supported," reported a football guide.

An era of new prosperity dawned at Southern Cal, once deemed unworthy and too insignifcant to join forces with northern West Coast teams. Southern Cal Coach "Gloomy Gus" Henderson shared in the new-found wealth, getting a $1,000 bonus from the school and a new car from the alumni for his

The opening of the Los Angeles Coliseum in 1923 acknowledged the startling rise of football popularity at Southern California. The fans came, and the Trojans won.

leadership. Of course Southern Cal officials would have liked things even better if Henderson was able to beat California. Henderson's old nemesis gave him another beating, 13-7, while 72,000 people paid to see the battle at the Coliseum.

A sportswriter joked after another of his perennial defeats by California: "If Henderson ever succeeds in bowling over the Golden Bear, the Trojans will make him a present of a couple of miles of Broadway frontage."

If Southern Cal was not able to pull one off against California, 1923 was a season of unexplained upsets in the West.

"The most notable of these was the California-Nevada scoreless tie and the defeat of Stanford by the University of Southern Cal," remarked Hub Huebel, president of the Pacific Coast Football Association. "The season as a whole was considered by many as the most remarkable in the history of the Coast."

After their impressive 1922 season, the Trojans opened a new year with the loss of 10 veterans—including linemen Leo Calland and Lowell Lindley, running back Howard Kincaid, and Harold Galloway, the pass-catching hero of the Rose Bowl.

"Henderson faced the task of building practically a new team," noted Huebel. "The biggest problem was the development of a backfield combination. The line material was good, but enthusiasts in the south were somewhat doubtful as to the real strength of the squad."

Chet Dolley developed into Henderson's team leader at quarterback, but glaring deficiencies prevented a repetition of

Willis O. Hunter (left), Southern California's athletic director, greets Coach "Gloomy Gus" Henderson in the Los Angeles Coliseum shortly before their Trojans go into battle.

1922 glories. Along with the California loss, the Trojans were also beaten rather soundly by Washington. Both defeats were particularly tough blows, since the Trojans were attempting to gain equality with the "establishment" teams of the Pacific Coast Conference.

While Southern Cal strove to reach this goal, spirit stayed at a high level. The era saw the birth of the card stunt, an imaginative trick of spelling signs in the stands. Created by Lindley Bothwell, the school's yell king, a small rooting section spelled out letter by letter its first card formation—"T-R-O-J-A-N"—to the delight of Henderson's young warriors. Although appreciated it was a far cry from today's colorful stunts which encompass weeks of planning, computer programming, and the coordinated work of 3,700 students.

ON THE SIDELINES AT THE COLISEUM (left to right): Student manager Coyle Briggs, playing-timekeeper Nate Morse, Harold J. Stonier, Assistant Coach John Thurman, Coach "Gloomy Gus" Henderson, and Southern California Athletic Director Willis O. Hunter.

The Trojans were given incentive in other ways. Ingenué Carmel Myers offered two free tickets for the Motion Picture Directors' Association costume ball to the Southern Cal player who scored the first touchdown againt Arizona. The Trojans took that offer to their hearts, burying Arizona 69-6 in a barrage of touchdowns.

Southern California ended the 1923 season with a 9-0 victory over Idaho while "powerful arc lights played from the parapets of the vast Los Angeles Coliseum and the phantom shapes of red and blue jerseyed athletes carried their battle into the fast descending darkness."

The game was one of the longest and bloodiest affairs in recent history.

"It required three hours to play," reported a newspaper. "On virtually every other play in the last half, time had to be taken out so that some player, usually two, might give temporary attention to his hurts. Both coaches, Robert Lee Mathews of Idaho and Gus Henderson of USC, announced their players in splendid condition, which causes suspicion to arise that about 70 percent of the time lost while ministering to prostrate players was due to using the strangle hold, the hammerlock, the kidney punch, the rabbit blow, and other methods barred in our best boxing circles."

That small football war, however, was nothing compared to the following season when Southern California went to war with California and Stanford on moral grounds.

The situation had long been simmering and was just about ripe for an explosion. Although both California and Stanford had approved Southern Cal's admittance to the lordly PCC, they retained a spirit of distrust about the Trojans.

"They intimated frequently that they did not believe that Southern California was maintaining such high scholastic standards nor enforcing such strict eligibility rules as they," noted an observer.

Whether real or imagined, this distrust came to a head before the Southern Cal-California game of 1924. The president of the California Associated Students handed the president of the Southern California Student Body a letter stating that California and Stanford were breaking off athletic relations with the Trojans at the end of the football season. Copies of the letter were distributed to the press box, and sportswriters instantly wired their newspapers. Word was then passed among the 60,000 spectators.

Further intensifying Southern Cal's humiliation, California beat the Trojans that day, 7-0. Bitter Southern California retaliated like a wounded animal and cancelled its game that year with Stanford.

"If we're not good enough to play Stanford next year, we aren't good enough this year," was Southern Cal's reaction in so many words.

Came this statement from Southern Cal's administrators:

"The University of Southern California knew that 70,000 people wished to see the game between Stanford and Southern Cal on November 8, in the Los Angeles Coliseum. The student body regretted that conditions over which they had no control made it impossible to play the game as scheduled.

"The northern institutions have seen fit to say that they do not feel that the best interests in intercollegiate athletics could be served by further contests with teams of the University of Southern California. It has become a matter of common knowledge that over a period of the last four years, northern institutions have looked with amazement at the growth of the University of Southern California and its athletic prowess.

"We have had intimations from time to time that northern institutions felt they had everything to lose and nothing to gain in playing us and would welcome opportunities to cancel relations. They have looked in vain for definite reasons to cancel such games. Southern California has lived up to every athletic agreement and contract into which it has entered. It stands willing to do so in the future."

Southern Cal called the act by Stanford and California "rash, heartless, and unwarranted insinuation."

"No respected institution in America would for a minute stand for the insult," said the Southern Cal statement. "We have looked in vain for any charges. There haven't been any."

Southern Cal's athletic affairs were dramatically changed in the aftermath of the unholy war. The most immediate and obvious change was the formation of the Trojan Club whose "sole purpose was to further the athletic program."

Henderson, although a campus hero, was caught in the

whirlpool of events that followed the "Big Three" breakup. Rumors circulated that Southern Cal, blinded by the successes of Midwesterners such as George Gipp, Harry Stuhldreher, and Red Grange, sought a new coach from that area.

"Unfavorable comment that has been common concerning Henderson's lack of offensive on his teams and the expressed desire of many for a championship team seems to have dragged forth skeletons from the Trojan closet," was the way a newspaper described it.

The rumor was denied by Southern Cal. A school administrator declared Southern Cal's official confidence in Henderson. He cited as proof of the university's trust the fact that the alumni had presented Henderson with an automobile and the school administration had raised his salary.

"This makes Henderson one of the highest paid coaches on the Coast," said the official. Henderson's salary was believed to be slightly over $7,000 a year.

The school official went so far as to intimate that other California colleges had started the rumor about Henderson, hoping to see the successful coach leave.

Ironically, this was all happening while Henderson was fielding his strongest team.

"Henderson's best team was definitely in 1924," says Leo Calland, who served as an assistant coach after playing for Henderson in the early 1920s. "I remember, once against Syracuse, they had a whale of a club, but we took them apart with our spread formation. We had a powerful running attack from that spread."

Southern Cal gained some national attention with that 16-0 victory over Syracuse and a 20-7 decision over Missouri to close out the 1924 season with a 9-2 record.

"Chick Meehan's Syracuse team came west with only one defeat and was completely outplayed by the Trojans," reported a football writer. "John McBride was the only Syracuse player who could make any headway against the Trojan defense. Hobbs Adams, a speedy Trojan end, made one of the most sensational plays of the year when he blocked a Syracuse kick, took the ball right off the punter's shoe, and sped 50 yards to a touchdown. Southern Cal showed a wonderful passing attack to defeat Missouri. Twice "Indian" Newman, a halfback, passed 45

The team of 1924 just before the start of a game in the Coliseum (left to right): Holley Adams, Hayden Phythian,

yards to a Trojan end for a touchdown. John Hawkins at quarterback and Henry Lefebvre at halfback were also the Trojan stars."

Mort Kaer, Jeff Cravath, Norman Anderson, Otto Anderson, John Riddle, Reginald DuPuy, and Hayden Pythian were among some of the others who made the Trojan season a winner.

As the season wound down, college officials came back to their senses, and California and Stanford called a cease-fire with Southern Cal. Their disagreements were settled amicably, and it was hoped, permanently, by a three-cornered agreement that became effective April 1, 1924. The agreement prescribed definite entrance and eligibility rules and requirements for

Ralph Cummings, Hobbs Adams, Norman Anderson, Otto Anderson, John Hawkins, Fay Thomas, John Riddle, Chet Dolley, Gordon Campbell.

athletes.

In the midst of this reconciliation, it became apparent that Southern Cal was not reconciled where Henderson was concerned. The early-season rumors became fact, and the university fired the mild-mannered coach and sought a Knute Rockne.

Southern Cal was not able to get a Rockne but came up with someone just as good in Howard Jones.

Time Out: Howard Jones

A female sportswriter was assigned one day to do a story on Howard Jones. The Southern Cal football coach found after a while that he was annoyed by her approach. So Jones told her about a "secret" new play he had devised.

"It's dynamite," he said. "We tried it last week for the first time. Went like a dream. Our fullback took the ball and ran clean through the concrete wall of the stadium."

"My heavens!" the writer said. "How ever did you stop him?"

Sighing with exaggeration, Jones thought for a while and said: "Yes, that's the tough part—the part we had to iron out. Couldn't stop that guy at all! Had to shoot him."

Anyone who really knew Howard Harding Jones would not have been surprised if the story was true. Ask his players.

"He was the toughest taskmaster I ever knew," says Nick Pappas, a tailback who played for the "Head Man" from 1935 through 1937. "Jones was the kind of guy who would tell you to run through a wall—and you'd ask him, how high? If you weren't ready when he called, boy, you'd never be ready. There was never a tougher man who ever put out a football team in my estimation. He didn't know what pain meant."

"If anyone had reason to hate the old man's guts, I think I did," says Gene Clarke, a lineman in the early 1930s. "He rode me unmercifully for three years. I never did anything right as far as he was concerned."

But Clarke did not "hate the old man's guts"—rather loved

him. Like many others under the Southern Cal martinet, Clarke learned respect and pride.

"He was a great man, really," said Clarke. "He taught me to suck in my stomach and hold out my chest. He taught me things to carry along in life. He taught me to play it clean—we didn't know how to play dirty, how to cheat. We never learned."

Along with his outward toughness, the complex Jones had admirable qualities—more suited to immortality. "Impeccable integrity," "honesty," and "dignity" were some of the other words used to describe this aloof, withdrawn man.

That Howard Jones was less than colorful perhaps hurt his national image. Jones' brother, Tad, a coach of less accomplishment, "was a far more vivid personality, and the luster of his fame has been as lasting," wrote Allison Danzig in his book, *Oh, How They Played The Game.*

In another work Danzig noted: "For all of his success, Howard Jones has never had a system named after him, as has Warner and as did Rockne. And yet, his is one of the most ingenious and progressive minds in the game."

From the standpoint of accomplishment Jones was in a class with a lofty few. He won two national championships, five Rose Bowl games, and eight Pacific Coast Conference titles. Yet despite these accomplishments Jones was never a public figure in the strata of, say, a Knute Rockne, Amos Alonzo Stagg, or Jock Sutherland.

One could argue that Jones was a victim of geographical propinquity except that the Eastern football establishment gave much recognition to other Western coaches such as Pop Warner, for example, when he coached at Stanford.

If the lack of flamboyancy in Jones' makeup hurt his "image," it certainly did not hurt his football style. He translated his impassive personality to his team, and in his case it was perfect.

"His teams had more straight power than deception," recalls Nate Barragar, captain of the 1929 Southern Cal team. "He always believed that if the men did their individual jobs, the play should go. There was nothing fancy. We'd actually tell the other team where we were going to run the ball—and then just ran it through that spot."

Morley Drury, a Trojan star of the 1920s, remembers that Jones' teams were "easily scouted because everyone knew what we were going to do. He had great power to just go. The quarterback called the game, and Jones was a great fundamentalist."

"Football to me means power—massed power, functioning smoothly, driving forward relentlessly," Jones once said. "I feel that I should attribute much of whatever success I have attained in football, both as a player, and as a coach, to emphasis on the power attack."

Al Wesson, a longtime sports publicist at Southern Cal and a close friend of Jones when he coached the Trojans from 1925 through 1940, recalls that his teams played mostly out of a basic Single Wing formation.

"It was a darn, good blocking team," says Wesson. "He was the first to introduce cross-blocking where two of his players would block one guy on the other team to open a hole for his runners. He'd have about six or seven formations that were just a little bit varied. He liked the draw play, and he also had a pretty good short pass-running play where a back had the option of either."

Wesson was credited with giving Jones the nickname, "The Head Man." It was an obvious appellation.

"We had few assistant coaches, because Jones liked to do things himself," recalls Wesson. "He'd take over the whole works himself, despite the fact that he had people there to help him. He was very thorough. He couldn't help it—he was so intense."

This irrepressible drive was noticeable at an early age after Jones was born in Excello, Ohio, on August 23, 1885. He and his brother played football at nearby Middletown High School, then two years at Exeter, before entering Yale. Fierce competitors, the Jones boys excelled in college. While playing end for Yale in 1905, 1906, and 1907 Howard Jones was named twice on Walter Camp's all-America teams.

Graduated from Yale in June of 1908, Jones coached the Syracuse team that fall at the age of 23, compiling a 6-3-1 record. In 1909 he returned to his alma mater and coached Yale through an undefeated and untied season, with no opponent getting inside the Elis' 30-yard line. He produced six all-

Coach Howard Jones talks—and everyone pays attention. Included among the listeners is a young John Wayne standing in the background.

Americans that year.

Jones went to Ohio State as coach for the 1910 season and in 1913 returned to Yale in an effort to rescue his alma mater from an embarrassing slump. With inferior material he managed a significant 3-3 tie with Princeton. Jones retired from coaching until 1916 when he joined Iowa for an extended tenure. In eight years with the Hawkeyes his teams won 42 games and lost 17 while running up a staggering total of 1,082 points. Jones guided the Hawkeyes to undefeated seasons and Big Nine championships in 1921 and 1922. One of his Iowa highlights was a 10-7 victory over Rockne's Notre Dame team in 1921. It was the first time the Fighting Irish had lost in 21 games, and Jones always placed that one up there with his all-time favorites.

After a year at Duke, during which he compiled a 4-5 record with an extremely weak team, Jones was appointed as the head coach at Southern California at a yearly salary of $10,000. He was, actually, a second choice despite his dazzling accomplishments. Southern Cal had first sought the services of the great Rockne but had been turned down.

Jones was not only a good coach, but a lucky one. He received an inheritance of talent when he came on the Southern California scene. These players, most of whom were recruited by former coach Gus Henderson, soon became known as "The Thundering Herd" and won a national championship in 1928.

"It was among one of the best Southern Cal teams in standpoint of material," recalls Leo Calland, a player and assistant coach of the 1920s.

While posting impressive records right away, including an 11-2 mark his first year, perhaps Jones' most important early accomplishment was getting Notre Dame on the Southern Cal schedule. Jones and Rockne revived their early friendship and business association with a game in 1926. That first game, won by Notre Dame 13-12, kicked off one of college football's most glamorous rivalries.

An instant success, the series magnetized legions of fans at monster-size arenas. Southern Cal became a national drawing card in the 1920s because of the Notre Dame games. Enormous crowds totaling over 120,000 watched the contests in Chicago's Soldiers Field while the Los Angeles Coliseum played to capacity audiences and later, after expansion, pulled in 90,000 to 100,000 a game.

The Southern Cal-Notre Dame affairs usually decided status in the Top Ten polls and sometimes decided national championships.

Rockne's unexpected death in the spring of 1931 preceded one of Jones' greatest victories over Notre Dame—a 16-14 thriller that triggered the Trojans to a national title. An illuminating fragment of Jones' character was revealed in a warm story that surfaced after the exciting victory.

After Johnny Baker's winning field goal in the final

seconds at South Bend, the usually stolid Jones lost his composure. He knocked a friend from the bench, raced on the field, and kissed the first Southern Cal player he met—captain-center Stan Williamson.

Fighting his way through a mob of Southern Cal supporters, Jones gouged his way to the Trojans' dressing room. Right behind Jones was Jack Rissman, who annually presented his Rissman Trophy for the national championship.

Standing together in the pulsating, steamy locker room, Jones said to Rissman: "You're just the man I want to see. Can you direct me to the cemetery where Knute Rockne is buried?"

Within an hour Jones and his entire squad were at Rockne's grave in Highland Cemetery. Jones conducted impromptu services that raw November afternoon. Said Rissman: "This was Jones' shining hour."

But Jones never handled Notre Dame as he would have liked. He lost more times to the Fighting Irish than he beat them, although many of the losses were bitter, one-point or one-touchdown decisions. He had more success with Stanford and Pop Warner.

"Howard had great respect for Warner, and he always worked hardest to beat Stanford," recalls Wesson

The two first met in the east when Jones, fresh out of Yale, was coaching Syracuse in 1908 and Warner was at Carlisle. One of Syracuse's three defeats that year was by Warner's team, 12-0. And when they renewed acquaintances several years later, Warner's Stanford teams beat Jones' first two teams at Southern Cal, and the third game in 1927 ended in a tie. Finally Jones caught up with Warner's famous trick formations and won five straight games with Stanford from 1928 to 1932. Warner's inability to cope with Jones' teams in that period forced the disenchanted old master to leave Stanford for Temple in 1933.

Success over the schools of northern California meant a great deal to Jones, and Southern Cal as well. Not only was Stanford victimized in this early Jones period, but so was California. After being pushed around, and looked down upon as well by their northern brothers, the Trojans finally got off their backs. A 27-0 victory over California in 1926 ended a long victory drought for the Trojans. An article in the *Daily Trojan* indicated the feelings of the time:

"Long years of patient waiting were rewarded, long years of toil came to an end; long years of submitting to an oppressive yoke were avenged at Berkeley Saturday when the thundering hoofs of Troy's galloping Herd crushed the Bear of California into the turf of Memorial Stadium. While 7,500 loyal Trojans screeched a hoarse shout of triumph, the Thundering Herd crashed on its way to everlasting fame."

Jones was the man of the hour and soon became the man of the decade for Southern Cal. He not only built football powers, but character. Recalls Pappas:

"Jones lived football. He was highly intense, clean, had great moral values, and was ethical as the devil. There was no way that anybody was going to play dirty football for him. He instilled that in you. We didn't know how to play dirty, absolutely didn't.

"Of all the guys I know and like, outside of my father, I admired this man the most. He was completely honest, I felt. His integrity was unimpeachable, in fact. He was a brilliant guy. He wrote a book on bridge—the Jones system. And when he was 55, he was shooting in the low 70s in golf. His whole theory on football was fundamentals."

Pappas recalls a highly introverted man when not in his element.

"His personality off the field was practically nothing," says the onetime football star. "I remember, he hated to speak at banquets. He would probably go to about one or two a year. If the team would go, he'd try to tell a story. Well, it was usually the worst story you ever heard, but we'd laugh like hell just to make him feel good. He thought it was really something."

Once on a field, though, Jones changed from Jekyll to Hyde. His dynamic personality swallowed up everything and everybody.

"He was completely different while teaching football," Pappas remembers. "You could always sense the electricity when he came onto the field. You didn't even have to see him to know he was there."

Jones was neither classroom teacher nor counselor. He was strictly a football expert. As Pappas remembers: "We'd see him September 1 when practice started, and we'd see him through the end of the season. And that was it until next fall. He didn't even have an office on campus."

Jones whipped his players to the limit of their endurance, and sometimes beyond.

"He was the kind of guy who wouldn't take you out of a game if you had a hot hand," explains Pappas. "I played 58 minutes once against Illinois. I was so tired I didn't remember the last quarter."

Jones' stern visage often melted in post-game ceremonies.

"He enjoyed the espirit d'corps of coaching," says Pappas. "It used to upset him if another coach didn't meet him halfway and shake his hand. If he didn't do that, Jones thought he was a bad coach."

Jones never used expletives. Well, hardly ever. The man whose strongest expressions were "gol darn" and "by gad" was once betrayed by fierce emotion. Clarke vividly remembers the circumstances.

"He never swore, never took a drink," says Clarke. "But one time when we were playing California, they began to bad-mouth us and kept it up throughout the first half. They called us everything, I mean everything.

"At the half, Jones was trying to get us fired up with a fight talk. 'These people,' he said, 'are you going to let them come down here and son-of-a-bitch you!' Excuse me, I'm QUOTING Howard. Well, everybody almost fell into a faint. He never said anything worse than 'by gad' or 'gol darn!' Jesus, Ernie Pinckert turned around and looked at me and kept smiling. I tell you, that was something."

The players attempted to suppress laughter during this humorous episode because Jones frowned on fun-making.

"I caught more of it from the old man for laughing," says Clarke. "You couldn't laugh out loud on the field."

Jones' uncompromising personality is further illuminated in this story from onetime Southern Cal star Chet Dolley:

"Jones was a very stern taskmaster. He very seldom smiled or laughed. He was a perfectionist in blocking and very often would get down himself and personally show his boys how to do it. One boy, I remember, by the name of Charlie Boren, would not let Jones knock him down. Normally you make it easy for the coach—if you want to play, that is. But Boren wasn't going to lay down for Jones, no sir. Well, he knocked Jones on his fanny, and you didn't do that. I don't think he played much that year."

Many theorized that Jones was not as thick-skinned as he might have you believe. Although not given to sentimental speeches, he once cried because of malicious remarks made about the Trojans at a Stanford pep rally. He also showed deep sensitivity on many occasions. Early in his career he once lost a game because one of his halfbacks failed to cover a pass. "You know, that was your pass," he told his player. The player cried—and Jones spent nearly an hour consoling him.

Never one to berate his players, Jones kept his feelings under control, maintaining his dignity and bearing at all times. This failure to let off steam, however, eventually hurt the stoic Jones. He was constantly tortured by attacks of nervous tension. He tried to placate his nerves by chain-smoking cigarettes.

His most constant characteristic was steely concentration—a quality that he translated to his players. His whole presence was so geared to football that he forever found himself losing keys and socks, ignoring traffic lights, missing appointments, and stranding members of his family. His football teams were well prepared for every game. But everyone—and everything else—within Jones' sphere suffered for it.

"He was very, very thorough," says Wesson, who often played golf with the absent-minded Jones. "He used to go home and work a lot of his plays out with poker chips. He did a lot of this at night, making believe the poker chips were players...'this is Russ Saunders and this is what he does, etc...'"

Jones revered mental as well as physical attributes. The qualities that appealed to him the most: quick-thinking ability; ability to "sense" opponents plays; aggressiveness and courage; dependability; speed; agility; and stamina. Once asked who was his favorite player after six years at Southern Cal, the one who most exemplified his high standards, Jones named Morley Drury as his fair-haired boy. He turned out many more excellent football players after 1931, of course—many of them all-Americans.

In fact before Jones came on the scene, there had not been an all-America player at the school. Before he died of a heart attack in 1941 the "Head Man" had produced 23 all-Americans. His 29-year record as head coach showed that he had won more than 73 percent of his games—194 victories, 64 defeats, and 21 ties. He won 75 percent of his games at Southern Cal with a record of 121-36-13.

An anniversary of Jones' death prompted the *Los Angeles Times* to publish a stirring and revealing tribute by Wesson, the "Head Man's" constant friend and companion:

"The Head Man, being of retiring nature, hated to make speeches. But he was a pigeon for a service club and never refused an invitation to talk at a meeting, no matter how small and unimportant.

"He was so forgetful and absent-minded that he frequently lost his way driving home to North Hollywood. But he could tell you what every player did when it was first-and-10 on the 26-yard line in the S. C.-Stanford game of umpteen years ago.

"He liked people who stood up straight and athletic. But he himself was always in a slouch, and when standing in a group he always leaned on the guy nearest to him.

"He never paid much attention to criticism heaped upon himself. But he burned and had plenty to say if anyone panned the game of football or any individual player.

"He couldn't stand a guy who had had a drink. But he was the first to come to the aid of a confirmed rum pot who was helplessly under the influence.

"He told his boys that football was fun principally for the battling, hand-to-hand, rough-and-tumble combat in it. But when he wanted fun, he invariably got the littlest, weakest fish in the High Sierras on his line.

"He was a perfect gentleman to strangers. But he never said a kind word to his closest friends.

"He always told the athletic director that he couldn't prepare a decent schedule, his assistant coaches that they didn't know how to scout, the publicity boy that he couldn't write English, and the team doctors that they were quacks. But they liked to hear the 'Headman' talk like that, for they knew it was his good-natured, rough kind of ribbing and that out of their presence he swore by them.

"He would hardly glance at a boy coming off the field after playing his heart out. But when the game was over, in the privacy of the training quarters, he'd hunt out every boy who had played, thank him for what he had done, and be sure that any injuries, no matter how trivial, were immediately cared for.

"He never 'treated,' never carried enough money to buy anyone lunch, and always figured on plucking his golf opponents for enough petty cash to pay his caddy. But his check book paid out generously to almost any charity that sought him out.

"He was a napkin-twister, a silverware-fiddler, and a wordgroper as an after-dinner speaker. But his sincerity made him closer to his audience than any silver-tongued orator.

"He didn't belong to a church. But he lived every minute of his life according to the Golden Rule."

Howard Jones: "Football to me is power—massed power, functioning smoothly, driving forward relentlessly."

Time Out: Morley Drury

Of all the Southern Cal folklore that oldtimers thrash over, they still talk animatedly about the ovation that Morley Drury got in his last game.

On a sunny December afternoon in 1927 in the Los Angeles Coliseum, the public address announcer told the crowd of 70,000: "Morley is coming off the field for the last time, folks. Give him the hand he deserves." As Drury walked across the field to the dressing room, Southern Cal's game with Washington was frozen in limbo for four minutes while the cheers peaked.

Trotting toward the dressing room tunnel, Drury remembers: "I reached the track and looked up at all those people. I tried to wave, but my hand jerked so it wasn't much of a wave. My knees got weak even if I did feel fresh as a horse. And I bawled like a baby."

Drury had finished his wonderful college career by running for 180 yards and 3 touchdowns. Southern Cal beat Washington 33-13 that day.

"It was a nice way to finish," says Drury. "During the half I went to Coach Howard Jones and I asked him to take me out early and put in Howard Elliott. He sent Elliott in and I went out in the third quarter.

"We had just scored a touchdown and the teams were all lined up to kick when Jones grabbed me and said, 'You can go on into the dressing room, but you have to walk across the field.' Well, the whole crowd stood up as I started my walk.

Then the opposing team stood up. They were very wonderful.

"I crossed the Coliseum floor and the ovation lasted until I reached the tunnel. As I approached the tunnel, I knew that I couldn't hold back my tears."

The stirring ovation was a tribute to a darling of the crowds. Drury was known as "The noblest Trojan of them all," for obvious reasons.

He was Jones' golden boy from 1925 through 1927 and perhaps his all-time favorite player. "Aggressiveness, courage, agility, stamina, and durability" were some of the qualities attributed to Drury by the Southern Cal coach.

Jones might have added versatility, as well. Drury ran, punted, tackled, passed, and blocked with the best. In one game against California in 1927, Jones' premier power runner started at quarterback, moved to halfback, and finally to fullback where he scored both touchdowns in a 13-0 Trojan victory.

Drury's courage was exemplified in his senior year when he played with a broken jaw wired together and carried the ball 223 times for 1,163 yards. For all his running expertise, though, Drury ironically enjoyed playing defense more than offense. He said he preferred intercepting passes rather than throwing them.

"He was omnipresent, smart, powerful, and positively brutal in the way he banged and whanged at Stanford's line," wrote one journalist. "His defense against passes was phenomenal, his generalship above reproach."

Drury always called the signals because, as Jones put it, "He had that instinct."

Nate Barragar, a center who blocked for "The noblest Trojan," put it another way: "Morley was older than the rest of us. He was more mature, more settled, and better adjusted. He was a great leader. He was superb under pressure."

Drury was born February 5, 1903, in Midland, Ontario, Canada, and moved to Long Beach, California, "when I was quite young." He worked in shipyards there to put himself through prep school and entered Southern Cal at the relatively late age of 21.

"I thought at first that I might want to go to Stanford or the University of California," Drury remembers. "But I had some good friends who had gone ahead of me to Southern Cal. Chet Dolley was one of them."

Morley Drury, the "noblest Trojan of them all."

Dolley later revealed that it was his "job" to recruit Drury. Southern California football stars were given assignments to procure fresh talent.

Drury was some talent, to be sure. He had reached Southern Cal with ten letters in football, basketball, water polo, and swimming. His abilities were easily recognizable as a Southern Cal freshman, despite a year of agony.

"I broke my jaw twice," he recalls. "I fractured it first in one football game and then really broke it badly in the last game. A fellow from Illinois mailed me a special mask to play with—and I looked like a man from Mars."

Drury truly must have seemed like someone from another world in his next three years. A nerveless workhorse, the Southern Cal wonder player helped start the tradition of Howard Jones' "Thundering Herd" teams. Drury's stunning talents allowed the Trojans to compile a record of 27 victories, 5 defeats, and 1 tie from 1925 through 1927.

The Trojans seemed to be headed for an unbeaten season in 1925 when Drury injured his knee. He had to watch from the sidelines on crutches as they lost to Stanford 13-12. He passionately longed to play in a Rose Bowl, and the Trojans would have in 1927 had they done better than tied Stanford 13-13. It was not Drury's fault that the Trojans failed to win that one. He gained 163 yards rushing and intercepted 5 passes.

Despite a spate of injuries Drury played—and played well. He finished his career with 1,686 yards on 317 carries and one year compiled 1,240 yards of offense—running and passing. The figures may not be unique by today's standards, but Drury was much more than just a good runner and passer.

A Los Angeles sportswriter saw the quality of a brave warrior in this all-American player.

"Mark Kelly, the sports editor of the *Los Angeles Examiner*, pinned the 'noblest Trojan' tag on me," says Drury. "He just said, 'He's the noblest Trojan of them all.' The name stuck. All through the years, people have been very nice to me and always introduced me as such."

The "noblest Trojan" performed before enormous audiences who appreciated his special talents.

"I did everything—the kicking, the punting, and the kicking after touchdown, as well as carrying the ball," says

Drury, his pride showing.

He is also proud that he became the first 1,000-yard runner in Southern Cal history.

"Heck, 500 yards was a big thing then," says Drury. "They didn't have the wide-open play like today, and they didn't pass much in my day."

Notre Dame was the real enemy, the game that Drury pointed for. He played against the Fighting Irish twice, and lost each by a point. "They were always tough," he says, "because you had to play them hard for the full 60 minutes. You could never let down against Notre Dame."

In 1927 a game with Notre Dame in Chicago drew the biggest crowd in Southern Cal history.

"There must have been 127,000 people in Soldiers Field," recalls Drury. "That was quite a highlight. I had never seen that many people before in one place."

He played the full 60 minutes that day, a herculean task.

"I was forced to play the full game because my substitute was hurt," says Drury. "It was a tough day's work, believe me."

Drury surfaced at Southern Cal at the precise moment of a football renaissance. Coach Jones had taken hold of the Trojan ship and steered it in a new direction.

"When Jones got there, he started to cut the smaller colleges from our schedule and began scheduling really big-time schools," says Drury. "Jones felt it was bad to play against weak teams because it gave you false confidence. Jones wanted to change all that."

Teams like Whittier and Occidental, at one time a match for Southern Cal, were no longer competitive with the Trojans. They were more or less a tune-up in Drury's time.

"I remember we once played Whittier and Santa Clara the same day and beat them both rather badly, 74-0 and 42-0," says Drury. "We played the first-string against each of them in the first half, and then our second-string took over in the second half. We played 25-minute halves for those games."

A 6-foot, 185-pounder, Drury's steely frame punctured the pride of many good teams, as well as the weaker ones. Running out of Jones' Single Wing formation, he escaped for 250 yards against California in 1927. He does not take all the credit for that spectacular performance, however.

"People like Russ Saunders, Lloyd Thomas, and Henry Edelson opened the holes for me," says Drury. "They were some of the greats of my day."

When the end came at Southern Cal, he walked out in style, to that glorious ovation at the Los Angeles Coliseum. Symbolically, he was walking out of football.

He went into writing with the old *Express* in Los Angeles, then worked in a brokerage office and ended up in real estate until his retirement. Now 71, he lives an elegant life with his wife, Louise, by Santa Monica's beckoning seaside.

"We're right on the ocean," he says happily. "We go to the beach and I fool around the garage. I really don't do much of anything, except relax."

Football still excites him, though, and stirs giddy refrains.

"I try to see all the Southern Cal games, if I can," he says. "Gosh, they have a terrific amount of variation in the game today."

He is more enamored of the ancients, though.

"I wouldn't want to play today, with this free substitution rule of going in and going out of a game," Drury emphasizes. "I would want to play all the time—like I did in the 1920s. It was tougher then, but more to my liking."

The Sound Of Thunder

Once at a party Bob Zuppke told Howard Jones that he needed alcoholic inspiration. "Howard, you are a great coach, but you'd be a greater one, if you'd take a drink once in a while," he said. "You'd have more imagination."

The Southern Cal coach pondered the advice from Zuppke for a moment, then said: "I never heard of a drink yet figuring out a play."

"You haven't?" said the Illinois coach in mock astonishment. "Well, I've just had two drinks and have already figured out three new plays. They are the Flea Flicker, the Whoa Back, and the Double Jump. Here they are, I'll diagram them for you. I'm going to use them next season when Illinois plays Southern Cal."

The Illinois coach was having fun at the expense of a Trojan coach known for his sober dedication to the game. Though Jones built his Southern Cal teams around basic power plays, he had a lot of options in his repertoire.

"Jones ceaselessly broadened his offense," says Edwin Pope in his book, *Football's Greatest Coaches*. "In his first try at Iowa he had used only 16 plays. In his prime at Southern Cal his Trojans had upwards of 100 plays."

Jones' "unimaginative" image came from his style at Southern Cal, where the Trojans' heroic coach structured his offense around brute force and a gifted tailback. The triple-threat man could pass, run, or kick and carried the ball on most plays behind a clutch of brutish blockers. When the player got tired, Jones brought in another superstar in what he called his "relay system."

This style of play focused attention on the ballcarrier, and as a result runners like Mort Kaer, Morley Drury, Gus Shaver, Orville Mohler, and Cotton Warburton luxuriated in all the publicity.

The Southern Cal attack was likened to a rapier. "Swishing off-tackle sweeps, sharp thrusts through guard, and graceful gestures in the air," said one writer.

If mystical deception was lacking from Jones' offense, he nevertheless had a "secret" weapon—specialization.

"Jones' system is unique in that no two men on the team have exactly the same duties," a sportswriter once said. "If one man has brought specialization to football, that man is Howard Jones.

"On most elevens the duties of the two men playing a like position, for instance, tackle, have the same general duties. Not so under the Jones regime. There is a left and right tackle on a Howard Jones team, and it is rare that a man is trained to play both positions. The same is true of the ends, the guards, and the halfbacks. And, of course, the other men, the center, fullback, and quarterback have duties separate from the others.

"But Jones' most startling contribution to football is his backfield. In the Jones backfield, instead of four ballcarriers there are only two, the fullback and the quarterback. Except in rare instances the two halfbacks never carry the ball. Their duty is to provide interference for the ball-luggers. Generally the quarterback is a fast man who carries the ball off-tackle and around end, the fullback being used primarily as a line-bucker."

The running plays were not without innovation, despite what Zuppke said at that party.

"I believe that Jones was the first coach to use the trap play (sometimes called sucker play or mousetrap)," said Pop Warner, a fierce Jones rival. "It was around 1928."

Jones was sometimes forced to defend his conservatism.

"The biggest thrill in football to me is the long run," he once said. "A hole smashed open, a dart through the line, a block by an interferer, a side-step, a straight-arm, a race, and a matching of skill and courage and wits between a swerving, dashing ballcarrier and his flying pursuer.

"This, in my opinion, is fundamental football and the very heart of and reason for the game. It is my answer to those who continually harp on so-called wide-open football and wonder why the game is not almost completely turned into throwing the pigskin around."

He stuck to his guns, he said, "at the risk of being called a stodgy, old conservative."

Observers gazed in wonderment at the variety of plays that unfolded. Said one sportswriter: "It is the kaleidoscopic change in the pattern of his offense, screening the direction and nature of the thrust, to the confusion of the defense, that makes his attack so difficult to stop, plus the sound principles of line play inculcated and the tremendous power generated by heavy, mercury-footed backs who run with a stark fury that is almost appalling."

Football students marveled at Jones' exquisite inside tackle play. Some thought it was the best ever developed. Jones made it work with hefty linemen like Jesse Hibbs, John Baker, and Ernie Smith.

The runners were Jones' joy, though. Of the 23 all-Americans he produced at Southern Cal, 9 of them were backfield men. Their presence inspired the famous football appellation, "The Thundering Herd."

Leading these runners through the fields of battle were some of the toughest linemen on the West Coast. One such beauty was Brice Taylor, a guard who became the first all-American produced at Southern Cal.

Taylor opened holes for the guileful Kaer, the first of Jones' exciting runners. The two made life miserable for most of Southern Cal's opponents in 1925. The Trojans outscored the opposition 456 to 55 and won 11 of 13 games in Jones' first season. Kaer earned all-America honors in 1926, but he might have in 1925 for scoring 114 points. He once had 4 touchdowns in a game and twice scored 3.

The victory total was the most ever produced by a Trojan team, and Jones became an instant god to Southern Californians and a pain in the neck to everyone else. A new era began at Southern Cal while an old one slipped away at California. The once-supreme Golden Bears came off their high horse just about the same time that Jones arrived at Southern Cal. Then the

Hobbs Adams was captain of the Trojans when they won 11 games in Howard Jones' first year, 1925.

Trojans began fighting with Stanford for supremacy on the Pacific Coast.

Criticized at times for "undistinguished entrance requirements," Southern Cal could never be faulted for unrepresentative football teams. Despite its contributions to academics and civic development, Southern Cal, whether warranted or not, became a "football school" under the Jones' regime.

Some of football's most ardent rivalries were born in Jones' formative years at Southern Cal. The Trojans hooked up with Notre Dame and UCLA for the first time and enhanced a passionate marriage with Stanford.

Victories over Notre Dame and UCLA were always

Brice Taylor, Southern California's first all-American player. Howard Jones produced plenty more.

important to Jones but gave him no more satisfaction than when he caught up with Stanford. There were no more bitter rivals in the land than Southern Cal and its northern neighbors, Stanford and California. Jealousies and the struggle for state supremacy had fostered war-like feelings.

In 1926 Southern Cal defeated a California team, 27-0. It was something that Jones' predecessor, "Gloomy Gus" Henderson, could not do. Conversely, Jones at first had trouble with Stanford—a team that Henderson beat with ease. Pop Warner, with his deception and power plays, was a nemesis for Jones in 1925 and 1926, when Stanford beat the Trojans 13-9 and 13-12. When a Jones team tied the Indians 13-13 in 1927, it was a day of celebration at Southern Cal. Later that season the Trojans defeated California 13-0 and went on to tie Stanford for the Pacific Coast Conference championship.

But the Trojans' long-sought championship goal was somewhat anti-climactic for they had gone through a season without losing to either Stanford or California. That was as important as a championship to them.

Southern Cal and Stanford had met before a crowd of 52,385 at Stanford Stadium on October 15, 1927.

"All Trojan rooters as usual were sitting in the sun while the Stanford rooters, as usual, enjoyed the comfort of the west, or shady side of their stadium," recalled an observer.

Arnold Eddy, later to become executive director of Southern Cal's General Alumni Association, was a witness to that important meeting with Stanford.

"Pop Warner, by virtue of a fluke loss to Santa Clara in his opening game, had hypnotized the bay area scribes into making Troy a 10-point favorite," said Eddy. "Ours was a green team. Jones battled Warner to a standstill, and only in the closing minutes of the game did Stanford come from behind to tie it. Die-hard Trojan rooters still claim the fourth quarter was minutes too long (in those days time was not kept as accurately as today)."

Russ Saunders scored a touchdown after recovering a Stanford fumble and Drury scored another on an end run to give Southern Cal a 13-7 advantage going into the last period. The Trojans would have had a 14th point but for a Stanford defender who blocked the conversion attempt and broke his nose in the process.

In the fourth quarter, when "time was fast running out," the Indians scored the tying touchdown with a passing game. "Fleishacker passed to Vincenti who ran three yards for the touchdown," remembered Eddy. "Murphy missed the extra point."

It did not diminish the individual accomplishments of the Trojans that day, however.

"Jesse Hibbs was poison," said Eddy. "He opened enormous holes in the Stanford line all day for Captain Morley Drury. He messed up the Stanford reverse plays with regularity understandable only to Howard Harding Jones. Sophomore Nate Barragar received a special plaudit from the coach after the game and won the starting berth at center and kept it.

"Francis Tappaan became regular left end. Monday morning papers, both San Francisco and Los Angeles, hailed Drury and Hibbs as potential all-Americas. We had to wait until the end of the season to find out for sure whether they were or not, but somehow I think that Howard Jones knew then—he always seemed to know so much about so many things."

The erudite Jones had caught up with Warner after two initial losses to the Stanford coach. A new wrinkle in the defense turned the tide, according to this account by sportswriter Allison Danzig.

"After his first two years on the Coast, during which he lost both times to Stanford, Jones changed his defense to smash the wing-back attack, playing his ends in close in a six-man line and sending them in fast to mess up the slow-forming plays behind the line of scrimmage. Jones also added to his own defense until it put Warner's '57 varieties' in the shade."

The series with Notre Dame started in 1926, triggered by a casual gentlemen's agreement some years before between Jones and Knute Rockne. Just after Jones' Iowa team had upset Rockne's Fighting Irish 10-7 one autumn afternoon in 1921 the two shook hands in the center of the football field at Iowa City.

"Now, don't forget," said the Notre Dame coach. "You owe me a game."

"You'll get it," Jones replied.

That handclasp brought together two of the fiercest rivals in college football history.

Five years later the two met again on a football field—but not without some planning by Rockne. The Notre Dame coach, in putting his schedule together, had wanted a West Coast game—preferably in a big city like Los Angeles. He wanted his team, already well-known, to get even more exposure in a cosmopolitan area.

The story goes that when the Southern Cal coaching job opened in 1925, Rockne recommended Jones for the post. This cemented an already firm friendship—and a thankful Jones "rewarded" Rockne with a home-and-home series against Southern Cal.

The first game between the Trojans and the Fighting Irish would be typical of their heady future struggles. It was a one-point game, won by Notre Dame 13-12.

Notre Dame had won eight straight games in 1926 but was shut out by Carnegie Tech in game number 9 and was "fighting mad and determined to avenge this unlucky reverse." Southern Cal took a 12-7 lead into the fourth quarter. But with a minute to play a left-handed passer named Art Parisien was rushed in to save the Fighting Irish. His throws moved Notre Dame quickly to Southern Cal's 20-yard line, and then with seconds remaining he fired a touchdown pass to John Niemiec for the winning points.

The rivalry soared in 1927 when an estimated 120,000 jammed elephantine Soldiers Field in Chicago (Herb Jones, the Notre Dame business manager, said the paid attendance was "only" 99,198.) Morley Drury passed to Russ Saunders for the Trojans' touchdown, but they were unable to convert the extra point and thus lost 7-6. That inability to convert extra points would haunt the Trojans in future Notre Dame warfare. In this particular game, though, the Los Angeles press groaned about a touchback that they thought should have been a two-point safety for Southern Cal. The officials disagreed.

"We were robbed," said Drury upon returning from the trip.

The Jones-Rockne rivalry, although short-lived because of the premature death of the Notre Dame coach in 1931, was a sunburst on the football horizon. Their association produced legions of anecdotes.

One year when Southern Cal arrived in Chicago to play the

Yell king Paul Elmquist hands megaphone to Morley Drury prior to Southern Cal's departure for Notre Dame game in 1927. It was a wasted trip. The Fighting Irish beat the Trojans, 7-6.

Fighting Irish, Jones was greeted by a newspaper headline: "Knute To Start Shock Troop."

"If he does," Jones told reporters," we'll score in the first minute of the game."

The next morning Chicago newspapers announced: "Jones Says Will Score In First Minute Of Play."

Rockne started his so-called "shock troop," a band of his toughest, meanest players.

Southern Cal scored in the first minute.

Before another of their memorable meetings this laughable confrontation took place:

Rockne: "Howard, we've had a wonderful series, always close. We've lost two games and have a weak team this year. Now it wouldn't be right for you to humiliate us. I tell you—I'll give you a safety on the first play if you promise not to score any more. You know we couldn't score if we wanted to."

Jones: "What do you say we play the game and see how it comes out?"

Southern Cal won, 27-14.

Jones, usually stolid, engaged in an animated repartee with the witty Rockne on another pre-game occasion.

"My gosh, Howard!" Rockne said. "What are you so nervous about? You're chain-smoking!"

"Well, you're not the coolest guy out here," said Jones in one of his rare comebacks. "Your cigar looks like a shredded rope!"

The one-point defeat by Notre Dame was the only loss for Southern California in 1927—a season when Jones produced two all-Americans, the aforementioned Drury and tackle Jesse Hibbs, and a plethora of rich talent. When Stanford went to the Rose Bowl that season to face Pitt, many believed that the best team on the Pacific Coast stayed home.

Along with Drury and Hibbs, Jones' fine team included Frank Anthony, Nate Barragar, Charles Boren, Henry Edelson, Howard Elliott, Bert Heiser, Cecil Hoff, Lawrence McCaslin, Don Moses, Russ Saunders, Albert Scheving, Tony Steponovich, Francis Tappaan, Lloyd Thomas, and Don Williams.

It was one of Jones' best teams, even though it did not go to the Rose Bowl. Though tied by Southern Cal and beaten by St. Mary's and Santa Clara, Stanford was selected for Pasadena.

If not a bowl representative, Southern Cal found 1927 significant in other ways. The net from football income reached an all-time high of $300,000, mostly due in part to the 75,690 seating capacity in the Los Angeles Coliseum ("26 miles of seats," proclaimed the *Pigskin Review*).

The Notre Dame affair at Soldiers Field alone grossed in excess of $250,000, then an all-time high both from the standpoint of attendance and income for any single game.

It was a giddy, prosperous time, and it was to get better.

In 1928 Jones beat Warner's Stanford team in a memorable 10-0 game and also manipulated Southern Cal's first victory over Notre Dame. This became Jones' most successful season to date, for it produced an undefeated year, the first uncontested PCC title and the first national football champion in Southern Cal history.

Tackle Jess Hibbs made all-American teams in both 1927 and 1928. He helped Southern California's great runners find daylight.

Observers found the sudden success overwhelming.

"By 1927 we had arrived as an intercollegiate power," said one. "Howard Jones had already become a great football name, but little did we realize that he was soon to become a national idol and in one short year achieve his fondest desire—to coach a fine group of boys to a national championship."

That Championship Season

New York City newspapers, to say nothing of the Hollywood movie stars, championed West Coast football in 1928.

After Stanford beat Army that year, Vincent Treanor wrote in the *Evening World* that the game "had demonstrated the futility of the Eastern one-man offense against Western team play."

After Oregon State beat New York University, Ed Sullivan's column in the *Graphic* stated: "We learned about football from them."

Bill Corum wise-cracked in the *Journal* that the Californians "may come from Palo Alto—but they all sing bass."

And Grantland Rice, that dean of all sportswriters, joked: "The two Western triumphs demonstrated that the best teams in the East this season were Stanford and Oregon State."

The *New York Mirror* brought Southern Cal into the picture, even though the Trojans had not played an eastern rival. The point was, Southern Cal had beaten Stanford 10-0 and Oregon State 19-0 that season.

"In view of what happened to New York U. and Army," wrote *Mirror* Sports Editor Dan Parker, "I propose the following choices for all-America teams:

"First team—University of Southern California.

"Second team—Stanford.

"Third team—Oregon State."

If West Coast football was revered by the Eastern

establishment, then Southern Cal was the sun of its own world, shining brightly and in a higher stratosphere than the other stars. Marching forward the Trojans not only demanded respect from writers but gained admiration from the "beautiful people." Their heroics spawned a cult of followers in the movie industry. Howard Jones was bombarded by "fan mail" from such people as Oliver Hardy of the Laurel and Hardy comedy team, Gary Cooper, Vilma Banky, Mary Pickford, Douglas Fairbanks, Sr., Harold Lloyd, Norma Talmadge, Richard Dix, Hoot Gibson, Ronald Coleman, Nancy Carroll, and Reginald Denny.

Hardy asked in a letter: "Is the quarterback's value greater today than it used to be?"

"Yes," replied Jones, "because the introduction of the forward pass broadened the field for the employment of strategy."

Gary Cooper wanted to know what the penalty was for coaching from the bench during a game.

"Fifteen yards," Jones replied by mail.

Vilma Banky asked Jones who he thought was the greatest player of all time. Jones ironically did not pick a Trojan, but Tom Shevlin, Yale's 1905 captain and all-American end. Why? "Because," said Jones, "he not only was powerful physically, but also had great mental characteristics such as dynamic determination."

It was well known, though, that Jones deeply admired his own Morley Drury.

Victories over Utah State, Oregon State, and St. Mary's to open the 1928 season inspired exuberant confidence in Southern Cal. That confidence was not disturbed, either, when the Trojans played to a scoreless tie with California in their famous "mud bowl" game at Berkeley. Although no rain had fallen for days in the San Francisco area, California's field was layered with mud at game time. Southern Cal fans asserted that California followers had hosed down the field in order to stop the Trojans' quick running backs.

Not only was Southern Cal handicapped by a wet and heavy field, the Trojans also had three regulars out of the lineup due to injury—Charlie Boren, Harry Edelson, and Lowry McCaslin.

"They were three important cogs in Howard Jones' terrific power plays," remembered Arnold Eddy, who graduated from Southern Cal in 1924, fifty years before his present position as executive director of the General Alumni Association.

Eddy recalled watching the muscled warriors struggling in ankle-deep mud and frustration.

"With the advantage of the heavy turf and Benny Lom's brilliant spirals, the Bears were saved from serious trouble on more than one occasion," said Eddy. "Don Williams and Russ Saunders of Southern Cal spent most of the afternoon trying to dig the ball out from the California end of that wet field. Williams went out of the game early with injuries, not to return until the Stanford game two weeks later."

After that controversial California game, Southern Cal defeated Occidental and dutifully prepared for Stanford. The

Southern Cal blockers lead quarterback Don Williams (partially obliterated in the back) on a long gain against Oregon State in

Trojans went into the game as underdogs.

"It took only a couple of early-season games to convince nearly everybody that Pop Warner had one of his greatest teams at Stanford," Braven Dyer wrote in his book, *Top Ten Trojan Football Thrillers*. "Pop said so himself when he declared that he 'had more good material than I ever saw before.' Later, of course, he qualified this by pointing out that he previously had coached 11 better men. But the damage was done. Stanford became quite confident."

Stanford became even more confident after hearing of Southern Cal's unimpressive showing against little Occidental. The Trojans beat the underprivileged Tigers 19-0, a score they probably should have doubled, while Warner's Indians embarrassed Fresno State 47-0. "Dink" Templeton, Stanford's track and field coach, predicted that the Indians' winning margin over

this 1928 game won by the Trojans 19-0. Leading interference are, Henry Edelson, John Winfield, and Russ Saunders.

the Trojans would be anywhere from one to four touchdowns. The bookmakers agreed.

"Tremendous reserve strength, a substantial weight edge, and a blind faith in Warner's ability to work gridiron miracles—these were the things Stanford men talked about as the zero hour neared," said Dyer. "Pop had concocted a new formation—called Formation B—to distinguish it from what he had been using. It wasn't much of a departure, except that he stationed his quarterback and fullback a bit farther back, thereby getting more manueverability for reverses and double reverses.

"Herb Fleishhacker weighed 220 and Biff Hoffman 195. They were the two back men, and when sent into the line behind 240-pound Artman and 205-pound Sellman, the tackles, they were supposed to crumble opposing lines like so much papier mache."

Reports from the Southern Cal camp continued to buoy Stanford's spirits. Tackle Jesse Hibbs had missed two days of practice because of an illness. Center Nate Barragar had been handicapped by injuries and spent half the preceding week in a hospital. An epidemic of flu broke out on the Southern Cal campus and forced Jones to move his team into the Beverly Hills Hotel.

By game time in the Los Angeles Coliseum, which had been sold out for two weeks, the odds on Stanford had vaulted to 3-1. But the oddsmakers had not counted on Jones' zealous preparations. Jones had surrounded himself with lieutenants, and one of them—Clifton B. Herd—was commissioned to follow Stanford all year. Herd trailed the Indians all over the countryside and brought back a detailed scouting report to Jones.

"From Herd's scouting reports Jones decided that the best way to offset Stanford's 10-pound weight edge and the crunching power which Pop could generate, once his plays began rolling, was to get in there immediately and start belting somebody," Dyer explained. "They called it the 'quick mix' in those days.

"Perhaps it isn't very revolutionary, as we look back, but for the most part opposing teams, up until the Jones plan, had been content to sit back and wait for Pop's reverses to come to them. This, of course, was more or less fatal, because by the time the play had formed to that extent, it packed a terrific punch and no single defender could do much against it.

"Howard sent his ends and tackles crashing in immediately to batter down the interference. When the ballcarrier poked his head beyond the line of scrimmage he had been stripped clean, or nearly so, and hard-hitting secondary tacklers thus got a clear shot."

This brutish defense promoted five Stanford fumbles that day. Southern Cal recovered three—two by end Lowry McCaslin. Harry Edelson, Russ Saunders, and Lloyd Thomas galvanized the Trojan defenders with crisp tackling. Saunders and McCaslin had a hand in the scoring, too. After Hibbs intercepted a Stanford pass on the 35-yard line, the Trojans took the ball in on passes, the last one from Saunders to McCaslin.

With only seconds to play in the first half, Thomas came from behind to haul down Chuck Smalling on the 10-yard line and prevent Stanford from scoring a tying touchdown. The Indians' brutal running game was further frustrated in the second half, and the Trojans clinched it on a 15-yard field goal by Hibbs.

Dyer's story in the November 4, 1928, issue of the *Los Angeles Times* called it a Southern Cal miracle, wrought by its hawkish miracle-worker, Howard Jones.

"Rated considerably below what was touted as the most powerful team in Stanford history, the battling sons of Troy scaled the heights at the Coliseum yesterday afternoon and turned back the Red Horde, 10 to 0, in the most stunning upset ever recorded in these parts," Dyer wrote. "Howard Jones is the happiest man in the world today, and nobody will begrudge him his joy. The Trojan mentor wanted to win that game more than he wanted anything else in the world. He had never defeated Warner. In the past he had come close to it on several occasions, but something always happened. Often it was Lady Luck that deprived him of victory. But yesterday Old Dame Fortune was riding on the Trojan war horse, and what a ride the little lady got."

Ed R. Hughes, writing in the *San Francisco Chronicle* the next day, called it, "The day after Waterloo."

Warner gave praise: "USC was the perfect eleven. There

were no mistakes. (Quarterback) Don Williams was above reproach."

Saunders and Hill never forgot the day, and throughout their lives considered it their shining moment in football.

"It was my greatest thrill," Saunders said years afterward. "Yes, even greater than my 95-yard return of a kickoff against Notre Dame at Soldiers Field in 1930."

It was, perhaps, Jones' most significant victory of the 1920s, in terms of publicity as well as accomplishment. By popular acclaim the Trojans were the best team on the West Coast, and judging by writers in New York perhaps the best in the nation.

Southern Cal certified this thinking by rolling past Arizona, Washington State, and Idaho to win the Pacific Coast Conference title, and then put the national stamp of approval on its undefeated season with a two-touchdown victory over Notre Dame, albeit a weak Notre Dame team.

Knute Rockne had brought his Fighting Irish into Los Angeles with mental and physical handicaps. Rockne's son lay on an operating table back in South Bend, dangerously ill. And with that on his mind Rockne also was presenting the weakest of his teams to the formidable Trojans.

Russ Saunders showed the Fighting Irish what sort of an afternoon they were in for—scoring a Southern Cal touchdown on "the old 21 play." As Saunders explained it: "The hole was jammed so I cut to the right and went across the line standing up." Williams threw a touchdown pass to Marger Apsit, a little-used receiver. The Trojans took a 20-0 lead when Tony Steponovich intercepted a Johnny Niemiec pass and returned it 18 yards over the Notre Dame goal. Williams later threw to Harry Edelson for another TD.

The play of Williams and Hibbs fittingly closed out glamorous careers. Both had to leave the game with help—Hibbs with a twisted ankle and Williams with a kick in the head—but both were officially stamped as all-Americans afterwards.

Far Western football vaulted after Southern Cal polished off Notre Dame with clinical ease. Newspaper applause greeted the Trojans, especially.

"Southern California all but hugged the life out of the South Bend Irish, and made it harder than ever for the folks back over the Great Divide to forget Los Angeles," wrote the *Los Angeles Times*. "The tang of the sea and the heat of the desert do not make sissies. Men are not debilitated into softlings in the great open spaces."

Both Professor Frank G. Dickinson of Illinois and Jack F. Rissman agreed with that assessment, in so many words. It was Dickinson's rating system based on the idea of awarding points according to the strength of opponents that pronounced the Trojans as the best team in the land in 1928. And it was Rissman who presented to Southern Cal his National Intercollegiate Football Trophy, the official certification.

The Trojans were thus thrust into national prominence in one sweeping year. But the season unfortunately ended in controversy for them. They were the logical choice to represent the West in the Rose Bowl that season but turned down the invitation.

Southern Cal's public explanation was a policy that "frowned on any games after the closing date of the Pacific Coast Conference season." Only in the event "of unusual circumstance" would the Trojans play post-season games and then not later than the Saturday before Christmas Day, the school said.

Privately it was said that Southern Cal officials had a feud alive with the Rose Bowl tournament members, although the reasons were obtuse.

Les Henry, chairman of the football committee of the Tournament of Roses, accepted Southern Cal's snub with grace.

"We went out of our way to make it possible for USC to play," he said. "We deviated from our own policy by offering the game to the Trojans a year in advance. I very much regret Southern Cal's stand in the matter, but a representative team can always be found to play for the association."

Henry added that he held "no animosity toward the Trojans and would very much like to see them play" in the Rose Bowl at a future time.

California, despite a loss and two ties, was named to carry the West's colors against Georgia Tech that January, 1929, and was involved in a memorable game—but only because of a freak happening.

It was in this game that California's Roy Riegels was

stunned into running the wrong way on a play that ultimately gave Georgia Tech an 8-7 victory. "Wrong Way" Riegels became a Rose Bowl legend.

Time Out: Nate Barragar

The years have glowed for Nate Barragar. Movies with John Wayne, television shows with Bob Hope, the extravagant glamour of professional football.

His memory often locks into the distant past, though. It is frozen in his personal Twilight Zone. The time is 1928, and Barragar sees it clearly now.

"I remember the Stanford game that year as if it were yesterday," says the onetime Southern Cal football star. "Stanford was favored to beat us by a big margin.

"Biff Hoffman, their fullback, was the key to the Stanford strength. He caught a punt in the Coliseum, and I was running down the kick. Hoffman was a big man.

"Well, I'm expecting to be blocked by their players, but I wasn't—and here we are, Hoffman and me, running wide open and right at each other.

"I decided to go under him in a knot. He went over, and it just about finished Hoffman. With him out of the Stanford lineup, that was it. We won, 10-0."

Such jarring tackles created publicity and drew attention during Barragar's golden career at Southern Cal and eventually earned him applause as an all-American.

He still has scrapbooks from his college days and eagerly reveals newspaper clippings.

"This one's dated December 15, 1929," Barragar says warmly. "That's when I made Walter Eckersall's all-America team in my senior year. The team included Bronco Nagurski, the Minnesota star."

Barragar is urged to read the article. Haltingly, the modest Barragar proceeds: "Nate Barragar of Southern Cal is awarded the left guard position. The Trojan played consistent football and was an important cog developed by Howard Jones."

Barragar was the seventh all-American produced by Jones and one of two in the 1929 season. Born in Kansas in 1907 and relocated in California at the age of seven, Barragar eventually grew up thinking of Southern Cal but never dreaming he would get such national acclaim.

A star at San Fernando High School, Barragar recalls, "I wanted to go to USC, although I had a number of scholarship offers. There was a strong local tradition, and the team had started to come ahead under Jones."

Jack Hughes, an alumnus of Southern Cal, coached at San Fernando High school and steered Barragar into Jones' lap. And Jones turned a boy into a man.

"He was an outstanding fundamental coach who taught young men how to handle themselves," says Barragar about the Trojans' famous "Head Man." "He was a taskmaster, a strictly dedicated football coach. Personality-wise, he wasn't a man who had a lot of things to say. He was just very quiet and very dedicated to his work. There was nothing funny about Jones. He was serious as anything. Chewing gum sometimes bothered him.

"Jones taught us to get across the line first, ahead of our opponent. 'You're going to get across the line first,' he'd say. 'Watch the ball.' In practice he would be running with one team on Bovard Field, and if he saw someone not running with the ball properly on the other side of the field he'd go clear across the field and correct it. This was the reason for his success—intense dedication. That was Howard Jones all the way."

Barragar recalls this typical Jones story:

"Dick Arlen, the actor, was one of Jones' close friends. He lived a block away from him. He'd go over and talk to Jones, and Jones wouldn't even be listening. He'd be figuring out a play on a napkin. He was always thinking football."

So was Barragar for that matter. A fullback in high school, he fully expected to play that position at Southern Cal. But Jones had other plans for him after he graduated from the

Nate Barragar, 1929 Trojan captain: "You have to be a leader. All the boys on the team are pretty smart, but you have to keep after them."

freshman team.

"I had a pretty good reputation as a fullback," Barragar recalls, "and I hoped to play that position on the varsity. But they needed a center in my sophomore year, and they made me a center. My job was backing the line on defense. I guess you could say I was one of the original linebackers."

Barragar luckily was free from serious injuries in his career from 1927 through 1929, but there was no safeguard against exhaustion.

"We didn't get hurt, but everyone got tired together," Barragar quipped, referring to Jones' practice of playing his best players most of the time with little relief. "People who started the game hardly ever came out."

In his junior year Barragar played on a national championship team. The aforementioned game with Stanford helped vault the Trojans to the top.

In his senior year Barragar was made a running guard by Jones "because we were weak there." He also played defensive fullback and captained the 1929 team.

"Being captain of the team and playing defensive fullback, you are into an awful lot of things," says Barragar. "You have to be a leader. All the boys on the team are pretty smart, but you have to keep after them."

The Rose Bowl game with Pitt that season lingers in Barragar's mind. He remembers:

"On the first play the Pittsburgh halfback, Tony Uansa, broke loose, and Russ Saunders caught him from eight yards in the rear. We held them and marched down for a touchdown. Uansa, he was an all-American. It turned out to be a lopsided game (Southern Cal won 47-14), and I believe the whole thing turned on that play. We won, and I think on that particular day we could have beaten anybody."

It was one of the few games that Barragar remembers "we could actually laugh and enjoy." He gives one such example.

"Jones has the second team warming up on the sidelines, and they're bouncing up and down there," says Barragar. "I told Clark Galloway, who played guard, that we should knock a Pitt player into Jones' lap to let him know that we deserve to stay in there. We did it. We knocked this guy clear to the sidelines, and Jones turns to his second team and says, 'Sit down, just sit down. If anyone can play like that, they play on my team.'"

Talking about Pitt, Barragar says: "They came out with five all-Americans, and we were supposed to have our hands full. But our fundamental line play caught them flatfooted, and we did with them as we wanted. We just pushed them around."

After graduation the siren call of professional football beckoned. But Barragar at first had a hard time finding a team that stayed in business long enough.

"I started out with the Minneapolis Red Jackets, but they only lasted a half-year," recalls Barragar, grinning about those once-futile franchises. "I joined the Frankford Yellow Jackets when the Red Jackets folded up, and we had to play two games a week because we were also playing out the Minneapolis schedule. It was funny, we had to wear both colors—red when we played the Minneapolis games and yellow when we played Frankford's."

When Barragar returned for another year in the pros, he had similar sour luck with Frankford.

"They folded up in the middle of my second year," he recalls.

But the Green Bay Packers remembered a time that they had faced the talented Barragar, and liked what they saw. They offered the football wastrel a job.

He spent three seasons with Green Bay, and it was rewarding financially as well as artistically. The Packers won three National Football League championships while Barragar was there.

"It was a great team with a deceptive attack," Barragar remembers. "They passed a lot. One of the years I played with the great Don Hutson. The whole squad only numbered 22. Now they have 70 and 80 on a team."

As was customary Barragar was also called upon to serve in motion pictures. Football players often had part-time acting jobs as extras in those days because professional football salaries were not especially good.

This unique marriage with Hollywood often spawned wonderful stories. Barragar recalls an incident after working on a movie called *Salute* at Paramount with Richard Arlen.

"Arlen was in New York on a personal appearance tour,

and he came over to our hotel room one Saturday in 1931 and we listened to that Notre Dame-Southern Cal game which the Trojans won 16-14 on Johnny Baker's field goal. Later we asked Arlen to sit on the bench with us when we played the New York Giants the next day at the Polo Grounds. Arlen then invited us to join him on the stage after the game and we accepted...but we didn't know what kind of a time we were in for.

"Well, everything was going okay. Arlen sat with us, and he was introduced at halftime and got a great ovation. We knew that, since he was so popular, that he might have a hard time getting out of the stadium and making the theater. So I told him, 'Dick, when the game is over, just start running to the dressing room. We'll follow.'

"We beat the Giants in the last two minutes; it was a very exciting game. Arlen starts running for the dressing room while this mob descends. Russ Saunders, Marge Apsit, and myself all jumped into a cab with Arlen. We didn't even have time to change or shower.

"We pulled up in front of the theater in Staten Island with a police escort, sirens going and everything. There wasn't much time left, so we just ran into the theater. Someone said, 'There's a plate of sandwiches, boys. Grab some. You're on.'

"We rushed out on that stage with Dick Arlen and his wife, Jobie, and I tell you I never had a bigger thrill in my life when I heard that applause for us. Later, Dick and his wife took us for a steak dinner. What made everything so good was that we had this big night and won the game with the Giants, too."

Barragar's natural inclination toward theater people was soon put to profitable use. He left football after a short but bright career to pursue work in the "picture business." He had been working all along in the production department of RKO Studios while playing football and had a direct line to the movie industry when he departed football's violent world.

His Hollywood star climbed each year, and the onetime Southern Cal all-American became one of the most successful production managers in the game. He captained many well-known films, including *The Greatest Story Ever Told*, and a bunch of Wayne movies like *Hondo, The Fighting Seabees*, and *The Sands of Iwo Jima*. He has done several Hollywood television series, and his work also takes him to New York where he recently shot a Bob Hope spectacular.

"I'm still working, it's good for me," says the 67-year-old Barragar, whose duties as a production manager embody many of the qualities of a football leader.

He explains: "I set up the schedule for a movie. I make out a budget. I set a date to start the shooting, and I'm responsible for the money spent and for the time spent making it. I've done just about everything one can do in the industry."

But Barragar sometimes daydreams football, even in his busy world. He "comes home" to Green Bay everytime they have a reunion of players.

"Every year at Green Bay they have a homecoming game for the oldtimers," says Barragar. "And I've tried to get back to every one since 1935. One year recently they had 80 alumni from the Packer teams for a game. We sat right behind the team bench. It was terrific."

Displayed prominently in his home is a special lamp he once received from the Packers during a visit.

"They gave everyone of us oldtimers a rather unique table lamp," Barragar says, his voice ringing with pride. "The base of the lamp is a real Green Bay Packer headgear. It's really something."

For Barragar it is as good as any Oscar.

Time Out: John Wayne

Two John Wayne legends persist.

The most formidable, structured by Hollywood, is the American folk hero, the titanic figure swaggering through motion pictures.

The other legend, not as enormous but every bit as interesting, is the football player.

One talent has eclipsed the other, but many remember the young, black-haired Apollo in a Southern Cal uniform.

"He had all the football ability in the world," says Leo Calland, a Southern Cal player and coach of the 1920s. "He had the savvy, a great build, and the equipment."

Chet Dolley, another Southern Cal figure of the 1920s, remembers a "big, rough and tough" football specimen walking around campus "with patches on the seat of his pants."

"He could play football, no doubt about that," says Dolley, "even though he wasn't the best-dressed on campus."

"Duke was a good guard," recalls Normel C. Hayhurst, his coach at Glendale High School. "He played a big part in our winning the Central League and the Southern California championship. He was one of the seven players selected for a football scholarship at USC. Our 1924 team was a good one."

Other remembrances are not so kind. Says one associate: "Wayne was a great guy, and he hasn't changed any. But he really wasn't a top-notch player."

Another will tell you confidentially: "He didn't have the desire. I'm not criticizing Duke, but some guys have more desire

John Wayne, a "big, rough and tough" football specimen at Southern California. He might have been a football star instead of a movie star except for a swimming accident.

than others. He had too many distractions. He was a big, good-looking guy with black, curly hair and a great build, and had to fight the girls off.

"Now, Ward Bond, the actor and Wayne's close friend, was just the opposite. He had all the desire in the world, but he didn't have the same equipment. Both were tackles in college, and I always said that if you took Ward Bond's desire and John Wayne's equipment you'd have an all-American."

Gene Clarke remembers a fine football player who could have been outstanding, except for a freak happening.

"I had a hand in making him a picture star, I always say," jokes Clarke, a burly lineman of the 1930s and a close friend of Wayne's.

"In Wayne's sophomore year he was slated for first-string right tackle at Southern Cal, but he had a bad accident the summer before the season started. I was with him when it happened. Duke and I used to go down to Balboa Beach and ride those big ocean waves. One day we're all on the sand with pretty coeds all around. You know how everyone likes to show off, particularly Duke and me.

"These big waves started to come in. We called them, 'butt-busters.' I mean, they were BIG! They were washing the bottom of the pier. Duke says, 'Come on, let's go and ride them.' I said, 'You gotta be nuts, they'll kill us.' He said, 'Come on, you've got no guts!' And I said, 'Dammit, if you're crazy enough, I'll go.'

"It took us 15 minutes to get out past the breaker lines because when the waves hit they pound so hard on the sand that you have to dive down and hang on. So we finally got out to where they were breaking, and I warned Duke that the breakers cup hard and will drop you right straight down. I told Duke if they start cupping to back out of them. 'Okay,' he said.

"By this time there were a lot of people on the pier nearby wondering who these damn fools were in the water. The last thing I saw was this wave coming, and I mean it was a big one. It started to cup, and I screamed, 'Get out of it, Duke'. And I tucked my butt back in the wave as it came over, see. But when I last saw Duke, he was going straight down. He hit the sand, and if he hadn't pulled his head to one side he probably would have busted his neck. As it was it dislocated his shoulder.

"Now this is three weeks before football practice starts, and he was playing right tackle in the old Howard Jones power plays and in this system you used right shoulder blocking all the time.

"Duke couldn't block, and he was afraid to tell the old man he'd hurt his shoulder swimming. The old man would give him hell for it. With Jones you slept, ate, and drank football 365 days a year. He wouldn't understand anyone getting hurt in a foolish accident like that. Well, what happened was the old man thought Wayne didn't have any guts. He didn't know about the shoulder injury, of course. So he put him down on the fourth or fifth team. That took Wayne off the training table, and he had to scrounge for his own meals. He owed the fraternity house so much dough that they had to ask him to move out until he could pay. He dropped out of school and went to Fox Studios."

This stroke of economic necessity changed Wayne's life. From a promising football career and the study of law in college Wayne became a lawman in Hollywood films. It was as natural a transformation as anyone could make, really. He always played cowboy games as a youth and eventually hungered to be an actor.

He was born Marion Michael Morrison on May 26, 1907, in the small town of Winterset, Iowa. His father, Clyde Morrison, was a druggist and his mother, Mary Margaret Brown, an attractive woman of sturdy Irish pioneer stock. The family moved west in 1913, owing largely to business problems and the harsh Iowa winters. Suffering from nagging lung congestion, "Doc" Morrison opted for the warmer climes of California. The family found an ideal ranch near Palmdale, on the edge of the Mojave Desert, and in these wide, open spaces, a young boy's dreams surfaced.

Around the harsh life of a homesteader, Wayne played out a familiar scenario. Often while bringing home groceries on the old family horse, Jenny, the beguiling youngster would pretend he was a cowboy on a dangerous mission.

Mike Tomkies writes in the biography, *Duke, The Story Of John Wayne*: "There was a sharp bend in the road where it made a turn around a cliff, and he would pretend a gang of outlaws was waiting there to ambush him. The boy would manage to scare himself half to death, imagining that he'd been 'pumped full of lead.' Then he would dig his heels into Jenny, and she'd gallop home."

Later the Morrisons moved to Glendale, just outside Los Angeles, and once again entered the pharmacy business. This time Marion delivered medicines and had his own newspaper route after school to help with the family expenses. During the summer he spent almost every day swimming in Pasadena's Brookside Park and got an early taste of glamour by helping to decorate the Glendale float in the Rose Bowl parade. "Glendale used to win the big ones in those days," he says.

It was in Glendale that he got the nickname, "Duke." He received the appellation from firemen who watched his dog while he was in school. The dog's name was "Duke," and the firemen did not know the owner's name, so they called Wayne "Little Duke." As he started to sprout toward his 6-foot-4 stature, the "Little" was dropped.

As a teenager Marion Morrison's extroverted character spawned popularity. He had a part in the play, *Dulcy*, took a role in Southern California's Shakespearean contest, and was a member of the stage crew for some of the plays at Glendale High School.

That Morrison boy also had a reservoir of athletic and intellectual talents. He not only became a star lineman on the Glendale team but an honor student as well. He was president of the Letterman Society, president of his senior class, and a member of the debating team, too. With typical boundless energy he also found time to chair the senior dance.

The Duke came to Southern Cal on a scholarship in 1925 but still needed to work at various jobs to put himself through school. Once on the varsity, he was not too proud to hawk football tickets as a side living. He soon established himself as a scalper supreme.

He got two tickets as a player himself and then bought tickets from other students. He turned these into fast profits, buying them for $10 and selling them for $15. According to one story Morrison took his tickets over to the Hollywood Athletic Club one day to see if he could sell them for a higher price.

The enterprise looked like it was going to fail when he

waited around most of the day and no one showed any interest. Finally it was nightfall when a chauffeur walked in and asked for game tickets.

"How much?" he asked the enterprising Southern Cal student.

Deciding to gamble on the price, Morrison said: "I've got two at 25 bucks apiece."

"That's a lot of money," said the chauffeur, but Morrison refused to budge.

The chauffeur called his bosses and they finally okayed the inflated tariff.

Duke Morrison also worked for a telephone company at 60 cents an hour and did odd jobs around movie lots when he was not in school. One summer, football Coach Howard Jones got Wayne and teammate Don Williams a job helping cowboy star Tom Mix "train" for a movie. Their job was to run three miles every morning with Mix to keep him in shape for a picture called *The Great K and A Train Robbery*. The two also worked as set dressers—moving furniture and props around the studio—for $35 a week.

A fateful meeting with director John Ford on that old William Fox Studio lot eventually resulted in Morrison's dramatic change of life style. Working as a prop man for Ford, Morrison was prodded into taking a small part in his 1928 film, *Hangman's House*. The legend was soon to be incubated.

"It was a case of my having to work, and then they began paying me good money to be in front of the camera so I stayed with it," the Duke explains.

One year later Ford was making a football film about the Naval Academy called *Salute* and hoped to hire Southern Cal players for bit parts. He was having no luck with Trojan officials and asked Morrison to be a go-between. The main problem was that Ford wanted them out of school two weeks early, before the start of the summer vacation.

"Can you get me these guys or can't you?" he demanded.

Morrison answered, "Yes," without batting an eyelash—but he had no immediate solution for the problem.

Calling on his innate acting ability Morrison performed as never before when he went to the school authorities. He convinced them that the football players would broaden their education by traveling to Annapolis, and make good money to boot as bit actors.

In May of 1929 Morrison headed a train delegation that left for the East.

"The boys were given a rousing send-off by many attractive coeds and other friends," said a story in the *Los Angeles Times*.

Included in the group of Southern Cal players that day were Clark Galloway, Russell Saunders, Jack Butler, Tony Steponovich, Jess Shaw, Frank Anthony, Al Schaub, Marshall Duffield, and Nate Barragar. Duffield and Barragar shunned the publicity that went along with the event, afraid that this work may be construed as professionalism and hurt their college careers. They even refused to be photographed with the departing group.

Morrison's first significant role and the name of John Wayne were given to him by Director Raoul Walsh in 1929. He played the role of a wagon scout in an undistinguished, $2 million spectacular, *Big Trail*. Soon thereafter he became a singing cowboy, "Singing Sam," in a string of Grade B films, but his career soared with the role of Ringo Kid in John Ford's acclaimed 1939 film, *Stagecoach*. In 1949, exactly 20 years after he started his acting career, he made the Top Ten of film stars in box office draw. And he has been there ever since. Nominated for an Oscar for his performance as Sergeant Stryker in *Sands of Iwo Jima*, Wayne won the award in 1970 for his role as Rooster Cogburn in *True Grit*.

During all these years of lofty accomplishment Wayne has maintained close, personal ties with Southern Cal. He is a zealous Trojan fan and tries to attend football games when not working on a movie. He also is a member of the Trojan Club, an alumni group that supports the team, and several other school-affiliated organizations. He owns an Honorary Doctorate Degree from USC, too.

"John Wayne," says a friend, "never forgets. He always mentions the fact that he's a Trojan."

Wayne's fierce attachment to Southern Cal is mirrored in stories told by two compatriots.

Gene Clarke, Wayne's fraternity brother, remembers the time he visited the Sigma Chi house for a party.

"I had this derby that was given to the players after we beat Notre Dame in that famous 16-14 game in 1931," says Clarke. "I never wore mine—because I look enough like a thug as it is.

"One day Wayne comes over to the fraternity house, and I had that damn derby in there. He said, 'What the hell is that?' I said, 'Oh, it's just a derby they gave us back at Notre Dame.' 'God,' he said, 'Don't you wear it?' I said, 'No.' He said, 'Give it to me.' You know, he wore that derby for the longest time, hardly ever took it off."

Nick Pappas, onetime Southern Cal running star and now director of the Trojans' Athletic Support Groups, recalls another visit from the movie star.

"He's a fraternity brother of mine, and the night before a big game with Texas in 1966 we were having cocktails together," says Pappas. "This is in Austin, see, and he had come in just for the game. We drank until about 4 in the morning—Wayne's drinking scotch and soda all this time. All the guys at the party had gone to dinner and come back and then gone to bed, and we're still in there drinking.

"In the course of our conversation, he says, 'Pap, I want to talk to the kids at breakfast tomorrow.'

"I told him, 'You're in, Duke,' without thinking. I hadn't asked anyone whether it would be all right for Wayne to talk to our football team on the morning of the game. It was a big one—a season-opener, with Texas ranked No. 1 and us No. 2.

"But I remembered that Coach John McKay loved John Wayne movies. He used to talk about his big evening—sitting home with a peanut butter sandwich and a glass of chocolate milk and watching a John Wayne movie. And he never met him. I also remembered that McKay would awaken early on the day of games, he was always up by 6 o'clock, and read the papers, have breakfast, and go over his diagrams. He was constantly working on football.

"So I call McKay and tell him I had a problem. 'Look, John,' I said. 'I was with John Wayne last night. He asked me if he could talk to the kids, and I said, yeah.' And before I could finish, McKay says, 'Geez, great...bring him down.'

"The kids are all assembled in the locker room at 10 in the morning, and in walks Wayne. Damn, he was fantastic. He walks in with this white, 20,000-gallon cowboy hat and black suit—he looked just beautiful. The kids look up, and their eyeballs pop. Here's the REAL John Wayne. And Wayne walks over to the coach and gives him a big hello and squeezes him—you'd think he and McKay were long-lost buddies. They had never met before!

"It was beautiful. A former football player and all, Wayne gives one of the greatest fight talks you've ever heard—and the kids got out all fired-up. We win the ballgame 10-6, and back in the locker room after the game, McKay says, 'Hey, guys, how about it. Let's give the game ball to John Wayne.'

"For a moment Wayne stands there—nonplussed. It was probably the first time in his life that he couldn't think of anything to say. Then he looks at the ball for a minute and pumps it like a quarterback. Then he puts the ball under his arm, and the kids break into a cheer, 'Hooray, Hooray.' All the guys joined in. He's still a Trojan."

Ernie And The Boys

Possibly the best team that Howard Jones produced at Southern Cal never won a national championship and lost two games in a season. It is fascinating speculation, at any rate, that the team of 1929 falls into this sublime category.

Fueling such an argument are the staggering point total of 492—highest in Trojan history, a conclusive 47-14 victory over Pitt in the Rose Bowl, and a physical pitch not detected in other Jones teams.

As one sportswriter pointed out: "None of the subsequent Rose Bowl elevens brought more glory to Southern Cal, who scored this smashing triumph over Pitt. They were at their peak when the season closed. This was not true of some of the other Trojan teams."

Braven Dyer concluded in his book, *Ten Top Trojan Football Thrillers*: "The 1929 team was one of Howard Jones' best—perhaps the tops."

Of course there were those two defeats—games where the Trojans' high-powered offense inexplicably managed a composite of 19 points. The Trojans were beaten 15-7 by Pacific Coast Conference colleague California and 13-12 by Notre Dame. Both times the opposition stopped Southern Cal's supreme running game and forced the Trojans into a passing attack. This aborted, too.

Around these off-days the Trojans literally ran over everyone else, scoring victories by outrageous margins such as 76-0 over UCLA in the first game of their passionate rivalry. A

48-0 decision over Washington, 64-0 over Occidental, 66-0 over Nevada, 72-0 over Idaho, and 45-13 over Carnegie Tech were among the 10 victories that season.

Dyer recorded the noise of the thunder-makers.

"In those days some of us writers who followed the Trojans in their daily workouts hung nicknames on the stars and invented or copied catch-phrases or titles to describe the Jones juggernaut," said Dyer. "The late Maxwell Stiles coined one of the best when he named quarterback Marshall Duffield 'Field Marshall Duffield.' When a hard-running halfback from San Diego was the team's top ground-gainer in 1929 and set a record of 14 touchdowns, a chap named Dyer likened his stride and majestic running to that of a turf thoroughbred—and he became 'Racehorse Russell Saunders.'"

The most romantic of the nicknames applied to the team itself.

"Somebody suggested 'The Thundering Herd,' and it was an instantaneous hit," Dyer said. "Checking with several oldtimers as to its origin, I still can't identify the culprit who hung it on the USC gridders. My first guess was Maxwell Stiles, but I have been told that is not right.

"I thought of Al Wesson, the peerless public relations man who invented all manner of gimmicks to keep his alma mater before the public. But Al denies everything. Typical of his modesty, he downgrades his ability to rise to such heights."

(Wesson told Dyer: "It couldn't have been Old Man Wesson who did it because Jones always wanted me to play up how scared we were of the opposition.")

Wesson takes credit for other things, though. "I wrote the school song, 'All Hail,'" he says.

Whoever supplied it, the title of "The Thundering Herd," stolen from a movie of that name with Noah Beery, was an apt description of the 1929 team. The most prolific offensive team in Southern Cal history was one of awesome running power.

"Those 'Thundering Herd' teams didn't throw the ball around much," remembers Dyer. "They thought that was the sissy way to play the game."

The Trojans were so rich in talent that Jones had five sets of backs and designated two first teams, depending on the style of attack. The starting backfield usually was Saunders, Ernie

Pinckert, Harry Edelson, and Jim Musick. The replacements were normally Duffield, Jesse Mortensen, Marger Apsit, and Jesse Hill. But they were used interchangeably. Jones evaded the caste system.

"When the Trojans wish to gain by power, their best bets seem to be Saunders, Pinckert, Edelson, and Musick," wrote Stiles in a *Los Angeles Examiner* article in 1929.

For a speed attack the other backfield was better, particularly with Hill at fullback.

"I never saw a man who could carry 168 pounds as well as Hill does," said Jones. "He is the best-looking fullback I've got out there right now." (Jones joined in the nickname game and called Hill "Hula Hula" for the manner in which he wiggled his hips while running.)

This was a team that also harbored a future all-American, Gus Shaver. Shaver, in later years referred to as perhaps the best all-around backfield man in Trojan history, was a quarterback and fullback as a sophomore in 1929.

The 1929 team produced two all-Americans—guard Nate Barragar, who cleared the way for some of those powerhouse runners, and end Francis Tappaan. It was through no fault of Jones, however, that Tappaan made it that year. Recalls Wesson:

"Jones wasn't much of a publicity hound. He was a man of very few words. I remember once Grantland Rice was picking his all-America team, and he wired Howard for his opinion on Tappaan. Howard wired back to Grannie: 'Tappaan is the best end we have.' That was a lot for him. I saw the wire later and said, 'For Christ sakes, Howard, let me do the replies from now on.'"

On that 1929 team also was a player who distinguished himself in another field. Having failed to make it big as a tackle, Ward Bond became a well-known character actor in the movies.

But of all the players Pinckert was by far the most colorful. Recognized as perhaps the deadliest blocking halfback in Southern Cal's history, the inimitable Pinckert always threw a good quip, too.

"He once had a bad game against Washington State in 1930," recalls Gene Clarke, a lineman of the day. "He didn't make a good block all day, and we lost the game 7-6. Well,

Southern Cal's Francis Tappaan, one of two Trojan all-Americans in 1929, goes up for a pass in the Stanford game. He came down with it, and the Trojans came away with a 7-0 victory.

Jones was never a smiler, but he did smile when he walked into the locker room after that game and heard Ernie singing, 'I'm Nobody's Sweetheart Now.'"

Another time after Southern Cal had a bad afternoon, Pinckert told Jones: "Know what our theme song's going to be? 'There'll Be Some Changes Made.'"

If clownish at times, Southern Cal's court jester was never cloddish. The heroic halfback played with agonizing muscle tears and tortured ankles.

Remembers Clarke: "Pinckert hurt his ankle in the third or fourth game of the season one year, and our team doctor insisted on Ernie having his ankle taped before he went out for practice. They taped his ankles practically up to his knees, and

his half-socks didn't cover the tape. So you know what that guy does? He goes in and gets his long socks so nobody would know that he had his ankle taped.

"Another time I remember Pinckert played a game with a hip muscle torn apart. It's the type of injury where you can't even sneeze because it'll hurt so much. But he got a shot of novacaine and played with that injury. He was about 60 percent of capacity."

Pinckert was soft-natured off the field but in uniform gripped by a demon.

"I've heard him hit guys in a game and make them squeal," says a friend. "He just knocked the wind out of them."

Constantly joking and chattering during a game, Pinckert

discovered great fun in football. He could not play it grimly, as most did. But there were times when he got painfully serious. Clarke recalls one such incident when Pinckert recoiled after a mistake.

"We were playing Georgia, and the Bulldogs had this all-American end, 'Catfish' Smith," says Clarke. "First time they kicked, Pinckert backed up as a defensive halfback, and Shaver went back to get the punt. Smith comes down the field, and Pinckert tries to knock him over by doing one of these 'Fancy Dan' moves where he goes down low. Well, Smith hurdled over Pinckert and knocked Shaver right off the ground.

"Pinckert picks himself up, and I'm sitting on the bench with Orv Mohler and we're laughing like hell. I say, 'Look at Pinckert. Jesus, if that were you or me, we'd be so embarrassed we'd be climbing a tree somewhere.' I then told Mohler, 'Wait till the next time that they punt to us.'

"So they punted the next time, and Pinckert makes every move the same, see. He goes down like he's going to block, you know, and Smith starts to hurdle him again, and Pinckert gets up all at once and puts Smith up as high as the cheap seats. Smith came down on his head; it knocked him cold as hell. Well, it was perfectly clean. You're not supposed to hurdle anybody. And nobody made Pinckert look bad a second time."

Later, the story had a sequel when Clarke and Shaver visited Smith after the game to sympathize with the Georgia all-American.

"Man, I ache all over," said Smith, showing the two Southern Cal players vibrant, criss-cross marks on his body. "I'm pretty beat up."

Along with that shot from Pinckert, the Trojans had been giving Smith a rough time of it all day.

"We have a pretty tough system here," Clarke told Smith in sympathetic tones. "Jones has this power play where we have two of our linemen taking you out of the play most of the time."

A distraught Smith paused for a moment, then looked up at the two with glazed eyes. "Man, were there only two?" he said.

Another example of Pinckert's brutish football nature occurred in a 1930 game with California. Clarke remembers

One of the few players who made all-American on his blocking ability alone, Ernie Pinckert, "hit guys in a game and made them squeal," according to an observer.

vividly.

"They had an all-American guard, Ted Beckett, and every time another team had a big shot, we always tested him to see how good he was," says Clarke. "Beckett is going down the field on this kick, and Pinckert blind-sides him. Oh, Christ, we saw pictures of this, you wouldn't believe, in slow motion. Pinckert hit him on the side, and he caved in and his neck almost hit his ankle. He just about doubled him up and dropped him flat on the ground. And then Pinckert picks him up, slaps him on the back and says, 'Nice going, kid.' He didn't know what hit him."

Violent at football and sometimes a prankster of the tallest order, the puckish Pinckert had other facets. A man of boundless talent, he also was artistic and inventive. He painted splendid murals and once schemed himself into a small fortune by designing football pads. If he had an ignoble quality, it was frugality. But even then Pinckert brought it off with charm.

It was just an extension of his tight-fisted nature that Pinckert screwed cleats off his football shoes and soled them for everyday wear at school. He also took his football t-shirts home and wore them for underwear, a confidant recalls.

Pinckert could run and pass with unerring skill, but it was his towering talent as a blocker that made the 1929 team what it was. He was one of the few players who claimed all-America status on his blocking ability alone (in 1930 and 1931).

Galvanized by the ferocious Pinckert in 1929, this rough crew vaulted toward a Rose Bowl meeting with Pitt, considered one of the nation's best teams. Despite their loss to California, the Trojans were recognized as the best team on the West Coast. Pasadena authorities were strongly influenced by Southern Cal's close game at Chicago against Notre Dame and of course by the fact that the Trojans had won the PCC title for the third year in a row.

Pitt, coached by Jock Sutherland, brought an acclaimed team to California. Undefeated and untied, the Panthers boasted four all-Americans in their lineup—halfback Toby Uansa, end Joe Donchess, guard Bob Montgomery, and fullback John Parkinson. All four had played in the 1928 Rose Bowl game and lost to Stanford 7-6. Inspired by revenge, they led powerful Pitt to Pasadena.

"Uansa was a broken field runner who had stunned all foes with his speed and change of pace," wrote Dyer. "He ran 70 and 72 yards for touchdowns against Duke; scored 3 times on West Virginia; raced 74 yards through Ohio State; and scored on the Bucks again after receiving a pass. Donchess, Parkinson, and Montgomery were only slightly less frightening, chiefly because they didn't carry the ball as often as Toby, I suppose."

Knute Rockne and John W. Heisman, two of the nation's

football experts, picked Pitt to win.

"There is no question here in the East about Pittsburgh's strength," said Heisman. "They are almost out of the class of every other Eastern team. Pitt has a stronger team than she had on New Year's Day, 1928. They had no such power, versatility, and stars as at present."

The Panthers were generally conceded to be on a par with Notre Dame as national champions and came into the Rose Bowl game with a 9-0 record, an overpowering point spread over previous opponents, and the favorite's role in most minds.

Uniquely the game turned on the first offensive play.

"On the game's first scrimmage play, Uansa broke between end and tackle, got in behind his interference, and set sail for the promised land," wrote Dyer. "As Toby ran he left his blockers far behind.

"Early in the play Saunders was knocked on his rumble seat. Less inspired players than Russ might have been content to lie there. But Jones had drilled into his players the stories of Pitt's might and their four all-Americans. Saunders was a cocky individual and knew in his own heart that he was a much better football player than the all-American pickers had painted him.

"So he got up off the green grass and gave chase...after Pitt's fastest back. (Saunders actually started after Uansa eight yards behind him.) It was quite a race, but eventually Russ got his man...on the Trojan 14-yard line. That was a stunning blow, not only to Toby Uansa, but also to the entire Pitt team and all Panther fans."

Montgomery later told reporters: "What the hell...we broke our fastest runner into the clear, knocked down your safety man, and then he got up and caught our man!"

The Trojans halted the Pitt drive and siezed the psychological advantage. After Pinckert batted away a fourth-down Panther pass, Saunders took control of the game's rhythm. "The equal of any running back" that Jones ever had went to the air to stupefy Pitt. Sensing that Jock Sutherland had geared his team to stop the Trojans' running talents, the guileful back produced 2 touchdown passes in the first 10 minutes. The first was a 55-yarder to Harry Edelson and the second a 25-yard strike to Pinckert.

Southern Cal had a 26-0 lead midway through the game,

leading Dyer to comment in his game story in the *Los Angeles Times*: "The ease with which the Trojans amassed 26 points in the first half left the capacity crowd (of 71,000) stunned with astonishment. Many of us had looked for a tough first quarter, and not a few expected that the Panthers would be leading at the end of the second period."

Another Saunders-to-Edelson touchdown pass later in the game produced a glittering play.

"Standing on Pitt's 39-yard mark Saunders gave Southern California another touchdown when he threw a perfect shot to this same Harry Edelson, who made one of the greatest catches ever seen in the Rose Bowl. Harry literally took the ball out of the hands of Edwards, Pitt quarterback, made a spiral turn to do it, and then came down running like mad to continue on from the point of the catch on the 15-yard line. It was 40-7 and more yet to come."

The Panthers were prepared to stop Saunders, the runner, but it was Saunders, the passer, that stopped them.

"I want to praise Saunders for picking their defense apart," Jones said after the game. "Their great fullback Pug Parkinson played close to stop our running, and Saunders

Pittsburgh tacklers close in on a Southern California runner in the 1930 Rose Bowl game. The Trojans won this one, 47-14.

passed over him."

Sutherland and Parkinson joined voices in praise of Saunders.

"Saunders is the greatest back I have seen since Glenn Presnell," said the Pittsburgh coach. "They rate with the great backs of all time."

"Everytime Saunders hit us, we almost caved in under his drive," said Parkinson.

This attention brought some solace to Saunders, who hungered for all-American recognition but never got it because his finest efforts came late in the 1929 season.

"I couldn't find any weak spots in the Pitt line but sure found some in their backfield," said the elated player, grinning widely.

While Saunders played the salient role, others contributed heroic performances for Southern Cal. Garrett Arbelbide and Pinckert were singled out by sportswriters.

"The outstanding lineman on the field was Arbelbide, who made tackles from front and rear, knocked down interference with abandon, and rushed Pitt's passers so relentlessly that they must have wondered whether or not he had wings the way he came flying through the air," Dyer said in the *Los Angeles Times*.

"Pinckert was the most vicious tackler on the field. When he smacked them, they stayed smacked," Dick Hyland reported in the *Los Angeles Examiner*.

After his second Rose Bowl loss, Sutherland had no alibis. Wrote Dyer: "It was not the heat this time. USC has come ahead; we have gone back since Thanksgiving Day. The Trojans played beautiful football; we fell down. The Trojans are the equal of any team in the country."

Bitter Pitt supporters at once found excuses for the loss. There were rival factions on the team because of jealousies over all-America status, was one report. Another said that Panther players had been seduced by Hollywood glitter. Sutherland's pass defense was unsound, said still another.

A scientist of some repute went to considerable pains to show that "sunshine and vitamins" were the cause of the Trojan runaway. Ultraviolet light from considerably more sunshine and vitamins in California-grown oranges, fruits, and vegetables provided Trojan players "with more energy," the scientist pointed out.

Be that as it may, the plain truth of the matter was that Southern Cal's personnel was superior.

"Better football is played on the Pacific Coast than in any other section of the country," said football authority Walter Eckersall.

Many had to agree after that Rose Bowl game.

The Game

NOTRE DAME STADIUM (South Bend, Ind.) Nov. 21 *(Exclusive)—When Howard Jones is old and a darn sight grayer than now he will tell his grandchildren about the heroic fight his 1931 Trojans made against the undefeated Irish of Notre Dame. He will tell them how his boys, with the odds hopelessly against them and with a sound thumping staring them in the face, came back to do the impossible and score sixteen points in the last quarter to bring to an end the sensational winning streak of the greatest team in Irish history. (Braven Dyer, Los Angeles Times)*

It probably has been glorified in print, animatedly discussed, and generally immortalized more than any other football game in Southern California history. It has been called "the greatest Trojan triumph of them all," a rather enthusiastic statement considering the vast length and breadth of Southern Cal glories.

But if one had to choose one significant game in Trojan lore, then the dramatic 16-14 victory over Notre Dame in 1931 would be a formidable selection.

Consider the circumstances. The game was played at the Notre Dame stronghold before a partisan Fighting Irish crowd. Notre Dame was enroute to a national championship, having put together an unbeaten string of 26 games. Notre Dame led the game 14-0 into the final quarter.

"That 1931 battle between Notre Dame and the Trojans," said Arch Ward, sports editor of the *Chicago Tribune*, "was the most thrilling football game I ever saw."

Events leading up to the game made the victory all the more exquisite in the end.

The season before, Southern Cal had been regarded as one of the country's foremost teams. Russ Saunders and Francis Tappaan were gone, but other players of proven ability were still around—Gus Shaver, Ernie Pinckert, Marshall Duffield, Garrett Arbelbide, Johnny Baker, Stan Williamson, Jim Musick, Marger Apsit, and Bob Hall among them. An appealing sophomore back, Orv Mohler, had joined the team, too.

But somehow the chemistry did not happen, and the Trojans lost two games in 1930. This collection of stars was upset 7-6 by Washington State and humiliated 27-0 by Notre Dame. Prior to the 1930 game with the Fighting Irish, Stanford's Pop Warner called the Trojans "one of the greatest teams of all times." Obviously Notre Dame did not have the same opinion after beating Southern Cal by four touchdowns. It could have been worse had not Knute Rockne taken his regulars out of the game after Southern Cal was obviously beaten.

All indications had pointed to a Southern Cal victory in that one. Rockne had lost his two ranking fullbacks, Joe Savoldi and Larry Mullins, and was forced to use a second-string halfback, Bucky O'Connor, at the position. Notre Dame had won nine straight games but had shown attrition in the last two, and the tired Fighting Irish were apathetic prior to this final contest of the season. Rockne shook the team out of its apathy during a two-day practice stop at Tucson, Arizona, where he threatened to go back to Notre Dame rather than coach a squad that "did not seem interested in the game ahead." O'Connor went wild against Southern Cal.

Ernie Smith, a tackle on the 1930 team, recalls that Southern Cal was at a psychological disadvantage for the game.

"Rockne used great psychology with all the newspapermen," Smith remembers. "He told them that he had nothing with Savoldi out of the lineup. Savoldi, a great fullback, had gotten married and had to be kicked off the team because of it. Well, we believed what we read in the newspapers, and here comes this Bucky O'Connor. We never did get over that Notre Dame loss.

"I don't feel that we were ready for them that day,

though, not taking anything away from Notre Dame. I don't think our team consciously let down, but they didn't subconsciously build themselves up for that game like we did for the others."

The season of 1930 had a distasteful touch of scandal as well for Southern Cal. A player was expelled from the school for falsifying entrance requirements. He had entered the university as a freshman under the assumed name of "George Kirkwood" after playing two years at another school. His real name was Spencer Purvis. In the midst of this situation, a verbal war persisted between Southern Cal and California factions over "professionalism" in Trojan athletics. Charges were fired in the north and landed across the state. They said that Southern Cal paid money to its football players and thus ran a "professional" team. These charges, printed in the California student newspaper, were precipitated by a 74-0 beating given the Golden Bears by the Trojans. Peace prevailed when officials of the two schools stepped in and declared a truce.

The eruption came one year after the famed Carnegie Report, a revolutionary paper condemning the practice of subsidizing athletes. Based on visits to 130 schools in America and Canada, the report by the Carnegie Foundation in New York focused principally on what investigators called "the deepest shadow that darkens American college and school athletics"—the practice of giving athletic scholarships. Proclaiming that it was immoral to have a "professional" atmosphere in amateur sports, the Carnegie administrators urged an immediate cleanup.

King Football only bounded ahead at Southern Cal. The Trojan spirit was captured visually by sculptor Roger Noble Burnham, who modeled the famous "Tommy Trojan" statue. It was said that he based the figure, a campus landmark, on running back Russ Saunders.

In 1931 Duffield and Aspit were gone from the team, but Shaver, Musick, Arbelbide, Baker, Pinckert, Williamson, Hall, Smith, and Mohler were back along with comparable talents. Smith and newcomer Aaron Rosenberg buttressed a formidable group of linemen. Coach Howard Jones found "greatness" in Smith because of his "strength, desire, and courage...he always gave his best." He revered Rosenberg for his size, speed, and ability as a fighter. Both became defensive supermen on the 1931 team.

It was unlikely that this collection of golden talent would fall to little St. Mary's on opening day. But that is what happened. While 70,000 fans watched at the Coliseum, the Gaels upset Southern Cal 13-7.

"This may have been an expectant championship year for the Trojans, but they looked anything else but," wrote Paul Lowry in the *Los Angeles Times*. "True, it was an opening game, but it also was an opener for St. Mary's, and the lethargic, poorly directed team that carried S. C.'s colors has a long way to go before it will overcome conference rivals in games ahead."

From the Southern Cal side, another touch of sadness was added to the afternoon's events. At halftime actor Conrad Nagel read a tribute to Rockne, killed that summer in the explosion of a plane over Kansas. Taps were blown while the thousands in the Coliseum, including longtime friend Jones, stood in silence.

The Trojans recoiled from that stunning opening-day loss and started a winning streak that included victories over Oregon State, Washington State, Oregon, California, Stanford, and Montana. Notre Dame was next, and the Fighting Irish, now coached by Hunk Anderson, seemed an irrepressible force to Southern Cal scout Aubrey Devine.

"Notre Dame is so good that Hunk Anderson could lick any team he has played, Northwestern excepted, with his second string," Devine told reporters upon returning from a scouting mission of the Fighting Irish. "It is impossible to set a fool-proof defense for the Irish because they are such a versatile squad. Just when you think you have them stopped, they break out in another direction."

Jones, who had been putting his Trojans through a week of secret practice behind Bovard Field's locked gates, expressed similar respect for Notre Dame.

"There is every reason to believe that the team we buck up against Saturday is much stronger than the one which trounced us 27 to 0 last year," Jones said. "On the other hand, there is nothing to indicate that my boys are any better than they were that day Knute Rockne's eleven made us look so bad."

In the *Los Angeles Examiner*, Maxwell Stiles preceded his departure story with: "ABOARD THE TROJAN SPECIAL,

Bound For Heaven Knows What, Nov. 17."

"That big noise that you just heard down there at the Southern Pacific depot was not a bedlam of Southern California rooters cheering a Trojan victory over Notre Dame. The noble six hundred were merely seeing the gang off," Stiles wrote. "Everybody seemed to be taking a good, long look at most of us. As if they never expected to see us again—after Notre Dame's team, those betting on Notre Dame, and perhaps one of those Mid-West blizzards got through with us."

At evening time a special section of the Golden State Limited pulled out of a Los Angeles train terminal carrying 34 Southern Cal players and coaches, trainers, medics, alumni, managers, newspapermen, and "a few who will go anywhere the Trojans go."

"The big push starts tonight," Stiles said. "El Trojan of Southern California starts eastward in quest of victory over Notre Dame, generally recognized throughout the Middle West and East as the greatest American football team of the generation. Quite a mouthful to take in one bite."

Enroute to South Bend the Trojans almost lost guard Johnny Baker, their top field goal kicker. Having missed two previous games because of an injured knee, Baker had a hard time adjusting at first to Jones' tough defensive drills in Tucson, Arizona. When Baker blew an assignment, Jones blew his temper.

"I remember quite distinctly the bawling out which Howard gave Baker," recalls sportswriter Braven Dyer. "Johnny was quite mad about it. Later he told me that he came within a whisker of quitting the team right then and there and heading back for Los Angeles."

Ridiculed by the South Bend press and razzed by most of the 55,000 spectators, the Trojans took the field against the Fighting Irish on November 21, 1931. In the second quarter Steve Banas blasted 4 yards for a touchdown to give Notre Dame a 7-0 lead. In the third quarter the Fighting Irish made it 14-0 when quarterback Marchy Schwartz scored on a 3-yard run.

"The score looked as big as the population of China," Dyer wrote in his game story. "In fact it looked a darn sight larger than that, if possible, because of the consummate ease with which the Irish scored those two touchdowns.

"In other words the Irish were in command of the situation, and everybody, apparently, but the Trojans knew it. Schwartz had been whizzing around his own right end repeatedly for long gains. Banas, on a twisting, 32-yard run which ended up on Troy's 3-yard line, had made the Trojans look positively silly. And the ease with which Schwartz went over for the touchdown presaged others to come."

Through three quarters it had not been Southern Cal's day at all. Fullback Jim Musick even had his nose broken by Notre Dame's vicious gang tackling. Musick was led from the field bitterly protesting Notre Dame's "dirty football." The rhythm changed, though, in the last period.

With the clock, the crowd, and the odds against them, the Trojans struggled back to respectability—and finally, victory.

Orv Mohler, a replacement for Musick, alternated as ballcarrier with Gus Shaver in the last quarter, and the two drove the ball within sight of the Notre Dame goal line. Shaver carried it over from the one-yard-line for Southern Cal's first touchdown. Baker missed the extra-point try, and the Trojans trailed the Fighting Irish 14-6.

Later in the period a pass interference call gave Southern Cal a first down on the Notre Dame 24. Shaver and Mohler sliced through, moving the ball to the 9-yard line. Then Mohler lateralled to his brutish teammate, and Shaver soared around left end for a touchdown. This time Baker's conversion was successful, and the Trojans trailed 14-13 with eight minutes remaining.

Southern Cal was alive and doing well in South Bend.

"The fury of Troy's attack in the second half astounded everybody," wrote Dyer. "No man, unless it be Gus Shaver, stood out. Mohler's choice of plays was almost perfect, and the way the 162-pound Orv rammed into the Irish line inspired his mates immensely."

Neither team could make consistent gains until Southern Cal took possession of the ball on its 27-yard line with 4 minutes remaining.

After two aborted plays, Gus Shaver faded almost to his goal line and threw a long pass to Ray Sparling, who made a diving catch on Notre Dame's 40-yard line. Later tackle Bob

Hall took Shaver's perfect pass over his shoulder for a first down on the 18. The Trojans had used up two minutes of playing time in this drive. An offside penalty moved the ball to the 13, and Sparling drove around end to get Southern Cal into an ideal field goal position.

Sensing for some reason that his team was not going to try a field goal, Jones sent Homer Griffith charging into the game with instructions. "Field goal, field goal," Jones said, pushing Griffith onto the field.

"But Mohler waved him back to the bench," recalls Al Wesson, Southern Cal's sports information director of the day. "He knew what he was doing."

Jones was shocked by Mohler's action. "Cold sweat broke out on his brow, and his assistant groaned in anguish," a writer reported.

After overruling Jones, Mohler called the logical play himself. Mohler took the snap from center, held the ball on the 23-yard line, and Baker kicked it through the goalposts and into the bleachers for the winning points. One minute and three plays remained in the game, but it was really over at that juncture.

"Great! Boy, great! But why did you do it?" Jones yelled while happily embracing his disobedient quarterback.

A calm Mohler replied: "Baker and I have been practicing that play all year. I knew if it failed I'd be the goat and we would be licked, but old 'Bake' doesn't miss on those short ones. I knew he wouldn't fail me. Wasn't it a beaut?"

It was. It took the fight out of the Fighting Irish.

"Notre Dame was far from the Fighting Irish type when Howard Jones' Trojans got hitting on all eleven cylinders in the last period of play," said Tom Thorpe in the *New York Evening Journal*. "No one would have thought it possible for any team to tally at a greater rate of speed than a point a minute against a Notre Dame squad. This Southern California did without much trouble.

"Notre Dame has no excuses. The Trojans simply outplayed them during the last 15 minutes in a manner which left no room for alibis. 'Old Rock,' looking down from up above, must have wept with tears of genuine sorrow when he saw his former Irish playmates being pushed around. It has been years since any team has been able to manhandle the Irish as Southern California did."

Dyer wrote his wordiest game story for the *Los Angeles Times*. His dispatch finally ran out of superlatives.

"Noah Webster's diction book does not contain enough adjectives to describe the way the Trojans refused to be licked," he said. "Until the Trojans get home, you can paste this in your hat for future reference: Nobody ever saw a gamer battle than that which the Southern California players staged against supposedly insurmountable odds this afternoon. It did not seem humanly possible for them to win, but thanks to the indomitable fight of a great gang of kids, plus the cool nerve and steady hoof of Johnny Baker, the Trojans today achieved the greatest athletic triumph in Southern California history.

"Yours truly has run out of paper, his typewriter has broken down completely, and it's getting late. You'll have to wait until tomorrow for more about the stunning achievement of a bunch of boys who were rated no better than a 2-to-5 bet to upset the mighty Irish."

Deep in the confines of the Notre Dame stadium the Southern Cal locker room was a chamber of madmen. The players hugged each other and danced around. Some cried.

Pinckert led the team into the dingy room, his eyes glistening. Gordon Clark followed, the game ball tucked under his soiled, red jersey.

"I knew they couldn't stop us," Pinckert shouted and slapped stocky Tom Mallory on the shoulders. "I've waited for two years for this day—but, boy, what revenge."

A group of alumni had crashed the guarded entrance and discovered Baker in the shower.

"It felt great," he said, grinning and dripping as the alumni pulled him out of the shower and danced around the Trojan quarters.

Jones was part of the euphoria. His hat mussed and his coat hanging from his shoulder, dripping cold perspiration, the coach went around the locker room and shook the hand of each of his players.

"Honestly, I'm too flabbergasted to say a thing," he told reporters. "But I'll tell you that it was the greatest team in the world. I knew I had a ballclub, but the thing that pleases me was that we gave 'em fourteen points and then came back and licked 'em."

The merriment continued on the train ride home.

"Howard Jones has been like a kid let out of school ever since we left Chicago," Jack James wrote in the *Los Angeles Herald*. "The strain and worry of past weeks all fell away from him like a discarded garment the moment the gun ended that game on the Notre Dame greensward Saturday afternoon. From that moment he 'unlaxed,' as the saying goes, and he has been unlaxing more and more as the journey progressed.

"Can you imagine the usually grim and serious 'Head Man' indulging in such playful pranks as pouring snow down the necks of the athletic director, or any assistant coaches that came within reach—war correspondents, Santa Fe passenger agents, or other innocent bystanders? Well, that's what he was doing yesterday afternoon when we passed through the snow belt.

"You should have seen him conniving with Jimmy Smith, the proverbial Trojan sophomore, to get into Bill Hunter and Sam Barry's compartment, that he might later open the door to admit Jimmy with an armful of dirty snow. You should have seen him double cross his erstwhile aide a moment later, rubbing this same snow in Jimmy's face while Barry and Hunter held him helpless.

"I tell you, this special train was a regular madhouse for the past three nights and two days, and here's one camp follower who's glad to get back to a saner and certainly safer existence."

What insanity prevailed on the ride back to Los Angeles was minuscule compared to the insanity that awaited the Trojan party.

An unprecedented welcome of enormous dimensions awaited the conquering Trojans on the streets of Los Angeles. An enthralled populace prepared to greet its noble legions returning from a distant victory.

Hail The Conquering Heroes

"Men of Troy, conquering football heroes, came home yesterday to the plaudits of a city and 300,000 of its cheering citizens who shouted their welcome from the sidewalks and roof-tops."

The *Los Angeles Examiner*, and everyone else who was there, will never forget the welcome that Southern Cal's football team received after beating Notre Dame 16-14.

"I never saw anything like it in my life," says Ernie Smith, who shared in the victory over Notre Dame and then the victory march afterwards.

Smith was one of the players greeted at the train station by the thicket of worshippers. As a symbol of their spectacular victory, the players all wore bowler hats obtained from a Chicago haberdashery.

"We were all done up in these fancy hats, and they had these cars waiting for us," Smith remembers. "They put two players in each car, and we started to ride down Fifth Street to Main and then on up to City Hall. I had never seen such a big crowd in my life, and here I was in the center of it.

"There seemed to be a half-million people lining the streets. When we left City Hall and started down toward the school, ticker tape came flying out at us. We rode down Spring Street, I remember, and people had torn up telephone books, and they were throwing all this paper out of windows. It was a real thrill—it was unbelieveable. For a football team to get this type of reception, I mean it was REALLY something."

Another participant in the homecoming celebration remembers people "four and five deep along the curbs throwing all kinds of waste paper."

"It seemed the whole town turned out at the railroad station when we came in," recalls Al Wesson, Southern Cal's ebullient sports publicist. "I think Ted Husing's national radio broadcast of the game had a lot to do with that welcome. He had built up the last quarter to such a dramatic extent that Los Angeles people were running out into the streets during the game and screaming.

"It was the wildest sports demonstration that the city of Los Angeles ever had. Three hundred thousand? I don't know, there were at least 200,000 in the line of march to see the Trojans riding in their cars. Everyone got a helluva cheer—even me.

"We all rode in open cars. It was the day of those fancy touring cars, you know. As we came down one of the main streets, I could see people hollering out of office buildings, throwing all kinds of streamers and confetti. It was like a ticker tape parade down Broadway in New York. It was the only time I know of anything like that happening anywhere."

This is the way the *Examiner* described the stunning event:

"A reception never before equaled for athletic stars turned downtown Los Angeles into a half holiday as the triumphant Trojans rode through the city at the head of a three-mile parade beneath a barrage of confetti and flowers. At the first cry of 'Here they come' and the first notes of Harold Roberts' Trojan band, playing 'Fight On,' men and women poured from every building on Spring and Broadway and Hill.

"They jammed the sidewalks. They overflowed into the streets. They lined the roof-tops. Bankers and laborers...industrial kings and clerks...merchants and typists...they stood together as the band went prancing by. For a day USC was the adopted Alma Mater of the city. Through the jammed lanes of humanity, the Trojan warriors who fought the Battle of Notre Dame rode as heroes ride. Police sirens screamed to clear the congested traffic that for an hour tied up the downtown vehicular traffic."

These players had been spectacularly borne from their train by Southern Cal students and lifted into their touring cars.

Bowler hats, symbolic of Southern California's spectacular triumph over Notre Dame in 1931, sit atop a bunch of smiling faces. The bowlers were courtesy of a Chicago haberdashery.

Said the *Examiner*:

"The boys who went away for a football game in South Bend and came back national heroes attempted to step from their train, but an entire student body from their school was there to lift them bodily from the train and carry them to waiting cars. Beneath an 'arch of triumph,' fashioned from chrysanthemums and poppies—gold and cardinal, the school colors—the players were led to a fleet of cars. Upon them hailed a shower of flowers, serpentine, blossoms, and confetti."

Mayor John C. Porter officially welcomed the team in front of City Hall while 40,000 people filled the area. Bishop John J. Cantwell of the Roman Catholic diocese of Los Angeles and San Diego paid a dramatic tribute to the Trojan players. Coach Howard Jones was introduced, and the ovation was so overwhelming that it was minutes before he could speak.

"The applause of the crowd echoed down the packed canyon of Spring Street," reported the *Examiner*.

When the players reestablished their victory march through the heart of town, they were lovingly obliterated by flying objects. "At times the players and their coach could not be seen for the blinding rain of flowers and confetti thrown from office windows," the *Examiner* pointed out.

Later, much later, when the triumphal procession became only a sweet memory, the players had the luxury of reflection. Each revealed special moments of the game, and some revealed funny moments of its aftermath.

Captain Stan Williamson, who had played the full 60 minutes, announced blithely that he had been kissed by Jones in the celebrative locker room.

"My big kick came in the dressing room when I found someone hugging and kissing me, and I was kissing back, too. I came to for a moment and saw it was the 'Head Man' himself," Williamson said. "He was so excited—and I was, too, that he didn't know it."

Garrett Arbelbide was in the shower when Baker kicked the winning field goal. He had played most of the game, but missed the most important part.

"I'd left the game just before the end and heard a lot of racket. Somebody told me a field goal had been kicked," Arbelbide related, rather sheepishly. "I got my thrill when I found out that Johnny Baker had kicked it. I thought the other guys had booted one over."

The destruction of the Notre Dame citadel had been recorded by a movie camera, and as if to certify the Southern Cal achievement the game was soon shown as a full-length feature in Los Angeles. Sportswriter Braven Dyer did the sound track narration at the Metro-Goldwyn-Mayer studios between supper one night and the next day's breakfast.

"They rushed the film down to Loew's State theater, then the top movie house in downtown Los Angeles," Dyer recalls. "When the bill first went on, the football game was one-half of the double feature. After the first day business was so good and everybody admitted it was the football game that lured them to the theater, so the manager jerked the second feature and ran the gridiron picture over and over. It broke all house records at Loew's State."

The aftermath of the game produced a bizarre sidelight. It was revealed that a Southern Cal player had been imprisoned for a week prior to the game because the Trojan hierarchy believed he was leaking team secrets to Notre Dame.

Gordon Campbell, an assistant Trojan coach, ordered William Hawkins, a third-string center, into the custody of private detectives prior to the game. Hawkins went voluntarily into seclusion at a mountain retreat, although claiming he was no Benedict Arnold.

"I was suspected of snooping signals prior to the Notre Dame game," Hawkins later told reporters. "I had asked several of the other players about certain pass defense plans. When this was brought to the attention of the coaching staff, I was ordered before them and grilled. I had been hurt the week before in scrimmage, missed four practices, and naturally wanted to know what had gone on in my absence, so I went to Tipton, Barry, Stephens, Hammack, Shaver, Mohler, and Pinckert and asked for certain information.

"I never thought that anyone would question my right to do that in view of my enforced absence. Campbell insisted that I was sending out signals to Notre Dame friends, and I boiled over."

He was not any happier over the ensuing events. Detectives searched his home for "papers," and then two men watched over Hawkins in a cottage at Topango Canyon. The player missed school for a week, was shadowed constantly by his beefy companions, and did not even get a chance to hear the Notre Dame game on the radio.

When the story came to light after the game, Hawkins' parents demanded an apology from Southern Cal. He was eventually exonerated, and Jones gave Hawkins' parents their apology.

"I'm genuinely sorry that the thing occurred and have done whatever possible to make amends to the boy who came through with his honor unsullied," said the Trojan coach.

While their images played to packed movie houses, the real Trojans played out the rest of their schedule in 1931. They conquered Washington 44-7 and Georgia 60-0 to finish out the regular season with a 9-1 record.

The Georgia game was so void of pressure that players found time for humor. This give-and-take occurred between Baker and a Georgia guard named "Red" Maddox:

While leading Southern Cal's superb off-tackle play against the Bulldogs, Baker was constantly being tackled from behind by Maddox. Getting tired of being dragged down by this tough antagonist, Baker told Maddox: "Look, man, I'll have to belt you good if you don't cut that out."

The weary Maddox grinned and said: "Don't get mad, Baker. I haven't been able to catch up with you. All I want to know is where can a guy get a gallon of corn liquor after the game?"

As expected the Rose Bowl beckoned Southern Cal after that smashing Georgia victory. The Trojans were invited to play Tulane, a team that appeared to be a towering challenge.

Aubrey Devine and Francis Tappaan had scouted Tulane and secretly expressed their admiration to Jones. Others expressed their admiration of the Green Wave openly.

"Tulane is the best coached outfit I ever saw, and it will take a terrific team to beat the Green Wave," said Clark Shaughnessy, coach of Loyola of the South, Tulane's close neighbor.

"It'll be a close, tough game," predicted Tad Jones, Howard's brother and a coaching luminary in his own right. "Tulane is a sound team."

Bill Alexander, the Georgia Tech coach, rated Tulane among the best teams he had ever seen and acclaimed the Green Waves' Jerry Dalrymple as the best end in the country. The unorthodox Dalrymple, who roamed the field as he pleased and frequently wound up in his own backfield, was the subject of an amusing incident after the Green Wave arrived in Pasadena. A California football writer had composed a story about the Tulane star, but his sports editor was not happy with the lead. Previously ordered to jazz up the section, the editor changed the wording of the first paragraph and ran the story under this bold bannerline:

"Dalrymple says he'll stop Trojan attack."

Insomuch as Dalrymple did not say that, he was extremely distraught when he read it. And, as a matter of fact, so was the rest of the Tulane team and Coach Bernie Bierman. The article only served to force both Tulane and Southern Cal into more zealous preparations.

A few days before the game, Jones invited the Southern sportswriters to a Trojan practice session. The visiting writers were especially anxious to see Southern Cal, particularly since the Trojans had earlier beaten Georgia so badly. They expected to see supermen, but found all-too-human college students instead.

"You never saw such quiet, boyish looking chaps... polished gentlemen all," wrote Bill Keefe, sports editor of the *New Orleans Times-Picayune*. "Williamson, a great big kid with a baby face, looks as if his feelings could be hurt with a frown. We expected to see a gang of ferocious, cruel, and twin-headed monsters, but find only a band of fine young chaps. No university ever boasted a more gentlemanly or clean-cut set of boys. Barring Pinckert, Shaver, and Williamson, they are not much bigger or tougher-looking than Tulane."

But actually the Trojans heavily outweighed the Green Wave players and figured to push them around. Bierman reviewed the individual matchups and proclaimed that his team did not belong on the same field with the Trojans. "They'll beat us by four touchdowns," he said gloomily. His predictions, perhaps just pre-game psychology, became even more dire as game time neared.

If Bierman truly believed what he said, then perhaps he

found solace in the knowledge that no Southern team had lost a Rose Bowl game before. Alabama had beaten Washington and tied Stanford, and Georgia Tech had taken California.

A day of dazzling ceremony preceded the game. Trumpeting the impending Olympics in Los Angeles, the theme of the Rose Bowl parade that year was "Nations And Games In Flowers." A UCLA freshman, Myrta Olmsted, was queen of the tournament's salute to the Olympiad. For the first time the tournament's story was told to all parts of the world with the initiation of short-wave radio broadcasts.

In the *Los Angeles Times* sportswriter Paul Lowry told his readers about the impending struggle of regional football powers. "Watch out for Ernie Pinckert," he wrote.

It was good advice—and psychic at that. Pinckert, normally a blocking back and defensive star, carried the ball for a change and scored two touchdowns on end sweeps through Dalrymple's territory. Pinckert's scoring runs of 30 and 23 yards after Ray Sparling had made a touchdown gave Southern Cal a 21-0 lead and enough of a cushion to withstand a late Tulane rally. The Green Wave fell short, but not by much, 21-12.

"USC has more power than any team I have ever seen," said Bierman after losing his first game in 12 that year.

It was not only the Trojan power that had won the game, though. It was the Trojan planning as well.

Well aware that Bierman, like preceding coaches, would prepare to halt Southern Cal's awesome power running game, Jones added a new element to his attack. Instead of continually plunging straight ahead with a Gus Shaver, he used a unique reverse play with Pinckert as the ballcarrier. Tulane's defenders steadily crashed into the Southern Cal line to stop the expected off-tackle blasting but left the territory around the ends relatively free.

Dalrymple did not have an impressive game, but in his defense it must be pointed out that he played with a kidney injury suffered earlier in the season. He was handicapped by protective padding that required frequent adjustment.

Undaunted by this obvious deficiency and losing by three touchdowns, Tulane scared Southern Cal—and surprised the 84,000 fans at the game—by scoring two touchdowns before the end.

"Tulane went down to defeat with as much glory as Southern California acquired in victory," Mark Kelly wrote in his story for the *Los Angeles Examiner*. "Ask any of the 84,000 persons attending and they'll tell you that Tulane gave 'em plenty of dispute, argued fiercely and valiantly to the final bark of that gun which must have been the best news of the season to Troy and her thousands of supporters."

But at the same time Kelly called the Trojans "undisputed champions." This was certified shortly thereafter when they won their second national football title in four years.

"These players accomplished more throughout the season than any team I ever coached," said Jones after the Rose Bowl victory.

Later, when accepting the Knute Rockne trophy for his national championship accomplishment, Jones called the 1931 team the best he ever coached.

Pop Warner, Jones' arch rival at Stanford, was apt to agree.

"Going over the personnel of the USC team there cannot be found a weak spot," Warner said. "All the positions are filled by first-class players of more than average weight. Pinckert is probably the best blocking back in the country and a very powerful ballcarrier and defensive player as well. Shaver is an all-American if there ever was one—weighing over 190 pounds and yet being a clever open field runner as well as a powerful line bucker.

"There are very few if any more powerful fullbacks than Musick, who weighs about 200 pounds, while Mallory is a blocking back of more than ordinary ability. Mohler can change off with Shaver, and while he does not pack as much weight he has no superior as a ballcarrier in the open field. This backfield is comparable to the Notre Dame backfield of last year which I considered the best backfield of all time.

"With a line of experienced players averaging over 200 pounds to open holes and interfere for such a backfield, it is no wonder that the Trojans are a superteam."

Pinckert, the supreme team player, was covered in glory. He received the Douglas Fairbanks trophy for being voted the most valuable player in the nation by his peers.

The blond star was not only good, he was durable. That was important in Jones' all-out style.

In his final year Pinckert played the full 60 minutes against St. Mary's, Notre Dame, and California—three of the toughest games in 1931. He gave 59 hard minutes against Stanford.

"Truly he is a rare and valuable bird," wrote Dick Hyland in the *Los Angeles Examiner*. "Never did Mister Headman Jones take Pinckert out unless the game was well in the bag. He has removed all three of his other backs, but Pinckert always stayed in there until things were safe."

The bullish Pinckert had more than 1,300 minutes logged in his varsity career, hundreds more than Jim Musick and Gus Shaver, the other backfield stars. They were not easy minutes, either.

"He tackled all over the field, broke up interference, snagged passes, and made holes through which Trojan ball-carriers flashed to touchdowns and fame," noted Hyland.

Pinckert had played his last game for Jones. He went out as an all-American player, joining seniors Baker, Shaver, and Williamson in that sublime category. The Tulane game that season was also the finale for Garrett Arbelbide, Bob Hall, Tom Mallory, and Musick.

Gene Clarke thinks it might have been Jones' best collection of talent.

"Some of these guys were just legend," says Clarke, a substitute on that stunning Trojan team who might have been a starter somewhere else. "I've had guys say to me that the fellows I played with couldn't play with these kids today. Don't you believe that. Of course the biggest man we had on the team was Ernie Smith, a 225-pounder. The kids may be larger today, but don't tell me that we couldn't adapt to today's conditions. The guys I played with had good athletic ability—and guts."

Clarke recalls an amusing incident typifying the enormous pride and spirit of the 1931 Trojans.

"It's pretty late in one game when somebody from the opposition really whacks Mallory with a wicked block. This is after the whistle had blown," Clarke says. "Well, Mallory takes a crack back at this big guy and the guy's cracking back—blocking, not punching, you understand. All this is going on after the play had been blown dead.

"The referee walks up to those two and says, 'What's the matter with you guys, don't you know how to play football?'

Mallory looks at the ref, and after a little pause he says to him: 'Don't we know how to play football? For Christ sakes, look at the scoreboard, buddy.' We were winning by about five touchdowns at the time."

Time Out: Ernie Smith

The freshman football players had gathered for practice when a young man in street clothes came out of nowhere. Big and broad shouldered, he startled everyone by kicking the ball the length of the 53-yard field.

"Who is that kid in the sweater?" the shocked freshman coach asked excitedly.

It was Ernie Smith—and that was the beginning of his football career at Southern California. He later became an all-American tackle and one of the main ingredients of Howard Jones' famed "Thundering Herd" teams.

"It was interesting the way I got my start at Southern Cal," Smith remembers. "I had this bad nose and throat infection all spring, and I wasn't able to practice with the freshman team. One afternoon, though, I'm in the doctor's office, and he tells me that I can finally go out and play football. Well, this was right before the opening game with the Stanford freshmen.

"I got on a dinky street car and came on out to the practice field. I of course didn't have a uniform, just my everyday clothes. The freshman team was lined up on one side of the field and they were trying to get somebody to kick off, but nobody was getting the ball across the field. So I got in and kicked the ball over the fence.

"I guess I impressed the coach because I made the team right away. They couldn't get me eligible for that game, but I started the following week and eventually made my letter.

That's how I got started, honestly."

For three varsity seasons at Southern Cal, from 1930 through 1932, and later several years in the pros, Smith became a towering figure. He not only was recognized as an all-American in college but an all-pro tackle and eventually made the National Football Hall of Fame.

"I was very fortunate to be with some great ballplayers," says Smith, now a few pounds over his playing weight of 225 and a little lighter in the hair department. "I look at the pictures in my den and think, 'What a great group of fellows.' Many of them were all-Americans. Of course without them I never would have achieved what I did. You can't do it alone unless you've got some great men beside you."

Playing on a line that included Aaron Rosenberg, another all-American and Hall of Fame colleague, Smith was the superb instrument of Howard Jones' explosive off-tackle operations. Southern Cal's outstanding runners literally rode Smith's shirt tails to glory.

Jones, the teacher, and Smith, the pupil, were a perfect complement. The coach admired his star tackle for his herculean strength, courage, and desire. "He always gave the best," said Jones. Smith admired Jones for his leadership qualities and football knowledge.

"He was called the 'Head Man' and he was that in all respects," Smith says. "We weren't real close, but I always felt that he was quite fair in whatever he did. All you had to do was be ready when he called on you. If you weren't, then he'd call on somebody else. And you could observe that on the field. You had to get yourself ready both mentally and physically to do the job that he asked you to do.

"He taught me as a freshman how to play tackle, and I got very successful. He taught me how to use my hands on defense. It was his coaching that made all of us good players. He took time to coach us individually. And he had a great memory. It was said that he could virtually remember what every player did on all the plays from the preceding week's game."

Before being placed into Jones' magical hands Smith had been molded for other games. He was an ardent student of music and in fact played a "mean" trombone in the Gardena High School band.

He eventually played football in a Rose Bowl game, but saw his first one as a music maker.

"The first game I ever saw in the Rose Bowl was Notre Dame against Stanford, and I saw the famed Four Horsemen play, it was back in 1925," recalls Smith. "I was playing in my high school band at the time, and we marched in the Rose Bowl parade and got tickets for the game. It was really exciting."

Sports soon ruled his life.

"Of course when I started to play football the band had to get on without me," Smith says.

His instrumental talent later blossomed at Southern Cal, where he not only made beautiful music on a football field but on the stage as well. Smith played trombone for a while in the Trojan band and even had his own dance orchestra.

"I slid my way through college on a trombone," he likes to say. "And I also sang a little. Bass was my key. Don't ask me to sing now, though."

His dual talents were apparent as a youth. Shortly after he moved to California from South Dakota at the age of 12 Smith showed an affinity for both football and music. As a matter of fact, he came to Southern Cal on a music—not a football—scholarship, Smith recalls.

"I was introduced to the USC campus and they took me to the music store and the orchestra leader said, 'Sure I could use a trombone player up here.' And then I knew I would have enough money to get through school. I knew I was going to be able to make my way."

In those days a scholarship was almost negligible in terms of dollars and cents. But, Smith remembers, "it paid for the tuition and gave us a chance to work at various jobs." It opened the door, and the burly Smith barged through.

"I worked my way through school by digging up lawns and getting jobs as an extra in movies," Smith remembers. "I think the pay was about 40 cents an hour. I looked back one time and counted 55 pictures I had been in. I played everything—football player, cowboy, singer. I worked in all of Will Rogers' pictures through that era. I was a waiter in Charlie Chaplin's *Modern Times*."

One movie that Smith worked in, *The Spirit of Notre Dame*, ironically almost cost Southern Cal a football game.

Smith explains why:

"We worked out the football sequences at Loyola College, about 10 miles from here. It was going to be called *The Original Rockne Spirit of Notre Dame*. But they changed the name because it didn't work out for some reason. Anyway the Southern Cal players all worked with the Loyola football players, I think it was 1932, and when it was over, that fall we played Loyola in a regular season game.

"And their coach, in his fight talk, told them, 'Now don't you worry about those big Trojans. Remember, you played football with them in the movie all summer.' And you know, they almost beat us? We won 6 to 0 but came very close to getting beat. Their coach used that psychology on his team, and they did more than they thought they could."

There were not many teams that came that close to Southern Cal during Smith's tenure, though. In his 3 seasons Southern Cal won a national championship and 2 Rose Bowl games. The Trojans' accomplishments over the 1930-32 period were gold-plated with a 28-3 record. They averaged 30 points a game to 4 for their opponents, producing 19 shutouts in that span.

"With players like Orv Mohler and Gus Shaver, how could we miss?" Smith emphasizes, his eyes glowing. "Mohler was amazing. He would take that ball and get out and direct his blockers and it was just tremendous. Remember, this was before there was a lot of passing, and they were just beginning to do the fancy things in the backfield. We had Mohler at quarterback and Gus Shaver playing fullback. That's why we ran up such high scores. And to think, Mohler had his back broken in his sophomore year—and he played after that!"

Through seasons of content and astounding triumphs Smith discovered that he would never forget his first game as a starter. Excitement was high.

"The Stanford game in 1930 was the first game I started and probably my most exciting because of that fact," Smith says, drumming thick fingers on a desk. "Naturally I was apprehensive, but once we kicked off I settled down. I was usually the man who kicked off. It's pretty nice to be in that position because you always start the game. Sometimes the coach forgets and lets you stay in."

The modest Smith did not have to worry about himself, though. His position was secure once he played in his first game. He was not only good, he was durable. He stayed relatively injury-free for the rest of his career.

"I went through an entire career and never lost any teeth," Smith says. "I had my nose skinned, but I never had any nose bleeds. I really don't know how I did it. After all, I played offense as well as defense. And on offense you have your head tied up in a man's thighs all game. It wasn't easy. Normally in those days when you went in, you stayed in until you got carried out."

While a Trojan star, Smith was the butt of good-natured humor. Teammates continually taunted him about his enormous shoe size and appetite. But they never liked anyone more.

"There are so many jokes told about Ernie Smith that I don't know which one to select," Orv Mohler once said. "He's been kidded about his shoe size, his appetite, his orchestra, and about everything else that could possibly be thought of.

"When I first came to SC, it was reported that Ernie wore 12½ size shoes. Now the latest report is that they are 14s. Whether this comparison is actual or literal, I don't know. But one thing of which I'm sure—he does win the contest for having a LARGE size.

"Anyone couldn't help but like Ernie who knew him. He looks more like a boxer than a collar advertisement, it is true, but he has a heart that is big enough to take in everyone's sob stories. There isn't anything he wouldn't do to help out a person."

Smith's manners were above reproach.

"A characteristic of Ernie's is that he is always shaking hands with people," Mohler said. "Have you ever noticed him on the field? After he has nearly killed someone with a tackle, he'll help the fellow up and just automatically put out his hand to shake hands with him. He does that rather unconsciously, though, because when you are standing talking to him with a group of fellows he does the same thing."

One of the few times that Smith was not a gentleman got him into trouble. Mohler recalled the funny "barber chair incident."

"As had been the custom, a barber chair had been added

to our train to be used on road trips," Mohler recalled. "It was the usual thing when a member of the team was in the chair getting a shave and a haircut for all of the fellows who happened to be near the scene of action to stand around, giving advice and helping the barber out in a general way.

"One morning Ernie arose, full of vim and vigor, and stormed the barber shop. A man was reclining in the chair covered with the conventional barber's apron and a hot towel over his face. Ernie gave one look, apparently recognized the body, rubbed his hands together and lunged upon the body, landing rather forcibly near the solar plexus. He then proceeded to work the person over very thoroughly in a light massage. Seeing that the barber wasn't giving full attention to his customer, Ernie came to the latter's rescue and started 'giving him the works,' so to speak, as far as shampoo tonic was concerned.

"Realizing, too, that a facial would be in order, he started massaging through the towel. I have a sneaking suspicion that none of these actions was done in any light manner. At any rate the customer decided that he had better see just what sort of an ambitious barber he had. He sat up in the chair, took the towel from his face, and looked around.

"There was a sudden emptiness of people in that shop of the former occupants who had been standing along the sidelines. The man in the chair was Coach Howard Jones. I think that the railroad company is still sending Ernie Smith bills for a portion of the door of the barber shop he took with him in making his hasty exit from the car."

Smith survived that incident and finished his years at Southern Cal by wrestling opposing teams instead of his coach.

Seriously considering a career in music, Smith gave up that idea upon graduation from Southern Cal "because music was real rough at that time." He helped coach the school's freshman team for one year, then opted for professional ball. Most of his career was spent with the Green Bay Packers, but he left them in 1938 because of a salary squabble.

"It was maybe a difference of $5 or $10 a game," says Smith. "At that time I was trying to get to a level of $200 a week. So you can see it wasn't a great deal. But I left anyway."

Football's glamour eventually lured Smith back. He joined

a team called the Hollywood Stars, but that association was short-lived. While there he had the dual role of player-coach and represented an all-star team that played the Packers. He was invited back to Green Bay but turned his back on the offer.

"My life insurance business at that time was making it unprofitable for me to play pro football," Smith remembers. "Pro teams didn't have salaries then like they have today."

Smith's insurance business enticed the rich and the famous. "I sold Bing Crosby his first insurance policy," Smith enjoys telling you.

Football remained a part of Smith's life, though, and surfaced in his service days during World War Two—when he served as player-assistant coach for the Air Force Flyers of March Field. After the war he scouted for professional teams.

In 1970 Smith was inducted into football's Hall of Fame. The moment was shining triumph.

"Frank Leahy, Notre Dame's great coach, and I were inducted into the Hall together," says Smith, his broad face gleaming pride. "We got pretty well acquainted—and I found out that we were both born in South Dakota."

Smith's football interests continue even today. While his expansive insurance business is the dominating force of his world, Smith has found time to work with the Tournament of Roses Committee and with a foundation memorializing the memory of Howard Jones. The latter project is Smith's most passionate work.

"A group of his players got together about 1958 or 1959 and felt that we ought to have something to keep his name alive," explains Smith. "We formed a foundation, and we have regular meetings. Originally we started out with the idea of giving a national championship trophy, but we were kind of preempted by bigger groups. So we finally decided to just stick to a scholarship program. We give a scholarship to a scholar-athlete at USC. In order to qualify he has to have at least a 3-point average over 10½ years of school and be an outstanding football player. And he has to enter into a graduate school to get it. We've put a couple of boys through dental and law school, and so forth.

"We really got swinging on the project in the 1960s, and we kept it going. Jones was the finest coach we knew. We don't want people to forget, that's all. There's a tendency to shove the greats of the past into the past. I always admired him, and as I look back I see him clearly. He made me understand that a man who lives by his principles can't help but succeed."

The Whispering Herd

Between the herculean figures of Aaron Rosenberg and Ernie Smith, Southern Cal's opposition did not see much daylight in 1932. The common vendetta was to beat the Trojans. But you could not beat them if you could not score on them.

Every team on the schedule pointed for the defending national champions but hardly made any points at all. Despite pressure of their lofty stature the Trojans shut out eight opponents in 1932 and allowed only seven points to California and six to Washington. They won all ten games.

That formidable accomplishment was due in large measure to Rosenberg and Smith, the heart of one of Southern Cal's finest defensive teams. Rosenberg has been regarded as one of the greatest guards in Trojan history, and Smith was an enormously talented tackle.

"Rosenberg is still considered Troy's mightiest guard—on defense he stopped everything that came his way and charged viciously on offense," said an appraisal story of Southern California's golden players of the 1930s.

Smith stood out "as headline material," noted another story. "He was a hammer-'em-down 200-pounder who played a whale of a game" for the Trojans. "When he plants those size 14 shoes of his wide apart and starts swinging those hamlike hands there's very little that gets by him."

Once reviewing the 1930s Coach Howard Jones was especially enamored of Rosenberg. The Southern Cal coach

Aaron Rosenberg "stopped everything that came his way on defense and charged viciously on offense." Considered by some to be Southern California's mightiest guard.

All-American tackle Tay Brown captained the 1932 team that produced Howard Jones' only perfect season at Southern California.

noted: "I give credit to Rosenberg for playing a big part in the success of the team's defense against Notre Dame and Stanford in 1931 and 1932. He was delegated to watch the fullback. He went in and cracked him and messed him up."

In 1931 Southern Cal defeated Stanford 19-0 and beat Notre Dame in that memorable 16-14 game. In 1932 Southern Cal shut out both teams by 13-0 scores.

"The 1932 team was the strongest defensive team that USC ever had," says Al Wesson, Southern Cal's noted sports publicist of the 1930s. "There were only two touchdowns scored on us all season—and they were both by passes. No one could move, no less score on the ground against us. Smith was one of the greatest tackles we ever had. Rosenberg was a smart, fine athlete. You couldn't buy a yard against this team. I'd say without qualification that the offense of the 1931 team and the defense of the 1932 team were the best produced by Jones."

The Trojans' towering defense literally took the thunder away from the "Thundering Herd" in 1932. Runners like Gus

Shaver, Ernie Pinckert, Jim Musick, and Tom Mallory had graduated, and Jones sought in vain for new men of equal weight, speed, and quality.

From the period of 1929 through 1931 the Trojans had averaged almost 38 points a game. But in 1932 they only averaged 20. Point production was only half as good, but the defense was twice as good.

No wonder, then, that appraisal stories for the 1932 season focused on "another great Trojan line."

"Captain-elect Tay Brown and Ernie Smith, 200-pound behemoths who held forth so successfully at the tackle positions last year, are back in good condition," said one magazine article. "Larry Stevens and John Dye, alternate standing guards, also return. Ray Sparling, veteran left end who pulled two or three tough games out of the fire in 1931 on his famous end-around, or reverse play, threatens to have a great year, having added considerable weight during the past twelve months.

"Aaron Rosenberg, alternate running guard with Johnny Baker last year, is back in harness, and it actually looks as if he will make Trojan fans forget the stocky lineman who was the toast of the town last November after nudging the ball through the uprights for that memorable victory over Notre Dame."

The veterans would be pushed for their jobs by superb, younger talent.

"There is other good material available for the line berths, and if any of these players of prominence show signs of lagging, Jones will have somebody else in there in a hurry," said the magazine. "Once a team gets a winning reputation material is abundant, and such is the situation of Southern California. Players get one or two chances to make good, and if they fail it is a long time before they land on the first string again."

Summing up Southern Cal's prospects, the magazine said: "The line should be as powerful as ever, with adequate reserves; the backfield material is there but will probably lack cohesion during the early games at least. The team has no Shaver, who will probably be the man most missed from last year's eleven. (Homer) Griffith may come along to fill this all-around job, but he will have to improve tremendously if he does."

The writer of that story had not counted on Cotton

Warburton, who along with Orville Mohler stood out in Southern Cal's depleted backfield. Warburton, especially, might have been overlooked by anybody because of his diminutive size. His exploits, however, were much larger by comparison.

Warburton, whose playing weight ranged in the 140s, scored the touchdown that beat Washington 9-6, starred in the victory over Notre Dame, and made two touchdowns that led to Southern Cal's 35-0 rout over Pittsburgh in the Rose Bowl game. The defensive work of this demoniacal sophomore was no less astonishing. Warburton was deployed as safety and was almost perfect at the job.

"I was responsible for the only blemish on our undefeated, untied, and almost unscored upon record," he once said. (Warburton slipped while covering a California receiver, and the result was a touchdown for the Golden Bears. His memory was not perfect, either, since the Trojans also gave up a touchdown to Washington that year.)

In the Stanford game Warburton and his teammates knocked down ten passes in a typical example of defensive zeal. Mark Kelly of the *Los Angeles Examiner* was impressed. "Never has any Trojan secondary showed finer defense than they did this afternoon. This was a very masterful team, a tremendously impressive club," the sportswriter said in his game story after Southern Cal's fifth straight victory of the season. "The USC defensive power was absolutely astounding; their ability to out-dazzle Mr. (Pop) Warner's razzle-dazzle was uncanny."

Prior to Stanford, Southern Cal had beaten Utah, Washington State, Oregon State, and Loyola. Next came California, a "must" game, according to Mohler.

"To each team this game looms as of supreme importance," the quarterback said in a newspaper story. "The Trojans must win to stay on top in the Pacific Coast Conference race, as well as to stay up in front in the battle for another national championship. The Bears have no championship in sight, but they see their grand chance to regain the prestige that defeats by Santa Clara and Washington State have damaged. Both teams feel they just have to win. What a setup for one of the great football battles of the year!"

The only thing that California could boast about after that game was that it had scored a touchdown on the supreme

Trojan defense. Southern Cal won going away, 27-7.

The Trojans then defeated Oregon with ease and Washington with some perspiration for their eighteenth straight victory over two years. Only Notre Dame stood in Southern Cal's way for a perfect regular season, Jones' first. Ironically the gambling fraternity made the Fighting Irish favorites on the standing rule, "Never bet against Notre Dame or the New York Yankees."

Southern Cal took advantage of Notre Dame's vulnerability to punt returns to beat the Fighting Irish. Warburton ran back a punt 39 yards to set up a touchdown pass by Griffith. Later Southern Cal fell on a loose ball on the Notre Dame 26, and Griffith eventually took it in. The Trojans' stunning defense twice slammed the ball down Notre Dame's throat, halting enemy thrusts on their 5 and 9-yard lines.

The perfect season gave Southern Cal its second straight Pacific Coast Conference championship and fifth in six years. The Trojans were picked again for the Rose Bowl, this time against relatively weak Pitt. The Panthers, tied by Ohio State and Nebraska, were not one of Jock Sutherland's best teams. Rumors persisted that politics had gained a bowl bid for Pitt. It was said that Pitt Athletic Director Don Harrison "had friends on the Rose Bowl selection committee."

This was perhaps the year that Colgate should have been the eastern representative. The famous catch-phrase evolved from this situation: "Colgate: Unbeaten, untied, unscored on, and uninvited."

Said an honest Pittsburgh sportswriter: "That Pitt team had to be one of the poorest to play at Pasadena. My paper was on a poverty kick at the time, so I listened to the horrible details at the University Club midst friends and liquor."

Owing to Pitt's damaged reputation and Southern Cal's defensive orientation not many points were expected to be scored in that Rose Bowl game. Expectations were half right, since Pitt did not score any points. But the Trojans scored an astonishing (for them) 35 points.

The Trojans manipulated the Panthers with a bigger, tougher line, Griffith's passing, and Warburton's running. A 50-yard pass from Griffith to Ford Palmer gave the Trojans a 7-0 lead in the first period.

Describing the spectacular play in the *Los Angeles Times*,

Coach Howard Jones, second from left, flanked by several all-Americans posed for this picture prior to the 1933 Rose Bowl game with Pittsburgh.

Bill Henry said: "As the ball arched high in the air, Pitt's safety man Sebastian set himself to knock it down in the end zone. Palmer came charging in from his left at top speed, and he and the ball hit Sebastian at the same time. Both players were a couple of feet off the ground. There was a brief but decisive wrestling match in mid-air. Palmer, perhaps aided by the impetus of his run, wrenched the leather away from Sebastian and lit in the end zone for the game's first score. Mr. Sebastian and the 84,000 people were surprised, and they were still gasping when Ernie Smith's suitcase-size shoe nudged the pill squarely between the posts for the first of four perfect placements for the day."

Warburton shone defensively before scoring two touchdowns in the last period. On one particular play he saved a touchdown when he tackled a Pitt runner in the open after he had gained 32 yards. After that Warburton made himself unstoppable. The Panthers ripped off his shirt but could not prevent him from gaining 87 yards.

Sutherland never forgot the crushing defeat, nor the previous 1930 beating by Southern Cal, and did not let his players forget it, either. Four years later, when Pitt returned for a Rose Bowl game with Washington, the Panther coach ordered the team bus to make a special stop on a hill overlooking the Arroyo Seco stadium. "There it is," Sutherland told his players. "There's the place two Pittsburgh teams were beaten by a total of 68 points."

To be beaten by a team of Southern Cal's proportion, however, was no disgrace. The Trojans were considered the national champions for the second straight year in 1932. And many years later, when West Coast sports editors collaborated on an all-time Pacific Coast Conference team, they placed Rosenberg and Smith in that weighty group.

The Trojans would not get any better during Jones' time on the West Coast. More winning seasons and bowl teams were in the future, but none as exquisite as his last two. Jones peaked between 1927 and 1932. The decline lay not too far ahead.

Decline And Fall

In 1932 Stanford's freshmen football team lost a game to the Southern Cal freshmen, and this so embittered them that they took an oath never again to lose to the Trojans. The "Vow Boys" never did.

This unique resolution took shape in 1933, when those same freshmen were sophomores. They helped Stanford defeat Southern Cal 13-7 and thus stop the Trojans' 27-game unbeaten streak, the longest in their history.

The first loss since the Trojans' opening game of 1931 ended their dominance on the West Coast and started Stanford on a course for the Rose Bowl.

"The King Is Dead," announced the *San Francisco Examiner* in a bold headline. "Monarch Who Reigned Since 1931 Crashed To Earth," said a smaller headline.

The story was just as overly dramatic:

"Across the nation's football front that trite phrase echoed this afternoon as Stanford University crushed, and I mean crushed, Southern California 13 to 7.

"These words fell with a resounding crash. Unbelievable, but 90,000 pairs of eyes witnessed the feat.

"It was a strange sight. Not since 1931, when a little band of St. Mary's Gaels turned the trick, has the old Trojan warhorse showed signs of slowing down..."

While the *Examiner* seemed pleased with the Stanford victory, the populace was ecstatic. When the game was over, there was dancing in the streets of Palo Alto.

Stanford's famed "Vow Boys" had not only broken the Southern Cal jinx of five years, but eventually fulfilled their own prophecy. They defeated the Trojans twice more while visiting the Rose Bowl three straight years.

This was no ordinary team, to be sure. Tiny Thornhill had replaced Pop Warner as coach at Stanford and fell heir to a plethora of talent. Included were some of the Indians' all-time stars, Monk Moscrip, Bob Reynolds, Frank Alustiza, Bones Hamilton, and Bobby Grayson. They beat a Southern Cal team that was on the decline, despite a 10-1-1 record in 1933.

Many of the Trojans' brightest stars had graduated after the 1932 season. Running back Cotton Warburton and guard Aaron Rosenberg, two of the country's best players at their positions, were some of the few "names" left. With Warburton and Rosenberg doing the significant work, the Trojans' dazzling winning streak reached 25 midway through the 1933 season.

Then came an unexpected, scoreless tie with Oregon State and a near-loss to California, two schools that the previous Trojan power teams would have handled with ease. They were telling signs.

Oregon State's tie with Southern Cal was a superb moral victory for the Beavers. For one thing it stopped the Trojans' 25-game winning streak. For another Southern Cal had thoroughly dominated the series, winning the preceding 10 games. The Trojans were 19-point favorites in the 1933 game, as well. To Southern Cal's embarrassment Oregon State Coach Lon Stiner used no reserves in that game either. Battling on a muddy field 11 Oregon State players held 21 Southern Cal players to a standstill.

Some observers were inclined to consider it a fluke, pointing to poor field conditions. But, actually, the Trojans had lost much of their scoring punch. This was evident in the next game when Southern Cal was held scoreless for three quarters by California before rallying for a 6-3 victory on Cotton Warburton's dazzling 60-yard touchdown dash.

Knocked senseless by a tackle in the first half, Warburton came back to win the game for Southern Cal but, in fact, afterwards did not remember making the touchdown run. It was an unusual sequel to the dramatic victory.

Arleigh Williams' field goal in the first quarter had given

Cotton Warburton: He was knocked cold, but managed to beat California anyway.

the Golden Bears a 3-0 lead, and they held the close margin tenaciously. When Warburton was stunned making that tackle, he had to be taken out and was somehow overlooked in the locker room when the Trojans took the field for the second half.

Warburton had taken a shower and was sitting nude on a stack of blankets when discovered by John Lehners, an assistant to graduate manager Bill Hunter.

"Yes, I did find Cotton, but it was more or less by accident," Lehners explained. "The student managers had gone down to the field for the start of the second half, and I was arranging a few of the blankets that had been left in the dressing room. You'll recall it was a cold, foggy day, and I wanted to be sure all the blankets that were needed were down near the bench for the players. Much to my surprise I found Cotton sitting on the blankets, stark naked. He had just finished his shower and was trying to put on his civilian clothes. He asked me to help him. 'The game's over,' was what he said. 'Let's get out of here.'

"I don't know whether I finally convinced him that the game wasn't over or not, but I helped him get back into his uniform. It was an awfully tough game, you know, and although I never expected to see Warburton get into the game again I thought it would help our team's morale and keep Cal from thinking Cotton was through if he did nothing more than just sit on the bench.

"When we finally reached the bench, the second half was underway. I asked our team physician, Dr. Packard Thurber, to take a look at Cotton and check his condition. Quite frankly I had no idea that they'd allow him back into the game. Next time I looked up, there he was running for the touchdown. I was never so surprised in my life."

Neither was Warburton.

"I don't know what happened," he said after the glorious run. "I don't recall anybody being near me. I just ran, and the next thing I knew Ford Palmer and the rest of our team were slapping me on the back."

California players remembered every detail, if Warburton had forgotten. Said Red Christie, the Golden Bears' linebacker: "On Warburton's run I guess all of us Cal players had our one miss of the day. I know I did. I had a straight shot at him behind the line, but he got away. Then there was a succession of missed tackles—and that was the ball game."

Sportswriter Braven Dyer watched Warburton escape the California defenders with uncanny ease. "It will take somebody with more imagination than this writer to explain how Warburton wiggled away from two tacklers, one of whom had him nailed by one leg after a gain of about three yards," Dyer said in his game story for the *Los Angeles Times*.

Warburton's glittering run notwithstanding, the Trojans were lucky to win that game. Chuck Stewart almost scored a touchdown for California on the opening kickoff but dropped from exhaustion 20 yards from the Trojan goal line. Southern

Cal's Larry Stevens caught up with him from behind.

"Going down the field on the kick I was knocked to the grass," Stevens remembered, "but I got up and saw that Stewart had gotten through the other fellows. So I set out after him, and just as I went to tackle him he fell of his own accord on the 20-yard line. Golly, I was glad to see him go down."

Trojan happiness turned to despair the following week when Stanford stopped the glamorous unbeaten streak.

It was a moment that Warner would have savored. Frustrated by an inability to handle Southern Cal teams, the coach had left the year before for the east. He emphasized in all seriousness that Stanford was a poor place in which to coach because the Stanford players would never be like the players who enrolled at Southern Cal.

"You can never hope to beat USC with the kind of material that comes to Stanford," a grim Warner had told his successor.

But Warner was proven wrong on that November day in 1933. The loss caused Trojan Coach Howard Jones to shake his head and say: "We were outfought and outplayed."

Curley Grieve gave this account of the game in the *San Francisco Examiner*:

"It was not a deceptive attack that turned the trick and piled up yardage. It was baffling but not undecipherable to a Trojan eleven that had won 27 games straight. (Actually 26 victories and 1 tie.) It was based almost entirely upon Bobby Grayson's ability to outrun the ends and halfbacks. He did this. He spread that heavy USC line, and made gaping holes through which Bones Hamilton and Van Dellen darted.

"He threatened with a passing attack that functioned magnificently during that touchdown march when Van Dellen made two spectacular catches. Meanwhile, up front in the line, all-American guard Bill Corbus was brilliant. He was in the line, over the line, and under the line of Trojan advancement. He was smashing, battering, and even roaming to the flanks to haul down the USC runners that followed the powerful Aaron Rosenberg. He was deadly. He never missed a tackle."

He was just as deadly on offense. Corbus kicked two field goals in the fourth quarter for Stanford's deciding margin.

Warburton, as usual, was the star for the Trojans, scoring

on a 44-yard run. Win or lose, he was always the star.

"No player in the nation accomplished more thrilling deeds than the platinum blond speedster from USC," said a sportswriter. "Yet the tendency in some quarters was to play down his admitted prowess on the score that he was a jack-of-one-trade. They ignored the fact that in this specialty he was superb, the most sensational ballcarrier since the halcyon days of Red Grange. He is not a tactical genius as a field general. He hasn't the physique to be a sixty-minute man. There are better punters and passers. But he's a first-team all-American as far as I'm concerned.

"To paraphrase Sherman's words: 'Warburton is hell.' He is just that. The 144-pound scoring ace broke up half of the games on the Trojan schedule in 1933. He was the sole reason for the 6-to-3 defeat of California. He scored the lone touchdown against Stanford. He ruined Oregon and scored twice against Notre Dame. He started the Washington State rout and wound up with 12 points to his credit. In the closing game of the year, a tough one against Washington, he crossed the goal line twice with the tallies that enabled USC to chalk up a 13-to-7 win.

"That's a sample of Warburton—the most feared runner in these United States. He was a marked man all season, special defenses were constructed to foil him, but 'Cotton' came through the hard way."

Quite frankly the Trojans could have used three or four

like him from 1934 through 1937. Southern Cal finished out the 1933 season in high style by beating Oregon, Notre Dame, Georgia, and Washington, but it was Jones' last good year for a while. In the next four seasons the Trojans struggled for respectability, and the Southern Cal coach failed to produce a yearly all-American for the first time. Ironically, Jones' star dipped just as his annual salary was improved to $15,000.

Jones' records fell to 4-6-1 in 1934, 5-7 in 1935, 4-2-3 in 1936, and 4-4-2 in 1937. Declining attendance figures paralleled the declining performances. Despite enlargement of the Los Angeles Coliseum, which had exploded to more than 100,000 seats for the 1932 Olympics, there was a distinct dropoff in fan support in the mid-1930s. In 1933 the Trojans had played before 645,000, but in the next three years the figures were 468,000, 432,000, and 435,000.

While baffling to some supporters, Southern Cal's fall was no mystery to Paul Zimmerman, onetime sports editor of the *Los Angeles Times*. Analyzing why Jones' material was weaker in those years, Zimmerman said:

"Howard had a lot of fine stars who spent three years on the bench when they could have played at some of the other schools. The high school players figured that out for themselves, and many decided to go elsewhere. Of course, alumni and coaches at other schools were stepping up their recruiting. By the same token the Jones staff and the alumni naturally got to

Southern California's linemen are on their toes for the upcoming Notre Dame game of 1933. Left to right, Ford Palmer, Hueston Harper, Larry Stevens, Aaron Rosenberg, Curtis Youel, Bob Erskine, and Julius Bescos.

riding on their oars, assuming every great prep star would want to be a part of the 'Thundering Herd.'"

Jones' down years not only caused unhappiness among Southern Cal supporters but might have sparked some bad feeling at home as well. The coach's son, Clark, was sports editor of the school newspaper at the time and never hesitated to criticize the Trojan teams.

And while Jones was down, he was kicked repeatedly by vengeful coaches. One such bitter rivalry existed with Washington's Jimmy Phelan, who admitted he had no love for the Southern Cal coach.

"There was bad blood between us," Phelan said. "It dated back to 1922, my first year as coach at Purdue. Jones was coaching Iowa at the time, and the Hawkeyes crushed us, 56 to 0. We had a kid on the sidelines with a concussion. I was trying to help him, and Jones was still pouring it on. Well, he didn't come over to say anything to me after the game, and then that night we were having dinner at a hotel in Iowa City. Jones came in with his party and didn't even nod to me. The next year Iowa beat us only 7 to 0, and Jones came over to shake hands with me. I told him where he could go.

"I've never really held any grudge against anyone in my life—except Jones—and when I played him I played with heated vengeance. The record book shows it."

During Phelan's 12 years at Washington, the Huskies beat Southern Cal 7 times—on 6 occasions when Jones coached the Trojans. As an exclamation point to the Phelan story, his team beat Southern Cal 5 times in a row from 1934 through 1938.

Not all feelings were bitter during this period, however. Jones developed a friendly rivalry and a friendship with Bill Spaulding at UCLA. While their teams battled on a football field, Jones and Spaulding matched each other at cards and golf. This firm relationship was the spirit upon which the exquisite USC-UCLA series was built.

Though usually beaten by the Trojans, Spaulding revered Jones. He called him "the finest friend I ever had."

"We sure had fun together," Spaulding once said. "Howard used to outdistance me off the tee, but I had the edge on the greens. We had a running gag going before every round. One of us would say, loud enough for all to hear, 'Let's make it

50-50-50 today.' Naturally, everybody thought we were talking dollars, but we were really talking cents."

Because of the ready-made appeal of two Los Angeles schools, both Southern Cal and UCLA were anxious to resume their rivalry. Southern Cal and UCLA had originally started the series in the late 1920s, but aborted because of the Trojans' overwhelming strength. In the mid-1930s the teams were more equally matched.

In 1936 Southern Cal and UCLA played to a 7-7 tie. In 1937 Southern Cal beat UCLA 19-13—but not before some very anxious moments. Attached to the 1937 game is a classic story involving Jones and Spaulding.

Kenny Washington, UCLA's all-American halfback, drove Southern Cal to distraction in the fourth period. Washington's passing helped the Bruins score two touchdowns and brought

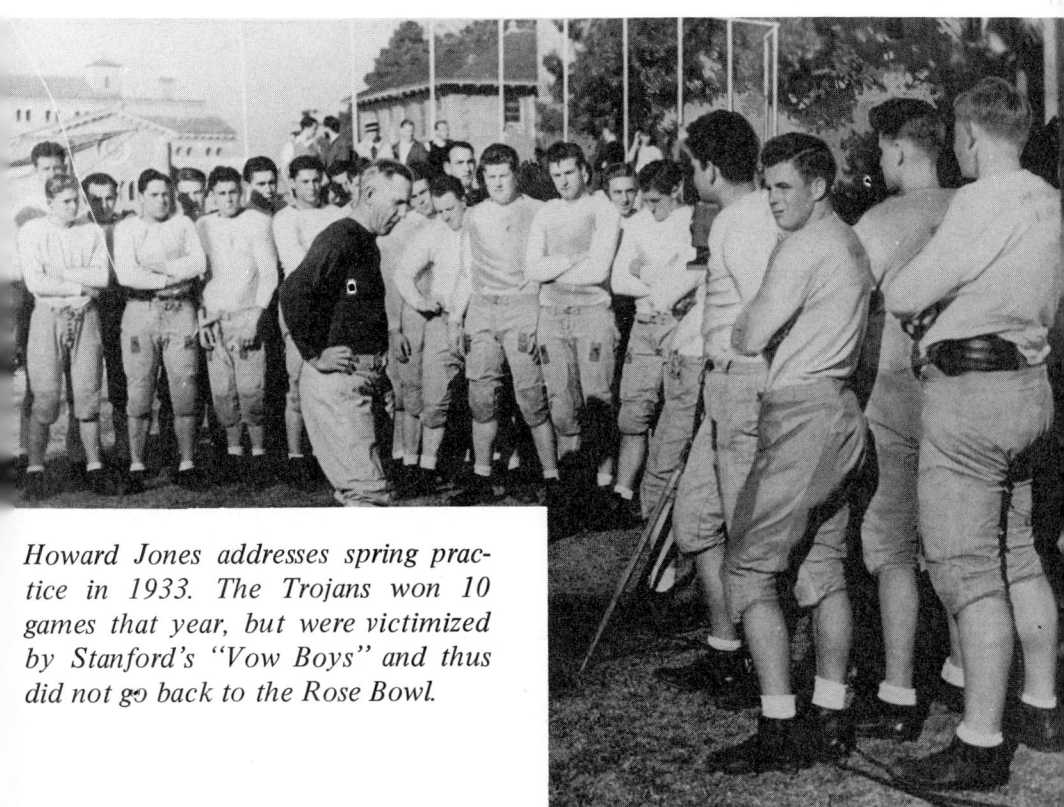

Howard Jones addresses spring practice in 1933. The Trojans won 10 games that year, but were victimized by Stanford's "Vow Boys" and thus did not go back to the Rose Bowl.

them to the fringe of another. The Bruin rally threw the Coliseum crowd into a frenzy and had Jones on the edge of nervous exhaustion.

After the game Spaulding paid a visit to the Trojan locker room and found the door closed. He knocked.

"Who's there?" a voice asked.

"Bill Spaulding," the coach said.

"What do you want?" the voice asked.

"Tell Howard he can come out now," Spaulding answered without missing a beat. "We've stopped passing."

Time Out: Nick Pappas

A boy growing up in Seattle fell in love with the Washington University football team. The boy nurtured a dream of someday playing for the Huskies. But fickle emotion destroyed that relationship. One day a radio program helped Nick Pappas find a new love—Southern California. The Trojans' fine tailback of the 1930s likes to recall the fateful day that changed his life.

"I used to follow Washington wherever they went, and I used to sneak in and see the ballgames from behind the fence," says Pappas. "I mean I really LOVED Washington. One day they were down there playing Southern Cal. I remember I was listening to the game on an old West radio, lying on the floor and my mother was reading nearby.

"They stopped the ballgame for about 10 minutes while Morley Drury was walking off the field for the last time. They gave him that tremendous ovation, and that stayed in my mind. I said to my mom, 'One day I'm going to be a Trojan.' Of course I never dreamed I would make it. But it was always in the back of my mind. I always thought if I could make it, that would be the greatest thing."

A boy's dream came true in 1935 when Pappas started a three-year career under Howard Jones. His early engagement with Southern Cal became a perfect marriage in later years, when Pappas took charge of the school's Athletic Support Groups.

Now a zealous alumni worker and a raconteur of the first

order, Pappas still looks as if he can carry a football. He moves around his gleaming office at Heritage Hall with the grace of a star athlete, broad shoulders thrown back and his beefy hands busy.

He enjoys recounting the 1930s and keeps his audience riveted for hours.

"Please bring in some coffee for us," Pappas says to his secretary. "Now, where were we? Oh, yes..."

Stories pour from the warm, friendly man.

"Southern Cal didn't seek me out, I came down here on my own," Pappas says, "I signed a note to come to the school, and in the first game I played with the freshmen I ran 65 yards for a touchdown. They offered me a scholarship after that run."

As a freshman, Pappas was duly impressed with the upper classmen. He enjoyed lingering in the fraternity houses, luxuriating in the life-size pictures of football players.

"They had one of Drury, and I thought, 'Gee, that's the guy who inspired me to come to SC,'" Pappas says, smiling.

Cotton Warburton also had Pappas mesmerized.

"I used to follow him around," remembers Pappas. "God, he must have thought, you know, I was a nut. One day I followed him into the locker room. He got undressed and put his jock on and climbed on a scale. You were supposed to weigh in and weigh out at everyday's practice.

"Just as I'm standing there at the scale, Warburton gets up on the thing and it measures 158 pounds. The manager standing next to the scale writes 175 pounds down on a chart. I say, 'Hey, it's 158.' Warburton looks at me and says, 'How much do you weigh?' 'One Forty,' I say. He says, 'Do you want to play for Howard Jones?' I said, 'Yes, sir.' He says, 'You weigh 175.' From that day on I weighed 175. But I never weighed over 160, really. Jones just thought you had to be at least 175 pounds to play football."

Pappas was at once caught up in giddy freshmen revelry. The enemy was cross-town UCLA, and a football player fought strange wars.

"Once I was told to go to sleep early one night so I could get up early in the morning," Pappas recalls. "We were on a mission to burn out a UCLA bonfire site. They had telephone poles and things stacked up 40 feet in the air on the field. Some guy in our fraternity house had this chemical and made a bomb out of it. So they got us out of bed about 3:30 in the morning, and we went up Sunset Boulevard, sneaking on our hands and knees. It was dark as hell, no moon out. Geez, we're finally going across this playing field on our hands and knees and all of a sudden I see feet. I looked up and here are these guys from UCLA. They said, 'What are you doing?' I said, 'Ah, nothing.' So this guy from UCLA says, 'If you've come to burn the thing down, you're too late. It was burned down this afternoon.'"

Another time, the Tommy Trojan statue on the USC campus was the butt of a UCLA prank. Pappas remembers: "They came in with a helicopter and dropped something on the statue that really smelled. It was the worst thing I ever smelled—some kind of chemical, just rotten, rotten. And we couldn't wash it off. But the payoff was, we get to the ballgame, and some UCLA kids have a banner right up in the Coliseum. It said, 'Didn't Tommy Stink?'"

The real battles raged on the football field, though. And the real enemy was Notre Dame.

"That was always a big game," says Pappas, "and sensational things always happened."

The Fighting Irish never lacked for trickery in Pappas' day. Their acts, according to some of their competition, sometimes bordered on the immoral.

"In the 1935 game we were leading at the half, and we came back on the field after intermission," recalls Pappas. "We were doing pretty well, because we weren't that good a football team. They're undefeated, see. We're holding on, and we're ahead and we walk on the field and they have a band covering the entire field waiting for us, and they strike up Ave Maria in the memory of Knute Rockne.

"So we all stand at attention, and they play it through twice. It was 18 degrees at South Bend, the last game of the season, and it was sooooo cold. In the meantime the Notre Dame team is huddling underneath a blanket, understand. Well, they finally kick off to us, one of our guys fumbles the ball at the 3-yard line, and they pick it up, get the ball, and go in for a score. The damn band beat us! That was 1935.

"In 1937 we go back there, and the same thing happens. We're either even or ahead, and we come out on the field after the half. Some guy, a Catholic, was killed in an auto accident prior to the football season, and they play the Ave Maria in HIS memory. We look across the field, and the Notre Dame players are huddled under those blankets again. But it didn't work that time. Jones says, 'Come on, boys. Let's warm up.' And we huddled underneath our own blankets. Notre Dame used every trick in the book to beat you."

In warfare the Fighting Irish went to rude extremes, was the claim. Horror stories of Notre Dame violence persisted. Trojan tongues cut by well-aimed elbows, punches thrown, shirts shredded, to say nothing of hurt feelings.

"Funny things happened on the field," Pappas says, meaning outrageous unethical conduct by the Fighting Irish. But it worked both ways. Once after a bitter half when Notre Dame players used illegal tactics, Southern Cal gave it back with interest. One Notre Dame player who had especially been taunting the Trojans had tobacco juice spit in his eyes and had to leave the game. The players were on their own, of course. Jones never condoned such buffoonery.

"Jones was very ethical and didn't put up with any dirty football," says Pappas. "You couldn't play for him if you played that way."

Pappas reveals this classic Jones story:

"We were playing Washington one year in the Coliseum—that was the year Jimmy Phelan was coaching the Huskies. And they called us every name in the books, SOBs, the whole works. They were not only badmouthing the hell out of us, but playing dirty as well. During the half, one of our assistant coaches came to us and said: 'Are you going to let those so-and-sos beat you up like that? Go out in the second half and give it back to them. Give them back what they're giving you!

"He was madder than hell, and the old man (Jones) heard him. Jones said, 'Just a minute,' and he kicked everyone out of the dressing room but the players and this assistant coach. He told this coach in a gruff voice, 'I don't know why you said that.' Then he turned to his players and said, 'I want to tell you men something. If anybody goes out there in the second half and does anything dirty or illegal, he's coming out of the game. He'll never play another gol-darn minute for Southern Cal.' He meant it, too. If you're holding and you get a penalty, he'd race you right off the field, and you'd be out of the ballgame. He was a completely honorable guy."

There were few earthly rewards for such goodness during Pappas' time, however. He played during a slump when the Trojans not only had trouble beating Notre Dame, but everyone else. Struggling to finish at .500 provided the team with character, at any rate.

"We didn't have any outstanding people like O. J. Simpson, people like that," Pappas says. "Everybody just played hard together. We lost, we won, we tied. We always played our best and played our hearts out."

Jones made up for loss of natural power by seizing every advantage.

"A thing that Jones always liked to do was kick off instead of receive, if we had the choice," Pappas says. "He felt that if the defense would hold the other team on the first series of downs and they'd be forced to punt, then we'd get the ball in good field position. It usually worked out that way. We'd get the ball at least to our 30 or 40-yard line."

Jones used the quick kick as another ploy, but Pappas wished he would have used the pass more.

"I loved to pass, but I didn't do much of it," Pappas says. "The rule at that time was you had to pass from five yards behind the line of scrimmage, and the second incomplete pass in a series of downs was a five-yard penalty. If you threw one pass and missed, you were not going to throw another."

With Pappas carrying the ball a lot of the time, Jones relied on safe, unelaborate plays.

"We used to run off tackle a lot," Pappas remembers. "Then we'd have a couple of plays where we'd go around the end. If the end was crashing, we'd try to run around him. If he was floating, we'd go inside. The way we blocked the play was that the fullback and the blocking back would take the end out and two guards would pull—one would go inside and one would go outside. The wingback and the end would take the tackle out, and the tailback, that's me, would hopefully find an open space.

"Jones used to tell us to run parallel to the line of scrimmage for two and a half steps, park the outside foot, and cut straight back. That gave the other guys a chance to do their job. Jones used to tell us, 'Run like you're going to shake hands with your girl in the stands.'"

No matter the game plan, though, Jones could not compensate for crowd noise. Road games were horrific for this reason. Recalling the unkind Notre Dame fans, Pappas shudders.

"We'd go to South Bend and that place holds 55,000—but there were always 60,000 or more in there," says Pappas, making a face of mock horror. "We might have had 5,000 fans there ourselves, but no more. It's a great scene, but, Jesus, you get that number of people, and it's awful trying to play there. They're constantly roaring—they keep it up all the time. If you get down within 15 yards of their goal line, you're going to have a hell of a tough time hearing signals. You're constantly stopping the game and going back into a huddle."

By the same token the Trojans' home field did not help them that much. Pappas explains:

"It's not the same at the Coliseum because it's a bigger park. The sections are a little bit more remote than at South Bend so you can't hear the noise that much. Back at South Bend, it's boom, they're right on top of you. Playing at Notre Dame was always brutal for us."

Ironically the same Trojan players who found distaste in Notre Dame methods later helped make a movie about the Fighting Irish with Pat O'Brien. In law school at the time, Pappas was called in as an extra.

"We worked in pictures every summer, used to make three or four football movies a year," says Pappas. "It was good money and no big labor. We made this one picture about Knute Rockne that I'll never forget. O'Brien was playing the part of Rockne, and he had the voice down pat. He had perfect makeup; his nose was flat anyway, and he looked exactly like him.

"We're filming the big pep talk scene. The guys are supposed to be in a locker room. All this is being done in a studio, on a sound stage, remember. They bring in O'Brien in a wheelchair, and he gives us a tremendous pep talk. And here are all these football players listening...they had been through a lot of these.

"O'Brien sounds so convincing and I'm getting all fired up along with the other actors, like it was a real game. I could feel myself grabbing the rubbing table I'm on. When O'Brien gets through, one guy says, 'Let's go.' It wasn't even in the script. And we roar off our seats and knock the whole set down! Honest to God. You know, we did the same thing the second time, and they had to shoot that scene three times before they could use it in the movie."

Pappas' football skills, honed by Howard Jones, were futher enhanced as a professional. He played briefly for a team in Hollywood. Pappas also worked as an assistant coach for the Southern Cal freshmen team in 1938 and 1939.

He became a World War II hero when he saved three lives in combat, coming home with the Bronze Star and Purple Heart. From 1953 to 1956 Pappas served as assistant coach on Southern Cal's varsity and later vaulted into administrative work.

Pappas was named alumni field secretary in 1957, Trojan Club director in 1959, and since 1962 has been director of the Athletic Support Groups at Southern Cal. He raises money to pay for athletic scholarships.

"I look for close to one-half million dollars every year," says Pappas. "But my job here is made easy because of what went before. Southern Cal has a great heritage and a great following."

Money-raising is done on a club basis, and you do not have to be a graduate of Southern Cal to join. Membership is based on the steepness of dues. For instance it takes a minimum of $1,000 a year to join the Associates, $500 for the Cardinal and Gold (Pappas' club), $100 for the Trojaneers, and $40 for the Trojan Club. A classier seat in the Coliseum, among other things, is a privilege enjoyed by the more exclusive club.

"Usually the first thing someone says to me when he joins is, 'Here's my $1,000—now where do I sit in the Coliseum?'" Pappas says. "Seats in the Coliseum are very, very important to them."

Not everybody can be satisfied, though. The Coliseum's makeup causes problems in seating arrangements. Of the 93,791 seats in the colossal arena, only 22,500 are between the goal lines. Some of the seats at each end of the field used to be 100 yards from the goal line before Southern Cal reconstructed them.

"It's still a tough problem," Pappas says. "You can't sit everybody on the 50-yard line, which is where everybody wants to sit. Those poor guys who pay $500 a year insist on sitting in second row, center."

Talking about his work, Pappas glows. He is eternally youthful, the kid with his first baseball glove, the eager boy with a new football.

"We've gone from zero membership in 1960 in Cardinal and Gold to 750," says Pappas, his eyes flashing. "So that's a pretty good piece of change. When I took over the Trojan Club, there were 550; now we have 2,500."

The clubs meet regularly during the football season, show game movies, and sometimes have "rap sessions" with Coach John McKay.

"The toughest thing to do in fund raising is to get the guy to give the first time," says Pappas. "Once he gives the first time, he'll give again."

The broad hands occasionally flap his tie. An animated man, Pappas rockets off his seat to greet a visitor, extends a friendly hand. He jokes with his two secretaries. He bolts coffee. He sweeps up a telephone and cradles it in his neck, talks, and waves visitors in at the same time.

The vista from his chic quarters reveals a rich panorama of campus life. The gorgeous sweep of Southern Cal University spreads below him. He has no time to look, though. Telephone calls and callers continually grip his attention.

"You'd be amazed at all the friends we have," Pappas says after hanging up from a long conversation with a Cardinal and Gold colleague. "In fact we have people who adopt us that are probably as rabid as any guy who went to school here. They're great people."

The boy from Washington had grown to a man now, and you could see that he was always meant to be a Trojan.

Frank Merriwell Arrives

After Doyle Nave threw a touchdown pass in the 1939 Rose Bowl game, he was awash in mail. More than 250 Dixie girls sent him proposals of marriage, and he received crush letters from ladies in such places as Omaha, Nebraska, Ellensburg, Washington, and Fairbanks, Pennsylvania. The mayor of Gordo, Alabama, dropped him a line, appointing Nave acting mayor of that municipality for January 16, 1939. A boy in Forestville, Connecticut, bedridden with infantile paralysis, asked for an autograph. And the National Association of the Deaf wanted a report confirming that Nave was hard of hearing. (He was not, of course.)

Normally a touchdown pass would not merit such attention—but the one that Nave completed was not a normal touchdown pass. He came off the bench in Frank Merriwell style in the last two minutes, and his dramatic pass helped Southern Cal beat Duke 7-3 on January 2, 1939.

Many years later a major magazine conducted a poll and found it to be the most thrilling bowl game ever played. That included not only the Rose Bowl but the Cotton, Sugar, and all the rest.

"I was nervous when I went in," Nave recalls today.

Nave had every right to be that way. He had been a reserve all season and played a total of 35 minutes and 22 seconds prior to the Rose Bowl game.

Grenville Lansdell, Mickey Anderson, and Ollie Day had all been used ahead of Nave at the position. Coach Howard Jones

Southern California quarterback Mickey Anderson runs into a Duke front wall in the 1939 Rose Bowl game. Doyle Nave later took over and showed how to do it.

admitted that Nave could pass but insisted that he lacked the all-around skills required for a quarterback.

Now came Duke, one of the nation's fiercest defensive teams.

"Duke had won every one of its games," Nave recalls. "They were not only undefeated, they were unscored upon. They were considered one of the greatest defensive teams then. We entered this game knowing well what sort of a team we were up against.

"They had Eric 'The Red' Tipton, a great punter. They would kick on first down deep in their territory if they had to. They played percentages and took advantage of breaks."

The Blue Devils finally got that break late in the game and worked the ball down to the 23-yard line. Tony Ruffa kicked a field goal on the second play of the fourth period to give Duke a 3-0 lead.

"His boot apparently sounded the death knell of Troy's fondest hopes," Braven Dyer wrote in the *Los Angeles Times*.

Everyone believed that. Then the rhythm of the game suddenly changed.

"We started fighting back," Nave says, his voice excited. "They fumbled, and we had the opportunity for a field goal with eight or nine minutes left. I thought Phil Gasper's kick was good, but the officials ruled it was wide to the right."

The Trojans later possessed the ball in superb field position.

"We had worked the ball to the 34-yard line when Jones put me in with about 2 minutes remaining," Nave recalls, "We then were penalized for too many timeouts, and the ball was put back on our 39."

Inexperienced but considered the best passer on the team, a shaken Nave was thrown into the biggest moment of his football life.

"Jones gave me a few minutes to warm up, and I was nervous, I'll tell you," Nave says. "He asked me what passes I could utilize. I thought the '27 Series' passes were the best. That's a pass to the left end on the short side. Al Krueger was the receiver I had in mind.

"I completed the first pass and made 12 yards on a button hook. That made it second down and 3 to go for a first down. The second pass was a '27' with a flair, and Al went down and did a pivot and broke to the outside. He caught that and gave us a first down."

The ball nuzzled near the left sideline, and Nave remembers, "We didn't have much room for Al to manuever in. We were on the left side, and Al was a left end. In those days the ball wasn't moved to the center of the field after a play. It was left exactly where the play ended. So we didn't have especially good field position even though we were closer to the goal."

Nave tried to move the ball closer to the center of the field on the next play.

"Krueger came behind the line of scrimmage and caught my third straight pass, but a Duke lineman picked him up and we lost a few yards," Nave says. "It was a '27 end-around' with Krueger. So we were down to second and 12 with very little time left."

Then Nave made history.

"We had about 50 seconds remaining," Nave recalls. "I told Al to get into the end zone in the corner, and I was hopeful we could hold the Duke team off. We called a '27 down-and-out.' When I got the ball, I faded way back over to the east side of the field. I was watching Al as he broke away from Eric Tipton. I threw the ball when he was on the 7 or 8-yard line heading for the left corner of the end zone.

"He had good hands, and I was praying that he could catch it—nothing's a sure thing in football. He made a terrific catch in the chest, and we just went berserk. We had 40 seconds remaining. We kicked to Duke. They tried to pass, they didn't have time to run. But they had no passing attack. And that was the game."

The famous touchdown play might never have happened, except for an intervening hand. Los Angeles sportswriter Maxwell Stiles revealed "strange events" that allowed Nave to come off the bench in the first place.

"The man who told me the inside story is Joe Wilensky, former Trojan running guard and tackle and an assistant coach at USC during the 1938 season," Stiles said.

In their book, *The Tournament of Roses*, Joe Hendrickson and Stiles reveal this story:

"Wilensky was manning the telephone on the bench,

relaying the messages of assistant coaches Sam Barry, Bob McNeish, and Julie Bescos, who had been observing the action high above in the press box. Suddenly Wilensky got an idea. He decided to take a chance to do something to pull out victory. He knew that the coaches above had already left the press box and were on their way to join the team. Nobody had scored a point all season against the great Duke line.

"'Our only chance is to get Nave in there to pass,' thought Wilensky. 'He has the arm to hit Krueger and dent this great Duke defense.' Wilensky snatched the phone. 'Yes,' he shouted so everybody on the bench could hear. 'Yes, yes—I get it. I'll tell him right away.' Wilensky slammed the receiver on the hook and excitedly nudged assistant coach Bill Hunter.

"'The word is to send in Nave and have him throw to Krueger,' said Wilensky to Hunter, who in turn passed it on to Jones. Nick Pappas, who helped Jones with the coaching and today is a member of the USC athletic administration staff, verifies that this is the true story of how Nave got into the game."

Once assuming control of the team, Nave had only Krueger in mind as a pass target. He was his favorite.

"Al was so clever when it came to breaking away from receivers that he was the most logical man to throw to," Nave says.

The Blue Devils had gone into a "prevent" defense, with many of their defenders placed strategically in the backfield to cut off long passes. Only one man rushed Nave.

"I felt sure that neither (Duke coach) Wallace Wade nor his players knew very much about Nave," said Clifton B. Herd, a Trojan scout. "If they had suspected his passing ability they would have rushed him more than they did. It looked to me as if Wade merely spread his defense, figuring that there wouldn't be time for the Trojans to score by running the ball. He wanted to be sure to pick up the receiver somewhere."

If the game was exciting, it was also controversial. The choice of Duke as a Rose Bowl team had been criticized in some quarters. Vociferous critics thought Texas Christian would have been a better choice. After the game Wade added more controversial fuel by slamming the Rose Bowl.

"This is a helluva place to bring a football team," Wade

said.

He also neglected to congratulate Nave, a subtle point that was not overlooked by angry writers.

But Nave himself defended the deflated Duke coach. Pointing to the pressures of an extremely tough loss and the fact that Wade's wife was seriously ill back home, Nave remarked:

"After all, he was preoccupied with the suddenness of Duke's defeat, and the one thing on his mind was to congratulate Coach Howard Jones. I wrote a letter to Mr. Wade...expressing my feelings. His reply is one of the most treasured possessions I have. During World War II I had a wonderful visit with him in his home. He is a fine man. I feel he was the victim of extremely poor taste."

Obscure before the touchdown pass, Nave became an instant celebrity. And Jones voted him a varsity letter on the spot, although the fourth-string quarterback was more than 100 minutes under the required playing time.

"He's played enough to win anything he wants from me," said the beaming Southern Cal coach in the joyous dressing room. "Sure, it includes a letter. (Actually the Athletic Board later officially voted Nave the letter in a special dispensation.)"

Appreciative for the opportunity to play, Nave expressed his gratitude to Jones. Wearing a wide piece of tape on his forehead from a pregame injury, Nave approached his coach in the dressing room and held out a hand.

"Thanks for the chance, coach," Nave said.

"No, Doyle, it is I who thank you," said Jones, "I hope that what you just did out there will make up for the rest of the season. I tell you, this was worth waiting for."

Blushing, Nave answered: "It surely was."

Later, Jones analyzed the game.

"Granny Lansdell was going great in those last few minutes, and I think that had there been more time he might have scored," the coach said. "But our only chance was to pass, and Nave is the best passer I have on the squad. I knew that Nave was the only man we had who might win the game for us at that time, and so I sent him out there and told him to get at least one of them off to Krueger."

The anonymous Nave made a lot of friends with his

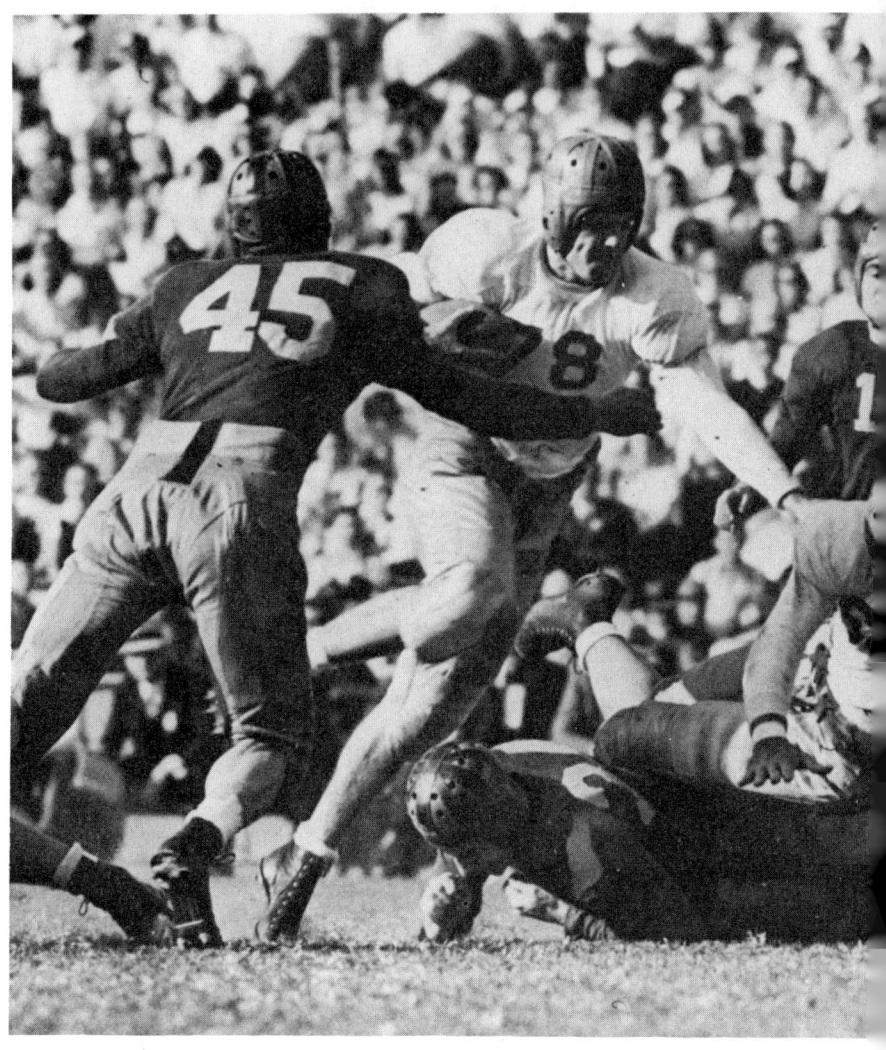

touchdown pass. One was Dr. Norman Topping, Southern Cal's chancellor, who recalls that the victory had theraputic value while he was hospital-bound.

"I was in quarantine in a hospital," Dr. Topping said later. "I had Rocky Mountain Spotted Fever, running a temperature of 105. I was dying, they had given up on me. No visitors, not even my wife. I wasn't aware of much else, but I asked for a radio to listen to the Rose Bowl game between USC and Duke.

"They said it was impossible. I insisted, demanding that

Southern California's Grenny Lansdell powers off tackle against California in 1938. Clearing his way is Trojan tackle Howard Stoecker. Southern Cal beat the tough Bears, 13-7.

they grant my last request. They brought me a radio. And then when Doyle Nave threw those passes to Al Krueger to beat Duke in the final minute, something remarkable happened. A miracle. It did more for me than any medicine. My temperature immediately started going down. I recovered. I also won $50 on the game."

Sports Editor Braven Dyer of the *Los Angeles Times*, a man who had vainly championed Nave's cause all season, ironically missed his protege's golden moment because of a newspaper deadline. Dyer, who had written publicly to Jones to "give my boy Doyle Nave a chance," was not there when he finally got it.

Dyer explained in the *Times*: "I had left with four minutes of the game remaining because somebody has to get out the paper. I was just pulling out in my chariot when over the radio came this announcement: 'Nave is back—he's going to pass—he's throwing the ball—it's in the end zone and it's complete to Krueger for a TOUCHDOWN!' There is no truth in the dastardly report that I promptly fainted at the wheel. The three gentlemen with me will testify that I kept right on driving into town just as if nothing had happened. The hell I did—I let out a yell which all but shattered the windshield and promptly began jabbering like an idiot. The gridirony of it all practically slays me."

Dyer did get to see the play eventually, though. Several weeks later he saw movies of the game and "noticed something that I might not have seen had I been there...that Krueger's marvelous catching was just as important as Doyle's accurate pitching. I have never seen a better job of snaring passes than the movies attributed to Al."

A few years later, during the Second World War, Nave produced a story attached to the memorable game. Nave was an officer on an aircraft carrier in the Marianas when he ran into an old acquaintance.

"I met Dan Hill, the fellow who played center and captained the Duke team against us," Nave says. "Naturally we had a lot of fun hashing over that game. During our talk I asked Dan, 'When I came into the game did you have any idea that I was going to pass?' Hill answered, 'Hell, no, we didn't even know who you were.'"

This game, possessed of poetry, almost did not happen. The appearance of both Southern Cal and Duke was an unlikelihood at one stage of the 1938 season.

The Trojans were soundly beaten 19-7 by Alabama on opening day ("Southern Cal actually looked much worse than the final score indicated," offered a sportswriter.) And later the Trojans were defeated 7-6 by Washington. ("They beat us much worse than the score reveals," said a follower of Southern Cal.) Southern Cal wound up in a tie with California for the Pacific

Coast Conference championship, each with 6-1 records. Finally the Trojans got the bid because they had beaten California that year. (The choice was further enhanced when Southern Cal closed out its regular season by beating a strong Notre Dame team, 13-0. That prevented the Fighting Irish from winning the national championship.)

A strong, if disjointed, bid was made for Texas Christian's appearance in the Rose Bowl. Los Angeles newspapers were bombarded by phone calls and telegrams from Texas asking to support the team. Texas Christian backers also contacted the governor of California and members of the state legislature. They intruded on big railroad and oil men, imploring them to use their influence in TCU's favor. One Texan sent turkeys as Thanksgiving Day presents to Los Angeles sportswriters. Dutch Meyer, the TCU coach, was quoted as saying: "We definitely want the Rose Bowl assignment and hope it comes our way."

But if Southern Cal authorities had first looked with favor on the Horned Frogs, they were soon turned off by this bombast.

"I do know that Trojan authorities gradually began to resent this brazen attempt to land the lucrative Rose Bowl nomination," said Dyer. "Bill Hunter, USC's director of athletics, began to look elsewhere for a foe."

When the choice of Duke was announced on November 28, Texas Christian was bitterly disappointed. "I am deeply sorry our boys couldn't go to the Rose Bowl," said Meyer. "My boys wanted it so badly."

The Southern Cal logic was obvious.

"Trojan authorities felt that they couldn't retain their self-respect as an educational institution if they succumbed to the pressure exerted by well-meaning friends of Texas Christian," Dyer later explained. "Never in all football history have I known of such a brazen attempt to land a game."

As it turned out, the Southern Cal officials were not sorry that they picked Duke. As a matter of fact, neither was Doyle Nave.

A $120,000 Kiss For Your Sister

Ned Matthews had 10 seconds to make up his mind while the persistent roars of 103,000 passionate fans filled the Los Angeles Coliseum. "Pass," the UCLA quarterback decided and led his team to the line of scrimmage.

The ball was five yards from Southern California's goal line when UCLA star Kenny Washington threw to Bob MacPherson in the end zone. Bobby Robertson flashed in front of MacPherson and knocked the ball to the ground. The roars swelled.

That aborted play turned out to be an expensive one for UCLA. It cost the Bruins a chance to beat Southern Cal and an invitation to the Rose Bowl, which was worth about $120,000 to each competing team.

By the same token the Trojans had salvaged a scoreless tie with UCLA. It was a little better than kissing your sister, as they say, because the tie vaulted Southern Cal into the December 9, 1939, bowl game with Tennessee.

The Trojans were actually lucky to come out of the game with a tie. Most everyone in the Coliseum knew that Matthews had called the wrong play. A field goal would have been safer and insured a victory for UCLA.

The Bruins actually had four cracks at the Trojan goal and failed. Coach Babe Horrell's team had driven the ball 76 yards in the last minutes of that exciting game and had every expectation of scoring.

Matthews, who had played a brilliant game all day, made

the wrong decisions in the end.

With first down and goal to go on the Southern Cal four-yard line, Matthews called for Washington to drive into the middle of the Trojan line. The halfback got nowhere.

On second down Matthews ordered Leo Cantor to slant over right tackle. He got two yards.

On third down Matthews called the same play. This time Cantor was thrown for a three-yard loss back to the five.

In the huddle for the fourth down Matthews called for a vote on the next play. Five players wanted to try a field goal, and five others opted for a touchdown. It was up to Matthews to cast the tie-breaking vote, and he decided on that pass.

"I considered sending a man in to call for a kick just before we made that first down on the four," said Horrell later. "But when my boys made the first down I changed my mind. After all, these kids were doing pretty well without my help.

Southern California's Grenny Lansdell is stopped by UCLA's Bill Overlin during the famous scoreless tie game of 1939. UCLA star Kenny Washington (No. 13) closes in on the play.

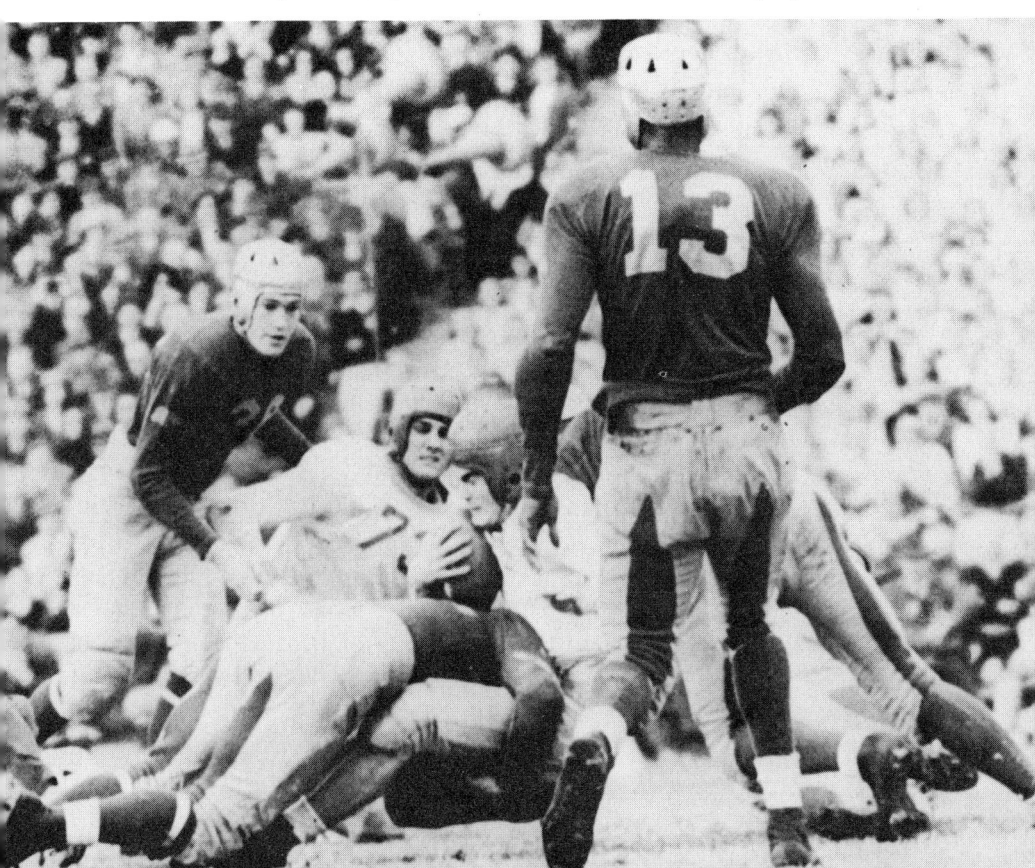

Anything Matthews did from then on was good enough for me."

The hero of the 1939 Rose Bowl victory over Duke, Doyle Nave, was a safety man for Southern Cal in this game. He was braced in the end zone, overly concerned, during UCLA's final drive.

"I really was worried," Nave said afterward. "I was trying to figure what I'd do if they tried a pass to Woody Strode, the big end. He was the man I was assigned to cover. Woody stands about six-five, you know, and I'm under six feet. I couldn't figure any way I could stop him from catching a high pass if they threw to him. Well, I was lucky. They didn't throw at him at all. I sure breathed a sigh of relief when it was over."

Southern Cal's goal line stand was a poetic finish to a game of building excitement. The Trojans themselves missed several golden scoring chances. On one play in particular, quarterback Grenville Lansdell fumbled the ball while going over the UCLA goal line in the first period. That gave the ball to the Bruins. The Trojans also had the ball on the UCLA 22 when Lansdell fumbled again. Another time they got as far as the 25 before dying.

Washington and Jackie Robinson, UCLA's other fine runner, created problems for the Southern Cal defense all day. In the fading minutes it was Washington and Robinson who spearheaded the Bruin drive deep into Trojan territory. But, ironically, neither got the call to run for the fateful last down.

"It was one of the cleanest, yet most bitter struggles in Coliseum history," wrote Paul Zimmerman of the *Los Angeles Times*. "In the dressing rooms, Bruins and Trojans were mingling after the contest to congratulate each other on fine play, which is the finest display of sportsmanship anyone could ask of this torrid crosstown rivalry. In the final analysis, there was nothing wrong with this ball game—but the final score."

If the score did not please Zimmerman, it was very satisfying to the Trojans. Aggressive at the start of the game, the Southern Cal power waned at the end, and the Trojans seemed to be very content with a tie. The decision provided the Trojans with the championship of the Pacific Coast Conference and a place in the Rose Bowl. On the verge of beating Southern Cal for the first time in history and landing a lucrative bowl bid at the same time, the bitterly-disappointed Bruins were forcibly retired from the limelight by the powerful Trojan defense.

Other teams suffered as well that year. After a 7-7 tie with Oregon to open the season, Southern Cal won seven games before meeting UCLA. The Trojans shut out four of their opponents and allowed as much as twelve points to only one team, Notre Dame. Part of the strength of that defense rested in the colossal figure of Harry Smith, a brutalizing 211-pound guard. "Harry stalked the ballcarrier from all points of the field," says an observer. "He was like a bull gifted with wings and had one of the keenest football brains ever in the line."

Smith was not only an imposing defensive force but an offensive monster as well. Big, fast, and aggressive, Smith was peerless among running guards. He made all-America teams both in 1938 and 1939 and later was voted into the National Football Hall of Fame.

Along with Smith, Lansdell was another all-American produced by Southern Cal in 1939. He, too, was Jones' pride.

"I've had few backs at Southern California as valuable and as versatile as Grenny," Jones remarked. "He combines power through the line with trickiness and speed in the open field. There's never been a more deadly straight arm. He deserves to be rated as one of the greatest backs in the history of football."

Accompanying Smith and Lansdell on a wonderfully balanced team were players of all-star caliber—ends Al Krueger, Bill Fisk, and Bob Winslow, tackles Phil Gaspar and Howard Stoecker, guard Ben Sohn, center Ed Dempsey and Nave, who showed in 1939 that he could run as well as pass. These players received constant acclaim from their opponents.

After the Trojans crushed California 26-0, Golden Bear Coach Stub Allison said: "We were playing to win and I thought we could. That is the best Southern California team I have seen. I'll have to hand it to the Trojan coaches; they had their boys ready."

A 19-7 decision over Oregon State produced this extravagant comment from Beaver Coach Lon Stiner: "At Nebraska, I played against Notre Dame's famous 'four horsemen' and 'seven mules,' against Illinois when Red Grange was his hottest and against Washington with George Wilson hammering from short-punt formation. And I've seen all the great teams of the Pacific

Southern California's Grenny Lansdell leaps over a mass of bodies to pick up three yards against Notre Dame in 1939. The

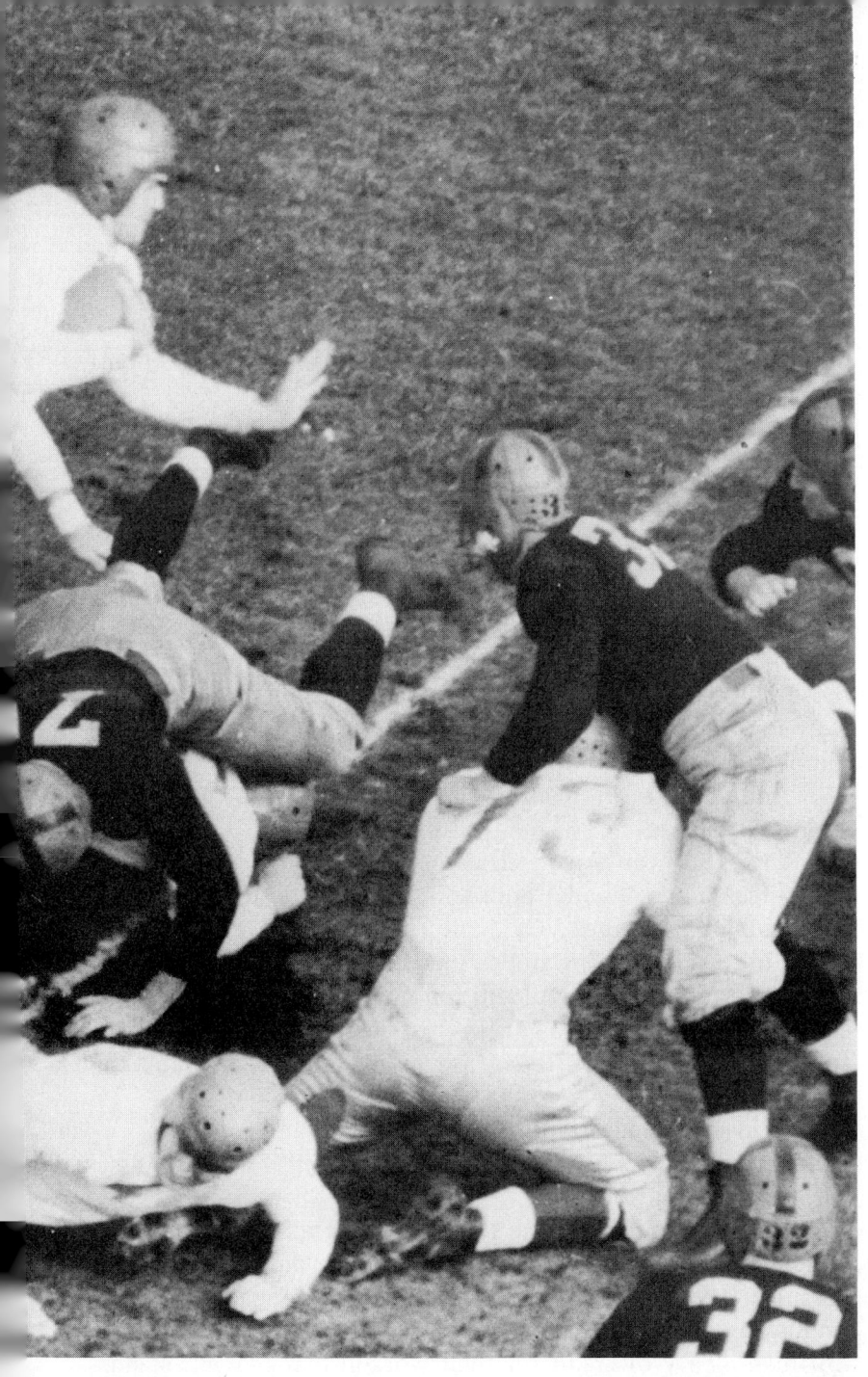

Trojans endured, 20-12.

Coast since 1928.

"All I can say is that the Trojans who beat us Saturday were better than all these other great ones—the greatest team I ever saw. I rate them not just because of their tremendous manpower, but because of their beautiful balance between their powerful running attack and brilliant passing. The Trojans who beat us are a much better team than the Trojans of 1933, whom our Oregon State 'iron men' tied 0 to 0."

The gambling fraternity also thought glowingly of Southern Cal and made the Trojans a big favorite over UCLA in their game of importance. The result shattered some illusions about Southern Cal, but Jones was quick to explain afterwards:

"UCLA was a much improved football team over its showing in the previous games in which I saw them, and the Trojans seemingly were not up to their physical peak so the result was a scoreless tie. My boys took quite a pounding in those Notre Dame and Washington games (Southern Cal beat Notre Dame 20-12 and Washington 9-7). And Smith, Sohn, Winslow, and Lansdell were far from in top shape."

And UCLA of course had Washington, a player of enormous talents.

"You just can't get a clear shot at Washington when you try to tackle him," said a Southern Cal player in the post-game discussions. "Just when you think you've got him cornered, he does a lot of hip-wiggling and gets away."

Suffering from shoulder and thumb injuries, Lansdell could not hold the ball with his customary strength. He apologized for fumbling away a sure touchdown in that first quarter.

"I'm sorry, coach," he said to Jones.

Jones took his hand and reacted warmly: "Forget it. You played a fine game."

UCLA acclaim filled the Trojan dressing room. Said Smith: "They're a tough team, but don't think we didn't know it in advance. It was a clean game all the way through, and those Bruins are a fine bunch to play against. Give Ben Sohn and Bob Hoffman plenty of credit for their work in that goal line stand. They were the ones that stopped 'em."

The Trojans were instantly selected for the Rose Bowl by Pacific Coast Conference members. Their record of 8-0-2 to

UCLA's 6-0-4 clinched the invitation. And Southern Cal just as quickly invited Tennessee to be the Eastern guest. (Coach Bob Neyland accepted "with pleasure.")

More luster was added to the season when the Trojans were named the national champions by the Dickinson System, one of the major rating services of the day. While just about everyone else picked Texas A&M that year, Professor Frank G. Dickinson decided on Southern Cal through a complicated point system that rated opponents' strength.

"The Trojans were the best team in the best section," said Professor Dickinson, who taught economics at Illinois. "USC was barely able to nose out undefeated Texas A&M."

Tennessee was selected No. 5 in the Dickinson System, a good choice considering what happened in the Rose Bowl game.

Although the Vols had a 23-game winning streak going, and were unscored upon in 1939, the bigger, stronger Trojans handled them with ease. Ambrose Schindler, a second-stringer at Southern Cal, ran and passed through Tennessee's supposedly immovable defense, and the Trojans won, 14-0.

"We weren't stale or off form," Neyland said afterward. "We were outclassed. We were badly beaten by a superior team, and my hat is off to Howard Jones."

The Trojans had beaten a team of reputation. The Vols' Rose Bowl squad included a clutch of all-Americans—guards Ed Molinsky and Bob Suffridge, quarterback George Cafego, and halfback Bobby Foxx. Each was outplayed by his counterpart. Schindler, especially, damaged Tennessee's reputation. He had a hand in both Southern Cal touchdowns, scoring one and passing for the other.

Cafego was the symbol of Tennessee's futility that day. Suffering from an injury, the quarterback was taken out for a replacement. "I couldn't have done any good against those big guys anyway," he admitted later.

The victory not only preserved Jones' perfect Rose Bowl record but predictably raised views of West Coast superiority. Henry McLemore of the United Press, for one, slammed Tennessee with this whimsical review of the game:

"They raise them rugged out here. Perhaps nature sees that they do so in order that they will be able to withstand earthquakes, unusual weather, and the taste of the water that comes out of the taps. There is a lesson to be learned from this Rose Bowl game. There is no sense in betting on a team that buys its clothes in the boys' department to beat a team that has to shave twice a day and is fitted for suits in the adult or grown-up section."

It was Jones' last hurrah. The Smiths and the Lansdells departed after the 1939 season and left Southern Cal in comparative poverty.

In 1940 the Trojans won only three games, lost four, and tied two. On July 27, 1941, Jones died of a heart attack, and some life went out of Southern Cal, too. Quite fittingly his last game was a close loss to Notre Dame, a team that had provided him with some of his toughest victories and defeats. Bill Earley batted down a Southern Cal pass in the end zone at the last second, and Notre Dame won, 10-6.

The death of Jones cost football a dear friend.

"With his passing, there ended an era of football in the West," said Los Angeles sportswriter Maxwell Stiles. "No man ever brought so much gridiron glory to the southern section of California. No man ever gave more of himself to the game he loved. To him, football was the first bright rays of dawn, the noonday sky, and the stars that shine by night. To him, football was a creed and he kept it clean and pure. Good sportsmanship and perfect execution of assignments on the field of play were sacred, and woe to any player on his team who failed to measure up to the full degree of either standard."

His death not only signaled the end of a monarch's reign but the finish of a school's monopoly. The city of Los Angeles now belonged to both Southern Cal and UCLA, for the Bruins were becoming more popular. The Trojans no longer would dominate the southern California area as before, would no longer be the only game in town. The 1940s not only brought war to the world, but a renaissance to football.

Howard Jones was gone, and the Trojans' brave, new world belonged to Sam Barry.

War And Pieces

In the opening game of the 1941 season between UCLA and Washington six members of a Southern Cal fraternity furtively joined the Bruin rooters. After the game they helped UCLA students load their Victory Bell into a truck for the trip back to the Westwood campus.

One of the Southern Cal students stole the truck keys. And while the UCLA students went for another set, the Trojans drove off with the truck and the bell. The theft of the 295-pound locomotive clanger and the subsequent search made the bell a fighting symbol between Southern Cal and UCLA.

For more than a year it was hidden, first in the Hollywood Hills and then in a Santa Ana haystack. The police were called in on the search, but were just as unlucky as UCLA students in finding the object. After a series of cross-town raids, the student body presidents of both schools met to negotiate an end to the search. Southern Cal agreed to return the bell—on the condition that it would be a permanent game trophy.

The next year Southern Cal lost it back to UCLA.

Beaten for the first time by the Bruins, 14-7, the Trojans came to a stark realization that the city of Los Angeles no longer belonged to them. Forever the king of southern California, the Trojans now reigned with another. The Victory Bell caper symbolized this new co-existence. And compared to other tom-foolery between UCLA and USC students, it was relatively tame.

Starting in the 1940s, Southern Cal-UCLA games transcended the football field and split the city of Los Angeles in half. UCLA was a football power on the rise, and Southern Cal was coming back down to earth after the Howard Jones years.

The fierceness of this unique rivalry was mirrored in campus pranks. The week after the football teams played to a 7-7 tie in 1941, a vicious scrimmage took place between students of UCLA and Southern Cal.

When four Southern Cal students took the locomotive bell over to the UCLA campus, they were pulled from their truck, dragged before the student body, and had their heads shaven. Later a large procession of UCLA students, who had attended a victory rally on the Westwood campus, drove their honking cars to a downtown Los Angeles intersection and blocked traffic for hours with varied stunts. Accompanying them was the school band.

Later in the day Southern Cal students got even for the UCLA indignities. When 20 carloads of UCLA students invaded the Trojan campus with the taunt, "Rose Bowl, here we come! Ex-Trojans, we're sorry for you!" they paid for it.

Irate Southern Cal students dragged their UCLA counterparts through a series of humiliations. They shaved their heads and painted "SC" on their skulls. They forced them to clean blue paint off the Tommy Trojan statue. (UCLA students had previously painted the Trojan symbol with the Bruins' color.) And they dumped them into a fish pond with the chant, "Fish Bowl, here we come!"

UCLA females were treated with disdain, although not as harshly molested as the males. They had their heads dunked. "Automobile spark plugs were pulled, motor hoods were ripped off, tires were deflated, and a jeep was pushed squarely in the middle of the fish pond," a newspaper reported.

Limping past police riot cars UCLA students promised: "We'll be back tomorrow—wait."

Since that raucous 1941 scene, this special rivalry reached innovative heights. Head-shaving was cut out after a while, giving way to sophistication. In later years mice were released in the UCLA library, a bomb went off in the UCLA rooting section, and the Trojan horse, Traveler, was painted blue. Tommy Trojan, the proud symbol of Southern Cal athletics, was an obvious victim. UCLA students painted him, dropped fertilizer on his nose from a helicopter, and welded his own sword into his back.

Campus frenzy became icily scientific when it pertained to Southern Cal and UCLA. Southern Cal "spies" infiltrated UCLA one season and schemed to disrupt the Bruins' card stunts at football games. A red-and-gold "SC" appeared in one corner of each card stunt picture, much to the puzzlement of UCLA students.

Another time, Southern Cal students pulled off an imaginative electronic job.

"How they did it, I don't know," says Athletic Support Groups director Nick Pappas. "But they somehow got into the classroom speaker system at UCLA. These guys wired into several of the buildings. Then, every 15 minutes or so, they'd play tapes of the Southern Cal fight song. At intervals, 'Fight On For Old SC' would blare through the UCLA campus. Oh, it just drove them crazy."

Dan Berger, a sportswriter for the Associated Press in Los Angeles, remembers another devious Southern Cal plot.

"The shop that printed the *Daily Bruin* at UCLA was invaded, stories were stolen and rewritten, pictures and captions were changed, and a bogus edition was printed by Southern Cal students," Berger says. "Then the Trojan pranksters kidnapped the truck driver who delivered the UCLA papers and replaced the genuine with the phonies. When UCLA students opened their daily paper the next day, they read the team's star quarterback saying, 'I'd feel much better about our chances against those terrific Trojans if we had a couple of players who understood the game.' The coach added, 'I can't see any hope for our team.'"

This type of sabotage is understandable considering the proximity of the schools and the passions involved. These games have usually been the emotional pinnacle of every season.

"You have to beat UCLA," says Pappas. "It's better for us to live in this town if we do."

The fandom is a unique species. Says one writer whimsically: "They are physically normal except for their mouths. Their mouths and what comes out of them defy description. The only thing known for sure about a USC-UCLA fan's mouth is that it is some kind of a cross between those of an army drill instructor and a circus barker."

There is the story of the ecstatic fan who poured green confetti on his hot dog and threw pickle relish into the air when his team scored. And a fellow who dislocated his shoulder trying to hurl a roll of toilet paper from one end of the field to the 50-yard line. And another who shaved the letters "USC" on his chest and wore them proudly until the temperature dropped to 45 degrees. He quickly turned to a UCLA shade of blue.

"They have supplies of confetti, toilet paper, signs, buttons, original cheers and, of course, heartening beverages," says an observer about these unruly fans. "The eccentric fan might even have a pair of binoculars and a program to follow the game with."

The USC-UCLA games are normally reserved for the last part of the schedule, lending more drama to the season. But during one abnormal period of the Second World War, the Trojans and Bruins uniquely played two games a season—one at the start and the other at the end. This was, of course, due to wartime limitations on travel. The appeal of the game was hardly lessened by overexposure. Monster crowds witnessed the events each season from 1943 through 1945, and the last year was especially successful in terms of crowd lure. In the first game of 1945, 81,000 fans attended the USC-UCLA game, and in the second there were more than 100,000 witnesses.

In forthcoming years Trojan-Bruin games would decide Rose Bowl berths and sometimes national championships. In 1941, however, their tie decided nothing other than the fact that UCLA was in the same league with Southern Cal. A down season for the Trojans, Sam Barry had taken over as head football coach after the death of Howard Jones and struggled to win two games. One of the victories was a 13-7 upset over Rose Bowl-bound Oregon State, and one of the six losses was a 20-18 thriller to heavily-favored Notre Dame.

In his defense Barry had been thrust into an uncomfortable position. The predominance of his work until that point had been basketball and baseball, two sports in which he continually turned out championship teams at Southern Cal.

A prep and collegian star of the highest order in Wisconsin, Justin McCarthy (Sam) Barry became both teacher and administrator in 1918 at Knox College in Galesburg, Illinois. He was named athletic director and coach of football, basketball, baseball, and track. While at Knox, McCarthy was befriended by Jones when the "Head Man" was at Iowa. Later when the Hawkeyes needed a basketball and baseball coach and an assistant in football, McCarthy was hired at Iowa upon Jones' recommendation.

Barry's fate once more was entwined with his friend when Howard Jones moved to Southern Cal. When Leo Calland resigned as the Trojan basketball coach in 1929, Jones' recommendation brought Barry to California. On Jones' recommendation Southern Cal President Rufus B. von KleinSmid signed Barry as head basketball and baseball coach and assistant football coach.

Barry specialized in basketball and baseball champions and was a superb helpmate in football.

"During his 12 years on the football staff under the 'Head Man,' Barry performed a variety of chores," explains sports publicist Al Wesson, confidante of both Jones and Barry. "Jones considered him particularly valuable for his scouting work and gave him many of his toughest scouting assignments. The 'Head Man,' famous for the strong defensive play of his teams as well as for their potent offense, always gave Sam plenty of credit for his skill in working out strategy to stop the squads that Barry had scouted.

"On the practice field under Jones, Barry usually worked with the Spartans, which is the polite name for the Trojan 'goof squad.' This group, which couldn't make the varsity grade, would learn the plays of the opposition and would also learn the opponents' defensive style under Barry. This team would scrimmage the varsity. Besides developing a squad that would give the varsity valuable scrimmage drill, Barry was always on the lookout for varsity material in what he called his 'Tigers,' and many of Southern Cal's greatest stars were discovered and developed by Barry from among this group of 'goofs.'"

But when Barry took over the team not many of these stars were left. As a matter of fact, there were not too many coaches around, either. Some of the assistants had left for more lucrative jobs elsewhere, and Barry had to search for teachers as well as pupils. He kept a stiff upper lip through it all, however.

"The job has been simplified by the fact that Howard

Jones set up our 1941 style of play during the last spring practice," said Barry optimistically. "All I have to do, therefore, is follow through with the system as outlined by Jones... carrying on as best I might without him."

Barry's best was not good enough. A sportswriter harshly pointed that out in the *Los Angeles Examiner*.

"The Trojans have stopped having representative football teams because they've stopped having representative football players," wrote Davis J. Walsh. "They haven't had the semblance of a breakaway runner in the last two years, nor has there been anybody on the squad who has been outstanding in more than a cursory few departments of play."

The losing year was not a wasted year as far as Barry was concerned. He whistled while he worked, even though he may have thought he was whistling in the dark.

"Congeniality, humor, and plenty of laughs punctuate the meetings of Trojan coaches as they map out work each day," wrote George T. Davis in the *Los Angeles Evening Herald and Express*. "They are hard-working, too, but never to the extent of taking themselves too seriously. Sam Barry is the kind of coach who inspires friendship and cooperation among his assistants without being a stern taskmaster in any sense of the word. And, through all the meetings one can sense the loyalty and admiration for the late Howard Jones as the motivating current."

The ghost of Jones could not help the lamentable Trojans in 1941, however. Things got progressively worse after Southern Cal opened the season by beating Oregon State on Ray Woods' 25-yard touchdown pass to Doug Essick in the last 13 seconds. The Trojans not only battled football teams, but injuries and illness as well.

Disfavored by the fates, Trojan spirit was bent, but not broken.

"I've coached a lot of teams in many branches of sports, but I've never seen a gang of athletes who refuse to become discouraged when breaks go against them like this year's squad," said Barry. "Injuries and illness have plagued us since the start of the season and at one time we had only 28 varsity players—an all-time low—out for practice. But what was lacked in manpower was made up by the fighting spirit of those who survived the injury 'jinx.' Believe me, it's a pleasure to coach boys of this caliber, and they deserve a few good breaks of their own to offset those that have gone against them. And if we do get 'em—watch us go."

But there were few golden moments in store for the Trojans. Observers found appalling weaknesses in Southern Cal football. Said one writer after a 33-0 loss to Ohio State:

"The Troys were so flagrantly bad all day that the crowd could barely believe the evidence of its eyes. They couldn't run with the ball. They couldn't stop the other guys, either running or with their passing. They, the Troys, hardly put a respectable block on the other side and, as for tackling, that seemed to be something with which they had very trivial liason...something very dire has happened to the University of Southern California in the last two years."

Southern Cal would have been even worse in 1941 without the services of Bobby Robertson, a gifted, all-purpose back nicknamed the "baby-faced assassin" by writers. The explosive Robertson, playing an average of 51 minutes a game, led the Pacific Coast Conference in total offense with 969 yards. He finished second to Stanford star Frankie Albert for all-coast honors.

Barry cherished Robertson for his durability and versatility.

"He's a battler," said the Southern Cal coach. "He runs. He kicks well. He passes. He blocks. He tackles—and he loves to play. I don't know what else you can ask from a back."

Robertson's fiercely competitive nature was evidenced in the Trojans' 7-6 victory over Washington State. Knocked out two times in the game, Robertson had to be argued into leaving the field. When he reached the sidelines he said: "What's the matter? I got a little knock. Give me a smell of that stuff, and I'll be all right." Robertson took a deep breath of smelling salts and rushed back into the game.

Such courage was the hallmark of the 1941 Trojans. But the season was a disappointment, laughably dismissed in a remark by comedian Bob Hope. He insisted, tongue in cheek, that the Trojans were not going to the Rose Bowl because they did not want to.

"Southern Cal beat Oregon State in the first game to show

its power, but eased up because it didn't want to fight the traffic to Pasadena on New Year's Day," joked Hope.

A deplorable season did not discourage fan support, however. While getting beat 13-0 by Stanford, the Trojans made a killing at the box office. A crowd of 86,305 paid to see the game at the Coliseum, and this figure set a national attendance record for 1941. The former high mark of the year was 85,753 at the Minnesota-Michigan game.

At the finish of the imperfect year Barry was given a backhanded vote of confidence. Commenting on the rumor that coaching luminary Jock Sutherland would be the next boss at Southern Cal, Athletic Director Willis O. Hunter said:

"There is absolutely not one iota of truth in the story about Sutherland being sounded out by us. It's not the first time that Sutherland has been mentioned as a possibility to coach football at Southern California. There never was anything to it, and there is nothing now."

President Rufus B. von KleinSmid, the gentle, white-haired patriarch of Southern Cal, was more pointed: "Sam Barry will be with us a long, long time. He has done a good job, and we hope that he will be with us many years more."

But von KleinSmid had not counted on wartime invasions. Barry was called away to the service, leaving the field open for Jeff Cravath.

Jeff Cravath begins his first season as coach of Southern California's football team with spring practice in 1942. He stressed speed and passing and introduced a new life style to Trojan football.

Time Out: Jeff Cravath

For some, he was a friend. For others, an enemy. Jeff Cravath was either adored or despised, idolized or held in contempt, but never forgotten.

Everyone who knew the Southern Cal football coach from 1942 through 1950 found extravagantly different qualities in the man.

"He believed in courage and had a tough, hard philosophy," says Don Clark, who played for Cravath in the 1940s and later became head coach himself. "He built character, but there were personal sacrifices that had to be made. Football was blended into a singular force on a Cravath team."

Clark, particularly, discovered two facets of Cravath.

"Jeff in his first year was very impressive and did an excellent job of coaching, and we had a great relationship," Clark remembers. "But when I later came back from the service in 1946, our philosophies had changed. His attitudes were different than mine. We had such a great relationship before I went away, but when I came back the whole climate was different. I didn't respond to him. I think he changed.

"Jeff had a hard time dealing with the ex-servicemen. They were a different type of individual, I guess, than the young, immature college boy. Another thing. He was not able to get into the service, and he might have had bad feelings toward people who did make it. So I saw both sides of him."

Clark found him unyielding.

"Jeff believed very strongly in doing things one way and

that was to go out and take the challenges of life head-on," says Clark. "He applied this to football. He never believed in open space, just running over the opposition. As a result certain types of players could not work in that environment."

Jim Hardy, who also played in the 1940s, remembers a funereal football scene under Cravath. The controversial coach was a victim of circumstance.

"It just wasn't fun after the war," he says. "There were a number of guys who came back to USC after World War Two...so many good football players. It was a particularly tough period to handle all this talent. Some of the players were particularly upset because they couldn't play. There was a conflict of personalities, too. And Cravath had a lot of talented, unhappy guys on his hands."

Hardy personally found Cravath heroic.

"He was a terrific guy, dedicated to the game and to coaching," Hardy recalls. "He loved USC and was a fierce competitor, an old-school type. He helped guys in and out of school as well as in football. I had an especially warm rapport with him."

An associate of Cravath's considered him a detriment to Southern Cal's football program, despite the fact that he had a 54-28-8 record in nine years and led the Trojans to four Rose Bowls. "He was a good guy, but he could get upset and eat people out," the associate says. "Instead of making players better, he made them worse. I don't think he was a big league coach."

But if Cravath had his detractors, he had his loyal supporters, too. People like Frank Gifford, John Ferraro, and George Davis revered the complex Cravath.

Gifford, who played two of his three years under Cravath, found him to be a "terrific guy" and eventually named his first son after him. John Ferraro, four years under the Cravath wing, discovered "a great person...a good psychologist..."

"Jeff lived football," says Ferraro. "He was very tough on the field, but he was warm and big-hearted off it. I loved him dearly and learned a lot of things about life from him."

Davis, who played three seasons for Cravath, says, "He was good for me."

"Outside of my father, he had the greatest influence on my life," says Davis. "I didn't think so at the time, but he really cared for the kids and for the principles of the game. He was a very moral man, a totally dedicated man. I had nothing but total respect for Cravath."

It was predictable that Cravath's harsh military style would

En route to an Ohio State game Southern California's football team stops off in Chicago's Union Station. Jeff Cravath (seated, center) takes a time out with some players and coaches. Left to right, front row: halfback Mickey McArdle, fullback Paul Taylor, Cravath, halfback Jim Musick, and quarterback Bill Bleeker. Coaches Shelby Calhoun and Gus Shaver stand behind Cravath.

produce scattered reaction. Life is never easy under a martinet.

"I can tell you stories about Cravath's practices that would really shock you," says Davis. "One time we went up to Ohio State and got beaten. They were good, but Cravath didn't think we played well. We took a train back and stopped over at Texas-El Paso University on the way home. Cravath wanted us to practice.

"We got there about 2 o'clock in the afternoon, and there were some Texas-El Paso players practicing, but not too hard. They did everything that they had to do, showered and came out in their street clothes, and we were still practicing. One of their guys said to me: 'Gee, do you always practice that hard?' That killed the West Texas area as a recruiting point for Southern Cal football. We were practicing so hard, that one of our guys got sick and threw up in the huddle. It was tough."

Cravath's steely character is further illuminated in this story told by Davis in his book, *The Fifth Down*, written with Neil Amdur:

"Stanford once ran back two punts against us in 1949, when the new punt returns with the wall blocking and reverse hand-offs first came in. They did something against us which we had not seen and were not prepared for. The result was that we scrimmaged punt returns for forty-five minutes the following Monday. The first team went out against the second team, and each was ordered to punt on first down during what was otherwise a game situation. At the end of the scrimmage, guys were crawling up and down the field between the two punters, unable to get back to the huddle before Cravath would run in and say, 'Center it, and kick again.'"

In another part of his book Davis writes: "When Cravath ordered his players through an impossible series of wind sprints, they moaned about 'that little sonofabitch.' But the players knew they'd have to kill Jeff Cravath to make him change or stop."

If Davis suffered with the others, he also discovered a special power in this all-too-human man.

"I matured more at USC than anything," Davis admits. "Cravath showed me who I was. He was such a wonderful man."

Upon Cravath's untimely death in an auto accident in the

1950s, Davis was moved to deep emotion.

"When I saw a news headline that he had been killed, my heart went down to my shoes," says Davis, now a high school football coach in California.

Friends OR enemies recognized a certain strength in the immovable Cravath. Early history revealed leadership qualities when Cravath captained a Howard Jones team in the 1920s. In some ways he was a lot like his teacher.

"Cravath holds firm to the Jones tradition," a writer once said. "Play the game hard, and play to win. But win or lose, play in the finest spirit of fair play which has made American football the great game we witness today."

Newell Jefferson Cravath was born in Breckenridge, Colorado, on February 3, 1905. He moved to Santa Ana, California, as a boy and soon gained stardom on his championship high school team. He enrolled at Southern Cal in 1923 and played football on one of the school's most outstanding freshmen teams. On the varsity from 1924 through 1926, Cravath became one of the finest defensive centers ever produced in the Far West.

His individual exploits were somewhat tempered, however, by Cravath's shattered dreams of reaching a Rose Bowl. The heartbreak was most severe in 1926 when the Trojans lost two games by one-point margins, 13-12 defeats to Stanford and Notre Dame.

After graduation Cravath stayed close to home as an assistant Trojan coach, then struck out on his own for Denver University. There he fielded representative teams in the Rocky Mountain Conference for a few years.

Cravath eventually returned to the southern California area to coach at a junior college and finally came back to the Trojan family. He was a line coach under Jones in 1939 and 1940 and was instrumental in bringing two Rose Bowl victories to Southern Cal.

When Jones died, Sam Barry was given the head coaching job at Southern Cal, and Cravath was offered the head coaching job at San Francisco University. Cravath turned out the Pacific Coast's highest scoring team in 1941 and was brought back to Southern Cal for the 1942 season after Barry went into the service.

Al Wesson, the sports publicist at Southern Cal, served as an intermediary to hire Cravath back. Wesson recalls:

"I had gone up to San Francisco to observe an indoor track meet because our track coach, Dean Cromwell, didn't like indoor track," says Wesson. "Athletic Director Bill Hunter told me that while I was up there, I should ask Jeff if he'd like to come back to Southern Cal as head coach on a temporary basis. Of course, I had known him a long time, and Jeff got permission to come to USC. When the war was over, Sam Barry came back, but Jeff had been doing so well that Barry just let him have the job."

Ironically, wartime helped—rather than hindered—Cravath teams.

"He had a big advantage because USC had a naval training program, and he had a lot of guys in the service who could still play football," Wesson recalls. "That helped build up Jeff Cravath and helped him get better players."

Cravath revered his war surplus, especially the freshmen.

"I discovered that it was the first-year men just out of high school who supplied the contagious spark of eagerness that ignited the desire of older students to play also," he said once. "An extensive Navy training program was put into operation at Southern Cal just before the season of 1943. Simultaneously, the Pacific Coast Conference voted to waive the customary peacetime regulation barring freshmen from varsity competition.

"Many of the Navy trainees, transferred from other colleges, had extensive backgrounds in football, but several of them were only mildly excited and others were completely disinterested in the game. It was the freshmen on the Trojan roster who saved the day. A pair of peagreen ends, in particular, provided the momentum which propelled us into the Rose Bowl for a conference championship playoff against the University of Washington in the 1943 season.

"There was Jim Callanan, only 16 years of age when he first reported for the team in mid-summer, and there was 17-year-old Gordon Gray, a Navy V-12 student just a few months out of San Francisco Poly High School. Another highly-excited freshman, and a good player as well, was Duane Whitehead. Callanan progressed so rapidly that he was a starter in the Rose Bowl game, and the next two seasons, he was a unanimous all-Coast selection and became our team captain. Gray, later to be developed into a high-scoring back, caught two touchdown passes in the Washington game to play a major role in the upset of the highly-favored Huskies, 29-0. Whitehead was first-string fullback for two seasons and rarely was substituted.

"When some of the older trainees saw how intense the squad was getting, they decided to report for the team, too."

Wesson recalls that Cravath was a superb line coach who was perhaps out of his element as a head coach. But his records were quite respectable, if not in the exquisite Jones class. His teams won Rose Bowl games in the 1943 and 1944 season, went undefeated one year, and collected Pacific Coast Conference championships in 1943, 1944, 1945, and 1947. He produced four all-Americans. He had only one losing season in nine, his last one in 1950.

Although a Jones student, Cravath was his own teacher when it came to play development. He stressed speed and passing and introduced a completely new life style to Trojan football in 1942.

"Call it the 'double T' or 'tease formation,' if you will," explained George T. Davis in the *Los Angeles Evening Herald and Express*. "The four backs line up in a box somewhat similar to the Knute Rockne formation, while the two guards form the other 'T' with the center. The team then shifts to either side, with an unbalanced line developing to the right or left.

"Certainly, with the twin-fake development in the backfield, the Cravath formation should 'tease' the opposition plenty. The fans won't recognize the Trojans as the team they've seen in past years. The Howard Jones idea was to have the quarterback carry the ball 75 percent of the time, the fullback 24 percent, and the halfbacks getting their hands on the pigskin only on remote occasions. All that is changed now with all four men handling the ball—and passing it, too."

Despite the innovation Cravath modestly debunked the importance of coaching.

"Football is not the complicated game that most coaches try to tell us," he said. "There are only three important factors to football: (1) blocking, (2) tackling and (3) handling the ball. Everything else dovetails with these primary fundamentals."

Cravath's simple football philosophy did not translate easily to his young warriors, though. "He had a lot of disruptions with his players," says Wesson.

Through this volcanic reign, however, an enormous number of successful people flowed. The logic was simple: Cravath cared.

"He built character," says Clark, "and that's the truth."

A Bunch Of Roses

"Life is very droll...the optimist sees the donut and the pessimist sees the hole."

Jim Hardy is reminded of that fluffy maxim and chuckles softly. He sees the donut.

"I wake up laughing every morning," says Hardy. "I am an optimist, no doubt about that."

With that irrepressible philosophy Hardy has reached high in his life and come down with a handful of stars. While playing football for Southern Cal and the pros in the 1940s and managing the Los Angeles Coliseum today, the ebullient Hardy has moved forward with brisk, meaningful strides.

"Pride" is another word in the Hardy bible.

"Many of my teammates thought of me as a square," he says. "But I have always taken pride in doing what I do best and constantly trying to better myself."

That is reflected in Hardy's values. He is quick to tell you: "First of all, I'm proud of being a native of Los Angeles; second, of serving on a battleship in the Navy during World War II; thirdly, of playing in the National Football League for seven years; and finally, I'm proud to be a Trojan."

He repeats the last milestone with reverence, as if to savor his association with Southern Cal. It was something to be treasured, all right. In his three years on the Trojan varsity, 1942 through 1944, Hardy was Coach Jeff Cravath's darling. He was the passing and total offense leader in 1943 and 1944, named the Helms player of the year in 1944, and cited as the outstanding player for both the UCLA game and the Rose Bowl in the 1944 season.

"It meant something to me to represent Southern Cal," says the prideful Hardy. "In a corny sort of way, I got turned on by the Trojans' fight song. I felt chills when I heard it. I still do."

Thinking about his Rose Bowl appearances in the 1943 and 1944 seasons, Hardy still pinches himself. He had dreamed about playing at Pasadena since he was eight years old.

"The biggest thing a guy could do was win a Heisman Trophy and play in a Rose Bowl," says Hardy. "I've gone to see every one of those Bowl games since I was eight. Since 1930 I've watched every Rose Bowl game—except, of course, the two I played in."

Respect for football was planted in a young boy by his father.

"When I was a kid, my dad was a telegraph operator for Western Union and he worked in the press box at the Coliseum," Hardy says. "Southern Cal was the big act in town, and my dad used to take me to see the Trojans play. From the moment I started watching them, I wanted to play for them."

While at Fairfax High School, the Los Angeles-born Hardy worked as an usher at the Coliseum. Later he came to USC as "a walk-on...I paid my own way." However, when Hardy showed Coach Cravath that he could play football, he was granted a scholarship.

Hardy got his chance in the opening game of the 1942 season. The Trojans were losing 27-0 to Tulane at the end of the third quarter, and Cravath called upon his untested sophomore. Hardy responded to the challenge by scoring two touchdowns and kicking an extra point for all of Southern Cal's offense that day. That was enough, because he became a starter after that.

"I was thrilled just to have been able to make the team and run out of the Coliseum tunnel with the silks on," Hardy says. "And I guess that was the beginning of a story-book college life."

In his sophomore year Hardy was a tailback in the Single Wing. In 1943 and 1944 he was a T-Formation quarterback with an exceptional arm.

"I liked the T-Formation because I was more proficient at it," says Hardy. "I was an exceptional passer, but just an average runner. I wasn't big enough to bowl anyone over, and I wasn't fast enough to run past anyone."

Hardy also was an extraordinary defensive player and one year led the Pacific Coast Conference in interceptions with 11. His career total of 13 ties him with 3 other Trojans for the school record.

"You had to have more endurance to play in my day," says Hardy. "We played most of the game. If you didn't have the ball, you were either tackling or rushing the other guys. The players get more rest now than we did. But on the other hand I think that the game is better today. Both offense and defense are played with a greater degree of intensity, and the players, of course, are faster and stronger now."

Hardy found himself in the midst of a dramatic transition at Southern Cal. From Howard Jones' run-oriented teams, the Trojans had turned to a more balanced offense.

"Jones' teams were all power—they just ran, never passed," says Hardy. "But we threw about 15 times a game, which was a little more than what Jones had been doing. Then they began throwing 25 to 30 passes a game after I left. So I was part of the new style there."

At the same time Cravath's teams reflected the Jones image on defense. "We gave that great concern," remembers Hardy.

With the help of Hardy, Cravath's first season was a qualified success—good when compared to 1941 but bad when compared with history. The Trojans won five games, lost five, and tied one in 1942. It was 1943 and 1944 that Hardy likes to remember. Those were Rose Bowl years.

"We had big games with UCLA each year," Hardy says. "Everything hinged on them. There was an enormous amount of pressure. It was a typical big game with the added ingredient of the USC-UCLA rivalry. I was nervous as anything."

But when Hardy played in a big game, it brought out the best in him. Owing to wartime restrictions on travel, Southern Cal and UCLA played each other twice a season in 1943, 1944, and 1945. In 1943 Hardy helped the Trojans beat UCLA 20-0 and 26-13, and the double victories put them in the Rose Bowl

THE TENNESSEE WALTZ—Southern California's Blake Headley, holding the football like a loaf of bread, dances away from a Tennessee tackler in the 1945 Rose Bowl game. The Trojans won easily, 25-0.

against Washington. In 1944 Southern Cal and UCLA played to a 13-13 tie, and then the Trojans routed the Bruins 40-13 for another Rose Bowl berth, this time against Tennessee.

"That last time we played UCLA was the most gratifying game of my career," Hardy confesses. "We had them 40-0 at the end of the third quarter. I scored two touchdowns, threw a touchdown pass, and intercepted a couple of passes. There were probably 90,000 people in the stands, and I loved every minute.

"I played a better game with more on the line. When I played in a big game, I was aware of the crowd and the electricity. It built up a week or two before the game. I went to sleep thinking about it and reading about it. And everyone's talking about it. It's a tremendously exciting experience. I guess there's a little show-off in me."

In 1941 the Southern California football record was a statistical disaster with a total of 64 points scored over the season—an all-time low. Just two years later the Trojans went to the other extreme and allowed only 58 points while making a school record of 6 straight shutouts.

The Second World War ironically had fleshed out the Southern Cal football program.

"Some schools were blessed with a great abundance of material because of Naval and Marine programs," Hardy explains. "We got transfers from all the other schools—kids from Oregon State, Washington State, Catholic schools. We really had an enormous amount of talent."

In 1943 Cravath produced an all-American in end Ralph Heywood. ("Heywood could do everything well," said a writer. "He was Troy's leading pass receiver two of his varsity seasons and was twice the top punter on the team, in 1941 and 1942.") In 1944 tackle John Ferraro made ten all-America teams.

"We had a better football team in 1944 than 1943," Hardy points out. "Not only did we have the transfers from other schools, but we also had some guys back who had been discharged from the service. We had a lot of good backs that year, including Pat West and Bobby Morris, both of whom went on to play pro ball."

No college team was able to beat the Trojans in 1943—but a couple of service teams did, San Diego Navy and March Field. The Trojans won seven regular season games, but it was the 35-0 loss to March Field that boded trouble in the Rose Bowl. Washington, the Trojans' opponent in the all-West Coast affair, had beaten March Field 27-7 that season.

Because of the war there was little hoopla attending the Rose Bowl game, which actually was a playoff for the Pacific Coast Conference title. A token "parade" was held with three decorated automobiles. In one rode Tournament President Frank H. Brooks, in the other Queen Naomi Riordan, and in the third Grand Marshall Amos Alonzo Stagg, one of the storied names of American football.

Hardy took the attention after that. Passing and kicking with power and calling signals with a flair, Hardy led the Trojans to a shocking 29-0 victory over the Huskies. It led Al Wolf to comment in the *Los Angeles Times*: "Southern Cal never again will be a Rose Bowl underdog."

"It was a special thrill," says Hardy, who completed three touchdown passes in that game to tie Russ Saunders' record.

Guard Norm Verry, who was out for the regular season

with leg injuries, came back heroicly to play in the Rose Bowl game and provided the Trojans with "the greatest defensive game of guard the Bowl ever saw," according to Cravath. Ferraro and center Bill Gray were also responsible for the upset. The Huskies were completely blunted and failed to move the ball beyond the Trojans' 28-yard line.

"You'll have to put that boy Norman Verry on the all-time Rose Bowl team someplace, somehow," Rube Samuelsen wrote in the *Pasadena Star-News*.

"Only one other guard ranks in all-time Rose Bowl class with Verry," said Los Angeles sportswriter Maxwell Stiles. "He is John (Baby Grand) Scafide of Tulane."

Washington had tried 19 passes against the Trojan defense and completed only 5 while having 3 intercepted. It was no accident that this happened, Cravath revealed after the game.

"The Washington coaches kept talking so much about Sam Robinson's and Al Akins' passing that I thought they were overplaying their hands to conceal the weakness that none of them was effective in that department," said Cravath. "So, acting on this hunch, I changed our pass defense on Thursday while working out in the gymnasium from a man-to-man to a zone, and I'm certainly happy that I did."

In the locker room Cravath told his players: "This day will always remain as a great memory for all of you fellows. I know you have made a former coach who has passed on very happy (he meant, of course, Howard Jones).

Southern Cal's enormous depth was even more apparent in 1944. Hardy says the Trojans were in a sublime class.

"I was not conscious of ranking at the time, but we were probably up there with Army, Navy, and Ohio State. Army, with Doc Blanchard and Glenn Davis, might have been better than us. Navy, too. Ohio State had an awfully strong team that year. But I do think that we belonged with the nation's best teams."

The Trojans won eight games and tied two behind Hardy's generalship. The most spectacular victory of the season was a 28-21 thriller over the San Diego Navy team, and the most significant was a 25-0 romp over Tennessee in the Rose Bowl. Both of these Hardy directed with aplomb.

Hefty and powerful, San Diego outweighed Southern Cal

at least 10 pounds to the man, and the Bluejackets were favored to beat the Trojans. But Jeff Cravath changed his offensive scheme with a new "stutter" play that trapped the fast-charging San Diego guards and tackles. And Don Doll and Milford Dreblow ran free, accounting for 257 yards between them.

The game came down to the last five minutes. The score was 21-21. The ball was in Southern Cal's possession on its 49-yard-line, fourth down with six to go. It was an obvious punting situation—and that was apparently what Hardy had in mind. The quarterback went back into punt formation. When the ball was snapped, however, Hardy danced in the backfield. It was evident he would not kick.

Cravath shouted to Hardy, "Punt the ball." Hardy threw the ball instead, and it landed in Doll's arms, almost 30 yards away. The halfback was stopped on the 11-yard line. On the next play Doll ran the final yards to the goal line past the astonished naval team.

Against Tennessee in the Rose Bowl, his last college game, Hardy was no less formidable despite playing with a stomach

Southern Cal's Ted Tannehill is on his way to a first down against UCLA in 1945. The Trojans beat the Bruins that day, 26-15.

disorder and a temperature. Hardy passed with reckless abandon—and with accuracy—and put the final stroke on the game with a touchdown pass to Doug MacLachlan in the last seconds. He became the object of most everyone's affection after that performance.

"Hardy was the greatest T-Formation quarterback I have ever seen in action," said Cravath.

"Hardy must be rated with the all-time Rose Bowl greats," said Al Wolf in the *Los Angeles Times*.

"Hardy's quarterbacking is on a par with the best of Sid Luckman of the Chicago Bears," said Chick Meehan, the onetime Syracuse coach.

Tennessee Coach Jim Barnhill ignored the Hardy superlatives and put it quite simply: "We were outclassed."

Actually, Hardy took advantage of a rather raw Tennessee team.

"We had more experience," he confesses. "They had younger guys on their team."

At one time during the game Tennessee had seven freshmen and three sophomores on the field. The Trojans also

Southern California's Don Burnside makes his way against Tennessee in the 1945 Rose Bowl. He took over the chief ballcarrying duties after injuries hit the more experienced Trojan backs.

Jeff Cravath meets with his backfield before meeting Alabama in the 1946 Rose Bowl. Next to the coach (from left) are: quarterback Jerry Bowman, fullback Roy Cole, right halfback Ted Tannehill, and left halfback Bobby Morris.

were studded with young players, if not as many as the Vols. Don Burnside, a 17-year-old, took over the chief ballcarrying duties against Tennessee after a wave of injuries hit the more experienced Southern Cal backs.

In 1945 the war ended, and so did Southern Cal's unbeaten Rose Bowl record. The theme of the Rose Bowl parade that year was, "Victory, Unity and Peace," but Alabama was anything but peaceful. With Harry Gilmer controlling Alabama, the Crimson Tide rolled to a 34-14 victory over Southern Cal. It not only stopped the Trojans' eight-game winning streak in Rose Bowl competition but made them look bad in the process.

The loss was the Trojans' fourth of the season, an unlikely figure for a Rose Bowl contender. One observer was quick to point out that the defeat by Alabama was not much of a surprise "because the Trojans had stunk out the joint most of the season." Actually, the manner of the victory was more

Southern California's Ted Tannehill makes a couple of yards against Alabama in the 1946 Rose Bowl game. The Crimson Tide made most of the yardage that day, however, while beating the Trojans 34-14.

surprising than the final score. Gilmer was expected to pass a lot, but did not. Instead, he ran a lot and accumulated 116 yards—110 yards more than the entire Southern Cal team. The Trojans had an embarrassing 6-yard net rushing figure and 41 petty yards in total offense, both negative Rose Bowl records.

Southern Cal's ineptitude was mirrored in comments by sportswriters.

"USC was the sorriest looking eleven that ever stumbled, fumbled, and groped its way through a game in the Rose Bowl," said one.

"The ushers were having trouble finding places in the stands for guys wearing white jerseys and red helmets who were constantly being thrown up there by the Alabamians," said another.

Time Out: John Ferraro

The telephone rang three times, and a secretary answered: "Mr. Ferraro is in the council chambers. I'll put you through."

John Ferraro answered and said he had some free time, but not too much. "We'll be in session in a little while, but I'd love to talk to you in the meantime."

The Los Angeles city councilman then drifted back into a time pocket of the 1940s and digested past glories. A tackle of soaring talents at Southern Cal, Ferraro was twice named an all-American and played in the East-West Shrine Game as well as three Rose Bowl games. Uniquely, he is just as proud of his academic achievements. He emphasizes that he singled out Southern Cal as an educational institution, not a football school.

"When I graduated, George Preston Marshall of the Washington Redskins negotiated a trade to get me, but I decided that I had not gone to school to become a professional football player," says Ferraro.

He went into the insurance business, joined the City Council in 1966, and is reaching for higher political office.

"The things I've learned from football I apply daily to my political life," Ferraro says. "Football disciplines you and teaches you that you must learn to give as well as take. Another thing I've learned from football is that you can drop out of the limelight in a hurry, and you must be prepared for it. I was pleased by the adulation and enjoyed the fact that people were nice to me, but I knew it would be gone as soon as I stopped playing football. It's the same situation in politics. I always try to give my best and not worry about anything else."

Ferraro has the distinction of playing five years of football for Southern Cal and could have played six. Few can claim that.

"In 1942 I was allowed to play as a freshman, and 1943 and 1944 were war years, so they didn't count against my eligibility," explains Ferraro. "When I came back after the service, I actually had three years of varsity eligibility left, but I compromised and played two of them—1946 and 1947."

A home-grown product from Bell High School, Ferraro "talked with people from Notre Dame and Santa Clara," but ended up going to Southern Cal because of a friend "who was a died-in-the-wool USC fan." In high school Ferraro was 6-foot-3 and weighed 210 pounds. In college he became a beefy 6-4 and 245.

"I was a big tackle on the team," says Ferraro. "I guess that gave me a push toward all-American status. It's a great thrill to be singled out and selected, but I realized that my chances were better because I played on winning teams. I have to give a lot of credit to my teammates."

Ferraro's all-American seasons were in 1944 and 1947, years when the Trojans played in the Rose Bowl. All-American honors were predestined after earlier performances.

"In 1943 we had played a service team, March Field, and they were great," recalls Ferraro. "We got beaten badly, but I had a particularly good game that day. I guess it set me aside as a future all-American. I got lots of raves from the press."

Later that season Ferraro played one of his best games in Southern Cal's victory over Washington in the Rose Bowl. "We went in prepared," says Ferraro. "I was a little nervous before the game started, but then it was all right once we got a few plays in."

If they sometimes made him nervous, large, passionate crowds also excited Ferraro.

"It was a terrific thrill to go into the Coliseum and play before those packed houses," he says. "One of the really great thrills of my career was when we went to Columbus to play Ohio State. That's really a madhouse up there. It's big and it was packed, and the people were really nice to us. We beat them, and the Ohio State fans were really wonderful. They

John Ferraro (center) is shown with teammates Duane Whitehead (left) and Jim Callanan prior to the 1945 Rose Bowl game with Tennessee.

started to cheer us. They appreciated what we had done. I remember reading the newspapers the next day. 'Magnificent Trojans Roll,' the headlines said."

Ferraro recites game histories with ease. The close ones, especially, stick in his mind.

"The 1944 season was exciting," he says. "We had some great games that year. We played St. Mary's Pre-Flight at Fresno. It was a tough game—we scored six points in the first half, and that was the extent of the scoring. But St. Mary's really gave us plenty of scares in the second half. They started running and they'd make six, eight yards at a crack, and when they got to the goal line they'd try to pass and fail. They just ran over us the entire second half but never crossed the goal line. The game with San Diego Navy was also tremendous. It went back and forth and had a 100-yard run in it before we won."

Southern Cal had an easier time against Tennessee in the Rose Bowl. The 25-0 Trojan victory conjures up an amusing incident.

"They had a very good team, but everything we did was right," Ferraro remembers. "Coach Jeff Cravath was clearing off the bench and letting everyone play at the end. This fellow George Davis came in, and he was really an eager beaver. George said, 'Hurry up, let's get another play off.' I looked at him and said, 'Relax.' I was pretty tired—I had played the whole game."

Against Michigan three years later, Ferraro could afford no such luxury as relaxation. The Trojans were beaten by the Wolverines 49-0.

"That was the year that Michigan used the platoon system and really beat us badly," Ferraro says. "It was really a shock seeing them come in and out of the game while we stayed in there for the whole time. And I was so tired after playing the full game. The platoon rule was new, and I think that Michigan was the only major school which understood it correctly."

The Trojans might have been better than that shellacking showed, but Cravath had a hard time harnessing all their power. Ferraro admits that there was a communications problem between the Southern Cal coach and the returning veterans.

"After the war, Southern Cal had a lot of returning servicemen who had led a rough existence, and they weren't about to come back to the discipline of football," he says. "A lot of us found out that there were other things than football. And some didn't adapt."

Even so Ferraro feels that the 1947 Southern Cal team was "a fantastic team...we got to the pinnacle in the California game (won by the Trojans 39-14) and then started going downhill. Notre Dame had a really great football team that year and beat us badly (38-7). They were superior, but I think that we should have played them a better game."

Ferraro was drafted by Green Bay of the National Football League and by the Los Angeles Dons of the old American Football Conference, but jilted the pros for the insurance business. He eventually left that to join politics, and before his present position as councilman served as chairman of the Police

Commission in Los Angeles.

The ambitious Ferraro recently announced his candidacy for the Board of Supervisors, a five-man group which runs the policies of Los Angeles County (population seven million).

He feeds on competition. Because of it Ferraro has reached high levels in his life. Recently he received the "Top Ten" award, a laurel given to athletes based on successful careers outside of sports.

"They cite five players from the current year and five from twenty-five years ago, based on what they have done with their lives after their athletic careers," Ferraro explains. "I made it one year with Stewart Udall (onetime Secretary of the Interior)."

Ferraro constantly shoots for the moon.

"Anyone who is in a competitive area tries for the highest," Ferraro says. "I was a football player, and I wanted to be an all-American. Now I want to move up in the political field, as high as I can go."

But in the political field you do not get too many chances if you fumble the ball.

"I'm prepared for the eventuality of losing," Ferraro says. "I know that things don't last forever."

The "old philosopher" then excused himself and went about the business of running a metropolitan city.

Thrown To The Wolverines

Braven Dyer was not a gambling man, but he felt that he had to do something drastic in light of the situation. Enroute home by train from a big victory over Ohio State in 1947, Southern Cal's players were in the dining car when the *Los Angeles Times* sports editor walked in. Dyer was at once assaulted by one of the smug Trojans. "What do you think of that? We gave Ohio State the business, didn't we?" the voice said.

Hoping to bring the players down to earth and better prepare them for the remainder of the season, Dyer recoiled: "Yes, it was swell, fellows, and you'll probably beat Oregon State all right next week, but I doubt if you can beat California."

Derisive snorts greeted Dyer's statement, so he challenged the cocky players.

"I'll bet you each a shirt you can't beat the Bears," he said.

"What kind of shirt?" retorted Ernie Tolman, a giant end.

"A $5 sports shirt for every man who plays in the game," snapped Dyer.

Two weeks after that Dyer lost $185.

"That man (Coach Jeff) Cravath used 37 players," Dyer said after watching the Trojans whip California 39-14. "I didn't bet a dime on the game, and I lost all that money. It took me a long time to make that up on my expense account."

There is little suspicion that a $5 bet inspired the Trojans that October day. But Dyer was happy he literally gave Southern Cal the shirt off his back. The game he saw was well worth it.

"California's Rose Bowl bubble burst with a loud bang here this afternoon as the magnificent Trojans all but ran the Golden Bears right out of the stadium, 39-14," Dyer wrote from Berkeley. "Don Doll, far and away the best back on the field today, provided the coup de grace when he returned the second-half kickoff 95 yards for Southern Cal's fourth touchdown. That did it, but good. I understand the Bear players were not impressed by the Trojans. They wouldn't be—they're still too stunned to know what hit 'em."

The game had been given the appropriate buildup, and the first-half scenario played exactly that way. Five touchdowns were scored, and the Trojans held a tenuous 20-14 lead at intermission. Then Doll's run stupefied California.

"That broke California's spirit," Cravath said. "I don't know what would have happened in the second half if Don hadn't made that great run. He really set the Bears back on their heels."

George Murphy, Southern Cal's quarterback, discovered an Achilles heel in the California defense at right tackle and aimed a lot of Trojan thrusts there.

"George found the weak spot in California's line and never let up," Cravath added.

The victory was the zenith of the 1947 season for Southern Cal. Unfortunately the Trojans would not reach such giddy heights after that. Inexpicably they struggled to beat Washington, Stanford, and UCLA and then were crushed 38-7 by Notre Dame and humiliated 49-0 by Michigan in the Rose Bowl.

In his book, *Top Ten Trojan Football Thrillers*, Dyer had an explanation of sorts for the comedown: "California probably wasn't as good as most of us thought in advance of the Berkeley game. And the Trojans undoubtedly weren't nearly as good as some of us thought after the Berkeley battle."

A former player has another explanation. "We had a good, well-rounded team," declared George Davis, who played center among other positions for Southern Cal. "We were better in the line than we were in the backfield, though. After Jim Hardy left at the end of the 1944 season, we never had a tremendous quarterback while I was there. We might have had three or four good quarterbacks—but the great teams always have this one guy that they can cluster around. We didn't."

Among linemen, however, tackle John Ferraro and end Paul Cleary seemed more than mortal. In 1947 they were voted to a total of 12 all-American first teams. "Cleary sparkled on both defense and offense and was particularly devastating on the end-around play," said an appraiser. "Ferraro was also a mighty man for the Trojans in the 1940s, a brute of a tackler with a killer instinct."

Both Cleary and Ferraro played in 1946, but the Trojans were not as effective that year. They won six games and lost four, including a 26-6 defeat at Notre Dame which led a

Notre Dame back Bob Livingston carries the ball over the 20-yard line on a run to the Southern Cal six before being stopped in this 1946 game at South Bend. Notre Dame triumphed, 26-6.

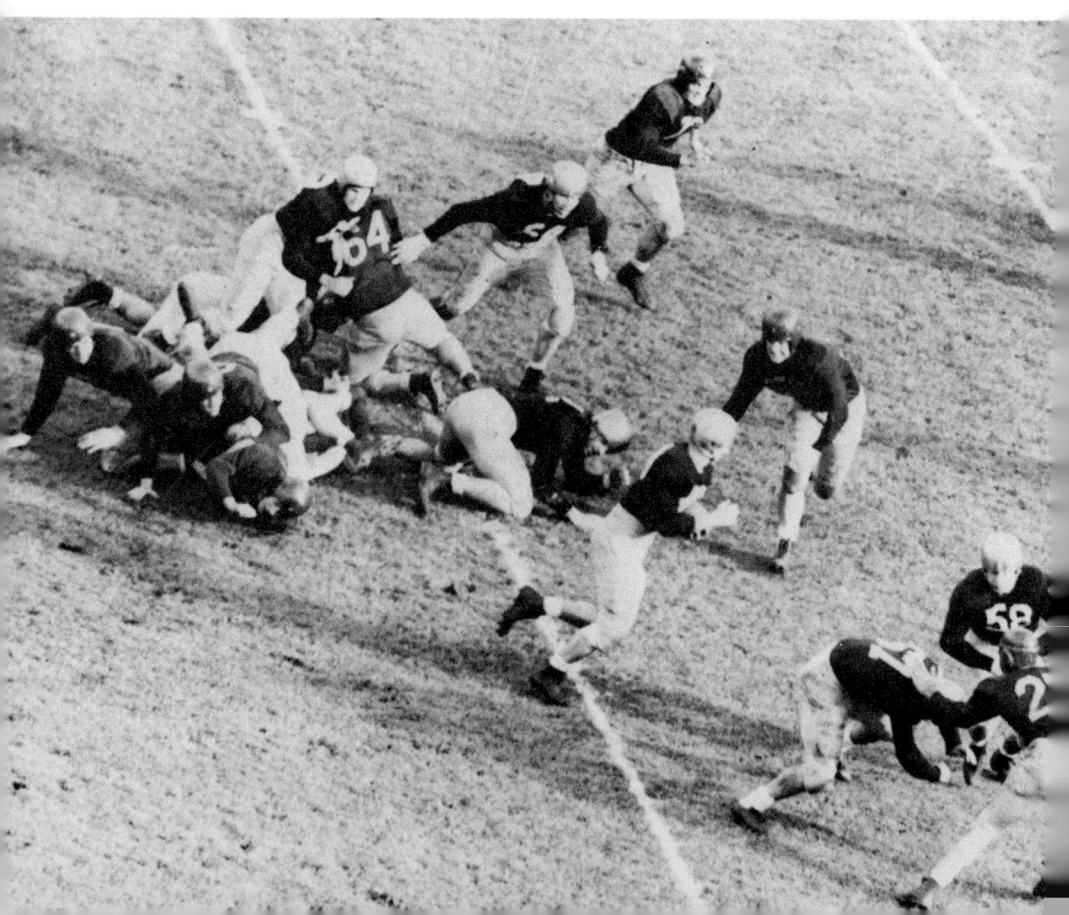

sportswriter to comment: "This Notre Dame team plays hard football. The Irish blockers are quite free with their use of hands and forearms...Some of my Midwest cronies who know their football say that's the way they play the game back here. It's different on the Pacific Coast, and until there is some standardization of this type of blocking our boys are going to take a beating."

The 1946 season did not provide an outstanding football team at Southern Cal, but it did provide excitement in other ways. It was the year of the Great Water Hoax, the emergence of the irrepressible Tirebiter as team mascot, and a time of exaggerated stories of Cravath's dismissal.

Prior to the USC-UCLA game, Los Angeles newspapers published stories that Southern Cal students, using fire hoses, had flooded the Coliseum field the night before to slow the Bruins' fine runners. Reports from self-styled "witnesses" had told newspapers of the flooding and a subsequent "bloody battle" that ensued between UCLA and USC students. Wire services picked up the story and sent it out nationwide, only to find out that it was a phony. Both schools and the Los Angeles police force later denied that such an incident had taken place—and the newspapers printed an apology.

The Trojans found a faithful companion and good luck charm in a dog named "Tirebiter." One of many mongrel pooches to roam the Southern Cal campus, "George Tirebiter" captured the imagination of the returning GIs with his penchant for chasing after cars and nipping at their tires. With the aid of a campaign by the school newspaper the dog soon became the team's unofficial mascot.

"George would ride into the games in a shiny convertible, stop in front of the rooting section among thunderous cheers, and then delight the rooters with appropriate barks over the public address system," recalled Bob Erburu, who worked for Southern Cal's Athletic News Service. "He really went into his act when the Trojans scored. Then his barks could be heard by everyone, without benefit of electrical assistance."

Tirebiter's place in Southern Cal's life style was further solidified when he was "dognapped" by UCLA students prior to a game. When finally rescued, the Trojan mascot had the letters U-C-L-A shaved on his back. Tirebiter went to the game that day with a Trojan blanket over him, much to the displeasure of UCLA rooters.

He earned a kind of immortality and a place in Trojan hearts at the California game in 1947 when he stood up against the Golden Bears' mascot.

"Before the game, California's famed mascot, Oskie, appeared to taunt the poor dog," remembered Erburu. "Oskie is a student dressed in Cal colors with a papier-mache bear head. The Bears' rooting section was in an uproar as Oskie proceeded to give George the bird. But then the noise died down as George decided that enough was enough and chased Oskie out of the stadium with an occasional bite at his heels to make the flight hurried, to say the least. That did it. George was made an official mascot, and his paw prints were enshrined in Troy's 'all-American Row' along with the cleat prints of SC's all-American footballers."

Tirebiter became a magical image. Newspapers wrote thousands of words about the famous mascot, and he was constantly being photographed with football stars and movie stars. He was a mongrel monarch on campus until his premature death. Killed by an auto in 1950, Tirebiter did not die in the personal sense. His charisma lived on in George Tirebiter II, "a smaller and perhaps cuter version of his father," according to Erburu.

While Tirebiter was making friends, Cravath was reportedly losing them. Prior to the Trojan's game with Stanford in 1946, one San Francisco newspaper predicted that he was finished as the football coach at Southern Cal. It turned out that reports of his demise were merely bombast. Cravath got out of town with a 28-20 victory over Stanford, savored all the more for the circumstances. Cravath lived to coach another year, and 1947 was his year.

A 7-7 tie with Rice in the second game of the season was the only blemish in Southern Cal's fast start. The Trojans tied the game in the closing minutes when a long pass by Jim Powers set up a touchdown run by Verle Lillywhite. The next week Southern Cal smothered Ohio State 32-0, one of its most significant intersectional victories in the 1940s. Don Doll's running helped the Trojans break that one open.

Victories over Oregon State and California the following

The mongrel monarch of Southern California in the 1940s: "Tirebiter."

two weeks set the Trojans on a course for the Rose Bowl. This goal was reached when Southern Cal defeated UCLA 6-0 later in the year and won the Pacific Coast Conference championship. Powers threw a 45-yard touchdown pass to Jack Kirby midway through the second period. And Gordon Gray preserved that margin when he intercepted a UCLA pass in the Southern Cal end zone with less than a minute remaining.

Undefeated against Western opponents, proud Southern Cal prepared for the Notre Dame invasion with a noisy "Homecoming Day." Joined by Tirebiter, more than 1,000 Southern Cal students mobilized forces and paraded through Hollywood and Los Angeles in a myriad of vehicles which included fire engines, hearses, trucks, floats, jeeps, and gold-fringed surreys.

"For a while traffic was hopelessly snarled in downtown Los Angeles as more than 1,000 USC students, singing and cheering, converged on the Biltmore Hotel in Pershing Square," reported a newspaper. "Proceeding on to Hollywood and Vine, the celebrants started several bonfires in the middle of the street and tore down a couple of traffic signals. Next they invaded the Ambassador Hotel where they filled fountains with bubble bath solution and paraded through the lobby."

As with many Southern Cal-Notre Dame games, this one had a notable story attached to it. It involved a whimsical Notre Dame tackle, Zygmont Czarobski.

Aware that he would be facing Southern Cal's great Ferraro most of the game, Czarobski proceeded to send his adversary daily telegrams. The first one stated that he was leaving South Bend and that Ferraro should begin to get ready for him. At every train stop another telegram was sent, emphasizing that Czarobski was another day closer to Los Angeles and that Ferraro should worry more.

On the morning of the game, Czarobski was in a barbershop getting a manicure when an associate walked in.

"Why are you getting a manicure on the morning of the game?" he asked Czarobski.

The tackle replied: "That will be my final message to Ferraro. On the first play of scrimmage, when I get down to my three-point stance, I will call his attention to my nails, have him notice how clean and polished they are, then I will tell him:

'When I stick these fingers in your eye, you needn't worry about infection.'"

As it turned out, Czarobski need not have concerned himself with psyching out his opponent. Emil Sitko scored twice, Fred Early kicked a field goal and added five extra points, and Notre Dame belabored the Trojans by 31 points before 104,953 fans in the Coliseum.

After that debacle, the Trojans got a worse beating from Michigan's Wolverines. Southern Cal was a victim of circumstances. Michigan, fighting with Notre Dame for the national championship, set out to prove that its team was better—and what better way than to beat Southern Cal by a bigger score than Notre Dame? That 49-point drubbing caught the eye of three national championship authorities—the Dunkel System, the Litkenhouse System, and the Football Thesaurus. But Notre Dame was generally conceded to be national champion after making No. 1 in the Associated Press, Helms, and the Williamson System polls.

Cravath confirmed the general feeling that Notre Dame was a better team than Michigan in 1947.

"Cravath and most of his Trojans claimed Notre Dame hit harder and was better than Michigan," said Joe Hendrickson and Maxwell Stiles in their book, *The Tournament Of Roses*. "Notre Dame played power football against USC. Michigan employed speed, deception, a whirling fullback as its ball handler—and the forward pass."

Reminding some of Michigan's fabled "Point A Minute" team that devoured Stanford by the same score in the 1902 affair, Fritz Crisler's team had a field day in the 1948 Rose Bowl game. The theme of the Rose Bowl parade was "The Golden West," but there was nothing golden about Western football that day. While Stanford had held out for 23 minutes against Michigan 46 years earlier, Southern Cal could not contain the Wolverines that long. Michigan fullback Jack Weisenburger scored a touchdown from close in with 9 minutes gone in the first quarter, and Jim Brieske kicked the first of his 7 extra points—a Rose Bowl record.

Weisenburger scored two more touchdowns later in the game, and Bob Chappuis, Michigan's all-American halfback, figured in five of Michigan's seven touchdowns. Weisenburger and Chappuis each rushed for 91 yards, and Chappuis added 188 yards by passing. The Trojans, meanwhile, were only able to manufacture 91 yards net running and 42 through the air. They did not make a first down until 24 minutes had elapsed.

This shocking inadequacy was prime joke material for newspapermen.

"The Trojans stood up on one play—the playing of the National Anthem," wrote Bob Hunter in the *Los Angeles Examiner*.

"Well, it wasn't as bad as we expected—it was worse," said Braven Dyer in the *Los Angeles Times*.

Ned Cronin remarked in the *Los Angeles Daily News*: "Southern Cal's football club needs one of two things, and possibly both. Reading from left to right, they are (1) a couple of barrels of plasma, and/or (2) a new matchmaker. The one they've got is going to get somebody killed if they don't get him out of there."

Chappuis came under special praise. "He looked every bit as good as Dixie Howell did when he gave Stanford a passing lesson a dozen years ago," said Dick Hyland in the *Times*. "His receivers, all of them, were great, making almost unbelievable grabs."

"A football squad that just about defies comparison," was the way the *Examiner*'s Vincent X. Flaherty saw Michigan.

"A terrible thing happened here this afternoon," he wrote. "They threw the Trojans to the Wolverines in full view of 95,000 horror-stricken onlookers. And it shall go down in history as the most macabre spectacle ever beheld since they fed the Christians to the lions rare. And by golly, it was awful...the Wolverines gave USC the worst defeat in the history of the school."

That ignominious game seemed to set the tempo for following seasons of discontent. While the Trojans never tasted such outrageous defeat in the next few years, decline was evident under Cravath, and his days at Southern Cal dwindled down to a precious few.

Earthquakes

Two earthquakes hit Los Angeles on December 4, 1948. A handful of scientists took note of one on a seismograph, and more than 100,000 people watched the other in the Los Angeles Coliseum.

While the earth literally trembled under their feet, Southern Cal and Notre Dame erupted on a football field. Chances are that nobody noticed the real earthquake while watching that marvelous 14-14 tie.

Some called it the "biggest upset of the decade." It might have been. Notre Dame had gone 27 games without a defeat and came into Los Angeles with a richly talented team that included four all-Americans—guards Bill Fischer and Marty Wendell, end Leon Hart, and Emil Sitko, the great runner. Southern Cal had no all-Americans and was virtually the same team that these same Fighting Irish had humiliated 38-7 the year before.

Prior to meeting Southern Cal, Notre Dame had routed Washington 46-0 in a game described by one sportswriter "as a riotous occasion on which the lambs were led up, one by one, to be dealt with as the executioner chose." The Trojans came off an unimpressive victory over UCLA, and their 6-3 record compared to Notre Dame's unbeaten mark established them as three-touchdown underdogs. That was being kind.

Southern Cal's game plan included a diversity of running plays at the outset to test Notre Dame's defensive style.

"When you get the ball," Trojan Coach Jeff Cravath had told quarterback George Murphy, "I want you to try out these plays. They probably won't gain much yardage, but after you've used 'em, we'll have a pretty good idea of how Notre Dame intends to defense us."

The Trojans at once put Cravath's idea in motion—or tried to, at least. The first play against Notre Dame gained them one yard. On the second they fumbled and lost eight yards. On the third they got nothing. And on the fourth down the Trojans punted.

A long touchdown pass from Frank Tripucka to Hart produced a 7-0 Notre Dame lead later in the first half. The brutish receiver bounced off half a dozen Trojans enroute to the goal line.

"Of all the college ends I've seen since 1919, Hart is the greatest," commented a sportswriter. "He caught that ball, swung off to his left, and set sail. He went all the way, after several Trojans bounced him. Several times it seemed they had him cornered for sure, but big Leon's tremendous power enabled him to break away. It is doubtful if any end in college football save Hart has the power to accomplish such a run—with the Trojans hitting as they were."

The complacent Irish fumbled several times in the first half, and Tripucka was forced to leave the game with a broken bone. It seemed like an ideal situation for the underdog.

Still trailing at the start of the fourth quarter, Southern Cal came to life behind the running of Bill Martin. First he blasted over from the one-yard line to tie the score and then gave the Trojans a 14-7 lead on a four-yard slant over left tackle. With little time remaining, Southern Cal was on the verge of a big upset.

At this point Notre Dame's cocky sophomore, Bill Gay, approached a referee.

"Mr. Referee," he said, "how much time is there left to play?"

"Two minutes and 35 seconds," replied the referee.

"That will be plenty of time, sir, if they will just kick it to me," said the swaggering Gay.

The Trojans did—and that was a mistake.

Gay sucked up the ball on his one-yard line and followed blockers down the right sidelines. He ran all the way to the Southern Cal thirteen-yard line before he was dragged down from behind by Don Doll.

With the game dying, Notre Dame quarterback Bob Williams cracked through the middle of the Trojan line for five yards. From the eight Williams threw a pass that sailed over Gay's head in the end zone. On the next play Williams again misfired to Gay, but Trojan defensive back Gene Beck was called for pass interference and the ball was put on the two-yard line.

There was less than a minute to go when John Panelli crashed over left guard to the one. Then Sitko finished the dramatic drive by plunging into the end zone over right tackle. Steve Oracko kicked the tying point for Frank Leahy's team in a deadly-silent stadium.

The tie kept alive Notre Dame's three-year unbeaten streak but cost the Fighting Irish a third straight national championship. (Michigan won it that year.) It was a huge moral success for the Trojans.

"That the Trojans had enough stuff to tie these babies speaks volumes for their fighting hearts...and their coaches," said one writer.

"Notre Dame may have had its Hart...but Southern California had heart. That made it a draw," commented another.

Leahy realized that he was lucky to come away with a tie. He said of Southern Cal: "That team could have played any team in the country to a standstill. I've never seen a better coached team more ready mentally than the Trojans were against us."

It was Cravath's last big moment at Southern Cal. The Trojans steadily declined after that and in 1950 plunged to their lowest level under Cravath—and one of the worst in the school's history—with a 2-5-2 record. Included in that totally frustrated season was a 39-0 loss to UCLA.

Cravath became an unpopular figure along alumni row. Rumors persisted that powerful figures held "secret meetings" to shake up the coaching staff. While this intrigue was acted out backstage, Cravath received the support of Southern Cal's students. Because the situation had become so palpable they held a spontaneous rally for the coach one day, and Cravath thanked them "from the bottom of my heart."

"Like you, I want to do whatever is best for the school," Cravath told a crowd of 400.

Parading near the rally were jalopies with signs, "We're Behind You, Jeff," and "Win With Jeff."

Cravath had not only produced a losing team but had been discredited as a coach of expertise. Perhaps that was the real reason behind the discontent of the alumni and some university officials. Some accused Cravath of misplacing players' talents, and maybe the most oft-cited example was the case of Frank Gifford in 1949 and 1950.

"A strong case could be made that Gifford was the most ill-used college player of all time," the magazine *Sports Illustrated* once said. "Cravath put Gifford on the defensive unit throughout most of his career, although he was probably the best all-around offensive player on the squad. He was its best runner and passer, he punted and he placekicked, and yet Cravath rarely gave him a chance to do these things. It wasn't until well into Gifford's pro career with the New York Giants that he was able to prove his full potential on offense. It might be argued that if Gifford had played before the free-substitution rule and under a coach who knew how to utilize the full measure of his ability, he would have to be named the finest player the West ever produced, maybe the best anywhere."

The case of Don Burke was another example of a grevious Cravath faux pas, according to one writer. In his book, *The Fifth Down*, written with former Southern Cal player George Davis, Neil Amdur explains: "(There are) Don Burkes (that) play on every high school, college and professional football team. They possess all the physical skills: size, speed, strength, stamina. You keep waiting for them to explode, but sometimes they never do, and Don Burke never got off the bench at Southern Cal. This bothered George (Davis). Don was a fullback who weighed 225 pounds and ran a ten-flat hundred, which in those days was damn fast. He came to Southern Cal as a junior from Hartnell College with the same credentials that O. J. Simpson would bring from junior college years later. Yet Don Burke was a third-teamer and played only when others were hurt. There was nothing wrong with the ability of the athletes who were ahead of Burke. Maybe private reasons prevailed why Donnie never played at USC, because he went to the San

Francisco 49ers, made first-string linebacker immediately, and played exceptionally well."

Davis adored Cravath but also saw his shortcomings.

"When I started coaching, I figured that if Cravath could make a mistake like that, maybe I could, too," Davis said in the book. "You can use logic when you're drawing X's and O's—logic and experience. But there is never experience at dealing with a human being."

Rumors of dissension among players added more fuel to the situation, and it came to a boil on December 12, 1950, when Braven Dyer wrote in the *Los Angeles Times*:

"Jeff Cravath is through as Trojan football coach. He will be asked to 'resign' within a few days. The *Times* learned last night that powerful alumni interests have persuaded the administration to get rid of the man who has been head coach for the last nine years."

Just a year before, Cravath ironically had signed a three-year contract at $14,000 annually.

"Cravath was not available for comment last night, but this writer has known for weeks that Jeff has suspected the ax would fall," wrote Dyer. "A hush-hush meeting of top Trojan officials was held last night at which time it was officially decided to buy up Cravath's contract. Alumni pressure got Jeff. And the alumni weren't the only ones divided on the question of retaining or dismissing Cravath.

"Most of the high-ranking officials within the administration were 100 percent behind the grid coach, but so much pressure was brought to bear by outside 'advisers' that these executives finally decided, for the good of the over-all football picture at SC, to ask for Jeff's resignation. There were cries from alumni for Cravath's scalp last year when the team lost a toughie to California and then got bounced around by Stanford. These yelps were a mere zephyr compared to the hurricane of howls which arose this fall. So many critics had pegged SC for a Rose Bowl team that the final record was more than the customary die-hards could stomach."

Cravath's dismissal, though blessed by some, was seen as an inhuman act in other quarters. Broadcaster Robert Kelley particularly castigated university officials for their methods.

"They crucified Jeff Cravath," he said. "The worst

criminal in the world is entitled to certain considerations. A man as morally high as Cravath deserved a better lot. Jeff's only crime was—he didn't win every game. He had only one losing season in nine years. The trustees of the university, meeting last night, under pressure from certain strong SC alumni, brutally fired Cravath—a loyal alumnus of the university with a marvelous coaching record wasn't even given the common courtesy of a chance to submit his resignation. They crucified Jeff Cravath and his fine family just four days before Christmas."

Kelley asserted that Southern Cal had approached Frank Leahy and that the Trojan Club had shown a passionate interest in other "name" coaches such as Fritz Crisler and Paul Brown. No such national football figure replaced Cravath, however.

The eventual choice was Jesse T. Hill, the gentlemanly, respected alumnus and successful track coach. He showed great courage in accepting the post.

Time Out: Jess Hill

Hard by the Los Angeles International Airport, the sleek office building loomed, clean and white in the California sun. It was easy enough to find from downtown. The friendly voice on the telephone had said:

"Go down Fairfax, get on the Santa Monica Freeway West, go up the ramp that says 'Long Beach,' and that'll switch you onto the San Diego Freeway. Take the Century Boulevard exit and go west on Century until you hit Sepulveda Boulevard. We're on Sepulveda."

The elevator floated to the eighth floor, and just down the hall in Room 8203 Jess Hill waited in an expansive, chicly-appointed office.

"I can look out the window and see my house from here," he says, pointing to a rich panorama of land. "And I can be home in a matter of minutes. That's the nice thing about my job."

At an age when most stop speeding, the indefatigable Hill is commanding new vistas as commissioner of the Pacific Coast Athletic Association. His "job" is no ordinary job. That is quite natural—for Hill is no ordinary man.

As player, coach, and athletic director at Southern Cal, Hill has not only spanned decades—but done so with distinguished achievement. His staggering creations would seem enough for three lifetimes, but the energetic Hill forges ahead, unaware of danger signs, if any.

In his mid-60s, Hill rules a major league conference and is

confronted with its inherently tough problems. On this particular January afternoon he mulled probationary measures for an outlaw PCAA school.

"I just came back from downtown after a meeting about the situation," says a frowning Hill, "spent all morning talking about it."

Despite such distraction of labor, Hill took two hours out of his busy schedule to talk about Southern Cal—the school that made the man. And when the warm session was done, it was apparent that the man, to some extent, had made the school.

Born in Missouri, Hill and his family moved to Southern California when he was 16, and this bony teenager flourished in the Corona sunshine. While selling or delivering for the Corona Ice Company, working at the Union Oil Station, or going to school, Hill always found time to stop and knock cans off fenceposts. He developed his arm and his eye this way. His free time was preoccupied with athletics.

"Every spare moment in his school and spare-time work schedule he would devote to sports—either devouring sports pages, watching the school squads practicing on nearby fields, or participating himself," remembers a friend. "He used some of his earnings New Year's Day, 1926, in a rare indulgence. He and a friend drove to Pasadena and bought tickets to the Alabama-Washington game—an event marred by a reviewing stand collapse and highlighted by Johnny Mack Brown's heroics. The contest ended in a 20-19 win for Alabama—and instant addiction to big-time football for Jess Hill. And to a growing list of sports heroes, until then centered around baseball players like Ty Cobb, Jess began to add big-name college football players."

Hill became not only a supreme high school athlete but a scholastic superstar as well. He won 10 letters in football, basketball, baseball, track, and tennis but also was salutatorian and president of his senior class and vice-president of the student body; a prize-winning extemporaneous speaker in Riverside County; and a member of the California Scholarship

A familiar figure at Southern California: Jess Hill. He spanned decades as player, coach, and athletic director and did so with distinguished achievement.

Federation for four years. Later he made stunning contributions at Riverside Junior College in basketball, baseball, football, and track. A spectacular broad jump at one meet got him an invitation to visit the Southern Cal campus in 1926, but Hill went home shaking his head. "I stayed about 10 days and went back with the feeling that USC was just too big for me," he says.

Hill finished the football season at Riverside and played part of the basketball season in 1926-27 when he was finally lured to Southern Cal by a friendly assistant track coach and a scholarship. While romanced by Tommy Davis, Hill admits that the $300 scholarship and 50-cent-an-hour part-time janitorial job had a lot to do with his decision to come to Southern Cal. The family budget was tight.

Track and baseball commanded Hill's attention at first at Southern Cal, but he yearned to play big-time football, too. At first he was thwarted by track coach Dean Cromwell, who feared crippling injuries to his star.

"Cromwell wouldn't let me go out for football," recollects Hill. "He and I sat down and talked at length about it, and I said, 'Mr. Cromwell, I'm in physical education and I'm going to be a coach one of these years and I'm probably going to coach in football and it's going to be a help as far as my future is concerned to get out there and learn something about football.' And finally he let me go out in 1929."

Hill was not very big for football at 5-foot-10, 168 pounds. But he became one of Howard Jones' favorites. "Hula Hula" Hill was what Jones called him—for the way he swiveled his hips.

"He was the fastest man I have ever seen on Bovard Field," said Jones in the most supreme compliment.

Before Hill reached fame in football, however, he had established a track standard. At the Intercollegiate Athletic Association meet in Philadelphia, in 1929, he set an IC4A record in the longjump with a mark of 25 feet, 7/8 inches.

Hill recalls: "I had one jump left. I said, 'Well here goes!' I just leaped right into the air and threw all that I had into it, and there wasn't anybody more surprised than I when they told me I had jumped 25 feet.

In football Hill's beginnings were notable. Subbing for

starting fullback Jim Musick, who was injured in the first quarter, Hill averaged 12 yards a carry in 10 tries in a 48-0 rout of Washington in 1929. However, Southern Cal fans listening by radio to that Seattle game were not aware of Hill's superb performance—the equipment manager had forgotten Hill's regular jersey and he was forced to wear someone else's shirt. Cliff Thiede (No. 32), who did not even make the trip, was at first given credit by broadcasters for Hill's exploits.

"This fellow Thiede is the greatest open field runner we've seen in many a moon," said one announcer, "maybe even better than Red Grange. Where has Coach Jones been hiding him?"

Hill endured despite other great running talents at Southern Cal and established a Pacific Coast Conference record of 8.2 yards a carry. His defensive expertise was extraordinary as well—so fierce, in fact, that an ex-world wrestling champion thought he could learn from him. "If I could go out to the USC practice field and practice with some fellow like that tackling me until I could avoid him," said Ed "Strangler" Lewis after the Washington game, "I would be world's champion again."

Hill pointedly notes that he played in the first USC-UCLA football game in 1929. "We beat them 76-0, and they realized at that time they weren't quite ready," says Hill. "We had tradition, and we had heritage behind us that they didn't have. After we beat them in 1930 52-0 (Hill did not play in that game), we called off the series."

An athlete of myriad dimensions, Hill chose a baseball career upon graduation from Southern Cal in 1930. The New York Yankees beckoned, and Hill remembers his first game with their farm team, the Hollywood Stars. He should—he hit a home run on the first pitch.

"We were playing the Los Angeles Angels," Hill recalls. "I had been sitting on the bench several days, enjoying the game, when Manager Oscar Vitt fixed me with a grim stare. 'Grab a bat,' he said. 'You're hitting for Marlowe.' Well in those days you didn't just grab a bat. Some player was liable to crown you because bats were scarce, and nobody was going to take a chance on a punk rookie breaking his favorite stick.

"So I looked around and found an old, yellow drug store bat propped up in a corner. I was never so scared in my life. The only reason you couldn't hear my knees knocking was because it was too noisy. Beryl Horne—they called him Trader—was pitching for Los Angeles, and I remember thinking as I staggered up to the plate that he'd probably sneak a fastball past me for a strike. I made up my mind that if he did I'd be ready for it."

Hill then hit Horne's first offering over the left field wall at Wrigley Field. A pro rookie hitting a home run on the first pitch to him in a game provided an obvious thought for Robert Ripley, who printed a Believe It Or Not cartoon about it on April 8, 1932.

Climbing through the farm system, Hill spent springtimes playing exhibition games in Yankee Stadium alongside Babe Ruth. "I can't think of a bigger thrill in my whole life," Hill says.

By the time Hill was brought up to the majors in 1935, Ruth was gone from the Yankee outfield, but there was other celebrated company such as George Selkirk, Ben Chapman, and Earle Combs. Hill's speed attracted attention and admiration. Enthused one sportswriter: "He was the prettiest baserunner in the big leagues, if not the fastest."

A hitter of some dimension as well, Hill was soon forced out of baseball by eye problems.

"I'm sure I could have done better and played longer wearing glasses, but it just wasn't done in those days," Hill says.

The New York Yankees sold Hill to the Washington Senators, and eventually the Senators sent him to the Philadelphia Athletics despite a lofty .306 batting average in 1936. Under the critical eye of Connie Mack, Hill batted .273 for the Athletics in 1937 and "learned about outfielding." The next year Hill was back in the minor leagues in Oakland, and not long after that began a career in coaching.

Returning to his starting place Hill energetically embarked with a new ship on a new sea. He coached baseball and football at Corona High School in 1939 and then joined Long Beach City College, improving its track and football program until joining the Navy in 1942. Among his Naval associates was Bill Hunter, Southern Cal's athletic director. Hunter found leadership qualities in Hill and eventually brought him to USC in 1946 as freshman football coach and assistant track coach to the legendary Cromwell.

Upon Cromwell's retirement in 1949, Hill was named to succeed him and proved to be a worthy successor. In the next two seasons Hill won two national track titles for Southern Cal and drew praise in some quarters as "the best track coach at any American college."

Hill modestly refutes that superlative.

"I coached the teams, all right," Hill says, riveting his eyes on you, "but Dean Cromwell left me all of this talent. I didn't have to do much coaching."

More grandiose challenges awaited the gentlemanly Hill. In 1951 he accepted the job of head football coach after the dismissal of Jeff Cravath and showed strength in doing so. He left a familiar, comfortable position for one of far more pressure.

After a losing season in 1950, angry alumni had pushed Cravath out of the job with a power play. And Hill now sat in the hot seat.

"The team was in great shape," insists Hill. "We had some

Jess Hill huddles with his Southern California players in a 1953 practice. "Yes, gentlemen, that is a football."

fine football players. Frank Gifford, for one. Frank had played defense the year before. I had him for one year in 1952 and went in using a multiple offense—a Single Wing and a T. He was the tailback and a great one. Later on I had Jimmy Sears, in my opinion one of the finest small backs I've ever seen. He played defense, offense, made punt returns, kickoff returns. He was one great football player. And of course Jon Arnett was great, too. Jon had the best sense of balance of any back I've ever seen. He could fly, he could fly.

"We were blessed with some good teams. I don't know what my record was...it was something like .720 in six years."

Precisely, Hill's teams from 1951 through 1956 won 45 games, lost 17, and tied 1, a .725 winning percentage. He had made good a vow to "fight defeatism at every turn." Under Hill the Trojans visited the Rose Bowl twice—the first time beating Wisconsin 7-0 in 1953 to break the Big Ten's long domination of the affair. With Hill as coach the Trojans also defeated California 6 straight years and ended Pappy Waldorf's Pacific Coast grip.

Nurtured on old-fashioned football, Hill found himself adapting to a virtually new game. The two-platoon system was the rage, and even though Hill's teams were "primarily running teams" they developed a passing game for balance. Variety was the keynote.

"We had men in motion, flankers and split ends—just like today," explains Hill. "They were used in our day, just not as much."

Hill entered football coaching at an unpredictable time. Because of the nature of the sport in the early 1950s, upsets were common. After years of domination by World War II GIs, college football was given back to relative babies. Teenagers fresh out of high school studded rosters. Hill recalls, "freshmen were eligible to play in 1952."

"Anyone might jump up in the 1950s and beat any given team on any given day," Hill says. "I remember in 1951 we went up to play California at Berkeley. I think they were ranked No. 1 in the country and were undefeated. They had won something like 30 Pacific Coast Conference games in a row. We went up there as underdogs. They had us 14-0 at the half, and we beat them 21-14. That was an upset, no question about

Jess Hill and some of his warm-blooded Trojans arrive in nippy South Bend, Indiana, for a game with Notre Dame. Just off a plane from sunny Los Angeles are (chilled, from left to right): Charlie Ane, Al Carmichael, Hill, Leon Sellers, and Jim Sears.

it, that was an upset. It was probably my most satisfying victory. Those things could happen in those days, though, more so than they do today.

"In my last year, 1956, we lost to Oregon at Eugene and to Stanford at Palo Alto, and I thought that we had a better team than either of them. Those were the only games we lost that year. You see your top teams today. It isn't often that any of them slips up. But in those days it was possible."

Philosophically, Hill was perfect for football.

"The amazing thing about it, I never missed any sleep," he says. "Coaches vary, you see. I never missed a meal, and I never was upset or vomited as some do before or after a game. Never!

When I took the job as football coach, I always had a philosophy that God himself couldn't please everybody and I didn't expect to please everybody. I just made up my mind to give it the full effort. I don't believe in 110 percent. I believe 100 percent is enough. Come what may, I wasn't going to let it bother me.

"I didn't take the football home at night, or during the season. I spent many, many hours at work. I'd get home 11, 12 o'clock on Monday, Tuesday, and Wednesday nights. But on Thursday we sort of figured the hay was in the barn. We kept thinking, of course, but we didn't continue to have meetings after Wednesday night. If we weren't prepared by Thursday, we weren't going to be prepared."

Winning was never critical to Hill—a life style at odds with many of the nation's successful coaches. Hill was more philosopher than he was coach. He preferred turning out winning people more than winning teams.

"I hate to lose," he says, "but I don't believe there's any disgrace in it unless one is satisfied to lose. I've never been satisfied to lose. I think you should try to win but should also know how to lose. We sometimes learn and profit from adversity. I enjoyed my six years as coach. I worked with wonderful young men. I see a lot of them every now and then today—they're very successful in business and professions. One of the satisfactions, although we always talk about winning, is to have youngsters play football at college or high school, wherever, and in later years be equally successful in business as they were on the athletic field. To me that's a great source of satisfaction. You have to have a deep attachment for those youngsters."

His players verify Hill's sincerity.

"Jess is one of my favorites," says Jim Sears, who played fullback for Hill. "He treated me like a father. He was a good organizer, and I enjoyed him. He had a lot of confidence in me and gave me the confidence I needed. He's the only person I know who remembers anyone he ever talks to."

At a time when Hill was coaching, his wife Betty described the aura at home. It was exactly as Hill had said.

"Jess is an even-keeled individual; winning or losing, there's not too much difference in his action," Mrs. Betty Hill explained. "Jess is this way: It's a job to be done; if we lose, the house doesn't go into a pall of gloom. If we win, we're happy but don't go through the ceiling. We certainly don't relive games into the night."

Hill's wife and son, Jess, Jr., learned to put up with his bizarre working schedule that not only included long hours at the office but long hours at home. Hill constantly watched football movies in his den—sometimes for 12 hours a day.

"Movies were an indicator of raw talent, but I always wanted to talk to a youngster," says Hill. "When you talk to him, you get something about his desires, his motivation and his attitude, whether he's willing to work, willing to sacrifice, willing to perspire. We were concerned about the type of young man we were recruiting and many times said no to a youngster if we thought he wasn't the kind of man that we wanted at USC."

Hill's talent search discovered black power. Not by design, Negro players at Southern Cal had been rare before Hill came on the scene.

"We hadn't had many black football players at USC, I guess, until I had four or five," he says. "I brought in Addison Hawthorne in 1952, and we had C. R. Roberts."

The mention of Roberts provokes a story.

"We played in Austin, Texas, in 1956, and things went smoothly. No racial problems at all," says Hill. "We beat Texas really badly, something like 44-20, and Roberts had gone crazy that day—ran for 257 yards. After the game, Roberts was sitting in a restaurant with some of our people, and this guy who had been at the game walks up to the counter and says: 'I don't know too much about this thing, segregation, integration, and that. But whatever it is, I've been watching that Roberts guy—and I believe in HIM.'"

When Roberts combined with Arnett, Hill agrees that he probably had his strongest backfield. Gifford and Sears are two others that Hill considers his all-time best backfield men. If making up a personal all-star team, "then no doubt linebacker Pat Cannamela would have to be considered." Hill, however, detests selecting the "best" of anything.

"You're bound to have a lot of good players at Southern Cal over all those years," says Hill. "I don't know how people can select an all-time USC football team. How in the world would we ever pick it? Situations and conditions vary. It's academic—you just can't do it."

After raising the standard of football—and upholding it for six years—Hill was elevated to the post of athletic director upon Bill Hunter's retirement. From 1957 through 1971 Southern Cal's athletic achievements soared under Hill. During his tenure Trojan teams won twenty-nine NCAA championships and almost double that number in conference titles. Hill's leadership stamped him as "Athletic Director of the Decade" by the Columbus Touchdown Club in 1969.

"You don't accomplish these things only with outstanding coaches, or even with superb athletes on the field," Hill says. "Athletic success, as with everything else that has made USC a great institution, also comes from friends and alumni across the nation who give this campus unparalleled support. Witness the 1,200 people we had at a football kickoff dinner one fall. No other school in the country has that kind of turnout for such an event.

"But long before most of us took up the reins of support and leadership, there were the Bill Hunters, the Gus Hendersons, the Dean Cromwells, the Howard Joneses, the Sam Barrys—you can't begin to name them all—who laid the groundwork with their patience, energy, judgment, and leadership. Those who come after them are only working over ground prepared by their great efforts."

Forced to leave Southern Cal at the mandatory retirement age of 65, Hill made his way back into the mainstream with the PCAA in 1972. "I'm too young physically and mentally to go out to pasture," he said at the time. "I'm looking at my new PCAA job as a challenge, not a sinecure."

Activity never ceases, the mind remains alert, and the only noticeable difference is the physical makeup. The hair is no longer abundant, a little greyer. The body has thickened some, the walk is still brisk, but a step slower. But Hill stays on course, hardly swaying. It is the new challenge that has gripped the new man.

California, Here We Come

"Oskie" was missing. His disappearance was discovered following receipt of a telegram from Los Angeles. The telegram read: "Weather is fine. Think I will stay—Oskie."

It took no detective to figure out who had stolen the famed papier mache mascot bear from the University of California. "Oskie" had been "bearnapped" by Southern Cal students in retaliation for an act of thievery by California students. They had lifted the Trojans' stadium banner during a game at Berkeley.

Peace talks resulted after Southern Cal came up with Oskie as a lever, and student officials from each school finally effected a settlement. The objects of their affection were returned to each by mail.

That was 1949. Two years later Southern Cal stole a football game from California. When the Trojans defeated the Golden Bears 21-14 in 1951, it had to be classified as one of the most memorable—and delicious—conquests in Southern Cal history.

It came at an appropriate time—Jess Hill's first year as coach in 1951, a season when the Trojans were rebuilding from the bitter defeats of 1950. Hill courageously tackled an imposing challenge and took Southern Cal a long way in his first year. Frank Gifford and Pat Cannamela became Southern Cal's first all-Americans since 1947, and the Trojans won their first seven games before losing their last three.

"The biggest game in my time was the California game in

Frank Gifford, "the best all-around back in the country in 1951."

1951," says Gifford. "They were ranked No. 1, we were 14 points behind at half time—and we came back to beat them."

Pappy Waldorf's Golden Bears had not lost a regular season game since 1947, a span covering 38 contests. Bill Mais' passing enhanced that unbeatable aura and helped California take a 14-0 lead at the half. Still, the Trojans were not resigned to defeat.

"We thought all along that we'd win," Gifford said at the time. "No, we didn't have any doubt, even at the half."

Taunted by chants of "dirty Trojans" from the crowd, Southern Cal came to life under Gifford's spark. Midway in the third period the triple-threat tailback broke around right end and followed his blockers 69 yards for a touchdown. Early in the fourth period Gifford passed to Captain Dean Schneider on a 6-yard touchdown play and kicked the extra point to tie the game at 14-14.

Later, Gifford kicked and ran the Trojans to victory. He put the Golden Bears in an impossible position with a punt to their 8-yard line. Unable to budge, California kicked out, and Johnny Williams returned the ball 20 yards to the Golden Bears' 22. Southern Cal advanced the ball in 3 plays and called on Gifford to get the final inches for the first down. He made it, with a few inches to spare.

Gifford then got three more yards, Bob Buckley drove to the two, and with two minutes and forty-four seconds left in the game Leon Sellers smashed over for the winning touchdown. Gifford's extra-point kick provided the perfect ending for Southern Cal.

"Heart, spirit, morale—that's what did it," said Hill. "Determination won it for us."

Determination—and guys named Gifford and Cannamela.

"Frank Gifford was the outstanding back on the field today, and Pat Cannamela was the outstanding linebacker," said Hill. "John Olszewski is great and hard to stop. And Les Richter is fine backing up the California line. But I'll pick Frank and Pat over them."

Cannamela, a stubby, 205-pounder, was not physically cast in the heroic mold of the sleek Gifford but nevertheless shared top billing.

"I know the other Trojans will understand if I say that Pat

Cannamela must be accorded equal ranking with the great Gifford," said a sportswriter. "Murderous Pat knocked Johnny Olszewski, Cal's famed back, clear out of the game the first time Johnny-O carried the ball. One scout in the press box said: 'If Les Richter is an all-American, then Cannamela is an all-Everything."

Gifford credited others for his success that day: "Those fellows up front were wonderful to me. Boy, were we fired up. California didn't seem to hit me as hard as the Oregon State tacklers did."

On his 69-yard touchdown run: "I didn't think about much of anything except how wonderful it was to get those great blocks out there in the open. The blockers certainly made me look good."

After the game a national picture magazine nicknamed the Trojans "Murder, Inc." They certainly looked that way until the last three games of the year, when they lost to Stanford, UCLA, and Notre Dame.

Along the way Hill cultivated Gifford's talents. A defensive player in 1949 and 1950, Gifford was literally turned loose as a tailback in Hill's Single Wing offense. In 1951 Gifford was the team's rushing leader with 841 yards and also the total offense leader with 1,144 (303 yards passing).

Jim Sears, Gifford's gifted running mate who later made the all-America team himself, found an irony in it.

"It's kind of funny," Sears says. "I came to USC as an offensive back and became an all-American defensive back. Gifford, who came to USC with me, began as a defensive back and ended up as an all-American offensive back. In my sophomore year I was a starter and Gifford was a little-known quarterback. In my junior year Gifford became a star. It was just a case that he was more fitted to the style of play. He was a combination passer and runner and fit right into the Single Wing."

Gifford's latent offensive brilliance was not in the least explored when he first came to Southern Cal from Bakersfield High School. He started out as a "second-string defensive back" in 1949, he recalls.

"I didn't think I'd be playing," he says, "but then one of the defensive backs got hurt, and I got into a game and intercepted three passes."

Gifford brought rich talents but empty pockets to Southern Cal in 1949. He remembers that he lived in a garage in his first year because he could not afford an apartment.

"I didn't have the money," says Gifford, "so I moved into Nick Pappas' garage."

Pappas, a onetime football hero himself, recalls an old boarder.

"Frank has never forgotten what USC has done for him," says Pappas and then ties this in with his own role as director of Southern Cal's Athletic Support Groups. "He's the kind of a guy who still helps us recruit players. He ALWAYS mentions the fact that he is a Trojan."

About Gifford's football ability, Pappas says: "He could really go. He was a steady, always-get-your-yard runner."

To Hill, Gifford was more than that. "He was the best all-around back in the country in 1951," Hill once said. Gifford never got the chance to prove it before Hill arrived with his Single Wing. Under Jeff Cravath in 1949 and 1950, "Gifford never seemed to quite fit into the T-Formation," a sportswriter pointed out. "However, in 1951 he found himself in the new formation and ran up adding machines with his ground-gaining antics."

Gifford usually had butterflies playing before large audiences, even after he made good in the National Football League with the New York Giants. At Southern Cal in his senior year Gifford functioned before more than a half-million people, including over 81,000 in the California game. "I just never got over the awe of playing before big crowds," says Gifford, who now speaks before big crowds as a television broadcaster.

Unfortunately Southern Cal never made a Rose Bowl appearance during Gifford's time. He would have liked that. The year after he left, Hill had his best team and a Rose Bowl berth.

Time Out: Jim Sears

A "10th-string halfback" has to be a philosopher. "You have to wait it out," says Jim Sears, "and as long as you stay healthy, you move up."

Fortunately for Sears—and for Southern Cal—he did not have to wait too long. Injuries moved a lot of people out of his way, and all of a sudden he found himself in the starting lineup as an extremely nervous sophomore.

Once he got his break—he was not nervous any more. Merely great.

From 1950 through 1952 Sears usually bore the sobriquet, "master of the big play."

Against Notre Dame in 1950 he ran back a kickoff 44 yards for a touchdown to inspire Southern Cal to a 9-7 victory.

Against California in 1952 he took a punt on his own 31-yard line and raced for the winning touchdown in a 10-0 Trojan victory.

Against UCLA in 1952 he was responsible for both touchdowns to lead Southern Cal's 14-12 triumph. One time he took a lateral from Al Carmichael and ran 72 yards for a score. Later in the game he threw the winning touchdown pass to Carmichael.

"I was just hit as I released the ball and thought that it had been intercepted," Sears says.

Such dynamic exploits were not expected from this sunny Californian. He was too small, the detractors pointed out.

"Everyone said that I would get lost in the shuffle because

USC was so big," says Sears, who weighed 163 pounds and stood 5-foot-9½ in high school. But he grew a couple of inches and gained a couple of pounds by the time he was a sophomore in college.

"Size doesn't mean anything," Sears told his critics. "You have to get the chance."

Some people had believed in Sears. That was all he needed.

"My high school coach knew I had promise," Sears says. "He had gone to USC and told me to try to get as much recognition as I could at a junior college. So I went to El Camino JC and played...and USC started coming around. Ray George, who was an assistant coach then at Southern Cal, rushed me into coming."

Sears impressed people with his courage instead of his physical stature. "Jeff Cravath, my first coach at Southern Cal, said he liked me because I had heart," Sears relates. "If anyone bled or showed guts, he made the team. You learned how to be tough under Jeff Cravath. We spent three or four hours a day practicing sometimes."

The Los Angeles native who called himself a "prune picker" made the team as a lowly reserve. Not long after, he was playing everyday, an inflamed sophomore.

"I remember in my first year when we played California, the crowd excited me so much that I couldn't work out because my legs were so tight," Sears says.

The Trojans lost to California that year, as well as several other teams. But after a crushing loss to UCLA, Sears' dramatic work in the finale against Notre Dame helped salvage some respectability for the season, Cravath's last.

"We were supposed to beat UCLA, but they won a game (39-0) for a guy whose wife died," Sears remembers. "But we came back against Notre Dame. I fumbled and they scored, but then I ran back that kickoff for a touchdown.

"First I looked to see if there was any penalty. It's like anyone who runs very far in a football game. You're afraid the run is going to be called back. I didn't feel the crowd at first. When you run you don't feel the people; you are too anxious to outrun the man. Then after it's over, you feel the people. Boy, there must have been about 95,000 in the Coliseum that day."

In 1951 Frank Gifford was the star and Sears lost a job,

Jim Sears, carrying the ball against Wisconsin in the 1953 Rose Bowl game: "The Single Wing was better for me as a runner. I was able to get a lot of off-tackle runs for five or six yards."

but not his confidence.

"Frank and I were very close even though I played behind him," says Sears. "Frank was a very hard worker; he wanted to do everything perfectly. While sitting on the bench in 1951, I didn't like it. And I made up my mind that I wasn't going to do the same thing in 1952. So I learned how to pass. I really worked at it."

When Gifford left, a refurbished Sears was there to take his place. The eminent runner was now an eminent runner AND passer in 1952. "It wasn't all running, because now I could throw as well," Sears remembers. "I threw 100 passes that year, completed 53, 9 for touchdowns."

Southern Cal's new multi-threat back was not only the Trojans' offensive and passing leader but also ran back kickoffs and punts. He also was safety man on defense. All of these polished talents singled him out for all-American status.

"The biggest reason I made the all-America team was that I was picked by the school at the beginning of the year and the school stayed with me," Sears points out. "I was fortunate to have had a good year. I led the nation in punt returns for most of the season."

Another reason that he made all-American was the presence of a new coach at Southern Cal, Jess Hill. After taking over for Cravath in 1951, Hill installed offenses more suited to the talents of Gifford and Sears.

"The Single Wing was better for me as a runner," Sears says. "I was able to get a lot of off-tackle runs for five or six yards."

The California "prune picker" led the Trojans into the Rose Bowl but ironically did not get to play much in the 7-0 victory over Wisconsin. He was injured early in the game and replaced by Rudy Bukich.

"I only played four minutes and got hurt, and then Bukich came in and threw the winning touchdown pass to Al Carmichael," Sears recollects. "I still wonder, after all these years, if we would have still won if I had gotten to play.

"I felt bad about missing most of the Rose Bowl. It's one of the biggest things you can point to in college. If you play in it, you remember it for the rest of your life."

The agony of losing a big moment was later tempered when Sears played in the College all-Star Game and was voted the Most Valuable Player.

Sears coached freshman football at Southern Cal in 1953 and then had a checkered career in the pros. The service interrupted a four-year stay with the Chicago Cardinals of the National Football League, then Sears came back to USC as an assistant coach under Don Clark before rejoining professional football. He joined the new American Football League with the Los Angeles Chargers in 1960.

"Sid Gillman enticed me," Sears recalls. "I wanted to get some notoriety at home. People never heard from me—I had been away so long. Playing in Los Angeles helped bring my name back."

Sears played in the AFL's championship game in 1960, but that was his last big moment. The next year the Chargers moved to San Diego and Sears went along, but only played a few games there. He was then traded to the Denver Broncos, his last stop in the pros. "I hurt my shoulder and just couldn't come back," he says.

Sears became a car salesman and then started a golf club business. "We make personalized clubs," he tells you. "I'll probably be making a set for Frank Gifford soon."

The onetime "prune picker" remains a staunch Trojan. He is forever grateful for the doors opened by football.

"It's definitely an advantage to have played football," Sears says. "People know you. They say, 'Hey, I remember when you ran back that kickoff.' It helps a lot in business."

He is also grateful for the friendships. Sears' younger son is a living reminder of that. Sears named him Gifford Troy—after his friend and the university. He also keeps contact with Jon Arnett, another dazzling back of the 1950s. "Jon and I are very close," Sears says. "I see him often."

The ball has taken lucky bounces for Sears over the mellow seasons. He is glad that he caught the wind when he did. He explains:

"The only reason that I made football at USC was that I was adequate in all phases of the game: punting, catching, returning kicks, and passing a little better than average. I probably would not even come close nowadays. You have to have a specialty today."

He is not excusing himself, though.

"We had a different attitude toward football in my day," he says. "You ate and slept sports. You really worked at it. The kids don't like to do that today. You had to be a pretty tough character 25 years ago, too. The equipment wasn't as good as it is today, and you didn't go into the line unless you were a tough son-of-a-gun. I definitely think we were more competitive."

The "old" philosopher still has a message, it seems.

Daring Young Men

Unusual things happened in the 1953 Rose Bowl game.

First, an amateur photographer bailed out of a plane trying for unique aerial shots. He missed the stadium and missed his pictures as well. He landed 20 feet outside Gate 9 at half time, into the waiting arms of police. He was eventually released because there was no ordinance prohibiting the stunt.

Secondly, Southern Cal beat Wisconsin 7-0. That ALSO was unusual because a Big Ten team had never lost a Rose Bowl game before. Like the daring photographer, the Trojans took to the air for their purposes. A Rudy Bukich pass to Al Carmichael provided the only scoring in the game.

Of course it was unusual, too, that Bukich was in there. He got his chance only because all-American Jim Sears broke his leg on the ninth play of the game.

It was the indomitable Sears who had driven the Trojans to nine victories in ten regular season games during 1952, the best record that Coach Jess Hill produced in his six years at Southern Cal. The tough, little tailback soared to heroic heights in most of the games that year and helped finish off UCLA 14-12 for the Pacific Coast Conference championship and the Rose Bowl berth.

The Trojans not only took the Rose Bowl nomination away from the Bruins, but also kidnapped the UCLA mascot, "Mr. Bruin." The 8-foot teddy bear, loaned to UCLA by movie star Shirley Temple, was removed from the lobby of the Westwood theater on the Bruin campus and placed under guard at a Southern Cal fraternity house. About 30 Southern Cal students were in on the heist and just managed to escape in a getaway car, which stalled precisely as a group of UCLA students appeared. A push got the getaway car rolling, and the thieves were pursued in a wild chase all the way home.

It was nothing, however, compared to the excitement that happened on the football field.

Southern Cal had defeated Washington State, Northwestern, Army, San Diego Navy, Oregon State, California, Stanford, Washington, and UCLA before losing to Notre Dame. The Fighting Irish spoiled the Trojans' national championship dreams with a 9-0 decision, and a writer whimsically pointed out: "No. 10 turned out to be USC's unlucky number."

Number 11, however, was luckier. Rose Bowl Day dawned unseasonably cold, so cold in fact that queen Leah Feland wore "long johns" under her flowing white gown. It was 35 degrees at 5 a.m. and not much warmer as the day blossomed.

The teams warmed up the chilled crowd of 101,500 with competitive football. Deep in the third quarter the Trojans drove 73 yards in 9 plays for the winning touchdown. Bukich set up the scoring strike with a series of passes to the outside and finally reached Carmichael for the last 22 yards. Sam Tsagalakis, who kicked the extra point, had missed a 23-yard field goal another time when the ball struck the crossbar.

"I almost sent in my great punter, Desmond Koch, to attempt that field goal," Hill said after the game. "Sam had been good all year from inside the 25-yard line, although Koch was better from longer distances. I first called for Koch to go in but changed my mind when I saw the ball was inside the 25."

The game was not decided until the last minute, when Southern Cal blunted a Wisconsin drive. Two long passes from Jim Haluska just missed Harland Carl's outstretched hands. Carl then got his hands on another Haluska pass in the end zone, but dropped the ball as he skittered out of bounds into the stands. Officials ruled that he did not have complete control of the ball when he left the playing area.

The winning pass play and Richard Nixon were topical after the game. Nixon, newly elected vice-president of the United States and confirmed football addict, had been grand marshall of the Rose Bowl parade that year and took a gentle ribbing along with Southern Cal from one sportswriter.

"USC was as potent on the ground as an airplane," wrote Jack Geyer in the *Los Angeles Times*. "Victory came to the Trojans in the third quarter when they forgot what laughingly can be called a running attack and struck by air. Nixon's party won this year, too, after a long wait—24 years, to be exact."

Hill admitted that Geyer was right—about the passing, that is. "I guess we should have passed more," he said.

During the contest Nixon was a thrilled—and animated—spectator. A friend told a revealing story about the man afterwards. "When the game started, he got excited," said William Nicholas, Rose Bowl Tournament president at the time. "He started bopping the people in front of him with his program. He really enjoyed the game. Afterward he visited both dressing rooms before we returned to the hotel."

Before the game, Nicholas was planning seating details for the honored guests and was advised by a member of the Nixon family: "Don't have mother and dad sitting in front of Dick at the game. He is a violent rooter. He would probably roll up his program and in the excitement knock mom out by hitting her over the head. Please put mom and dad in the seats behind him."

Elmer Wilhoite hit somebody, too, that day but unfortunately had to pay a penalty for it. The all-American Southern Cal guard was expelled for using his fist on defense.

"The official said I was using my fist, but I wasn't," Wilhoite pleaded. "I was using my shoulder."

Carmichael called the winning play "a beautiful pass...but it came to me so slowly I was afraid that some Wisconsin guy would pick it off."

The play was a late addition to the Southern Cal scheme.

"We first used it in the UCLA game, but it didn't work," Carmichael explained. "The manuever called for the ends to cross and for the right halfback, who was me, to delay two counts before taking off. Then I swung wide and cut back to the middle."

Bukich said he was well cared for most of the day by the Trojan blockers: "Man, oh man! Did you see the protection I got from Lou Welsh, Ed Pucci, Don Stillwell, and Bob Cox? Except for one pass I had all the time I needed to throw."

Wisconsin Coach Ivy Williamson had no alibis, nor any complaints. "It was a good, tough game," he said. "Our boys gave a good account of themselves, and I am proud of them."

Southern Cal was never as effective under Hill after the 1952 season, although some fine moments, and some fine people, brightened the montage in the succeeding four years. Extraordinary runners such as Jon Arnett and C. R. Roberts added sweep and depth to the broad Trojan canvas.

In 1953 a dramatic victory over Stanford added luster to an otherwise modest season. Called "one of the greatest gridiron games ever played" by one sportswriter, the Trojans defeated the Indians 23-20 on Sam Tsagalakis' field goal from the 28-yard line with 35 seconds to go.

"Little Sam, looking kinda puny out there as the giants ahead dwarfed his 5-foot-7½-inch frame, lowered his head and swung his foot," the *Los Angeles Times* reported. "The ball sailed high in the air, and most of the people knew it was good because Tsagalakis jumped about 8 feet off the ground and waved his arms to the heavens."

From 1953 to 1955 Southern Cal bowed to Red Saunders' powerful UCLA teams. The Bruins not only claimed supremacy in Los Angeles, but the whole West Coast. They won the Pacific Coast Conference title three straight years, but ironically their possible best team in history could not go to the Rose Bowl in the 1954 season. The undefeated Bruins, who had outscored nine opponents 367 to 40, were acknowledged as the best in the country that year, but the PCC barred repeat appearances in the Rose Bowl during those times. UCLA had lost to Michigan State 28-20 at Pasadena the year before.

Southern Cal, which incidentally had been beaten 34-0 by UCLA in 1954, finished as runnerup in the PCC to the Bruins. The Trojans were selected to play Ohio State in the Rose Bowl and also finished runnerup there. The Buckeyes beat the Trojans 20-7 in mud, and rain, and afterwards Ohio State Coach Woody Hayes had something to say about the weather, the bands, and Southern Cal's football team—none of it good.

"My coaches who sat in the press box said we would have beaten USC by a higher score on a dry field," said Hayes, not too politely. "They thought our men would have gone a little farther on every play."

As if that was not enough, Hayes also ungraciously commented: "There are about four, possibly five, teams in the Big Ten that could beat USC...Big Ten teams are better in the Rose Bowl because they are raised on tougher competition."

Annoyed that the bands had chewed up the field and supposedly made conditions more impossible than they were, Hayes said rather heatedly: "The bands should have been required to stay on the sidelines instead of putting on the show where we were going to play. I think bands are a fine thing, but they owe their popularity to football, not the other way around. If you don't believe that, invite the bands out to the Rose Bowl some year without the football teams and see how much of a crowd they would draw."

The chattering Hayes went on: "Ohio State definitely is No. 1 in the nation."

Hill took issue only with one remark, the one about Big Ten supremacy. The Southern Cal coach did not believe that four or five Big Ten teams could beat the Trojans. In fact he did not believe that Ohio State could beat the Trojans on a clear day.

"Just say for me I'd like to play Ohio State again on a dry field," Hill said. "The rain hurt us a lot. We planned to throw and rely on our speed. We were handcuffed both ways by the rain."

Actually the bad weather restricted both teams. A sportswriter described the 89,191 spectators as "waterlogged lunatics" and marked the playing conditions as "the worst in Rose Bowl history."

While fumbles hurt USC, Ohio State quarterback Dave Leggett managed to hold onto the ball, and he took the Buckeyes on touchdown drives of 77, 68, and 35 yards. Hopalong Cassady, Bob Watkins, and Dick Harkrader did the ballcarrying for the most part.

Southern Cal's only touchdown came on a long punt return by Aramis Dandoy late in the second quarter. Describing it in the *Los Angeles Times*, Paul Zimmerman wrote: "There was little more than five minutes of the second quarter remaining when Dandoy cut loose with the most brilliant run of the afternoon to put the Trojans temporarily within striking distance. Hubert Bobo, back to kick, had to duck away from

two charging Trojans and barely got the ball away. The punt was a line-drive affair that went fifty-five yards before Dandoy fielded the dribbling ball on his fourteen. The Trojan eluded two onrushing Buckeyes and fought his way to midfield where George Belotti, 231-pound tackle, served up the key block. The fleet Trojan did a neat job of eluding Bobo after that as he sped toward the end zone."

The Rose Bowl became a "Mud Bowl" in 1955 when Southern Cal met Ohio State at Pasadena. The Trojans skidding and sliding are Gordon Duvall (No. 40), Jon Arnett (No. 26), and Leon Clarke (No. 81). The Buckeyes beat the rain and the Trojans, 20-7.

The ease with which Ohio State dominated Southern Cal in that game brought protests from West Coast sportswriters who felt that UCLA should have been there. They scored the "ridiculous" PCC rule that did not allow champions to make Rose Bowl appearances in successive years. "We should play our champion each year or get out," said one writer. "If we can't beat them with our best, we shouldn't try to do it with our second best."

But in the next few years it did not matter which PCC team was in the Rose Bowl arena. Big Ten teams continued their stunning domination and, one year after they had won their 10th game in 11 at Pasadena, sportswriter Maxwell Stiles protested in the *Los Angeles Mirror*:

"It beats me why the team that is rougher, tougher, and more aggressive always comes from the Big Ten. Why can't our own men hit harder, run harder, just once in a while?"

Time Out: Jon Arnett

Jon Arnett lives an idyllic life near the sea, drinks wine, reads Ralph Waldo Emerson, and writes poetry in free verse, a newborn Socrates. He also plays volleyball, watches hockey on television, and debates freely with wanderers.

Football is hardly spoken at the Manhattan Beach retreat—it is a prehistoric game of Arnett's past, no longer chic in his household.

That this poetry-loving, wine drinker once played football as well as anyone in the world is unrecognizable in the man. Tap the subject and Arnett will tell you quite frankly:

"I'm not down on football...I'm down on what people try to make out of it."

In Arnett's theory, football is, or should be, a game for children—not grown men with corrupt morals.

"I'm not bitter about the game," says Arnett unhesitatingly. "I just woke up to the way people treated people. I know what I was promised in football—and I know what I got."

Almost 20 years after the infamous payoff scandals shook Southern Cal and 3 other West Coast schools, Arnett is alive and extravagantly well in Manhattan Beach. Arnett and several other Trojan players were accused of accepting illegal financial aid from school-associated booster clubs, but bore the brand heroicly.

The Southern Cal seniors were given the courtesy of playing in five of the games that year, 1956, and selected the first half of the season. ("I guess they figured we were only half wrong," Arnett jokes, "so they let us play half a year.")

The penalty was severe enough; it probably cost Arnett the Heisman Trophy that year. ("I was averaging 150 yards on 12 carries a game at the time," he says.)

However, it did not hurt his professional football career. Playing with the Los Angeles Rams and Chicago Bears during 10 years in the National Football League, Arnett was recognized as royalty, the cream of runners.

He played it well but did not find it especially aesthetic.

"I was realistic," Arnett explains. "I knew that we were chattels. What is the NFL? Entertainment...guys who pop pills. I was mature in the pros, and I was able to swallow the game better. Some people took themselves too seriously. Sundays were fun, but you had to have the ability to be able to walk away from the game once it was over. It's not really that BIG a deal. You should worry about your family, worry about dinner. But after the game was over, they were still talking about the game. The next day they were still talking about the game. It wasn't that important."

Maturity came early for Arnett. He was in his first year at Southern Cal in 1954, he remembers.

"I had a great start and they're talking about the first sophomore all-American and all that, and then I sprained my knee in the sixth game against California," says Arnett. "All of a sudden I didn't see my name in the paper anymore, and the coaches weren't coddling me anymore. And I can remember crying myself to sleep at night thinking that I might never play football again. I think I began to know then, that when you were through with football you were through. My fame was here today—and gone tomorrow. I'll tell you, it was the best thing that happened to me. That's when I became a student first and a football player second. It gave me a new perspective on my life."

Despite the injury Arnett was Southern Cal's top rusher with 601 yards. It was an indication of future accomplishments and confirmed the faith of Southern Cal officials.

Years before he starred in a Trojan uniform, he had a sense of direction. Arnett grew up in a "semi-ghetto area" of Los Angeles, nurtured on Southern Cal success.

"USC was No. 1 in my backyard and always had the

Jon Arnett in the pros: "Sundays were fun, but you had to have the ability to be able to walk away from the game once it was over. It's not really that big a deal."

heritage," says Arnett. "I went to every Southern Cal game when I was young; I sold papers, tried to do anything to get into the games. I didn't have any idols. I couldn't even tell you the names of the stars of my day. I just wanted to go there because of the school's reputation."

The classy product of Manual Arts High School got his wish and joined Southern Cal on a scholarship. He majored in finance but pretty soon began majoring in football, too.

"I coached Jon in his freshman year," recalls Jim Sears, Southern Cal's all-American back of the 1950s. "I told him he'd be an all-American if he didn't let his head size get any larger. He was really good."

Arnett's aspirations were not especially high, though.

"All I wanted to do was make the team behind Aramis Dandoy," Arnett reflects. "All I wanted to do was play a little and get Dandoy's autograph."

But Arnett accomplished more than that in his sophomore year. He carved bold headlines across sports pages and at one juncture was named National Player of the Week.

"My first game was thrilling," Arnett recalls. "I got to play in the second quarter and scored three touchdowns."

Arnett's knee injury in his first varsity season was disappointing but not destructive. It had theraputic effects on his psyche. "I started to put the game in its proper context," he says. "I started not to take myself seriously."

He played serious football, though. As a junior, Arnett again was Southern Cal's rushing leader with 672 yards. He thought his talents were undeveloped at that. He did not carry the ball enough, he says.

"I never carried the ball more than 20 times in a game—at least I can't recall if I did," Arnett says. "One time in a big game with UCLA I carried the ball only 8 times; I would have loved to play for John McKay (the present-day coach). I know that O. J. Simpson had twice as many carries in 2 years at USC than I had in 3."

The 1956 scandal bit deeply and cast a shadow on Arnett's early life.

"It was a traumatic year for me," he says. "I was only 20. We were getting under-the-table payments that all the schools in the Pacific Coast Conference got; even with the payments and the maintenance jobs, I had to work summers to pay it all back. All of a sudden USC opened its books, and it came out."

The schools involved along with Southern Cal were UCLA, California, and Washington. They were all penalized by the PCC.

"There's a sidelight to the story that's kind of funny," says Arnett. "One of the reasons that I went to USC is that USC

The payoff scandal of 1956 bit deeply and cast a shadow on Jon Arnett's life.

offered the least of all the schools—and some of the schools that pointed their fingers at us in the 1956 scandal had offered me much more...'the simon-pure' schools such as Stanford, 'the Harvard of the West,' was among them. Those were the schools that really put us under."

Arnett was offered $50,000 to play football in Canada, but turned his back on that temptation because he felt he "owed allegiance" to Southern Cal. "They asked me to stay and play half a season in my senior year instead of going to Canada for $50,000," Arnett says. "USC showed me what allegiance was—they dumped me and dumped my family."

Arnett's younger brother, who wished to do post-graduate work at USC many years after the scandal, was denied entry.

"USC was the only school to turn him down," Arnett says. "When he came back from Heidelberg University to further his education, he couldn't get in—and it was a political thing. So I got disenchanted with Southern Cal. I remember he cried because USC wouldn't accept him."

The school also cost Arnett a job as a broadcaster, he says.

"I was doing color for Southern Cal games, and they bounced me because I talked about pro football on television and that was taboo," says Arnett. "This is the same university that stopped me perhaps from winning the Heisman Trophy and jeopardized my career and money-earning capacity. I'll never understand it."

If Arnett sounds bitter, he says he is not.

"It's been great in some ways," he insists. "I loved the university when I was there. I had a super time. Actually what happened at USC was a blessing in disguise. In sports there is a tendency to fall into the false illusion that people are going to give you something for nothing. But that's just a false illusion."

Arnett's last game was memorable. He rushed for 157 yards against Stanford, and at the end of the game, which incidentally Southern Cal lost, Arnett was leading the nation in rushing. In addition, for the season he had completed 8 of 11 passes for 133 yards, had kicked 7 extra points, and was leading the Trojan team in tackles. Although he did not play the rest of the year, he also led the team in scoring for the third straight season.

When the Stanford game ended, Arnett was summoned to

a microphone by the Trojan rooting section which continually chanted, "We want Jon." On his way to the dressing room, he changed directions and trotted across the field to address the Southern Cal students.

"He stood there with his head bowed, crying," remembers Joe Jares, who was the *Daily Trojan* sports editor in 1956. "Dann Angeloff, a super patriot kind of cheerleader, was next to him, chin up and lips set in a grim line. All the mourning USC fans milled around in the stands and on the sideline grass."

Arnett spoke softly: "Right now the seven of us find it pretty hard to say what we feel. We can only thank you for the 100 percent support you gave us. We're sorry that we let you down today (Noooooo, screamed the students), but all we can ask is that you stick by the team the rest of the way and give 'em everything you have. Thank you."

Jares recalls: "Well, no, it wasn't the Gettysburg Address. However, at that moment he could have recited cake recipes and been cheered mightily."

"I'd live the college life over," Arnett says today. "I loved that part of it."

Arnett signed a lucrative contract with the Rams but kept his feet on the ground at the same time.

"I started working as a stockbroker during the off-season in my second year in the NFL," says Arnett. "I did that for seven years while I was a player. It gave me a chance to see the real world while I was still a player. A lot of players weren't prepared for the fact that they weren't going to make $40,000 a year after they retired from football. But I could see the transition. In the 1950s most of the guys were just thinking about playing. If they gave any thought at all to anything, it was that they'd open a bar or something when they retired. Now players see that they must prepare for the future."

When Arnett left professional football, he was prepared. He continued as a stockbroker for a few years, then became a national sales vice-president for Global Van Lines. He finally went into partnership with former baseball player Billy Cowan in a real estate investment firm in Los Angeles and struck gold.

"We're building buildings and having a helluva time," Arnett says. "We laugh a lot."

Arnett does not miss fame. He has found something more

important—himself.

"I felt I was well prepared to handle retirement from football," he says. "I saw after I graduated from USC how quickly the alumni forgets. You can't rely on anyone just because you played football.

"The hardest transition you have to make after you retire is to get yourself scheduled. When you're playing ball in high school, then college and the pros, you always have a person imposing the discipline. Most of the athletes I know are undisciplined in their outside lives. In our firm we don't do business with any athletes because they're so irresponsible. If I had gone through five more years of catering, I would never have been disciplined."

Quite naturally Arnett's world does not pivot around business. He is a romantic, too.

"I write poetry and I'd like to write a book some time to capture something from the eyes of a young man who came out of a ghetto and found out what life is all about," Arnett says. "An autobiographical novel, that's it. We look at ourselves and it's a big enough story. We have to know about ourselves, that's important. I started writing when I was 22 or 23 because I was questioning if what I was doing was really important."

Arnett is engulfed in writing talent. His father-in-law, Dave Lott, has written a book, and Arnett's wife, Vicky, owns and writes for several magazines along with Mr. Lott. Arnett is duly proud of his wife. ("She was a debate major at California," Arnett says. "I debate with her and lose. I tell her it's the only way that Cal can beat USC.")

For a recent birthday Arnett received a unique present from his wife. She compiled several of Arnett's poetic efforts and had them bound.

"I get into jags when I write for three or four months," Arnett says. "They wanted to publish my stuff at USC."

Since Arnett has left football, he has forgotten that it ever existed. "I've become a super hockey fan," he says. "I haven't been to a football game for four or five years. They've so commercialized it and made every player the 'greatest.' They think the athletes are so great nowadays in football. There's no way I'm going to pay $10 to watch a game. I get turned off by jocks demanding these huge salaries."

Arnett's press clippings have gone the way of all junk.

"My mother kept a collection of stories about me in a big, brown box somewhere," says Arnett. "I don't even know where it is. I don't even care."

He has his memories stored elsewhere.

"I wouldn't take $10,000 for the games I played," he says. "I loved the game when I played. But I don't condone the sport."

Arnett keeps a special faith and wishes that others would, too.

"The only important thing in life," he says, "is how we treat one another."

Time Out: C. R. Roberts

"USC was known as a place where blacks couldn't get in to play ball. I got hate mail. They used to tell me I was the first black in the starting lineup since Brice Taylor in 1925. There was definitely prejudice when I was there."

Unpleasant memories stir C. R. Roberts at times. But football achievements in 1955 and 1956 washed away the taste of bigotry that lingered at Southern Cal.

Roberts was no Black Avenger, yet felt he had to go there to cure the disease of prejudice.

"I felt that somebody had to go and it might as well be me," Roberts says. "I wanted to contribute something."

His contributions soared above the obvious physical achievements. Books tell you that Roberts gained 1,309 yards in his Southern Cal career, including a still-standing record of 251 in a game. His average of 6.5 yards per carry is the second best in Trojan history.

But if he was one of the best fullbacks produced at Southern Cal, he was also a man of stature in other ways. He considered others' feelings. "People sometimes forget that the most important things are people," he says. Roberts towered above ordinary man in the philosophical sense and brought a sublime humaneness to Southern Cal.

He did not get it back in kind right away, though.

"I played freshman ball. Gordon Duvall was ahead of me and so was a guy named Cooke," he remembers. "I felt my situation (color) had something to do with my not starting. I had to make all sorts of adjustments. I would get letters, and the letters were all racial, all hate mail to the effect that I was a black boy going to a white boys' school. About the second to the last game of my sophomore season they let me play the whole game. In 1955, in the UCLA and the Notre Dame games—that's when I knew I was going to play regularly."

But there were still problems in practice, Roberts recalls.

"My blockers laid down for me and made it tough carrying the ball in practice sessions," Roberts says. "It was a sacrifice I had to make. They would make me run a play, I remember, and they were stacking the line, and someone tipped the defense where I was going to go and they racked me up time and again. Coach Jess Hill wasn't aware of the situation."

The situation became more bearable in his junior year. Roberts had won the respect of teammates. It was obvious when the Trojans went to Texas for a game.

"This was one of the rare times when an integrated team came down to Austin, and I was supposed to stay somewhere else than where the team stayed," Roberts remembers. "But the team said they'd prefer to have me with them, and the team wouldn't go unless I stayed in the same hotel. It was quite a problem then, because the whole team got hate mail after that—all from California. The guys didn't get excited, though."

Roberts recalls a trip without incident.

"Black people from Texas came in and took me out," he says. "That took the edge off everything. It was one of the most wonderful road trips I ever had."

It was one of the most productive, too. Roberts only played 12 minutes against Texas and rushed for 251 yards, the aforementioned school record. ("There was a joke after that game whether I'd get enough playing time the rest of the season for my letter," he says.)

"During the first quarter I was lucky enough to make a couple of touchdowns on long runs," he says. "Most of my runs were like for 60, 50, and 47 yards. Hill took me out early because he thought there might be trouble. Actually I was glad to get out. The other players said a few bad things. I expected it."

After Roberts went over the 250-yard mark later in the game, he remembers: "Then the other players started saying

C. R. Roberts runs for a 22-yard gain against Notre Dame after taking a screen pass in the 1955 game.

nice things."

Later in the year Roberts also ran wild against Washington, and although his yardage total was not as high as the Texas game he enjoyed that performance more.

"I felt that was my most productive game because I did everything physically well by beating my man one-on-one," he says. "Everything went well for me that day. I remember I fumbled the ball once and it popped way up in the air, and I was able to catch it on the fly and continue running."

He also found teeth marks on his thigh after the game, won by Southern Cal 35-7. "I think it happened in a pileup," Roberts says. "Some guy was out to get me, I suppose."

Ever since he learned to carry a football, people were "out

to get" C. R. Roberts. Few actually did, though, on a football field.

Born in Mississippi, Roberts moved with his family to the southern California area before he remembers. He grew up in Oceanside, and his passion was hunting, not football, as a youngster.

"One day I came back from hunting, and the boys were playing in the streets and they coaxed me into playing football with them," Roberts remembers. "I made some touchdowns, but I didn't know then it was such a special accomplishment. I guess that was around the sixth grade."

Roberts' natural talents developed, and the colleges came to him.

"I wanted West Point originally," Roberts says, "but I finally decided on USC because the people impressed me. I was impressed with the way things were done at USC, the way people were very close. I wasn't girl-crazy and I wanted to study, and I thought that USC would be the best place for that. USC provided a tutor in math, which I needed."

Because of prejudices Roberts found the beginnings "very hard...friends wanted to know why I wasn't playing more."

Besides bigotry Roberts' career was involved in other unpleasantries. He lost a year of eligibility when the notorious 1956 payoff scandals exploded through the West Coast.

"The players involved in the scandal had jobs and were making over $75 a month, more, I guess, than what they were supposed to be getting," says Roberts. "I didn't play in 1957 because of the scandal, but I was happy that Jon Arnett was able to get five games out of it in 1956. Jon was a senior and given the option of playing either the first five or last five games of the season. He and some other seniors made a deal for some information. Everyone else lost their eligibility. There were something like ten or twelve players involved.

"I was very hurt; I didn't know what to do. I guess I matured in that situation. I learned that you have to find things out for yourself. It's a shame, if everyone had stayed together in my senior year, we would have had the most fantastic team. I believe Coach Hill wanted to leave because of the scandal. (Hill moved up to the position of athletic director in 1957.)"

Since Roberts could not play in college in 1957, he played in the pros. Roberts spent a year with the Toronto Argonauts of the Canadian Football League and later came back to advance his business studies at Southern Cal.

A tempting offer by the New York Giants of the National Football League soon lured him back into professional ball. ("It was a matter of eating," he says.) He was drafted, signed, and traded the same year. The Giants dealt Roberts to Pittsburgh, but he would not stay. "I couldn't take the intolerable racial situation in that town," he explains. "They got rid of me quickly, and I was back on the West Coast."

Roberts was picked up by the San Francisco 49ers and was relegated to the taxi squad his first year. However, in the next five years he became a regular in the famed "all-initial" backfield that included Y. A. Tittle, R. C. Owens, and J. D. Smith. Roberts also played with John Brodie, whom he had known as a fierce opponent in college. "It took quite a while for Brodie and me to get to like each other after all our battles in college," Roberts says. "He played for Stanford."

After five illustrious years in the NFL, Roberts turned to Canadian football once more. Among other things, he "enjoyed the people in Canada very much." He played with the Hamilton Tiger-Cats until "I got tired of being away from home." He worked as a real estate salesman and a loan officer trainee in a bank before going into the teaching field.

"School teaching is sometimes hard, but I do it and I like it," says Roberts, who teaches accounting and business at Lawndale High School in a suburb of Los Angeles. "The thing is, you have to have a special love for kids. And I've always gotten along well with kids."

Looking back over the years Roberts sees some pain, but mostly pleasure.

"I'd do it all over again," he says. "It was a tough row to hoe—but it was worth it."

The "C" stands for Cornelius after his father and the "R" stands for nothing, he tells you.

More to the truth, the "C" should stand for courage and the "R" for royalty.

Scandal

In an exclusive story on the front page of the *Oakland Tribune*, football player George Stephenson revealed why he took illegal money from UCLA and the University of California.

"I have found that in most cases, athletes of conferences cannot make ends meet for even $100 a month," he said. "It cost me $80 a month for room and board, not counting meals on weekends, and that doesn't include laundry or personal necessities. At UCLA and at the University of California I found it ran me $125 a month for bare living expenses."

Stephenson received $115 a month, $40 more than he was supposed to be getting under Pacific Coast Conference rules. He was one of several players caught and branded.

The athlete payoff scandal of 1956 hit the West Coast with locomotive force. Players from UCLA, California, Washington, and Southern Cal were penalized for taking under-the-table aid, and the schools themselves suffered temporary exile from the PCC, to say nothing of tarnished integrity.

Jon Arnett was the most famous name of 12 seniors found guilty of accepting excess aid at Southern Cal. After facing that option of playing only half the schedule in 1956, and selecting the first 5 games, the seniors were relegated to scrimmages and sideline duties the rest of the season. About his publicized refusal of that golden offer from Canadian football in his senior year, Arnett explained: "It's much easier to ignore a flattering offer than to turn my back on my teammates, coaching staff, and university."

The Trojans also were crippled by the losses of tackles Fabian Abram and George Belotti, end Chuck Leimbach, quarterback Frank Hall, fullback Bob Isaacson and halfback Fred Pierce. The bombshell event decimated the four schools beyond recognition, making it possible for Oregon State to win the PCC title and a Rose Bowl berth for the first time since 1941.

Along with declaring several players ineligible—many lost an entire season, not just half—the PCC ordered stiff punishments against the schools.

On May 6 Washington was placed on a two-year probation. On May 23 UCLA, which had been warned three times previously of laxity in its athletic employment program, was placed on three years probation and fined $15,000. On July 8 both Southern Cal and California were put on probation and fined. Southern Cal got a two-year probation and a $10,000 fine, and California was hit with a year's probation and a $25,000 fine.

(A review of the situation was later undertaken by the PCC and a reduction of penalties recommended. In Southern Cal's case the Trojans had sanctions removed in all sports but football. The league acted benevolently because Southern Cal had cooperated fully in the investigation, furnishing a complete list of its players involved in the payoffs.)

The situation had been simmering since 1952 when the PCC started a cleanup program of recruiting abuses. The years after the Second World War had become the golden era of nationwide recruiting and subsidization, and the lordly National Collegiate Athletic Association hoped to stop overreaction with its famous Sanity Code of 1948. In 1952 the American Council on Education presented a report on the situation, and the PCC took up the cudgel, "embarking upon a policy of further accenting enforcement." That year the league "authorized the commissioner to employ professional assistance for purposes of investigation," and in May, 1955, established the Athletic Code Enforcement Board to "assist the conference and commissioner in developing facts and information on certain cases of violations."

Not long after the Rose Bowl on January 1, 1956, the PCC began procedures against UCLA, California, Washington, and

Southern Cal. Stories of illicit payments, phony job rackets, and illegal raffles made national headlines for months.

J. Miller Leavy, a Los Angeles County deputy district attorney, reported that some California football players received a minimum of $50 a month for virtually non-existent, off-campus jobs. This was in addition to the $75 per month allowed for campus work by the conference.

"It is a phony job in which a coach promises and provides the athlete with an 'outside' job that pays a minimum of $50 per month with a businessman backer of the Berkeley school to pick up the tab," Leavy told the press.

Leavy had substantiating statements from the mothers of two boys rushed by California proselyters. The Associated Press reported:

"He (Leavy) cited the alleged instance of one boy who received regular $50 payments for five months and worked a total of two hours during the entire period. The boy disclosed that his buddy enjoyed a similar deal, and Leavy noted, 'Among the football players, the athlete indicated, the job program was considered a farce, a cover-up.'"

In another instance Leavy revealed that an athlete's grades in junior college were "helped" by the "Berkeley registrar's programming."

"(Head Football Coach Pappy) Waldorf told the athlete that Cal was trying to build up a good football team and that the boys never had any financial worries and that his family's medical expenses would be taken care of, too," Leavy said. "The $75-and-$50 pattern established at Berkeley is borne out by the sworn statements of the other prospective athletes and their mothers."

Leavy revealed that one mother was given a better job offer to move to Berkeley if her boy accepted an offer to play. The mother refused, according to Leavy, because she told the man, "it was just like selling your own child."

"There were instances where whole families would be moved to Berkeley, brothers of athletes would be 'sponsored' in the university, brothers and sisters would be flown to Berkeley, expense-free, to watch home games...summer jobs offered to top athlete prospects ranged from $400 to $600 a month," Leavy said.

UCLA and Southern Cal were accused of running illegitimate raffles to make money to pay off athletes. UCLA made $50,000 a year and Southern Cal $30,000 from these events, according to reporter Ed Schoenfeld of the *Oakland Tribune*.

"The money (for athletes) is obtained as a direct result of the raffles staged by the two institutions' major athletic booster clubs," Schoenfeld wrote in February, 1956. "Offering Cadillacs, a thousand dollar mink stole, and a holiday in Mexico as prizes, the raffles are among the best unkept secrets in southern California. They have been conducted for the past several years without interference."

Schoenfeld pointed out in his story that such events were against the state penal code. "Raffles are illegal, and a misdemeanor, with maximum punishment of a $500 fine and six months in jail, or both," Schoenfeld said.

Both UCLA and Southern Cal spokesmen disputed Schoenfeld's story, but it did not stop California attorney general Pat Brown from looking into the situation. That, of course, added more explosive material to the building drama.

A "downtown fund" operated by alumni was disclosed at the University of Washington. "Several athletes said they had received money from the fund in addition to the income from college jobs," reported the AP. In the wake of the scandal there was a wholesale revolt by football players and later the dismissal of Coach John Cherberg and the resignation of Athletic Director Harvey Cassill.

Of all the accusations one of the most starkly dramatic was Stephenson's. The 22-year-old player explained in detail how UCLA made secret cash deals with its football stars. Stephenson was a star fullback at Hoover High School in San Diego and was named on the National High School all-American Football Squad. He was contacted by nine West Coast schools and visited the campuses of Southern Cal, UCLA, Stanford, and California.

"While visiting the UCLA campus for the second time, an assistant football coach told me I would be getting $115 a month while attending school as soon as I enrolled," Stephenson said. "The coach said the reason UCLA athletes were given $115 a month was because the coaching staff felt that amount was necessary for a student to live at Westwood. I was told not to say anything about the money given me over $75. He told me about the Coast Conference's ruling that athletes could be paid a maximum of $75 a month for campus work. But he said UCLA felt it had to break this rule because a boy who did not get financial help from home would need more than $75 a month to live at UCLA.

"At the same time I asked the coach if he could get me a summer job, and he said he would see about it and let me know. A few weeks later the coach wrote me a letter and told me I had a job at a Los Angeles warehouse starting at the end of that month. He also made arrangements for me to live in a campus fraternity house during the summer, but I had to pay for my room and board out of my salary."

During the school year Stephenson worked as a file clerk in the football coaches' office, but not too hard. "An assistant football coach told me to put in as much time as I could on the job," Stephenson said. "Try to work the 50 hours required by the conference, but don't do it if you feel it will interfere with your studies, he said."

The "warehouse" job during the summer consisted merely of picking up a check, Stephenson revealed.

"The same assistant coach gave me a slip of paper with an address in Westwood on it," said Stephenson. "He told me to go to that address about the third day of each month and pick up $40. He told me to go into the office and see a man who would ask me to sign my name to a list of football players and collect the $40."

In his statement to the press Stephenson also revealed that a similar situation existed at California when he later attended that university.

The scandal not only blemished the four schools involved but created enormous bitterness between universities in the PCC. This extreme feeling once prompted the president of a northern university to refer to a California school as a "bastard that has the bark of a purebred but the innards and hair of a mongrel." The melodrama reached higher circles, involving men of state, and rumors circulated that USC, UCLA, California, and Washington were on the brink of secession from the PCC.

"A rebel football government seemed on the verge of setting up shop in Sacramento under the protective wing of Governor Goodwin (Jeff Davis) Knight," reported a national sports magazine. "Knight, an honest, forthright man of even temper, was hopping mad. The fact that the PCC fathers had barred USC and UCLA from Rose Bowl competition for two and three years respectively had raised the hackles on his red-blooded neck, and he said so. 'Set up our own league,' he screamed."

Knight appealed for a new, realistic approach to athletic scholarships, calling for a higher ceiling on the monthly payments to players. It is the $75 maximum that is at fault, not the people, protested Knight, a football player for Stanford before World War I. This attitude did not sit well with Oregon governor Elmo Smith, who said: "If California standards are incompatible with ours, maybe they should pull out."

Uncharitable feelings such as these and alumni pressure eventually led to the dissolution of the Pacific Coast Conference in 1959. In the period prior to the agonizing death of the PCC, there were immediate changes noticeable in the West Coast football scheme. UCLA, a West Coast bully in the early 1950s and a national champion in 1954, became an also-ran. Southern Cal, which had a moderately successful 8-2 record in 1956, was able to win only one game in 10 during 1957, a year when Jess Hill left coaching to become the athletic director and Don Clark became head football coach.

Time Out: Don Clark

With the arrival of Don Clark as coach at Southern Cal in 1957 came an intense style of race-horse football. The players ran back to the line of scrimmage from the huddle crying, "Five." The indication, of course, was a determination to make at least five yards on the play.

Everything worked as planned—up to the line of scrimmage. When the Trojans put their lamentable offense in motion, five yards seemed as far as a mile.

"I had tremendous problems as football coach in my first year," Clark remembers. "The thing is, I took over right after the payoff scandals, and Southern Cal was under penalties. There was no recruiting players. I didn't even have a quarterback. I was working with seniors and juniors who were not even permitted to play. Not only that, not any of the school officials was interested in the athletic situation. We had minimum facilities, a minimum budget, and I started with nothing in my favor. So here we're talking about a really low position."

Football was suddenly no longer king at Southern Cal. The payoff scandal of 1956 deflated football to such an extent that it was treated as something of a step-child. Clark remembers that relationships with school administrators "weren't working properly...they were very trying times and nothing could be resolved because no one wanted to do it."

Clark recalls that he even had to renovate his own quarters. "I went to engineering school, so I knew a little bit about renovation," says Clark. "I had to get the money myself. I got tired of waiting for it from the school."

The 1957 team record was as deplorable as the conditions. The Trojans won but one game and lost nine, the first time that had ever happened. Clark tried to make up for it in practice sessions.

"He (Clark) was very demanding and ran practice sessions that were quite long and quite exhausting," remembers Ron Mix, a tackle who played under Clark from 1957 through 1959. "He tried to make up for a lack of talent by conditioning us better. We were more sound fundamentally than other teams— but the lack of talent was too great a deficit to make up. I hated football. The amount of work we did was just unusual. Clark was the adult in charge and we respected him, but the amount of work we had, it completely took the enjoyment out of the game. The fact that I didn't like football was no reflection on Don Clark, though. He was a good coach."

Lou Byrd, a fine guard in the Clark years, recalls the hard times, too. "Don Clark hired an assistant, Al Davis, to make us run, run, run. We ran to the line of scrimmage. We would run out of the clubhouse. You were so sore that no one could touch you. It was a tough, miserable year, and they just beat us to a pulp. We kept losing, and the coaches got madder and madder."

The first year, insufferable as it was, prepared Clark for more pleasant days. A sunburst came to Southern Cal in the person of Dr. Norman Topping in 1958.

"Dr. Topping came in as president and got tremendous support groups for athletics," Clark says. "Dr. Topping cared about the situation."

Mindful of the place of athletics in university life, Topping appointed a representative from his faculty to act as a liaison with the National Collegiate Athletic Association. With the appearance of an athletic-minded administration, Southern Cal's football teams accordingly got better. The Trojans had a 4-5-1 record in 1958, and in 1959, Clark's last year, they won 8 of 10 games.

He had started with a loser and gone out with a winner in three short years. It took a man with a positive attitude—and a towering devotion—to do that.

"I believed that success was built out of habit," Clark says.

"When we played or practiced, we didn't take our helmets off until we were off the field. Our practice sessions were highly structured—no wasted time. I was kind of heavy on organization."

Clark related to his players easily because of his relatively young age. He was in his mid-30s.

"I kept a relationship with the athlete," Clark says. "I was young and could demonstrate anything I wanted done on a field. I was personally involved. I called a lot of the offense and the defense on the sidelines." Clark adds, "I never was involved in a player revolt."

Clark's teaching methods were a carryover from his playing days at Southern Cal where he was an outstanding lineman in the 1940s. "I always felt I had to do things in the most fundamental fashion because of my size," says Clark, whose high school coach at one time thought that he was too small to make the grade at Southern Cal.

Clark believed strongly in defense as a player, just as he did as a coach. ("The Southern Cal teams of the 1940s won the championship games on strong defenses and the easy ones on strong offense," he reminds you.)

Marriage with Southern Cal was fostered in Clark's boyhood days on an Iowa farm. "I listened to USC play in the Rose Bowl when I was once milking cows," Clark recalls. "I had taken the radio out to the milk shed. The game really excited me. I hoped some day that I could play in a Rose Bowl."

Clark eventually did after his family moved to California in 1939 when he was 15. Continued success at George Washington High School in Los Angeles earned Clark all-city honors as a prep lineman and a meeting with Southern Cal coach Howard Jones.

"I was greatly impressed with meeting the man," Clark says. "I'd heard about Jones in Iowa when he was a coach back there. Hearing all my life about Jones and the Rose Bowl, I was delighted to accept a Southern Cal scholarship."

Clark remembered at the time that "Jones didn't look too good." Not long after, Jones died of a heart attack, and Clark eventually played for Jeff Cravath.

"It was primarily all running on those Cravath teams during the war," Clark recalls. "Cravath did not believe in the forward pass."

After playing his first year of varsity ball in 1942, Clark's career was interrupted by the war. He joined the army and took part in the Battle of the Bulge. He spent 18 months in the combat zone and won a battlefield commission. Clark returned to Southern Cal after the war and played football in 1946 and 1947, particularly distinguishing himself as a guard in the last year. He was Trojan captain and won two prizes—the Davis-Teschke Most Inspirational Award and the Peter K. Thomas Outstanding Lineman award.

"I always say I came back from the service just to play Notre Dame," Clark emphasizes. "The Notre Dame rivalry was always a fantastic one. It has been one of my all-time great athletic experiences. I know I coached at Navy when we beat Army one year. But I put the Southern Cal-Notre Dame series on a higher plane."

In 1947 Clark got his long-cherished wish to play in a Rose Bowl game. It was not a particularly pleasant experience, though.

"We got trounced by Michigan (49-0)," Clark recalls. "Our club lost its momentum just before the UCLA game. (The Trojans were undefeated through eight games but just managed to beat the Bruins 6-0 prior to a 38-7 loss to Notre Dame.)

"We had a great team that year but there was a problem coming into the Rose Bowl game. We had a lot of injuries to key players. Michigan had an exceptionally well-balanced team, but it was disappointing that we couldn't put it together for that Rose Bowl game."

It was small consolation that Clark himself had a good game. "All I got," he says, "was a better contract in the pros."

Clark alternated between the football field and the classroom in 1948 and 1949. While playing for the San Francisco 49ers of the National Football League, he finished his schooling and graduated with honors in mechanical engineering. He began a coaching career with the Naval Academy in 1950, and after one year as an assistant there came back to Southern Cal. Clark served six years as assistant line coach under Jess Hill before taking over the head coaching job.

"When I got the head job, I changed the relationship with the athlete," Clark explains. "I was very close with the players.

I worked with them, and there was a special feeling between us, I think."

When Clark took over, the Trojans had lost 19 lettermen from the 1956 team—11 by graduation and 8 who were ineligible because of the recruiting penalties levied by the

Coach Don Clark: "I was very close to the players...there was a special feeling between us."

Pacific Coast Conference. After the prohibitive bonds of the first year, Clark was able to recruit. But he had problems ("We could never get any speed.") He did manage, however, to bring important talent to Southern Cal. "I recruited the McKeever twins (Mike and Marlin)," Clark says. "It was tough, though. My wife wanted them to go to Notre Dame. She said that all good Catholic boys should go to Notre Dame."

Clark also produced Ron Mix—"the finest offensive tackle of the day." "Talk to the pros," Clark says, "and ask them who the finest tackle was. They'll tell you, Mix."

(Mix later credited Clark with his successful professional career: "I didn't like football tremendously when I was at Southern Cal, but whatever success I had in the pros, I'm certain that the foundation came from my college training. It was what stirred me in the future.")

A philosophical change forced Clark out of coaching prematurely. "I don't even know what prompted it," says Clark. "I was 36, and I didn't want to sign a five-year agreement. I just decided I was going to quit coaching—I didn't even tell my wife about it. I just said to myself, 'I'll find something else tomorrow.'"

Clark eventually took over a family business from his ailing brother and turned it into a winner. Prudential Overall Supply ("You can't rent a Trojan uniform, but we CAN rent you the finest in industrial and career apparel.") exploded to seven California plants and 500 employees in a relatively short space of time.

The "captain" of a new team, Clark sees a game similar to his football days.

"I feel the same challenge exists in our company that existed in football," Clark points out.

Many years after leaving football, Clark's race-horse style has not left him.

Byrd's Last Game

"I don't do any talking. Might tell myself to get going maybe, but coach always says the kind of talk he likes to hear from me is the pop of the pads on a good hit."—Lou Byrd, 1958.

Lou Byrd went about his work on the Southern Cal line with silence and efficacy, "popping" and "hitting." UCLA might remember 1958. Byrd was voted Player of the Game then.

"That UCLA game was beautiful," Byrd recalls. "I had a fantastic defensive game. Everytime they ran the Single Wing I was there. I made a lot of beautiful tackles. That game was telecast coast-to-coast, and we had 97,000 people in the Coliseum. It was my biggest thrill."

Moments almost as golden rush to Byrd's tongue. Stanford might remember 1956. Byrd was John Brodie's nemesis then.

"It was a game that broke my heart because I really wanted to play more than I did," Byrd recalls, wistfully. "I cried because I wanted more action—I only played three plays against Stanford. All the way through the first half I didn't get into the game. Brodie was throwing, and I knew I could kill him. When I finally got in, I hit him for a 5-yard loss and a 7-yard loss, and then I recovered a fumble. My family was there. The next day the newspapers had headlines saying, 'Tough Guard Named Lou.'"

Uniquely, Byrd only played 49 minutes in 1956 and made

Honorable Mention on the Pacific Coast Conference's all-league team.

"I didn't even play enough time for a letter," he says, chuckling. "It was a helluva year."

Byrd surfaced dramatically as an outstanding guard at Southern Cal with no fanfare. Born in Mississippi and brought up in New Orleans, he played well in high school, but his direction was uncertain, his steps unsure. He joined the navy and played four years of service football before he was pointed toward a goal.

"I met the coach from Ventura Junior College, and he recommended that I come to California," Byrd recalls. "I promised him that I would."

Determination burst from a young man. Byrd took a test to get his high school diploma, then attended junior college to "prove myself." "It was beyond my wildest imagination, playing junior college ball," Byrd says. "It was quite a thrill for me."

From an unsuspected source Byrd was pushed in the direction of Southern Cal. He remembers:

"I went to this dentist, a Doctor Temple, and he said that he knew all about me. He was a USC alumni, a scout. I was kind of suspicious when he asked me, 'How would you like to go to USC?' The next Saturday, Doctor Temple and his wife put me in their big Cadillac and drove me down to USC and introduced me to all the coaches. They treated me to lunch, and here I was, all of a sudden, a little, old country boy thrust into the limelight."

Byrd answered, "Yes," almost before they asked him to play Trojan football. "They told me to go home and work," Byrd recalls. "I did."

Byrd played middle guard on defense and running guard on offense, and he recalls, "I was nervous in every game I played—my first one and my last one. I always went to the bathroom before every game." He reached emotional peaks against UCLA. "I seemed to have my best games against them," he says. "I always got jacked higher than a kite because of the crosstown rivalry."

Unfortunately for Byrd his prodigious talents peaked at a time when Southern Cal football plunged. In a sense he was part of a lost generation trapped in a vacuum of indifference.

In 1956 the notorious payoff scandals created steep problems for the Trojans. Byrd missed the scandal but suffered nevertheless because in 1957 he played on the most ineffective team in Southern Cal history. ("I was a day late and a dollar short," Byrd kids about the black events of 1956.) The Trojans not only had their problems on the field but off as well in 1957. While still carrying the demeaning title of outlaw school, Southern Cal was further stamped as a renegade by the National Collegiate Athletic Association in a new development. The ruling body found that Southern Cal had violated NCAA bylaws by paying illegal transportation costs to two football players.

The NCAA ruled that "1—The Trojans will be unable to enter athletes or teams in any national collegiate championship event, or any invitational events which cooperate with the NCAA. 2—In addition, SC will not be allowed to participate in TV programs subject to NCAA control. 3—Any further violation of NCAA rules will be cause for expulsion from the association."

Byrd's last game for Southern Cal in 1958 had a negative touch of history attached to it. While the superb guard knocked the underpinnings from UCLA, the Pacific Coast Conference also was on its last legs. The end of the game signaled the end of the 43-year-old conference as well.

Cancer spreading from the 1956 recruiting scandal eventually destroyed the grand, old league. "The mistrust that had existed since the end of the Second World War among some of the institutions intensified into an almost incomprehensible bitterness during the scandal," a writer pointed out. "It was feelings such as these that led to the end of the Pacific Coast Intercollegiate Conference."

At a meeting in Portland, Oregon, on August 10, 1958, the conference was officially dissolved (effective June 30, 1959). Later in the summer of 1958 the four outlaw schools involved in the recruiting scandal announced that they would form a new league. Southern Cal, UCLA, California, and Washington called it the Athletic Association of Western Universities, or the "Big Four" for short. It promised an uneasy relationship, however. At one point UCLA coach George Dickerson charged that California was trying to steal athletes from his school by making under-the-table cash offers.

Reporting on the situation, sports editor Curly Grieve of the *San Francisco Examiner* wrote that "UCLA has virtually torpedoed the so-called Big Four...the group is likely to be known as the Big Fourflushers...and may be stillborn. The PCC, with a resounding death rattle, could conduct its own investigation of Dickerson's wild charges and UCLA's own recruiting and proselyting practices, or ask the NCAA to do it for them. In that event, one, both or all four schools just might be put on the shelf again for a long time."

By 1959 Stanford joined the "Big Four," and the AAWU, forerunner of today's Pacific-8 Conference, was officially established on July 1. The league was at first loosely governed.

Reported *Sports Illustrated* in September, 1959: "Article VII of its code carries the astonishing proviso that 'there shall be no central enforcement agent of this association.' The members hired as executive director Admiral Tom Hamilton, the onetime Navy star and coach who left a job as director of athletics at Pittsburgh. His duties are exceedingly vague, to say the most.

"As one official of a member school put it, 'In Hamilton you have a powerful, forceful guy—with no power and no force. He will be a little like Mr. Anthony on the radio. He will talk over problems and quarrels between schools and try to get them together to resolve their differences before they hit the courts again. Each school will govern itself under the honor system. The expression for the AAWU is 'mutual confidence,' and believe me, it will be a confidence game."

The AAWU endured, however, despite such cynicism, and eventually secured its own contract with the Tournament of Roses for the Rose Bowl games. Northwestern schools were angry at being shut out of the affair, and animosity toward AAWU members was discernible. "UCLA and profanity are synonymous," said an official of Oregon University. "The real animosity is toward the Los Angeles people. UCLA is an s.o.b. to everyone."

The McKeever Incident

Steve Bates lay on his back, sipping liquid food through his wired jaw. His nose was broken, and there were multiple fractures of the bones on the right side of his face. His face was flattened and twisted by the fractured parts.

Under normal circumstances it would have been considered an unfortunate football accident. But these were not normal circumstances.

The California player was injured in the cause celebre of the 1959 season with Southern Cal's Mike McKeever acting as the heavy in the story. McKeever, a brutish Trojan guard, was alleged to have hit Bates with his elbows after a play was over.

"It was a bad situation," remembers Don Clark, the Southern Cal coach then. "California wanted to outlaw this boy. It was a very vicious thing, the McKeever incident...tormenting to the squad. We had lawyers here. He was called a gorilla. But I feel very strongly for the athlete in that situation. I felt he was doing his job."

At the time, Clark was quoted as saying: "A review of the films...indicates no misconduct on the part of Mike McKeever. He played one of the greatest offensive and defensive games of football that I personally have ever seen."

McKeever was generally regarded as a villain in the case, but Ron Mix, a tackle on that team, recalls: "The accusations were absolutely and entirely unjustified. I still recall the play. The referee was right on the spot and did not call a penalty. It was just an unfortunate situation that the player was hurt. Bates was tackled and hit by a player I don't recall and was also hit by Mike McKeever, and it was alleged that Mike hit him late. He hit him in the jaw with his elbow.

"I recall the play from the game and from seeing it many times in films. All one had to do was to review the films. The films negate the charges. The boy was seriously hurt, and Mike was the second tackler and it's understandable how it could be reported as a vicious thing. It tarnished a boy's reputation. Perhaps the story drew greater attention because it was USC."

When it happened others were not so kind. From the governor of California to the press, McKeever was roasted in speech and print.

"To me this is a very serious thing, the whole question of dirty football playing," said governor Edmund G. Brown. "Because if these coaches are teaching these young men to play dirty, why it's another step in the direction of cheating and playing the game unfairly."

Pete Elliott, the California coach, called it "one of the most flagrant violations I have ever seen in football...the only reason I'm saying anything at all is that this type of play has got to be stopped."

California University president Clark Kerr and Chancellor Glen Seaborg issued a joint statement condemning McKeever. "McKeever was ejected the week before from the Stanford game," they said. "Films of last year's University of California game with the University of Southern California show McKeever undertaking the same tactics against Joe Kapp as were used against Steve Bates. We feel that amateur athletics deserves better than this from its participants."

Sports Illustrated printed an editorialized story, pleading with McKeever to "Lay those elbows down, Mike." One of the *Sports Illustrated* writers reported after the game: "The press viewed the flickering game movie in appalled silence. It was run and rerun. It was like watching Richard Widmark hitting a cripple in a gangster movie." Another *Sports Illustrated* writer commented: "Bates hit the out-of-bounds marker flat on his back, and the play was clearly over. McKeever kept running and piled on top of Bates, smashing him in the face with his elbow as he landed. He had plenty of time to stop. But he didn't."

"McKeever's injury of Bates was but one of many

occasions where his bony elbows have caught the chin of an opponent and the eye of an official," the magazine noted. "Mike, who along with his identical twin, Marlin, an end, has been touted as USC's spearhead in a crusade to regain lost glory, was ejected from last year's game with Cal for elbowing Joe Kapp. He was thrown out of the USC-Stanford game on October 24 for striking Doug Pursell, a center, and from this year's Cal game for twice using his elbows against quarterback Pete Olson. This seemingly calculated mayhem, according to USC's way of thinking, is all part of the game—after all, USC wasn't even penalized for the Bates incident. But it is a game its opponents at California will not soon forget."

Southern Cal had not conceived of such notoriety before the McKeever twins played their first season in 1958.

"The McKeevers, twin holy terrors of Los Angeles' Mount Carmel High School (both were schoolboy all-Americans), were recruited by Clark to lead USC back to glory," said a writer. "The press built up the brother act with enthusiasm. Galahad and Lancelot were coming to the Trojans' rescue. USC was dubbed 'The University of Southern McKeever.' Said Marlin, before Mike's lethal elbows earned their undistinguished reputation: 'We get sheer pleasure out of football—out of knocking people down...it's just plain fun.'"

As expected their presence accelerated Southern Cal's football accomplishments. In 1958 the McKeevers helped the Trojans win three more games than they had won in 1957. And by 1959 they sparked Southern Cal to eight victories before season-ending losses to UCLA and Notre Dame. Both were picked on all-America teams that year, along with Mix and tackle Dan Ficca, but Mike McKeever's status did not diminish criticism from certain quarters. McKeever was selected as an all-American player, but he was not an all-American boy, according to one critic.

"Intimidation, of course, is an integral part of modern football tactics, as important in its way as an adequate passing attack," the critic said. "To get an opponent to flinch (as many must at the mere mention of the University of Southern McKeever) is to establish an incalculable advantage over him in football. If intimidation becomes deliberate jawbreaking, however, football has ceased to be a game. When a boy misconstrues aggressiveness as modified manslaughter, the game is better off without him. Mike McKeever seems unclear on the point, possibly because Don Clark, a genuinely fine coach, has never taken the time to drive the point home."

The McKeever twins played another year, under the new reign of John McKay, and eventually were drafted by the Los Angeles Rams. However their lives followed distinctly separate paths after that.

Marlin McKeever went on to pro football glory with the Rams, Minnesota Vikings, and Washington Redskins. Mike McKeever followed a cruel fate. A head injury sidelined him from pro ball, and he eventually died from an auto accident in 1967 after laying in a coma for 18 months.

Time Out: John McKay

"Winning is tougher than losing"—John McKay.

John McKay is as complex as his offense, and sometimes as hard to explain. He is not always the Jolly Green Giant (at 5-foot-9 he could not get the part, anyway) nor the Good Humor Man. McKay admits that he is not that easy to know.

"I don't know any person in the country more irritable," he tells you. "I don't smile as much as I used to."

McKay has built football champions at Southern Cal with sublime arrogance. It is this icy aloofness from his players that has allowed him to be more objective through the years, much like an army general. In accomplishment the end has more than justified the means.

Hal Bedsole, who played three years under McKay from 1961 through 1963, found him intolerably uncommunicative.

"I didn't know him," says Bedsole, an all-American end in 1962 on the national championship team. "He didn't talk to you. His style was to tell one of his coaches to tell you something. He was very quiet, very serious, and very sincere. In those days he was very much a loner and a quiet type of person.

"McKay coached through his coaches, not his players. I think I had more ability than I showed on the field. Had I played for another coach, I might have been showed my mistakes, where I was screwing up. I just feel that I wasn't all that I could have been."

Bedsole wishes that McKay would have been more

John McKay, "the prototype of the perfect football coach—clean-cut, articulate, and enthusiastic."

personal.

"One day I was in the locker room," Bedsole recalls. "McKay walked in and said, 'You've been elected to all-America. Here's your medal. Have a good day.' And that was it. It didn't bother me because things were going so well. I was having so much success, and I guess my ego got in the way. But when I was going bad as a senior, I could have used a man-to-man coach. I had some bad games and I got benched, but McKay didn't tell me why. It confused me. It was very humiliating, very embarrassing."

Despite harboring such intense feelings Bedsole discovered a "fine coach" in the man. "I give McKay all the credit for making me an all-American," he says.

Steve Sogge, quarterback of McKay's national championship team of 1967 and a participant in the Rose Bowl three times, found a similar remoteness in the white-haired coach.

"He was a little aloof from his players," Sogge says. "Nobody knew him well enough because he was that way. McKay always had excellent people working for him, and he could sit back and objectively evaluate the whole situation."

Sogge, too, found exquisite coaching abilities in McKay.

"He was a tremendous coach," Sogge says. "I respected the man's coaching ability tremendously. He was a great one."

Associates indicate that McKay has mellowed through the years, become more player-oriented. ("I think he has changed," says one. "He talks to players now about their problems.")

He has not lost his lordly manner, however. "He is still a little arrogant," points out a sportswriter.

McKay himself admits that he does not especially worry about "communicating" with his players.

"So many coaches today are talking about communications with their players, and this and that," McKay says. "It's nonsense. Athletes should be told there are certain things they are going to do if they want to play at a particular school (like USC), and if they don't want to do them they can go somewhere else and play. I will not recruit a boy unless I feel the boy wants to attend USC and play for us. We don't beg anyone to come here. This is a great school of opportunity, scholastically and athletically."

McKay is his own man. He brooks no interference from the alumni, a powerful lobby that controls athletics behind the scenes of most schools. Once asked if he uses alumni to help him in recruiting players, McKay said: "We don't use alumni too often. They just don't know the rules; something also seems to get lost in the translation." McKay has also told them sweetly what they could do with their advice about game plans.

Despite this haughty mien, McKay continues to reign as a

popular monarch at Southern Cal. His success has had something to do with that.

McKay's teams have won three national championships, finished in the Top Ten nine times, won eight Pacific-8 Conference championships, and appeared in the Rose Bowl seven times, winning four of them. Under McKay's leadership the Trojans have had only two losing seasons in 14—his first two—and have won about 75 percent of their games with a record of 109 victories, 35 losses, and 7 ties. He has produced two Heisman Trophy winners and a fistful of all-Americans and holds numerous Coach of the Year awards.

When he first took over as Southern Cal football coach, he was an unknown quantity. "Now he could probably run for mayor of Los Angeles and win," notes a sportswriter.

Success came with stunning swiftness for McKay. A backfield coach for one year, McKay was promoted over other likely candidates at Southern Cal when head coach Don Clark retired after the 1959 season. In three years McKay not only built up the football program but built a national champion as well. One of the lasting contributions of the innovative McKay is the "I" formation, one of the most productive offenses in college football.

"The attack should be as complex as possible," explains McKay. "That's why I favor the 'I'. The fullback, No. 2 behind the quarterback, and the Z deep man are able to break in either direction."

In McKay's "I" formation the quarterback stands over the center, as in the "T." The fullback is a few steps behind the quarterback, and the tailback is behind the fullback.

McKay's offensive schemes have been "borrowed" from time to time by the nation's top coaches. Says Woody Hayes of Ohio State:

"No coach in the country does as good a job tying up his running game with his passing game as John McKay. Year after year he has the best receivers in the country, too. Not among the best—the best. I think John McKay has done more to open up college football than any other man. What he does is a beautiful thing to watch...unless you're playing against it. I have learned a lot of football from McKay, and I've borrowed a lot from him, too."

Frank Broyles, the Arkansas coach, took tips from McKay in the "I" and went through 21 games unbeaten with it. Bear Bryant at Alabama also took note of the McKay innovation. "I don't think McKay's ever borrowed anything from us, but I certainly have from him," he said. McKay was offered $200 a day by some eastern and midwestern schools to install the formation there but pleaded that he had no time.

McKay continues to run as hard as ever in his 50s, which just proves that old halfbacks never die. He flourished as a player at the University of Oregon before striking gold as a coach at Southern Cal. As in the case of most enormously successful men, he overcame early hardship to do it.

One of five children, McKay lost his father when he was 11 and was forced to help support the family. "I swept out restaurants so I could eat," McKay says about his difficult boyhood days in Shinnston, West Virginia.

McKay was an honored high school player in football and basketball before entering the Air Force during the Second World War. Remembering combat duty as a tail gunner in the South Pacific, McKay reflects: "A job like that gave me a lot of time to meditate and made a cigar smoker out of me."

McKay played as a freshman at Purdue in 1946 but left after head coach Cecil Isbel was fired. McKay moved to Oregon and starred as halfback in a backfield that included Norm Van Brocklin. In 1948 McKay scored eight touchdowns, and he and Van Brocklin led the Ducks to a 9-1 record and a berth in the Cotton Bowl. (They lost to SMU.) In 1949 McKay and Van Brocklin led Oregon to a Pacific Coast Conference co-championship with California, but the Bears eventually were granted the Rose Bowl berth. In his time at Oregon, McKay made the all-coast first team and all-American honorable mention.

The New York Yankees of the old All-America Conference drafted McKay, but he decided to stay on at Oregon as an assistant coach. He directed the Oregon offense and pass defense and soon became one of the top recruiters in the West. During the summer of 1959 McKay was invited to join the Southern Cal staff as backfield coach, and when Clark left the following December he surprisingly became head coach.

"Southern Cal broke the mold when he became head coach," recalls one-time Trojan football star Jon Arnett. "At one time the only way to become the USC coach was to be an alumni."

McKay's attractive blonde wife, "Corky," remembers that her husband arrived home with a special glow the day of his appointment.

"He came home looking 6 feet tall," she says, "and he's only 5-9. I was bursting with excitement, but I couldn't say anything until the official announcement was made. I had to keep quiet for five or six hours, and you know how hard that is for a woman."

McKay's first two years were losing seasons but not wholly unexpected. In the time-worn terminology of coaching, 1960 and 1961 were "rebuilding years." Extravagant success followed, however. In 1962 McKay's Trojans won the national football championship with an 11-0 record, capping the marvelous season with a dramatic 42-37 victory over second-ranked Wisconsin in the Rose Bowl.

Another national championship season in 1967 culminated with a 14-3 triumph over Indiana in the Rose Bowl. In 1972 McKay's Trojans were mythical national champions again, their third title in 11 years, and enhanced that royal status with a 42-17 whipping of proud Ohio State at Pasadena. By then the ultra-successful McKay had succeeded to the dual position of coach and athletic director. He became one of the most honored men in college athletics and one of the most coveted as well. Professional teams, especially, have bid for McKay's services, but he has turned aside lucrative offers from the Los Angeles Rams and San Francisco 49ers.

"I thought about the offers very seriously," says McKay. "In fact I damn near took the Ram job when it was offered. There was that time and one other I almost accepted. I won't say I'll never go into pro coaching, a man should never say 'never.' (But) Southern Cal is the school that gave me the opportunity, and I'll forever be grateful. I'm athletic director, and that's another reason why it's hard to leave. I have a say in how the department is run, and I enjoy this. How could I go out and recruit a boy, tell him what we have in store for him, and then take off and leave? It just wouldn't be right.

"I like it better the way it is. Lean years come and go like they do for farmers. I want to stay at USC because it's a fine school. We wouldn't live anywhere but here if we could avoid it. I might still go pro if the right opportunity comes along. But I would miss the college game. The players develop more in their college years, both as athletes and human beings, than they do later. I like to have a hand in their growth."

(At least McKay should not be concerned over a job. He has been given tenure at Southern Cal with a professorship.)

McKay is a tough guy only in practice sessions. Otherwise his players are left alone. He has no rules on curfew or hair, two of the modern curses of American football coaches.

"I assume these people are men," McKay says. "At least they say they are. During the season I couldn't go all over the city and see if the players are sleeping. They are students first. It wouldn't be right to have a 10:30 p.m. curfew for a pre-med major who would have to stay up late studying. You must give them some leeway. I don't have a lot of strict rules. I never had. I had kids with mustaches in 1962. Now it's a big fad."

McKay is untroubled by player revolt.

"Everybody says that youngsters are tougher to coach today," says McKay. "I'm not so sure they are right or wrong. We haven't seen that much difference at USC. Our youngsters still say, 'yes, sir,' and 'no, sir,' and are very polite, and we are very polite to them. We've never been one of those hard-type coaches. We've always said that the youngster is out for the team. He's trying his best. If he doesn't do well, there is no reason to get angry with him. He just isn't as good as we hoped he would be, so we don't worry about that."

The athletes regulate their life styles, so long as it does not interfere with the business of winning football games. Toward the ultimate goal McKay sharpens their physical abilities considerably.

"McKay feels that he has a moral responsibility to see that the young players under his charge are physically ready for the demands of spring training," reports a national magazine. "He says he would be negligent if there was not some type of organized conditioning to get them ready. USC players are 'invited' to enroll in a January-to-June physical education class—including weight lifting, running, and agility—open to all students. Players out for spring sports, about 25 percent of the football team, normally do not take the class."

"We're No. 1!" exulted Southern California players cry, carrying John McKay on their broad shoulders at the end of the 1972 season. It was McKay's third national title in 11 years.

McKay explains his feelings on the subject: "If you don't have this type of winter program, and you leave it up to the players, they will show up on the first day of spring practice in terrible shape. It would be a bad health practice on my part to allow players to begin with pads on the first day of spring practice without proper conditioning."

While revering physical stamina, McKay is just as concerned about mental strength.

"We always look at a person's physical ability first," McKay tells you. "But you have to have someone who concentrates on what he is supposed to be doing and can play the game well mentally. That means that sometimes the guy with the most physical ability doesn't start. The fan will look at a player once and say, 'that guy really made a good play.' But we have to have someone who will do what we want on every play and not just once in a while."

McKay's revolutionary theories astound provincial football people. He is an atypical college coach.

For instance he believes that teams—especially his—would be better off not going into a huddle.

"Basically we feel that the only reason you go into a huddle anymore is for the formation," McKay says. "We really don't know what we want to run until we come up and see what kind of a defense that they are going to play against us. Over the years we've audibilized a lot. In some games we've audibilized as much as 75 percent of the time. In other words we have changed the play that we called in the huddle up on the line of scrimmage. So, basically, we're really taxing the mentality of our youngsters. We'd be better off a lot of times not even going into a huddle except just to go in and say, 'the formation is this,' and go out and look at what they present to us. Then call the play we think would be best to run against that defense."

McKay also opposes the common practice of sending plays into his quarterback.

"I've believed for years that, if the game is what it is supposed to be, to develop character and leadership in young men, then you should train them and then go out and see what's developed," McKay says. "I train our quarterbacks to call the play themselves. If he doesn't like a suggested play, he is going to change it and try something else, whether it's right or wrong. He's still going to have the right of leadership and change the plays.

"I want to give my quarterbacks on the practice field the final examinations without giving them the answers. It seems to me, if I trained a quarterback and say, 'this is what we want to do and why and such,' then I want to send him out on the field and see if he listened and learned the lesson. If I call every play, he doesn't have to know anything, except how to take the snap from center and throw a forward pass."

McKay has a sharp mind and a sharp tongue, and does not

hesitate to use either. He delights in the controversial new rule that allows freshmen to play varsity ball. Many others do not, especially educators. He would prefer second-place teams in the Pacific-8 Conference to get bowl bids. The Pac-8 now only allows the conference champion to go to the Rose Bowl. McKay believes that the safest way to win is by throwing the ball, a theory not in keeping with most everyone else.

"This sounds radical," McKay concedes. "Ordinarily you think ball control on the ground allows you to stagger in. The statistics we kept at USC averaged 7 yards a pass and only 4.1 a carry. During the test period we ran 497 times and lost possession some 18 times on fumbles. We threw 199 times and had only 3 interceptions."

He is an outspoken critic of Southern Cal's tough schedule, and in effect blames himself since he helps with its formation.

"A good schedule is one where you don't play somebody that can beat you every week," he says. "I think our schedule is a bad one in that respect. When you play Arkansas, Illinois, Michigan State, Notre Dame, those are good teams. What you need to play are people that you would beat just by walking out of the huddle and lining up. We don't play those type people. When you play a good team week in and week out, you have more chance of injury. There is more intensity in the game. Emotion plays a big part in football. You can't be up week in and week out. What you'd really like is a real tough game, a couple of easy ones, a real tough one, a couple of easy ones. This way you have a better chance for a great record."

When recruiting, McKay makes his choices count since "we have fewer football scholarships than any university in the country playing bigtime football." McKay says that 24 or 25 players are brought into Southern Cal each year. "Eighteen will be freshmen and six or seven are junior college transfers," he explains. "Out of that number we figure that 18 will start before they leave USC."

McKay debunks a popular belief that Southern Cal is "super rich" and can "buy" any player it wants.

"Stupid," McKay insists. "I could stand on a soap box for the rest of my life trying to explain our situation as a private school, but what would be the use? Our athletic department supports itself. We rent the office space our desks are in, we rent our practice field...even pay for our training table meals. This goes for all our athletic teams. Our situation is vastly different from that of any other institution of our stature. If we got to keep money taken in by our athletic teams we'd be the richest department in the world. But as it is all our profits go into a general fund that helps support the entire university."

McKay has reached heights that men in his profession dream about, yet all is not roses with a winner, he says. This heroic figure reveals a human frailty.

"Winning is tougher than losing," McKay insists. "It's the fear of defeat. The more you win the more you can't stand the thought of losing. I'm sure this is the same sort of feeling that forced Vince Lombardi out of coaching when he retired from Green Bay, and I know it was the reason Frank Leahy (of Notre Dame) eventually had to move on to something else.

"I've been beaten before and beaten badly. I know there are millions of people on this planet who don't even know or care there is such a thing as football. It's not that important. But the fear of defeat crawls at you. There's not a coach I know who can relax during the season. At least four months every year you're completely separated from your family. You end up in a little world of your own, and I've always felt that people who do that are on their way to oblivion. I stop and ask myself if I'm becoming such a bad person. The more you win, the worse it gets. Your personality changes. I catch myself thinking 'I can't lose...I can't lose...' Why can't I lose? The world won't come to an end."

Perhaps McKay's ability to laugh at himself counterbalances his fears. Called the "prototype of the perfect football coach—clean-cut, articulate, and enthusiastic" by one sportswriter, McKay's most shining quality is his sharp humor.

"Without a gag writer he still has about as many one-liners as Bob Hope," says an observer. "He never has taken himself seriously. Not even now when he's at the heap's top."

"On campus McKay is the man," said another. "His wit and humor would be rated 10 on a scale as high."

McKay throws a quip about as well as he used to throw a forward pass.

Once noting that opening games give him the jitters McKay said: "I'd rather open with a second game."

Talking about emotion in football he told a reporter: "I keep hearing how much emotion plays in winning football games. To this I can only say that my wife, Corky, is an emotional person, and she can't play football worth a darn."

McKay once recalled a recruiting experience he had with a linebacker from a suburban Los Angeles high school. "When it came down to brass tacks and we asked him if he'd be interested in attending Southern Cal, he replied: 'Well, gosh, I think I would, but there's one problem: My dad doesn't like your television show.' Honest! The kid went elsewhere. So we may not have the best football team in the country this fall, but I'll guarantee you one thing: My television show will be a whole lot better."

On another occasion McKay was lucky enough to land a terrific 250-pound tackle from Cleveland. A reporter asked him, "How in the world did you get him away from Woody Hayes at Ohio State?"

"Gary Jeter's dad is a photographer," McKay remarked, referring to Hayes' noted run-in with a photographer at a recent Rose Bowl game.

A fledgling sports reporter once interviewed McKay and asked him if his children had any interest in sports. "Only moderately," McKay answered. Of course he was kidding the reporter. McKay's son, John, Jr., is an outstanding receiver on the Trojans.

Some other McKayisms:

—"If you have everyone back from a team that lost 10 games, experience isn't too important."

—"Experience at losing isn't as important as experience at winning."

—"The American youth loves competition—but not at his position."

The irrepressible McKay has his own television show and, characteristically, writes his own script. Much of the material is joke matter directed at himself.

"If we don't go to the Rose Bowl again this season," he once said, "they ought to fire the coach. I don't care if he is a professor."

In his free time McKay plays golf "poorly" and watches John Wayne movies. ("He likes to curl up to a late show with a glass of chocolate milk and a peanut butter sandwich," says an associate.)

He is a man of few superstitions. ("For a while he wore what he called his lucky pants, but he hasn't put them on since the day they split down the seat at a Notre Dame game," says his wife.)

McKay does not need symbols, he makes his own luck. That is seen in his philosophy.

"Football is like life," he says. "You only get out of it what you put into it. You don't have to be big to play the game. Look at me. I'm only 5-9."

People have been looking at McKay—with wonderment—for some time.

Hooray For Hollywood

John Wayne, William Bendix, and Robert Young showed up for just about every game. Andy Devine was seen rubbing elbows with Southern Cal players in the locker room. Randolph Scott ate breakfast with the team on Saturdays.

Discovering a winner the Hollywood crowd—and a lot of other people—joined the Trojan bandwagon during the 1962 season. After two losing years under John McKay, the Trojans were destined to be loved.

Not much had been expected of the 1962 team, but an upset of Duke on national television in the opening game provided a dramatic springboard for Southern Cal. The Trojans crushed SMU, shut out Iowa, and then beat California and Illinois handily. When they defeated powerful Washington in the sixth game of the season, "ticket manager John Morley had to start getting up at 3 a.m. to meet the demands of alumni he hadn't heard from in 10 years," said a sportswriter. Newspapers discovered the Trojans. "Look," said Southern Cal publicist Don Simonian, rather excited one day. "We made all three columnists in the (Los Angeles) *Times*!"

"We knew we had a good football team," recalls Hal Bedsole, an all-American end that season, "but no one felt that it was a national championship caliber team—you don't think of things like that before a season, anyway."

Several sophomores, including Bedsole, halfback Willie Brown, and quarterback Pete Beathard, had been elevated to the starting unit in 1961. "And that led to our success as juniors the next year," explains Bedsole.

Beathard was favored over Bill Nelsen, another quarterback of extraordinary ability who was a year his senior.

"Nelsen was a fantastic leader," Bedsole says. "And it didn't affect his play that Beathard took over. Nelsen could perform better as a substitute. He observed and immediately took the offense over. Pete was working off raw physical ability; Bill approached the game scientifically.

"Beathard was as fine an athlete as played college football. Today there would be a struggle for first-string quarterback between Beathard and Nelsen because of the difference in the game—but in those days McKay went to Beathard on all-around ability because you had to play both ways. He even returned punts. Nelsen didn't have the foot speed and the agility that Beathard had."

Craig Fertig, a quarterback who distinguished himself in later years, also was a member of the 1962 team, and Bedsole remembers: "They must have had 11 good quarterbacks. I was recruited as a quarterback, and I asked McKay when I was a sophomore if I could play another position. I voluntarily moved myself to wide receiver. I had never caught a pass in my life, but I thought it would be easier to play on the varsity that way."

The personality of the 1962 team was heavily defensive, according to Bedsole.

"When McKay prepared us to play, we were conscious that we could not expect a lot of points on the board so we stressed stopping the other team," Bedsole says. "We were not a racehorse team. We were a very small team, too. I was biggest at 220 pounds. We played some very good teams all over the country that year—teams that were representative. I don't think we could run it up even if we wanted to."

"I know we're playing a lot better defense," McKay said at the time, "I feel our defense against Iowa forced them into a good many errors. You've got to be stubborn to win against top competition, and that stubborness should begin on defense."

While the temperature rose among Southern Cal's growing legion of fanatics, the Trojans ran their winning streak to nine with victories over Stanford, Navy, and UCLA. "We beat the Bruins for the Rose Bowl 14-3 with a great comeback," Bedsole remembers. "They were ahead 3-0 in the last five minutes, and then Brown made a miraculous catch near the goal line and they turned the ball over and we scored again. We had 93,000 people in the Coliseum."

Southern Cal claimed the No. 1 spot in the polls but had to beat Notre Dame in the final game of the regular season to keep it. A victory would mean the national championship and the first undefeated season since 1932.

McKay told his team before the game: "It's like the poker player. He's won all the money, and then somebody challenges him to a showdown, all or nothing."

On the third play of the game Beathard threw a swing pass to Brown, and the trim-legged, 170-pound halfback with amazing balance raced 34 yards to the Notre Dame 18. Fullback Ben Wilson, a 228-pounder called the "hardest-hitting predental student on the Coast" by one sportswriter, slashed eight yards on a rollout. Three plays later Wilson leaped over a pack of bodies into the end zone for the Trojans' first touchdown.

"Though Notre Dame had moments of sassiness, it was, thereafter, USC's game," reported John Underwood in *Sports Illustrated*. "When the Irish began to adjust in the second quarter, Beathard ran 28 yards on a busted pass play, Brown whipped around end for 21, and the irresistible Wilson got eight and five and then one for the second score. Typically for luckless Coach Joe Kuharich, whenever Notre Dame threatened to become unruly there was a fumble or a penalty or a pass interception or an injury (defensive back Frank Budka broke his leg) to wreck things...Beathard didn't complete a pass to his all-American end, Hal Bedsole, but then he really didn't have to."

A 25-0 victory over Notre Dame that day confirmed Southern Cal's No. 1 ranking. Wilson also confirmed it in a post-game speech to students. "Some people—a lot of people—doubted we were No. 1," he said. "If you know anybody who still does, tell him I'd appreciate meeting him outside after we're through here."

Though the menacing Wilson made war-like remarks, there were those who were not entirely convinced of Southern Cal's supremacy. People from Wisconsin, quite naturally, disputed it. The Badgers were ranked No. 2 and hoped to settle matters in the Rose Bowl. The emergence of Ron VanderKelen as a star

In the midst of one of the most dramatic Rose Bowl games ever played, Southern Cal's Hal Bedsole catches a touchdown pass from Pete Beathard against Wisconsin in 1963. The Trojans survived a tremendous fourth-quarter rally by the Badgers and won, 42-37, to secure the national championship.

passer and the Big Ten's domination of past Rose Bowl games gave Wisconsin's followers good cause to be optimistic. Some of the press felt that way, too.

"Wisconsin had a 10-0 record and had won the Big Ten championship and we were 10-0, too, and were champions of our league (Athletic Association of Western Universities) and also ranked No. 1, but I had the feeling from the press that we were underdogs," Bedsole recalls. "Yet our team was quietly confident that we were going to bury those people."

The pre-Rose Bowl days seemed like a "picnic" to Bedsole.

"McKay had trouble getting us ready," he remembers. "He feels that it's more important getting to the bowl than winning it. McKay says it's an honor, a reward for having a good year. As a result we didn't practice that hard for the game. We had a short schedule to practice, but we didn't even use our allotted days. We just threw the ball around and talked about lineups. I looked at films. We approached the game like it was an exhibition. That was the atmosphere...a kind of picnic."

It was not played that way, however. The Tournament of Roses parade paid tribute to America's achievements in space, and later that day, VanderKelen put on a matching aerial show in the football game. In one of the most spectacular finishes of all Rose Bowl games the Badgers scored 23 points in the last quarter behind their gifted passer but came down to earth at the end. The Trojans had the ball in the last two minutes and punted successfully on the last play of the game for a dramatic 42-37 victory that corroborated their No. 1 ranking. The penalty-filled game lasted three hours and five minutes, ended in haze, and, paradoxically, had the Trojan players in a darker state of depression, though they won the national title.

"There was no feeling of elation for winning the national championship," Bedsole recalls. "It was really unfortunate. It was discouraging after they came back like that. All the stories in the papers were about the great Wisconsin comeback. We felt we were national champions before the Wisconsin game. And we knew we were far superior than the Badgers. And we should have won by more. But that comeback took a lot out of us."

Southern Cal had opened up a 42-14 lead when the fourth quarter began. Two touchdown catches by Bedsole, one a spectacular, leaping grab in a corner of the end zone in the third quarter, had helped the Trojans forge the big lead. Ironically he was not supposed to be in the game. ("I had three personal fouls called on me," Bedsole remembers. "You were supposed to get thrown out of the game after two. For some reason the officials blew it. Wisconsin was complaining like hell. And I scored both my TDs after the third personal foul. I had gotten a foul early in the game when I blasted someone. Then I was anxious to get VanderKelen. I hit him after a kick, plowed into him. Then he was rolling out, and he stepped out of bounds and I cuffed him.")

The Trojans relaxed by nature and design after running up the 28-point lead. "We got too lackadaisical," Bedsole says, "and I think McKay wanted to let up. It was quite obvious to us. He told us to just do running plays. He didn't want to run it up. He didn't want to embarrass these people. McKay didn't say it, of course, but I know that's what he thought." (The passing of Beathard and Nelsen had burned Wisconsin through the first three quarters. Beathard had four touchdown passes.)

McKay was not prepared for what followed, however. Injuries and incidents had knocked the heart out of the formidable Trojan pass rush by late in the game and led to its wild conclusion.

"Freaky things had been happening," Bedsole remembers. "One of our starting front four hurt himself in a hotel accident. He rammed his finger and split it and couldn't play. Another guy was thrown out. We lost a kid to injury, and some other crazy things happened—and all of a sudden we had people playing inside who hadn't even lettered. We had an interior line with no experience, no pass rush, and VanderKelen had all day to throw. We got tired...and it got dark."

And VanderKelen got hot. Writers agreed that it was Wisconsin's (and VanderKelen's) finest 15 minutes.

VanderKelen completed 8 of 10 passes in a long drive, setting up a 13-yard scoring strike to Lou Holland. After Wilson fumbled the ball on Southern Cal's 29-yard line, VanderKelen seized advantage of the break with another touchdown pass.

Wisconsin gained possession not long after and drove toward the Southern Cal goal line again with VanderKelen directing an aerial attack. Brown saved a touchdown by intercepting a VanderKelen pass in the end zone. Southern Cal was unable to move, and a bad pass from center produced a safety for Wisconsin. The score was now 42-30 in favor of the Trojans, but VanderKelen was not through. The Wisconsin ace threw a touchdown pass to Pat Richter in the dying moments of the game. Then the Trojans squeezed the ball in the final two minutes.

"When Wisconsin was making those drives in the last quarter, there was a lot of holding going on in the offensive line," Bedsole recalls. "The officials didn't stop it though. I kept screaming at them: 'What are you letting all that holding go on for?' The officials really had a hell of a time in that game."

While startled by Wisconsin's efficiency in that fourth quarter, Bedsole was not overawed. "In my heart I didn't feel they'd win," Bedsole says.

The Trojans looked like losers, though, when they filed into their locker room.

"We had our heads down and were depressed like we had lost it," Bedsole remembers. "McKay said, 'Get your heads up, you didn't lose.' There were two teams in the Rose Bowl that day that felt as if they had lost the game."

VanderKelen broke Rose Bowl records with his explosive performance that included 33 pass completions in 48 attempts. He was named co-player of the game with Beathard.

VanderKelen was optimistic that he could catch Southern Cal, Bedsole relates.

"He later told me, when we were on the Minnesota Vikings, that he was confident that they would overtake us. He told me, also, that they had a total breakdown in their defense. We could have scored 50 or 60 points against them if we had wanted to. We didn't throw a pass in the last 20 minutes. When they started to come back, McKay had told us to be conservative. I know if he had to do it again, he'd go to the whip."

Reporters pressed the Trojans from a negative standpoint in the dressing room, but got positive answers. "What happened to Southern Cal?" one asked Brown.

"We won, that's what happened," snapped Brown. "We relaxed when we got way ahead, but we still won. Why do people always want to downgrade the Trojans? We weren't supposed to win, remember?"

Ray George, the Southern Cal line coach, was just as testy. "I don't understand it," he said. "We worked our bellies off to win, and nobody seems to appreciate it. We're tired, but not too tired to go out there and beat them all over again."

McKay's comments were abrupt: "We came in No. 1. They came in No. 2 and lost. That makes us still No. 1."

Indeed the Trojans were No. 1 and, as proof of their indisputable status, swept every national award that year. Considering the circumstances—a rugged schedule, new admission standards, and strong competition for southern California high school talent—a perfect season was almost a miracle. McKay had become the miracle worker, though, with a team that included Beathard, Nelsen, Brown, Bedsole, Wilson, and a tough linebacker named Damon Bame.

Importantly, his players believed in McKay.

"Coach McKay is never wrong," one of the Trojans said before the Notre Dame game. "You think, 'Now, now he's made a mistake,' but then you find he's right—he's always right."

Others also believed in McKay.

"After two years of struggling with another man's material, he has won the respect of the game's best technicians, and perhaps won himself a new contract to top the $15,000 he now receives," said a sportswriter. "He is jaunty, personable, and incisive, quick to quip ('I'll never be hung in effigy—I sent my men out to buy up all the rope in town') and late to get home at night during the season. McKay is a believer in the three-team system—he calls his red, gold and green—most of all because it gives everybody a chance to play. He made a sidearm passer out of Beathard to improve his running passes, especially to the left."

The emergence of McKay as a viable force coincided with a rise in Pacific Coast football. The balance of power appeared to be swinging toward the Far West with the ascension of Southern Cal, Washington, and UCLA. Earlier in the year UCLA had beaten top-ranked Ohio State, and at one time during the season those three teams from the Athletic Association of Western Universities were ranked among the first eight in the land. "Never before had three West Coast teams been ranked so high," pointed out a magazine.

Nor was the power discernible only in the ranked teams. Oregon, Oregon State, and Washington State—the newest member of the AAWU—boasted impressive intersectional victories in 1962.

Before losing to Southern Cal, 14-0, Washington was thought to have the strongest team on the West Coast. "The Huskies are so quick and tough they demoralize the opposition," said one writer.

The Trojans beat the Huskies—and everyone else that year—with those precise attributes.

The Old 84-Z

"Fourth and eight...Fertig with the snap. He's rolling...he throws...complete to Sherman. A touchdown for USC! (voice rises sharply) What an amazing comeback this has been. The snap. Brownell tries the extra point. It's up...it's good. There's a minute, 35 remaining unofficially on the scoreboard clock, and Notre Dame finds themselves trailing 20 to 17 to a band of USC Trojans that refused to quit."—Broadcaster Tom Kelly, November 28, 1964.

John McKay gave you the impression that he would have preferred to shoot golf or watch a western movie that Saturday. The Monday before the 1964 game with Notre Dame, he told reporters: "I studied the Notre Dame-Stanford film for six hours last night, and I have reached one conclusion: Notre Dame can't be beaten."

McKay's outward pessimism enlarged as the week grew short. On Tuesday the Southern Cal football coach was even more dour: "I've decided that if we play our very best and make no mistakes whatsoever, we will definitely make a first down."

On Wednesday he told the world: "We can't run inside on Notre Dame. Their tackles weigh 262 and 245, and nobody has blocked them yet." While cutting into a huge steak, McKay added: "The condemned man ate a hearty meal."

All this was just McKay's subtle bombast. He fervently believed that Southern Cal could beat Notre Dame and, in fact, planned on it in fierce practice sessions behind closed doors. The matter, especially, about running on Notre Dame inside was McKay's chief strategy. He told the public that his Trojans could not run through Notre Dame's elephantine guards, but privately believed that they could.

While Southern Cal's intense players tore photographs of Notre Dame stars off their locker room walls and danced on them, McKay provided more practical voodoo to counteract the nation's top-ranked team. He confidently explained his offensive game plan to his players:

"They play a split 6 defense with those big tackles slanting in. Everybody has tried to double-team their tackles, and their linebackers have taken advantage of the hole that creates to slip in and do a good job. We'll block down on the tackles with just one man and pull our guard behind him to take the linebacker. Then our ballcarrier can follow another back into the hole. We ought to be able to gouge our men through. And if we can make our inside running go, we can make our passing go."

McKay's concern with Notre Dame's offense was just as passionate. The Fighting Irish, behind quarterback John Huarte, used tactics similar to McKay's power I that had taken the Trojans to a national championship two years before. Only this formation was more diversified, and it took Southern Cal scout Mel Hein two inches of paper to describe it. McKay had never seen a scouting report that thick. Nobody could stop Notre Dame completely, but the Fighting Irish could be slowed down on the strong side running, the screen pass and the deep pass, McKay thought.

"We'll use a confusion rush," the Trojan coach decided. "We'll loop our tackles outside, use criss-cross stunts, and play a three-deep secondary—very deep."

On the morning of the game Southern Cal linebacker Ernie Pye came up with another stunt: the "broken glass" play. At the Trojans' 10 a.m. brunch Pye accidentally walked through the plate glass window of a motel dining room.

"The shattering of glass could have been heard for blocks, and the crash was followed by the slow, building noises of blended laughter and alarm," noted a writer. After McKay found that his wounded warrior was not seriously hurt (he cut a heel and missed the game), the coach strolled to a blackboard that had been set up in the dining room for last-minute plans. "Okay, fellows," McKay said airily. "Ernie's given us the idea for today. We've got to crash their glass."

Incentive was there for both teams. The Fighting Irish fiercely coveted their first national championship in 15 years. The Trojans badly wanted a Rose Bowl berth and, in fact, had been given an implied promise for one if they defeated Notre Dame. The Fighting Irish were installed as 14-point favorites with the second best offense in the country, the best defense, and three players—Huarte, end Jack Snow, and linebacker Jim Carroll—named to a myriad all-America teams. The Trojans had a mediocre 6-3 record but superb individuals in runner Mike Garrett, quarterback Craig Fertig, and receiver Rod Sherman. In addition an open date had given the Trojans two weeks to prepare for the contest.

Despite McKay's elaborate preparations, Huarte drilled passes through the Southern Cal defenders to help Notre Dame forge an early lead. Huarte hit on 11 of 15 throws for 176 yards and one touchdown—to Snow—and the Fighting Irish added a field goal by Ken Ivan and a TD run by Bill Worski to take a 17-0 lead at half time. The Trojans, meanwhile, whacked away at Notre Dame's formidable line but did not get far enough for a score. It was apparent, though, that they were running on Notre Dame inside and making the Fighting Irish defense aware of this power.

At the half an amazingly confident McKay told his team: "Our game plan is working. Keep doing your stuff, and we'll get some points." Later he confessed to a companion: "If we can get on the scoreboard quick, we can put some pressure on 'em. They've won nine games without any duress. If we can make this thing close, they might not know how to react."

The power blocks by Southern Cal's tackles opened holes for Garrett and running mate Ron Heller in the second half. When Notre Dame swung its defense to the strong side, Fertig threw to Sherman over the middle. Fertig's passes moved Southern Cal quickly within scoring range, and Garrett ran it over to cut Notre Dame's lead to 17-7.

Huarte rallied Notre Dame on a crackling drive to the Southern Cal nine, but that failed on a fumble. Later a holding penalty hurt Notre Dame even more. The Fighting Irish had

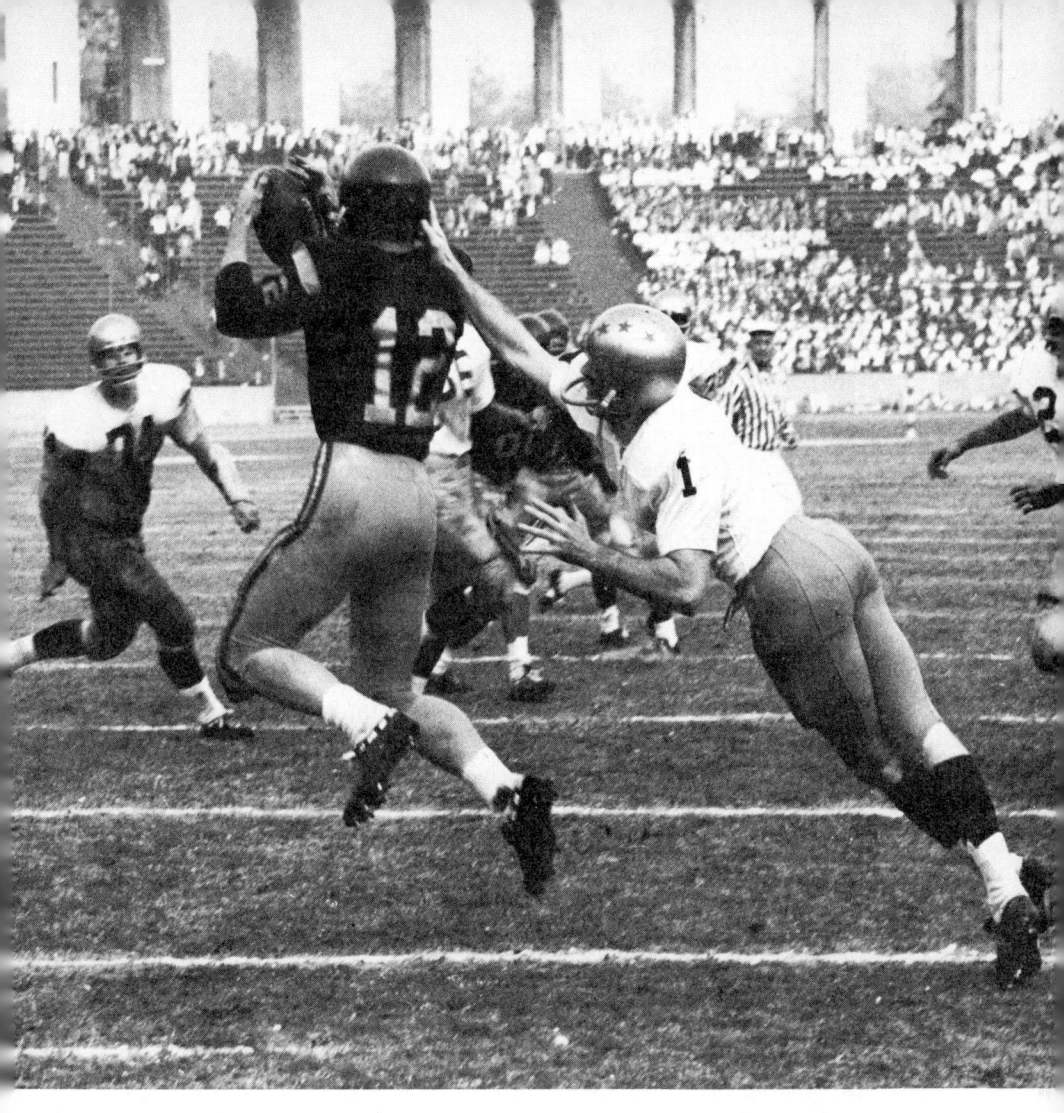

Rod Sherman catches a pass from Craig Fertig in one of the most dramatic plays of the 1964 season, or any season for that matter. It gave Southern California a touchdown and a glorious 20-17 victory over Notre Dame.

scored a touchdown, but the penalty nullified it and thereafter the momentum of the game changed. The Trojans recoiled with an 82-yard touchdown march behind Fertig's passes. He completed the last one to Fred Hill for a score, and the Notre Dame lead was down to 17-14.

McKay was extravagantly optimistic at this point. "I knew we had 'em then," he said. "The momentum was all ours. In a situation like that, the No. 1 rating is a fairly suffocating thing."

Southern Cal translated McKay's thoughts into action. With about five minutes left in the game the Trojans literally squeezed the life out of Notre Dame. Huarte had the ball but had to eat it. Unable to budge against hot Southern Cal, the Fighting Irish were forced to punt. Snow kicked to Garrett, and he returned the ball 18 yards to the Notre Dame 35. Now there were only two minutes and 10 seconds left.

Garrett plunged into the middle of the Notre Dame line but could not get an inch. Fertig called time. Then Fertig, termed "the best pure passer in college football" by McKay, went to the air. He found Hill on a down-and-in pattern for 23 yards. The play gave the Trojans a first down on the Notre Dame 17 and lifted many of the screeching crowd of 83,840 out of their Coliseum seats.

Fertig called time again. Then the quarterback threw a flat pass to Garrett which carried out of bounds at the 15. On the next play Fertig shot a pass to Hill, who was wide open in the end zone. The end grabbed it and fell. It looked good at first, but an official ruled that Hill was out of bounds on the catch. On third down Fertig threw again and missed. The enormous clock below the Olympic torch at the Coliseum showed one minute and 43 seconds remaining in the game, and Fertig had one play left.

On fourth down and eight it was an ideal situation for a field goal, but the Trojans did not want a tie. Sherman told McKay that he wanted to run an "84-Z delay." The pass play was an old one in the Southern Cal playbook. The receiver splits wide to the left, delays for one second after the snap, sprints straight ahead for five steps, fakes outside, then cuts sharply down and across the middle of the field. The quarterback drifts straight back and throws to the spot.

"I watched the way their halfback reacted, and I figured that I could beat him," Sherman later explained.

The play unfolded perfectly. Fertig found Sherman clear of Irish defender Tony Carey and drilled a chest-high pass to his receiver for 15 yards and a touchdown. Now the Coliseum crowd whooped and danced in the aisles and ecstatically threw missiles of all shapes and sizes into the air.

The 20-17 victory gave the Trojans expectations of playing

in the Rose Bowl. Anticipating an almost certain bowl bid a player had written "Beat Michigan" on a locker room blackboard. Inexplicably, though, Southern Cal did not go. Oregon State was curiously chosen although all implications had pointed toward Southern Cal. Faculty representatives from the Athletic Association of Western Universities had in fact waited purposely until after the Notre Dame game to make their decision. Actually Southern Cal and Oregon State had tied for the AAWU title that year, but the Beavers had a slight edge on their overall records, 8-2 to 7-3.

The news of the AAWU's decision came just as McKay and his team were in the middle of a celebration dinner at a restaurant. Stunned silence greeted the announcement, but then USC athletic director Jess Hill said: "So far as I am concerned, this is one of the rankest injustices ever perpetrated in the field of intercollegiate athletics."

Later Fertig expressed the feelings of the team: "We really got taken! The players are thinking of pooling our money and going up to Oregon and playing those guys."

Paradoxically one of the sweetest victories in Southern Cal football history ended in one of the most bitter defeats.

Time Out: Mike Garrett

"I sort of shake like a leaf in the wind as games approach. The night before a game I lie awake hoping they don't hit me too hard. Sometimes I get hit so hard that I lie on the ground and wonder why the hell am I doing this? You have to accept getting kicked and knocked down and run over all through life, just to get by. But it's like you're in a dark alley, and you're running from trouble and you know you can get hurt if you get caught, so you keep running. I'm not chicken, though. I keep going back into that alley."

Exquisite feelings such as these tortured halfback Mike Garrett all through his career at Southern Cal and later in the pros. He knew, though, that if he was not playing football his life style would be warped.

"If it hadn't been for football, I'd have been a bum," Garrett tells you. "I'd have to work to survive so I suppose I'd have found some job for $2.50 an hour, and I'd be slugging along, hating it, the rest of my miserable life. Thanks to football I lead a good life."

A fierce determination to succeed grips Michael Lockett Garrett. It was reflected most profoundly one day after Southern Cal defeated Colorado 21-0 in 1964. Garrett rushed from lineman to lineman, apologizing for the holes he missed during the game. Quarterback Craig Fertig remembered the situation and understood it completely.

"Mike's the whole player," Fertig once said. "He's all out, even when he's not carrying the ball. Why, he knocks himself out faking for you."

At 5-foot-9 and 200 pounds, Garrett was not of heroic proportions but blended astonishing balance and quickness to become the Cadillac of runners in his time at Southern Cal. In three years Garrett produced enormous offensive accomplishments, things that had never before been done at the school, or anywhere else, for that matter. That O. J. Simpson eventually erased his national collegiate ground-gaining record of 3,221 yards does not, of course, diminish Garrett's heavenly glow.

In all, the irrepressible Garrett amassed 4,876 yards from 1963 through 1965—3,221 by rushing, 48 passing, 399 on pass receptions, 498 on punt returns, and 710 on kickoff returns. His best year was his senior year, when he rushed for 1,440 yards and collected the Heisman Trophy in the process.

"I don't think anything is more exciting than winning the Heisman," says Garrett, who has also played on a Super Bowl winner with the Kansas City Chiefs. "It's important to me because when I die, or whatever happens to me, they won't call me Mike Garrett, Super Bowl winner, they'll call me Mike Garrett, former Heisman Trophy winner. I wanted the Heisman so much. It was a million-to-one shot, and I did the impossible— and I'm very, very happy about it."

The Heisman symbol significantly represented wealth as well as grandiose achievement. This football demigod had climbed Mt. Olympus and discovered riches. He had once said as a poor boy, "I could not have the things I wanted." Now, with an expensive professional contract, he could have anything.

Early hardship motivated Garrett to soaring accomplishments. Product of a Los Angeles ghetto, Garrett hardly knew his father. His parents separated when he was 16, and his mother eventually remarried. Ella Garrett worked part time as a domestic to help support the family, which included six children. They lived in a four-bedroom, $36-a-month government housing project near a cemetery.

"I didn't know then that I was poor, but I remember that I put newspapers in my shoes to cover the holes in the soles," Garrett says.

Football was Garrett's missile out of the ghetto and the sky was the limit at Southern Cal. From the beginning his star climbed. His running talents were superbly mated to John

In college or in the pros, Mike Garrett has not stopped running. "If it hadn't been for football," he says, "I'd have been a bum."

McKay's I Formation.

"I really didn't know what the I Formation was all about when they got me into it," Garrett recalls. "But I just blended into it very easily."

His sophomore year produced 833 rushing yards and extravagant comments.

"Garrett does not pass or punt or call the plays," noted a sportswriter. "He just runs—like no USC man before him."

Coach Tommy Protho of UCLA found the omnipresent Garrett terrifying. "There may be better ones around," he said, "but I can't name you two real quick. His broken-play patterns are hell for a defensive man."

When Garrett shuttled back and forth and forward some 60 yards to advance the ball 24, leaving Michigan State tacklers sprawled behind him on their bellies one day, McKay noted with deep admiration: "It was incredible. There was no way that run could be made, yet Mike made it."

McKay saw extraordinary qualities in his wonder player: "He was the best from Monday to Friday, as well as on Saturday. If I'd wanted to use him at guard, he would have been the best guard. If I'd made him a linebacker, he'd have been the best linebacker. If I had taught him to pass, he might have been my best quarterback."

Garrett's junior year produced 948 rushing yards and more extravagant comments, but the player himself was not impressed that much by his achievements in 1964. "I was not playing as well as I could," Garrett says. "I don't remember anything specific...I just played much better in my sophomore and senior years. I had games where I ran well and did things I never thought I could. As a senior, especially, I was very happy with myself."

Of course no small part of that happiness was his Heisman Trophy, the Holy Grail for college football players. Garrett continues to taste the moment.

"The public relations man at SC told me, 'Mike, tomorrow they select the Heisman Trophy winner. Do you know where you'll be tomorrow morning?' I told him I would be in my apartment. He said, 'Yeah, if I give you a call, you've won the Heisman.' So I slept very well that night—thinking that I played the best I could all year. If I didn't win it, it would be unfair. I

Mike Garrett displays a handful of professional achievements—a 1,000-yard rushing season and a 5,000-yard career mark.

could think of a few other people who deserved it, but as I lay there in bed I said to myself, 'You're going to win it, Mike. You're going to win it.' And I woke up the next morning, and I expected the call about 8 or 9...and I got it. I called my mother right away."

Despite his mountain of achievements Garrett had never thought of himself as anything special to that point. "It's like you're a star from then on," he says. "It's like winning a Pulitzer Prize. You don't have to worry about anything else once you've won that Pulitzer."

When interviewed by newsmen, Garrett said: "I am overpowered." Told that he was only the second Negro to win the honor—the first was the late Ernie Davis of Syracuse—the soft-spoken Garrett replied in characteristic modesty: "Well, that's a marvelous thing. He was a great man."

He was hardly a swaggering hero. Asked what he thought about a sub-par game against Notre Dame (Garrett only gained 57 yards) he noted with chagrin: "All I was thinking about was getting up off the ground. That's where I was most of the time."

Like his classy performances Garrett ran away from the rest of the field in the Heisman voting. Such outstanding names as Tulsa's Howard Twilley, Jim Grabowski of Illinois, Donny Anderson of Texas Tech, and Floyd Little of Syracuse were left far behind.

Fortunately for the elegant halfback he could achieve such a glamorous dream. His royal status somewhat diminished the pain of a gnawing disappointment. Garrett never reached the Rose Bowl, something else he dearly wanted along with the Heisman Trophy. When he realized that the Rose Bowl goal had passed him by, he sat and cried in the Southern Cal dressing room after his last game.

"We were strong, but not as strong as teams before us with Pete Beathard and not as strong as the teams after us with O. J. Simpson," recalls Garrett.

The team of 1963 probably had the most talent of any that Garrett played on, but was not hungry enough to go to the Rose Bowl, he says.

"Basically the team of 1963 was almost the same as the national championship team of 1962, but wasn't eager," Garrett recalls. "I felt that the seniors had lost their desire in 1963, since they had already won a national title. I was a sophomore and was just learning what was going on. I really worked my behind off to make that team. I felt we should have gone to the Rose Bowl that year—and then the roof fell in. (The Trojans lost three games.)"

In his next two years the Trojans had less muscle than 1963, and their Rose Bowl hopes diminished accordingly.

"We didn't have talent like some of the other teams in the country had," Garrett says. "As a senior we had the worst of our teams when I was there. We didn't have a good quarterback at all. I think that hurt us. And we didn't have an outstanding fullback, either."

Surrounded by less talent Garrett ironically had his most successful year as a senior. He credits hard-working offensive linemen for that. (He has said on more than one occasion: "I don't give a damn what kind of defense they put up there. Just give me linemen who'll block for me, and give me an opening and I'll do it.")

The quick and nimble Garrett could not only run through holes, he could hit baseballs through them as well. Recognized first as a football player, he also received more than passing acknowledgement as a baseball player in his senior year. It gave him second thoughts when professional sports beckoned. "I played outfield on the baseball team and hit seven home runs and batted .309," Garrett says. "By mid-season I had really come around and was hitting the ball well, and I was happy with myself. Coach Rod Dedeaux, in fact, advised me not to sign with a professional football team because he thought that I could become a major league baseball player."

Garrett was a wanted man in his senior year. "The Pittsburgh Pirates baseball team told me they planned to compete with the pro football teams in the bidding for my services," Garrett recalls. "No firm figure was made to me, though."

The Los Angeles Rams of the National Football League and the Kansas City Chiefs of the American Football League also wanted Garrett's famous running legs. Garrett finally decided on football. ("I like baseball, but I like football more," he said then. "I think I can play it better, and I don't like the idea of playing in the minor leagues in baseball.") The Kansas City Chiefs had the most alluring offer—a $300,000 bonus spread over 20 years and a yearly contract of $150,000. Garrett signed for five years.

Garrett's association with the Chiefs was a paradoxical blend of sweet and sour. He had the ultimate success of a Super Bowl victory and the rare accomplishment of a thousand-yard rushing season. But he suffered through some down-beat times, too. After one particularly rough year during which Garrett was tormented by injury, he noted: "People doubted me. They were unaware of my injuries, and when I came back they weren't aware I wasn't totally healed, and when I was healed they weren't aware I wasn't in great shape. But they doubted."

Relations with Coach Hank Stramm were not the best, either, and Garrett decided that "I just got tired of football in Kansas City. I just wanted to play my last year out and get out. Kansas City wasn't healthy mentally for me."

New interests took hold of the bright, young man. Garrett showed a preference for politics and a renewed desire to play baseball. "Life is too short to put off doing those things you want to do before you die," he said at the time. "And I want to try something else now."

Although Garrett did go into politics, he found out that he did not like it. ("I helped with a couple of campaigns, but I decided that I didn't need all that attention," says Garrett. "I'm a private person.") And although Garrett had announced that he would join professional baseball in the Los Angeles Dodgers' organization, he decided that it was not his shangri-la, either. Happily he found a new football life with the San Diego Chargers, his present team.

Forever concerned about racial injustice Garrett is a nobleman by instinct. His sense of fair play transcends the football field and has given vent to a part-time career in San Diego social work. During the off season Garrett works with black children in an institution called "Harambee House" (Swahili for "coming together.")

"We're pretty community-oriented, and we deal with kids within the community," Garrett explains. "Instead of sending them away we deal with them right here. It's sort of nice. It's the only thing that can be done for a lot of black kids that are mentally distorted and discarded by society. When I retire from football, I'll probably do this for the rest of my life."

Whether attacking football players or social problems Garrett does it lustily and intelligently. He has grabbed life with both hands. And while his body functions, his mind works, too.

Garrett, a free-wheeling runner, is a free-thinking man. He formulated a rush of ideas while at Southern Cal, where he studied sociology. He read most anything pertaining to the origin of man.

He says, "I want to get more profound. I want to know the background of how man thinks. If you can find how he first started, you may be able to find why he thinks the way he does."

Garrett defines himself as "a realist, an idealist, and a pragmatist." He explains, "If they contradict, that's the way I want it. I'm an idealist in setting goals, a realist in trying to find out what our problems are, and I'm pragmatic in dealing with them."

He is more concerned with others than himself. "As far as being rich and famous anymore, that's out the window," he says. "I just want to live a quiet life and do what I can for people."

"Involved" is the word for Garrett. It is a word not usually associated with 30-year-old Americans in today's world. Stronger than his dreams of a Heisman Trophy is his passion to see some of man's problems licked in his lifetime.

"I look at poverty for example, and I think you should be able to alleviate that," Garrett says. "Look at foreign aid and the amount of food we send to those countries overseas. We have people in this country who need food. The Mormons have a saying for it: 'Clean up your own house before you go somewhere else.' I look at us landing on the moon, and I know when we're dedicated we can alleviate any problem. John F. Kennedy said we're going to land on the moon, and in 1969 we landed on the moon. There are pollution, traffic, and racial problems—if we're dedicated to them, we can alleviate them."

From the playing fields of Southern Cal to the ghettos of San Diego, Mike Garrett has not stopped running for a goal.

Where Have You Gone, Mike Garrett?

"You can't run into the middle of Texas"—Frank Broyles, Arkansas coach. "Yes, I can"—John McKay, Southern Cal.

Bill Bradley could broad-jump 23 feet, dunk a basketball with either hand, and switch-hit in baseball so efficiently that he was offered a $40,000 contract with the Detroit Tigers. He was at his ambidextrous best on a football field, though. There he could throw with either hand, kick with either foot and, as someone said, "think with either brain."

The Texas quarterback was the most heralded sophomore in the Southwest Conference since SMU's Doak Walker. Bradley seemed a mountainous problem for Southern Cal on opening day in 1966, and Trojan coach John McKay joked that he would have to think up a "superdefense" for "Super Bill."

But while the eyes of Texas were on their adored golden boy, the eyes of the rest of the country watched the Southern Cal team operate out of McKay's fanciful and virulent I formation. If 42,000 Longhorn rooters could not, a national television audience could appreciate Southern Cal's 10-6 upset over the Longhorns in damp, muggy Austin.

"USC was better than the 10-6 margin by which it won an opening game over a tough, uncompromising team, and that means that the Trojans are up there among the best in the land," said a sportswriter.

To be sure Bradley had not been a bust. He had shown great poise, considering the pressure of the buildup for his first varsity game and the hypnotism of national TV. He had scored a touchdown "on a three-yard run that practically nobody saw because the fake was so nifty," said a writer.

But Southern Cal's quarterback, who had no such buildup as Bradley, was a more commanding figure that day. Troy Winslow passed to Rod Sherman, Ron Drake, and Rich Leon and handed off to Steve Grady and Don McCall in the first half "and all but ran the Longhorns out to the L.B.J. ranch," noted one observer.

Prior to the contest McKay had asked Arkansas coach Frank Broyles for some advice about playing Texas and was told: "John, you can't run into the middle of Texas. Nobody can." But that was exactly what the Trojans did to save the day.

Late in the game Bradley punted to the Trojan two-yard line, and the Longhorns hoped to keep Southern Cal sewed up there. But Winslow sent his runners straight into the teeth of Texas' hefty line, and the Trojans blasted out of the hole and kept the ball, which they eventually presented to movie star John Wayne.

Sherman hit for three yards, then six more. Mike Hull plunged one yard for a first down at the 12 with six minutes left. Three more running plays brought USC out to the 27 and secured another first down with four minutes to go. With two and a half minutes on the clock Southern Cal had the ball on the 36, but it was fourth and one.

"I've got to have enough confidence in my offensive line to make one yard," McKay thought, "or we shouldn't be out there."

The Trojans made four yards on the play and finished off Texas right there.

"When they brought it out from their goal line, ramming it right at us and kept it for eight minutes, they proved they deserved to win," said Texas coach Darrell Royal. "If I'd known we were never going to touch the ball again, I'd have tried anything on a fourth and four at the 50—even a quarterback sneak."

McKay said later that Royal's decision to punt seemed like the proper thing to do at the time.

"Texas made the right call," McKay noted. "I'll guarantee you they're not going to get the four yards running, because we're up there in a goal line, nine-man line. They might have hit us with a long pass, if they wanted to gamble on it. But by punting they had us right where we didn't want to be."

Ball control was Southern Cal's magic. "When you can't get the football for more snaps than we got," said Royal, slightly ruffled, "all you can do is wait until they shoot the gun and go congratulate somebody."

While Winslow provided the impetus on the field, Wayne led the action on the sidelines. Attired in a black suit and huge white cowboy hat, the movie star swilled liquor from a bottle in a brown paper bag and led the cheers.

With Wayne there it could not have been Texas' day, anyway, pointed out a whimsical writer. "When, really, did anyone ever get the best of John Wayne?" he said.

The triumphant Trojans came home to applause and recognition after the big opening day victory over one of the nation's top teams. Their image soared, but quite frankly it was a false image. Actually this team was not as distinguished as the Texas game would have you believe. Although the Trojans won the championship of the Athletic Association of Western Universities (now expanded to eight teams with the addition of Oregon and Oregon State) and went on to the Rose Bowl in 1966, they obviously lacked the dramatic impact of past years. No quarterback in the class of a Pete Beathard or Bill Nelsen, or even Craig Fertig, called plays. No one of Mike Garrett's astonishing talents ran in the backfield. There was no Hal Bedsole to catch passes.

With defensive back Nate Shaw, tackle Ron Yary, and Sherman, a flanker of expertise, the Trojans of 1966 were not poor, but not indestructible, either. This personality was evident in three losses en route to the Rose Bowl, including a cruel 51-0 beating by Notre Dame—their worst defeat in history. That game returned Notre Dame to the top of the wire service polls and chased the embarrassed Trojans into a post-season bowl date against Indiana.

A situation similar to the earlier game against Texas faced Southern Cal in this one. Precisely like Texas, Indiana had a quarterback of extraordinary capabilities.

"Without Bob Griese, well, we just wouldn't be here," acknowledged Badger coach Jack Mollenkopf.

Griese was accepted as a total player. A writer noted: "He gets the ball away faster than any other college passer and also punts, kicks off, kicks extra points, kicks field goals, and runs with the ball like a halfback."

Predictably it was Griese's arm and toe that secured a 14-13 Indiana victory. The star quarterback moved the Badgers on two touchdown strikes, each time giving the ball to fullback Perry Williams for the final yardage. Griese kicked the extra points for each touchdown. Don McCall scored in the second period for Southern Cal on a run, and Winslow passed to Sherman with two and a half minutes left for the other Southern Cal touchdown, but the Trojans gambled and lost on a two-point conversion attempt.

"We had no thought of playing for a tie," McKay said afterwards. "Even if we had tied it up, Purdue could have

Purdue's George Catavolos intercepts a pass intended for Southern California's Jim Lawrence in the 1967 Rose Bowl. The two-point conversion try nullified, the Boilermakers escaped with a 14-13 victory. Others in on the action include Southern Cal's Rod Sherman and Ray Cahill and Purdue's Eddie King and John Charles.

worked Griese's short passes to the sidelines after we kicked off, and they could have moved within range of a field goal."

After Sherman got behind Purdue defender George Catavolos to catch Winslow's touchdown pass, the conversion play was set up with Jim Lawrence as the intended receiver.

"We put Sherman, Lawrence, and Ray Cahill on the right side," McKay later explained. "Sherman and Cahill criss-crossed in the end zone, and Lawrence flared to the right. Troy threw the ball perfectly."

But at the last second Catavolos stepped in front of the Winslow pass and intercepted it. Catavolos gave his story of the play to a reporter:

"They had to go for two points in a game like this. And they had to throw because they couldn't run on us down there. John Charles, our other defensive halfback, broke up Sherman on his pass pattern. This enabled me to step in front of Lawrence to intercept. I was playing between Winslow and Sherman. When Charles took care of Sherman, I went behind and took care of Lawrence. He and I were the only ones left."

Lawrence was astounded by Catavolos' timing. "I could almost feel the ball in my hands, it was so close," he said. "It was a perfect pass. Troy had me pegged all the way. But that Purdue fellow made a tremendous play."

McKay lost a game but won the admiration of writers and people with gambling instincts everywhere.

"John McKay, the old black-jack player, hit 13 and went broke in the Rose Bowl," said Bud Furillo in the *Los Angeles Herald Examiner*. Mel Durslag wrote in the same newspaper: "McKay reasserted the old credo that if a man must go, he should go with honor." Jim Murray noted in the *Los Angeles Times* that "The Trojans died with their boots on and their guns out...let the record show that the Trojans bet the hand, lost like men, smiled, pushed the chair back, and walked out the swinging doors like John Wayne. They showed up for the shoot-out."

The Rose Bowl game was the first of four straight for McKay, a record, and the "gambler's" luck was better in future years. He had an ace in the hole in O. J. Simpson.

Time Out: O. J. Simpson

When O. J. Simpson played at Southern Cal, a familiar scenario took place after every game. Coach John McKay knew the questions were coming from reporters and was ready with his famous one-liners.

Question: "John, the guy carried the ball 42 times today..."

McKay: "It's not very heavy."

Question: "Don't you think you're overworking Simpson a bit?"

McKay: "He doesn't belong to a union."

When McKay was through with the jokes, he pointed out most seriously: "If you don't have O. J. carrying 35 to 40 times a game, it would be like having Joe DiMaggio on your team and only letting him go to bat once a game."

If Simpson was overworked and underpaid in college, he made up for it in the pros. Now he is being overworked and paid handsomely for it.

"The kid loved to run," remembers Nick Pappas, a former USC runner himself, "and, boy, could he run."

Significantly, Simpson ran in McKay's exotic I Formation, which means that he hit the line six or eight different ways.

"It was O. J. once, O. J. twice, and all of a sudden, boom, he's gone and it's all over!" Pappas exclaims. "One of the greatest runs I've ever seen in football was O. J. Simpson going for 13 yards against UCLA. He broke about three tackles and carried about four guys over the line. It looked like when he got the ball, he said, 'I've got to score,' and by God, he did, against the greatest odds you've ever seen. It was a plowing through of nothing but bodies, and big bodies...a great run. And later he ran 64 yards for a touchdown. It was a typical Simpson run. He cuts, goes to the outside, cuts clear across the field, and outruns everybody. It was O. J.'s way of doing things."

Simpson's favorite play at Southern Cal was the "22-23 blast." He explains, "It's a quick opener. Nothing fancy, just straight ahead. The secret is hitting the hole (opened by blockers) as quick as you can. They hand me the ball, and we try to blast the other team right out of there."

Of course Simpson paid the price for over-zealous running. (Simpson carried the ball 674 times in two years, an average of 32 a game.)

"I felt the bumps, and they hurt plenty," he once said. "I remember after games I'd stretch the nights because I didn't want to go to bed. Once I'd get into bed I couldn't sleep. Every place I'd lay, every way I'd turn, I'd feel pain. The next day would be awful."

Towering success dwarfed the agony. Simpson led Southern Cal to a national championship in 1967 and in 1968 won the Heisman Trophy as the best collegiate football player in America. Along the way he set national records for most yards gained in one season (1,880 in 1968) and most gained in a career (an astounding 3,540 in just two years). He also scored 36 touchdowns.

"I'd feel pain, but I'd have a smile on my face because we'd win," says Simpson, now a star of higher magnitude in the pros. "That's what I remember best about playing at USC—winning. We had the teams, and we had the tradition."

At 6-foot-2 and 210 pounds, Simpson could run 100 yards in 9.4 seconds in college. "Against consistently rugged opposition, much of it stacked against him, few runners in college history ever combined the speed, power, elusiveness, and endurance that O. J. did," pointed out a writer.

"In the 100th season of intercollegiate football O. J. Simpson was, appropriately enough, all of the greatness that had come before him in one dynamic package. Over and over he made holes where there weren't any and created daylight out of tangled jerseys."

Recognized as the supreme college player of his day, Simpson carried his royal title with astonishing humility. Once after a particularly superb game against Stanford, Indians' linebacker Don Parish remarked: "I don't even want to talk about his football ability. We contained him for a half, but then we got tired and he just got stronger. What I want to talk about is this. You might think that a player that's as great as he is would be conceited and arrogant. But not him. He even complimented me when I'd hit him. He'd say things like, 'nice stop, Donny.' Maybe he was trying to psyche me out, I don't know, but he did it."

Such praise of Simpson's graciousness is not uncommon. A veteran sportswriter for the Associated Press recently remarked, "He's the nicest athlete I have ever interviewed." Another AP writer recalled Simpson's manner during a long talk session. "I was student editor of a college newspaper at the time, and I had come in to talk to Simpson long after he had been interviewed by dozens of professional writers," the AP man recalls. "You know, he sat and talked to me for 45 minutes, probably answering the same questions that he had been answering the hour or so before? It was the greatest interview I ever had. And I was only a student."

When he won the Heisman Trophy, Simpson did not take full credit. "I want to emphasize that this was a team award, and the guys on the team won it as much or more than I did," he told a news conference. (His class had not deserted him as a pro, either. After recently breaking the record for rushing yardage in a season, Simpson would not be interviewed without his entire offensive line. He claimed that he could not have broken the record without those players and that they deserved the acclamation as much as he did.)

Such noble characteristics were not indicative of Simpson's early life in San Francisco, however. While an untamed youth, Simpson fled to the fringe of juvenile delinquency. Roaming through the Potrero Hill section of San Francisco as ringleader of a gang—he had leadership qualities even then in junior high school—he led others into street fights. Simpson recalls he "got his kicks" throwing rocks at buses, pulling fire alarms, fighting, and crashing parties and sports events.

O. J. Simpson: "I'd feel pain, but I'd have a smile on my face because we'd win."

Coaches soon harnessed Simpson's outstanding athletic ability and put him to more productive use. Aware that his talents could pull him away from ghetto living, Simpson figuratively and literally took hold of a football and ran away from his past. Simpson followed a pattern epitomized by many of America's great black athletes.

Simpson—born Orenthal James Simpson in Stanford University Hospital on July 9, 1947—developed an early affection for sports and played games at every free moment. "It was always sports with that boy," recalls his mother, Mrs. Eunice Simpson. He learned early how to fight. With a name like "Orenthal" he had to. The unique name was contributed by an aunt, who strangely enough gave her own children more conventional names such as "Stewart," "Stanley," and "Pam."

Simpson kids about his aunt: "She must have been sick once, and my name just came up." Simpson's mother insists that the aunt dubbed her boy after a French actor. At any rate it was all very confusing to O. J.

"I didn't know my name was Orenthal James until I was in the third or fourth grade," he says. "One of the teachers happened to say, 'Orenthal James Simpson' instead of O. J. and I guessed it was me."

Since then Simpson himself and others have further compounded the issue. He signs autographs, "O. Jay Simpson." And newspapermen use "Orange Juice" as a catch-phrase in reference to the star running back. Headline writers have a lot of fun with the sobriquet—you know, "Rams Squeeze Orange Juice," and so forth.

At one time of his life the idea of Simpson playing football was unthinkable. He suffered from diseased legs and had to wear braces. "He had been a heavy baby, the fattest of my four," his mother recalls. "But he lacked calcium in his bones. The doctors said that it might have been rickets. That's why his legs are so bowed today."

Simpson's father and mother separated when O. J. was just five years old, and Mrs. Simpson raised the children on a low budget. The family moved frequently, in and out of government projects and low-cost apartments in San Francisco. Throughout this tenuous existence Simpson never lost sight of sports. Baseball was his preference and Willie Mays his idol when he captained the Everett Junior High School team, but Simpson turned to football in later years.

At Galileo High School in San Francisco, Simpson was originally assigned to play tackle but did not stay there very long when Coach Larry McInerney noticed his exceptional ballcarrying skills. He made the all-city team at fullback but did not contemplate a college football career until after a serious talk with an assistant coach at Galileo. Simpson, who at one time thought earnestly about army duty, was urged by Jack McBride to go to college. "You'll never get anywhere letting people give you stuff," McBride told Simpson. "You've got to work for everything."

An exceptional two-year career at a junior college thrust Simpson in the direction of Southern Cal. Simpson attended the City College of San Francisco for two reasons, to pull up his grades and prove to himself—and some detractors—that he could play junior college football. In his time at CCSF, Simpson broke national rushing and scoring records for junior colleges with 2,552 yards gained and 54 touchdowns. Mays, his boyhood hero, and Marv Goux, an assistant Trojan coach, then steered Simpson to USC. "You have an unusual talent," said Mays. "Recognize it; don't mess it up." Goux told Simpson: "We aren't going to offer you a darn thing. We'll give you a chance to play for USC and to become a Trojan. I watched you play and, if you want to, you can star here. But you'll have to work. You're the one who has to make it your own way."

Referring to Goux's approach, Simpson said: "It was straight—and I liked it."

Although a proven football player, Simpson had to prove himself all over again. McKay gave his new player new assignments.

"He'd been a flanker, running once in a while," McKay explains. "We had to make him something he had never been—a running back. It was a complete rebuilding of his way of life. When he first got here and ran inside, he fumbled too often. Those big men up front like to take a man apart."

The atmosphere of Southern Cal practice sessions was comparable to Marine training camp for Simpson. He recalls brutal drills under the California sun. McKay, the drill instructor, stood by impassively while Simpson went through his paces.

"Two guys held two big, five-foot-long bags," Simpson explains. "They gave you a stiff belt as you took off. You banged through with power. Another big bag was about two yards away. Now you must turn light-footed. They then threw heavy air bags at your feet and knees. You learned to hit, elude, and make moves on the defensive backs."

McKay recalls: "He kept at it and at it, as if to say: 'This is where I am going to make my name.'"

A big day against Texas in the second game of the 1967 season gave Simpson national attention. Carrying the ball 30 times he gained 164 yards, and USC won, 17-13. Texas coach Darrell Royal acknowledged Simpson's gifts: "I doubt if there is a back with more ability than Simpson in the country."

The next week Simpson gained 190 yards against Michigan State. USC won, 21-17. Against Stanford the week after Simpson collected 163 yards on the ground. USC won that one, 30-0. A 169-yard day against Notre Dame in the following game helped the Trojans beat the Fighting Irish 24-7 and started O. J. on the way to all-American status.

Simpson's qualities of power and speed made him a combination of two backs in one. He could run outside like a halfback or inside like a fullback, and McKay utilized these possibilities to the fullest extent. In addition Simpson's uncanny peripheral vision made him even more dangerous.

"Most backs are 'blinders,'" McKay once said. "They see what's in front but can't see what's at the side. The great ones see the color and numbers of an opponent's jersey. O. J. is the only man I've known who can come back to the huddle and tell who made the key blocks."

Injured later in the season, Simpson recuperated in time to lead the Trojans to the national championship. The most-recalled run of his college career was a 64-yard touchdown dash against UCLA that gave the Trojans a 21-20 victory, a Rose Bowl berth, and the national title all in one grand swoop.

In the Rose Bowl that year Simpson scored both touchdowns in USC's 14-3 victory over Indiana and was named the game's most valuable player. His rushing yardage figure of 1,543 for the season led the nation and attached more glitter to his name. But as majestic as his first season was, his second had even more sweep. It became so after a while that people expected a colossal performance every week. In fact that is what they got.

Southern Cal beat Minnesota 29-20 on opening day in 1968 with Simpson contributing 367 yards—236 by rushing. "Don't ask me to describe him," said Minnesota coach Murray Warmath. "Everyone already has. There is really nothing more to say."

Running on a bruised left leg Simpson chalked up 189 yards in Southern Cal's 24-7 triumph over Northwestern. "He approaches a hole (in the line) like a panther," noted Northwestern coach Alex Agase. "Then, when he sees an opening, he springs at the daylight." Northwestern linebacker Don Ross exclaimed: "Simpson's the greatest back in college and the greatest I've ever played against."

When Simpson scored three touchdowns in USC's 27-24 triumph over Stanford, Indians' tight end Bob Moore reflected: "I guess O. J. Simpson showed us on a couple of those runs why he's the man."

Against Washington, Simpson scored both touchdowns and rushed for 172 yards in a 14-7 Trojan victory, leading Huskie coach Jim Owens to say: "We knew that Simpson would be coming at us, but there was nothing we could do about it. He is one of the greatest backs ever to play football. Because of his size and speed, he probably improvises better than any runner I've ever seen."

Before Southern Cal played California, Golden Bears' coach Ray Willsey pointed out: "O. J. Simpson probably is the greatest back of our time. USC beat us by twenty points without him last year, so I guess we're about forty down this year going in." (Southern Cal won 35-17, and Simpson scored two touchdowns and rushed for 164 yards.)

Performances such as these earned Simpson the Heisman Trophy—an honor that had eluded him the year before when he finished second to UCLA's Gary Beban. In 1968 Simpson was light years ahead of his nearest competitor, Purdue runner Leroy Keyes. "I'm not disappointed," Keyes said. "It was just one of those things. I figured that O. J. would win."

Simpson stood beaming at a Heisman Trophy news conference with his wife Marguerite, fielding reporters' questions. Don't you ever get tired carrying a football 40 times a game? he was asked. "During the game you don't think about how many times you carry the ball," Simpson responded. "You think about the situation—the score and the down—but you do get tired at times, especially if you have to run too many end sweeps."

Another questioner asked Simpson if he was born with his football talents. Glancing toward McKay the Heisman winner noted with a radiant smile: "As Coach McKay likes to say, I was taught it all."

Simpson discussed his future, personal and private. He announced that he and his wife were expecting a baby and quipped: "A name like Heisman J. Simpson might be nice." Simpson also launched into his professional career and ultimately created some controversy over it.

"I would like to live in California, so I would prefer to play on a California team," Simpson told reporters. "I also would prefer the National Football League over the American Football League, so that would mean the Los Angeles Rams or the San Francisco 49ers. If it weren't California, my second choice would be New York, Chicago, or Dallas."

The problem was that none of those teams had any rights to Simpson. At that point it would be either Philadelphia of the NFL or Buffalo of the AFL. Both had the worst records in pro football, and it was just a matter of time as to which would get the first draft pick that season. Simpson negated the possibility of his going to either city, handing both Philadelphia and Buffalo what amounted to a public slap in the face. When Buffalo lost its remaining games and thereby won the "O. J. Simpson Sweepstakes," rumors abounded that Simpson would test the draft in court. He did not, though. At the end he was resigned to playing for the Bills.

"Sure, I always wanted to play in the National Football League," he said, finally. "But if there was any disappointment about being drafted by Buffalo, it's over. I know I should accept things as they are, and I'm anxious to get started. It's a great honor to be drafted No. 1. I'm awfully proud of that."

Simpson became the highest-priced rookie since the merger of the NFL and AFL in 1966. A long siege of negotiations between the player's agent and the Bills culminated in a juicy contract for Simpson. It was in the neighborhood of a half-million dollars, but Simpson actually became worth almost twice that much with fringe benefits that included the use of his name for commercial purposes. A one-man conglomerate, he himself said at one point that he had signed contracts worth $900,000 during one yearly period.

Simpson's glamorous name and his big money did not automatically mean immediate pro football stardom, however. Playing with mediocre teams in his first few years Simpson was at times disappointing, and he sometimes found life unbearable at Buffalo. Once comparing his pro career to college he said: "In pro ball I don't work as hard, but I'm hit just as hard, I hurt just as much, and the smiles come harder because the victories come harder. I have to say football has been fabulous for me. I never had anything before, and now I have almost everything. But after almost every game I have disappointment. And sometimes I envy my successor in sunny Southern Cal."

While struggling through his rookie season in professional football, Simpson was flagrantly disturbed. "I'm frustrated in two ways—because we've been losing and I'm not getting the ball," Simpson told an interviewer. "I feel helpless. I don't mind being a decoy if it helps. It's good if it works. But after you lose seven games, maybe you do something else. I would like to get the ball more when we're behind. I admit I haven't done anything spectacular in pro ball, but if Chicago gets behind, you can bet that Gale Sayers is going to get the ball."

Simpson not only missed not carrying the ball as much, but his relationship with McKay. Writing in his book, *O. J. The Education Of A Rich Rookie,* Simpson pointed out: "The most striking contrast between college and pro ball was between the head coaches. USC coach John McKay was dapper and witty, always breaking up meetings or press conferences with wry jokes. He was the kind of man who could make you feel close to him without using a lot of speeches; just a few words from him could let you know what you had to do—and also make you want to do it. (Buffalo) Coach John Rauch presented an altogether different appearance."

Simpson was not easily discouraged, however. Painstakingly he reached Olympian heights in pro football. His yardage totals expanded with the growing years, and in 1973

Simpson accomplished the heretofore sacred milestone of 2,000 yards in one season. Similar to his college achievements Simpson had done something that no mortal before him could do. Always cognizant of his helpmates on the offensive line, Simpson made sure that those players received due credit for the dazzling deed. Throughout his career he has always made it a point to personally thank his offensive linemen for their contributions to his yardage totals.

The herculean achievement of a 2,000-yard rushing season won Simpson not only more glory but more gold. The Bills gave him a new long-term contract, one, in effect, that binds him to the team for the rest of his professional playing days. Not that he needed the money. His outside interests have fleshed out through the years, so much so that Simpson no longer is just a football player. He is a movie actor, a television personality, an entreprenuer—in short, a walking business empire.

Running through this new and complicated life Simpson sometimes reverses his field and returns to his starting place. Poignant glimpses of history forever flash through his mind.

"He has never forgotten that he played for Southern Cal," says a school official. "With everything that he has to do, he still comes back to say hello and still has time to help us recruit new players."

Simpson plays for Buffalo but still carries the ball for Southern Cal, it seems.

The Tunnel Of Love

Steve Sogge envisioned the horrors of the Notre Dame torture chamber. "I thought the stands would be a mile high, and they would throw rocks and bottles at us," the Southern Cal quarterback had said.

Upon his arrival his worst suspicions were confirmed. The arena at South Bend did seem like an endless pit, with thousands of fierce Notre Dame worshippers on hand. While nobody threw rocks and bottles, the Notre Dame people threw something far more lethal—their support.

It had been referred to by football romantics as the "12th man." "If you were an alien from California, you felt more or less like a man at a convention of lunatics," was the way one reporter described it.

Amid all this Notre Dame love and lore, the Southern Cal team arrived in the fall of 1967 to do battle with the Fighting Irish for fame, fortune, and the No. 1 ranking. It was not an easy setting to walk into, and despite the fact that the Trojans had superior athletes the Fighting Irish were installed as 12-point favorites because of the home field advantage. Psychologically it was quite an advantage.

The night before the game a typical pregame pep rally rocked the South Bend campus, leading one policeman to say: "On a clear night, and if the windows are open, I can hear them a half-mile away. But that's Notre Dame. I don't worry none about it."

This time Frank Leahy, the former Notre Dame coach, was

on the podium before a monstrous crowd at the campus field house. "I want to congratulate each and every one of you for being the greatest 12th man that any football team in the entire world has ever known," he said. The crowd erupted into wild cheers.

"It was a scene that would have made a psychedelic love-in look like a church social," observed one writer. "A Green Beret would have turned tail and run. Pregame pep rally? It was a riot."

Green, yellow, and pink toilet tissue soared into the field house heavens and bombed the crowd. Sirens went off, horns exploded, and voices erupted. Several other speakers, stressing Southern Cal blood, followed Leahy. "Southern California has an astounding football team," assistant coach John Ray was saying. "And they've got a big back named O. J. Simpson, too. But two years ago they had a back named Mike Garrett, and he only made 22 yards here. We respect all teams here, but we fear nobody. NOBODY!" More cheers.

Signs told stories of the ardent Notre Dame support. One, about 150 feet long, proclaimed boldly: "Garrett Juice In '65, O. J. Simpson In '67." "Irish Love Canned O. J.," said another. From the ceiling swung a dummy with no head. A note pinned on him read, "The Headless Trojan." Frenzied cheers belabored the ears throughout the religious ceremony. "Eat 'em up, Irish. Eat 'em up," the crowd chanted. And after a player had pointed to Notre Dame's 51-0 victory the year before, the crowd cried, "Do it again, do it again."

Such passions were moderate, considering what transpired in the stadium the next day. But despite the anger from a full-throated crowd of 59,000, banners ordering the Fighting Irish to "Get A Trojan For The Gipper," and other such distracting theatrics, some special ingredients were missing from the surrealistic Notre Dame montage this time. Mystique, ghosts of the past, and spirit notwithstanding, the Fighting Irish were short a runner, a kicker, and a passer. And the result was a thorough 24-7 beating from a decidedly superior Trojan team.

"We had them figured," said Southern Cal coach John McKay, who counted the victory among the most precious of his career. "Our people were able to get in the right places. (Terry) Hanratty was off, and we got him to throw impatiently on a few occasions."

Preceding victories over Washington State, Texas, Michigan State, and Stanford that season were not as sweet. Southern Cal placed the Notre Dame success up there with other golden memories—such as the 16-14 victory in 1931. It was, in fact, the first time that the Trojans had beaten the Fighting Irish at South Bend since 1939.

"The turning point of the 1967 season was that Notre Dame game," Sogge recalls. "Southern Cal feels that it has to beat Notre Dame, even though it's a non-conference game. There's a tremendous amount of pride going. Everyone talks about the UCLA game, but I never held UCLA in the same esteem as Notre Dame."

When the 1967 season began, Notre Dame was still light years away. The Trojans had to think about other teams first, and McKay had to worry about filling positions left by 11 regulars who had graduated. After inspecting the field, with such runners as O. J. Simpson and Earl McCullouch, quarterbacks such as Sogge and Toby Page, and other personnel of the caliber of defensive end Tim Rossovich, tackle Ron Yary and linebacker Adrian Young, McKay announced: "We'll be better than last year in all ways. Better defense, better offense, better passing, better running, better punting. What else is there?"

Of course McKay also looked at the treacherous schedule and remarked about the first five or six games, "If we live through that, you'll hear from us."

A 49-0 romp over Washington State on opening day did nothing to assuage McKay's cautious optimism. Watching game films the coach thought out loud that the Trojans' offense was lucky and that the defense was sour at times. There was no question that Southern Cal had dominated outmanned Washington State, McKay noted sharply, "but when you have men open 15 yards and you overthrow them 15 yards more, you have to think you might not get away with that against a team like Texas."

This disgruntlement carried through the week's practice before the Texas game. Unhappy at his team's poise against Washington State, McKay seemed irritable while building toward the meeting with the admired Longhorns.

One day watching a passing practice go flat, McKay

screamed at one of his players: "If they double-team you, you gotta get it to him right now, the hell with anybody else..." Then he turned to an assistant coach and said: "Dave, I want you to impress that boy that 12 yards is two more than 10, see? Twelve is two more than 10...This is a passing attack, baby, get the ball out there...Damn, sometimes you have to hit a guy with a ball bat just to get him to pay attention."

Later in the week McKay saw flaws in the defense. After repeated instruction had failed at one point, McKay rushed into the line and grabbed a defensive player by his shoulder pads and forced him into the proper position. He commanded another player off the field. "Just get off the damn field," McKay snapped. "You're not showing me a thing as a football player." One day he uncharacteristically left practice early in disgust. "Got two kids hurt in five minutes because they didn't seem to know what the hell they were doing," he said. "I figured they'd been out there long enough anyhow, and there's no use practicing when you're going that bad."

Seemingly endless meetings and thousands of feet of filmwork preceded the Texas game. McKay and his staff looked at old Texas movies, but Texas had the advantage of watching an updated USC film, the Washington State game. The Longhorns had not played yet in 1967.

McKay pointed out the virtues of Texas quarterback Bill Bradley and tailback Chris Gilbert, especially Gilbert. "The best thing that happened to us last year was that Darrell Royal didn't find out what a great tailback Gilbert was until the second half of the game," McKay noted. "Gilbert gained 103 yards on us in the second half." Intermittently hot and cold all week, McKay occasionally pumped up his own team. "Listen, you want to know how good O. J. is?" McKay, in a good mood, said one day before practice. "He's bigger than Gale Sayers. And faster. I don't exactly know what out-quick means, but he'll out-quick you, too." And Ron Yary was "as good (a tackle) as I've ever seen," the coach said. "Ron has far better movement than a boy his size (6-foot-6, 255 pounds) should show. He is fast and hard to move out, he is so strong." (Yary later confirmed that assessment by winning the Outland Trophy as the best lineman in the country.)

McKay was not a barrel of fun most of the week, though.

Ron Yary, Southern California's Outland Trophy winner in 1967: "As good a tackle" as John McKay ever saw.

Until the last day, he refrained from giving talks about Texas because he thought it was not necessary. "If you continually talk to the team it becomes a matter of oh, Dear God, what's he going to say now. Same thing, over and over. I'm not one to talk to the team all the time."

The Friday night before the game, however, he became analytical and more specific. Texas is a far better team than the Trojans faced the previous week, he pointed out. He said that you supposedly were not able to run on the Longhorns, but that the Trojans could—and would.

On the bus ride over to the Coliseum Saturday, McKay sat with Sogge, his starting quarterback, and rehashed strategy. Toby Page, the first-string quarterback, had a bruised rib cage and could not start.

Once in the bowels of the Coliseum, McKay sought his locker room, fronted by a green door, splashed with his name in chalk. He discarded a plaid coat and changed into his ridge-soled field shoes for the Saturday night game. McKay surveyed the list of officials for the night and noted that one was from Texas' territory, the Southwest Conference. "We'll get a holding penalty for sure," he said sardonically.

Pretty soon heavy noises, laced with occasional shrieks and yelps, filtered from the visitors' locker room. Lighting up a cigar McKay commented, "That will be Texas...Texas has arrived."

McKay soon sent his team out on the Coliseum floor to challenge the lofty Texans amidst a jumble of color and noise from the crowd of 67,000. Taking advantage of a Southern Cal fumble Texas scored first on an 85-yard drive led by the irrepressible Bradley and Gilbert. Simpson later scored around left end to give Southern Cal a 7-7 tie at the half.

In the locker room McKay stepped to a blackboard and made changes for the second half. He ordered a more wide open game, such as passes on first down. Also because double coverage had bottled up split end Earl McCullouch, McKay wanted to use two tight ends now. Finishing his analytical talk McKay suddenly turned inspiration man, shouting: "You ran in. They could hardly walk in. Now's the time to put it to them."

Rossovich was especially inspired. He rammed through the big Texas line several times and nailed Bradley and Gilbert with authority. Safety man Mike Battle pestered the Longhorn receivers. Simpson began rolling up yardage. And as the game went on, Sogge got better. Sogge completed a touchdown pass to Bob Miller to make it 14-7 Southern Cal, and Rikki Aldridge kicked a 30-yard field goal and it was soon 17-7.

Tim Rossovich storms a ballcarrier in the pros. At Southern Cal his talents helped the Trojans win a national championship in 1967.

Bradley directed a touchdown play for Texas, but it was too little and too late. Southern Cal won the game, 17-13.

Simpson, with 164 yards, had outrushed the entire Texas team. "He makes the three-yard run exciting," commented McKay, more relaxed than he had been all week.

Southern Cal's glamour runner was just as potent the following week against Michigan State, and the Trojans won another tough one, 21-17. He also helped Southern Cal beat Stanford with gusto, 30-0, and the first four victories put visions of sugar plums in Sogge's head. "We thought we were outstanding," he says. "Winning the No. 1 spot was in the back of our minds. Even though you don't shoot for the national championship, it's always there."

The Trojans then went to South Bend, and the journey turned out to be the road to the national title. The match was described as the "Poll Bowl" by some writers, since it meant stature in the wire service polls. Besides, Southern Cal-Notre Dame meetings more often than not decided national championships. Before the 1967 affair the winner of their game had ended up as national champion in somebody's poll 14 times. Prior to the 1967 game Southern Cal was ranked No. 1 in the country, and Notre Dame, because of a close loss to Purdue, was No. 5. But that had little bearing on the thoughts of the odds-makers. "They had talked about how USC hadn't beaten Notre Dame in South Bend in a long, long time," Sogge remembers. "It was a tough place to play in. Great for Notre Dame, of course. Their fans have such tremendous enthusiasm."

The Notre Dame players burst on the sunny field in their gold helmets and blue jerseys, eliciting frightening crowd noise. Southern Cal's warriors, in road white with the cardinal numbers and helmets, were greeted by comparative silence, although some of their followers held an icy fortress in the stands.

Nicknames flourished, adding color to the already color-saturated day. There was "Orange Juice" Simpson and Earl "The Pearl" McCullouch for Southern Cal. Notre Dame presented quarterback Terry Hanratty and receiver Jim Seymour, once called "The Baby Bombers," but now known in their maturity as "Mr. Fling and Mr. Cling." None of these formidable offensive weapons was obvious at first, though. Defenses predominated, forcing mistakes that produced a 7-7 tie early in the third period. At that point the stars of the game were two linebackers—Young of Southern Cal and Notre Dame's Bob Olson. Young intercepted three of Hanratty's passes, and the Fighting Irish quarterback spent most of the afternoon clutching his gold helmet in disbelief and trudging in despair to the sidelines, throwing his arms up before coach Ara Parseghian. Olson pestered Simpson and clung annoyingly to Trojan receivers.

Finally Simpson began running superbly late in the third period, wringing groans from the frantic Notre Dame sideline. Whenever the great runner broke loose, Notre Dame defensive coach Johnny Ray could be heard shouting to his players: "Too many yards, too many." Then Simpson took a pitchout from Sogge and found open land. "Too many yards," Ray screamed again, "too many." Then Simpson was by himself, flying away from the nearest pursuer. "Oh, no...No!... Ray moaned. "No!... Oh...damn...Geeawed!"

The 36-yard touchdown run broke the tie and unleashed more Southern Cal scoring. Simpson went over again (his third touchdown of the day), and the Trojans added a field goal to seal Notre Dame's fate and subdue the huge crowd. "Simpson's nickname shouldn't be 'Orange Juice,' noted Notre Dame sports publicist Roger Valdiserri. "It should be 'Oh, Jesus,' as in, 'Oh, Jesus, there he goes again.'"

Carried off on the shoulders of his players McKay crooned: "This is my greatest win."

The Trojans were a good team, but without Simpson might have been an ordinary team. And Sogge was apt to agree. "It was great to have O. J., not only because he was so good, but because he was so modest," notes Sogge. "We all felt very close to O. J., and we were happy that he got the publicity. We never had a morale problem. We were such a closely-knit team because O. J. was such a fine, fine person."

Galvanized by their star, Southern Cal won splendidly over Washington, Oregon, and California. Curiously, though, the Trojans were upset 3-0 in rainy Corvallis by Oregon State in the ninth game of the season despite a 188-yard rushing day by Simpson.

"It's difficult to go undefeated with our schedule," Sogge says. "That game against Oregon State was played in six inches of mud. It wasn't a football game—it was a brawl. We played a flat game. We just couldn't get going. Despite the loss, though, we still felt we could be national champs."

The loss to Oregon State cost Southern Cal the No. 1

ranking and left room at the top for UCLA. However it was academic at this point who was the top college football team in the land. That would be decided on the field of battle the following week, when Southern Cal met UCLA in the last game of the season. The nation turned its eyes toward Los Angeles.

More Important Than Life Or Death

In the Southern Cal playbook it was called the "23-Blast." O. J. Simpson lines up deep and goes straight ahead, taking a handoff from the quarterback. A guard and a tackle on the left side open a hole for him, and Simpson shoots through for maybe 5, 10, or 15 yards, if he is lucky. Simpson had heard it called plenty of times during the 1967 season. Then he heard it again.

"I was bent over there, and I heard him call it," Simpson said. "I said to myself, the 23-blast—oh, oh, that's me."

Quarterback Toby Page handed Simpson the ball, and he headed for the left side of the line. Guard Steve Lehmer and tackle Mike Taylor cleared Simpson through a huge hole.

"As it unfolded it looked like a five-yard gain," noted a sportswriter. "Then Simpson veered toward the left sideline. Oh, well, a 15-yard gain and first down."

But suddenly there was Southern Cal end Ron Drake blocking out UCLA's halfback, and the safety was out of the way, too. Simpson turned back toward the middle of the field, going to his right, and open land appeared before the great runner.

Soon he was exerting his famous 9.4 speed, accelerating toward the goal line despite a sore foot and a complete afternoon of torturous football. And everyone in the Los Angeles Coliseum knew he would not be caught.

"Of the remarkable 1,415 yards Simpson gained this season, those 64 were the most impressive of all, for they came after two hours of the toughest punishment he had endured— and they stretched all the way from Pasadena to Number Onesville," one writer said.

Simply translated it meant that Simpson's 64-yard touchdown run against UCLA in the last regular game of the season had not only given the Trojans a 21-20 victory over their bitter cross-town rivals, but a berth in the Rose Bowl and the national championship as well.

It was fitting that Simpson himself should settle the score with UCLA. This important game blended a myriad of implications.

Red Saunders, the onetime UCLA coach, once said that a UCLA-Southern Cal game was not a matter of life or death—it was more important than that. Taken at his word, the 1967 battle transcended even those outrageous values.

Hollywood could not have come up with a better script. It was improbable enough that Simpson and UCLA quarterback Gary Beban should emerge in the same city as Heisman Trophy candidates. Furthermore here were two schools in a divided city fighting for not only the championship of Los Angeles but the championship of their conference, a Rose Bowl berth, and top national ranking all in one splendid afternoon. "It is so garishly theatrical that it really should have started at a soda fountain in a Hollywood drug store," noted a sportswriter, whimsically. "It is strictly from the studio lots."

As with most Hollywood productions, this one had the accompanying hoopla and tinsel. There was Marvin Goux, the stern-looking assistant coach at Southern Cal, playing the part of an inspiration man. Perhaps not in the class of, say, a Knute Rockne, Goux had done some bit acting in films and prepared the Trojans and their followers with fiery speeches, soaked with college spirit. In a small dressing room jammed to the hilt with players and the Southern Cal band, Goux begged the Trojans to "win one for John." Then he held up a photograph of Coach John McKay looking dejected after the previous year's loss to UCLA. Raising his fist Goux said: "Listen, listen. The worst thing in life is to be a prisoner. I could never be a prisoner. Never. I would rather die. We've been prisoners to those indecencies over there for two years. Today's the day we go free." Everyone cheered.

One was reminded of the bittersweet association of these two fine schools through the years. There was no question in Los Angeles, no cross-town rivalry in America was as passionate as the Southern Cal-UCLA wars. So Goux said that Southern Cal had to go to the Rose Bowl and win the national championship, but more important than that the Trojans had to win the championship of Los Angeles.

Over at UCLA, Coach Tommy Prothro and others stressed the virtues of Beban. Prothro emphasized that Beban could beat you a number of ways—with a run, pass, fake, or call. "And his ability to change plays at the scrimmage line is perhaps his greatest asset," Prothro announced. UCLA's award-winning quarterback was a familiar sight, all right—his fierce royal figure bobbing behind the center, shifting his backs, checking, raising his head to survey the defense, contemplating last-second changes.

"There's something about the way he manages things out there that gives everyone confidence," said UCLA fullback Rick Purdy. "You just know whatever he calls is right."

Beban had been the class quarterback of the country for three years but denied any association with greatness. "I suppose I'm rather ordinary," he said. Others would have to disagree, particularly Simpson, who said: "Gary's the greatest."

Poise, Beban's supreme quality, was singled out by one professional scout: "He is about the most self-assured player I've ever seen. He knows exactly what he is going to do, and he will spot things out there, file them away mentally, and use them on you later. You don't judge Beban on how much he does, not on his statistics. He beats you with the 'when' he does something. Invariably it's at the perfect time."

Similarly acclaimed for his poise, Simpson had endurance and strength to match. When he first had come to Southern Cal from a junior college, Simpson was prized for his startling speed. But McKay also discovered something about his bullishness. "We wanted to see if he could take it inside," McKay said. "We ran him seven straight times in one scrimmage, and that was it. He busted people backward."

Simpson never imagined that he would be carrying the ball as much as he did in 1967, like 38 times against Notre Dame, 36 against Michigan State, and 30 against both Texas and Washington. Still, he did not buckle. "I don't get real tired," he said at one point during the season. "Maybe it's because I'm anticipating that on the next carry I'll break clear. I feel like I can go all the way every time, mainly because we've got such a good line."

No UCLA students rented a single-engine aircraft and strafed the Southern Cal campus with blue and gold paint as before. No Southern Cal students sneaked onto the UCLA campus with brick and mortar and sealed up all the doors and windows of a sorority house, as they once did. There was no dynamite planted in UCLA's bonfire this time, nor smoke bombs planted under the UCLA yell leader's platform in the Coliseum, nor a land mine planted under one goal line, as a depraved fanatic had once accomplished before he was caught. There were pranks, of course, but not as radical as the aforementioned. Actually the game did not need any embellishment. It had enough explosive material without any additives.

McKay particularly was vexed over insinuations that Prothro "had his number." Prothro had beaten McKay the previous two years, and there were feelings, whether warranted or not, that the UCLA coach had won with guile rather than talent.

Responding to this criticism McKay said angrily one day: "Well, we pushed 'em all over the field in 1965, but we fumbled on their 1, 7, and 17. I guess he planned that."

The teams' styles were as different as their campuses, as far removed as their coaches. Despite the presence of the superb Beban, UCLA was a fanatical defensive team. "UCLA swarms on its foe, sticks him, prods him, and buzzes around him. It stunts and squirms, hits and slides, penetrates and scrambles and forces mistakes," pointed out a pregame analysis. Although they played an excellent defense, the Trojans were offense-oriented.

Distinctly contrasting in personality, UCLA and Southern Cal were perfectly matched in talent. Using a special grading system McKay had weighed the value of the teams, player by player, and came up with the arithmetical equation that UCLA and Southern Cal were exactly equal. "It's going to be a helluva game," McKay decided in the most unscientific terms.

Southern Cal was installed as a three-point favorite,

although ranked second in the country to No. 1 UCLA. Analysts figured that the Trojans had faced a tougher schedule than the Bruins, pointing to victories over such teams as Texas, Michigan State, and Notre Dame. Southern Cal was upset 3-0 by Oregon State, a team that UCLA had tied. The Bruins, on the other hand, had beaten only Tennessee among the respected powers, and suffered narrow escapes against Penn State and Stanford, two dramatically weaker teams.

"We've been good when we had to," said Prothro. "We've had to be good," replied McKay.

Emotionally the UCLA players seemed higher than Southern Cal's. Prothro kept his charges in a demonstrative state of frenzy before the game. He encouraged them to "hop around on the sidelines like thieves trapped in a corridor," pointed out one sportswriter. The Trojans, on the other hand, appeared more businesslike, more professional. In the team meeting before the game McKay told his players that they would be coming back to the locker room in two hours or so. "It'll be the shortest walk of your life," McKay said quietly, "or it'll be the longest." It turned out to be the shortest, but not without some apprehensiveness.

For a while it seemed that UCLA was the only team in the place. Beban, playing with injured ribs, conducted a flawless touchdown drive and sent Greg Jones blasting over from 12 yards out to give the Bruins a quick 7-0 lead. The Trojans, meanwhile, could not break Simpson clear and thus were unable to mount any type of offensive threat in the first quarter. They did manage to tie the score, though, with a gorgeous defensive play. Beban threw a pass at midfield into the wide left flat, but it was intercepted by Pat Cashman. He shot in front of Jones, the intended receiver, and raced 55 yards for a Southern Cal touchdown.

Protho said later about that play: "I called it. It's a new one. He's supposed to roll one direction, turn and throw blind, hoping no defender's there. It's a stupid play. I'll never use it again."

Beban moved UCLA again in the second quarter but was racked up deep in Southern Cal territory. Powerful blows from Cashman sent the Bruin star writhing toward the sideline. At this point Zenon Andrusyshyn attempted a field goal for UCLA from the 20-yard line, but it was off target. Sparked by their vital defensive stand the Trojans found new life with Earl "The Pearl" McCullouch. The runner took off down the sideline on a daring reverse play, netting 52 yards. McCullouch then caught a 13-yard pass, and Simpson, an injured right foot throbbing inside a shoe with a special sponge cover, burst over guard from the 13 for the Trojans' second touchdown. Southern Cal had a 14-7 lead at half time "amid the most noise since D-Day," noted an observer.

In the third quarter Beban took UCLA on another long drive, only to be frustrated again by the riled Southern Cal defenders. Andrusyshyn tried another field goal, and this was blocked by Bill Hayhoe. Undiscouraged, Beban guilefully directed a touchdown play that tied the score at 14-14 later in the third period. Remembering a mistake that he made earlier the business-like Beban hit halfback George Farmer with a 47-yard scoring pass.

"Cashman had been waiting for another of those flat passes, so we sent Farmer straight down, right past him," Beban said later. "It balanced out. Cashman's interception earlier was really responsible for our second touchdown."

A poor punt by Southern Cal's Rikki Aldridge and a Beban pass later put UCLA in excellent scoring position again, but Hayhoe, a 6-foot-8, 254-pounder, dropped Beban for a big loss. And two plays later Hayhoe blocked another field goal attempt by the frustrated Andrusyshyn.

"Those things somehow weren't as discouraging then as they are now," Beban said after the game. "We knew we would score again."

The Bruins did, but so did the Trojans. As if sanctified by some Hollywood movie mogul, the teams battled toward an engrossing finish before an audience of more than 90,000 in the Coliseum and millions more on national television.

UCLA scored first on a typical Beban-inspired scheme. The star quarterback hit four passes in a seven-play drive covering 65 yards, the last one to Dave Nuttall for a touchdown. A subtle, calculating move by McKay (and Hayhoe) then provided Southern Cal with its most important play of the game. When the Bruins lined up for the extra-point kick, McKay inserted Hayhoe in the line because "we knew he (Andrusyshyn) kicked it low so we just put the tallest guy we had in there on defense. We told the kids it wasn't so important that they bust through and make him rush the kick as it was just getting to the scrimmage line and raising their arms high."

Hayhoe got his arms high enough to put a finger on the ball, deflecting it slightly. The kick was no good, and McKay said afterward with a wink, "I call that brilliant coaching."

Simpson, of course, made McKay look like a genius after that with his game-winning touchdown run. Toby Page had taken over at quarterback for USC from Steve Sogge and repeatedly sent Simpson whirling through the Bruin defenders. On this particular series of downs Simpson appeared winded after carrying the ball two straight times.

"Page looked at me as if I couldn't carry the ball a third straight time," Simpson recalls. "I looked at him as if I could."

Page originally decided not to use Simpson when the Trojans lined up. It was third down at the Southern Cal 36. Then Page noticed that UCLA's linebackers had anticipated the play he had ordered and changed signals at the line of scrimmage. He called the "23-Blast," Simpson's favorite. That sent the great runner through the left side of the UCLA line in the most remembered touchdown run of the 1967 season. Aldridge (who will not be remembered as much) kicked the crucial tie-breaking extra point for the Trojans.

Although neither Simpson nor Beban was in perfect physical condition, each star responded to the high stakes with efficacy. Beban, whose rib cage "looked like an abstract painting in purples and pinks," according to one writer, passed for more than 300 yards. Simpson, whose swollen right foot was described as something that should be "in a museum of natural history," drove for 177 yards. And Jim Murray of the *Los Angeles Times* suggested, "They should send the Heisman out here with two straws."

The players themselves agreed with that assessment in so many words, holding a Mutual Admiration Society meeting after the superb game. Visiting the Trojan dressing room Beban shook Simpson's hand and said: "O. J., you're the best." Simpson responded: "Gary, you're the greatest. It's too bad one of us had to lose."

Beban won the Heisman Trophy that year, but Simpson

got to go to the Rose Bowl. The UCLA quarterback would have given his arm for the chance to go to Pasadena. He had given everything else that brilliant autumn afternoon.

The Simpson Bowls

Approaching a Rose Bowl game with Southern Cal one year a Big Ten coach remarked with a trace of cynicism: "We are at a disadvantage. John McKay has the Rose Bowl on USC's schedule each year."

It only seemed that way in the 1960s—but at one point the Trojans did go to the Rose Bowl four straight seasons. During that time four different Big Ten teams visited Pasadena.

Each of the appearances from the 1966 through the 1969 seasons, win or lose, served to embellish Southern Cal's football program in one way or another. But broach the subject on the Trojan campus and you are sure to hear about the "Simpson Bowls" more often than not.

O. J. Simpson had always dreamed of playing in a Rose Bowl game and managed to play in two. That is two more than Mike Garrett, who ached for Rose Bowl magic and two more than another Southern Cal superman of the past, Frank Gifford. Simpson was a winner in the first one and a loser in the second, but a champion in both.

A spectator at the 14-13 loss to Purdue on January 1, 1967, Simpson remarked to a Southern Cal player: "Don't worry about it. We'll be back next year."

When Simpson kept his promised Rose Bowl date on January 1, 1968, he made it a memorable one, gaining 128 yards and scoring both touchdowns in Southern Cal's 14-3 victory over Indiana. That confirmed the Trojans' status as the national champion.

Voted the game's most valuable player, Simpson stood

alone on the battlefield amid an otherwise bland performance by Southern Cal. He gave noticeable electric presence to a Trojan team stripped of several regulars.

"Five of our regulars were out at the start of the game because of injuries, and we lost two more during the action," McKay pointed out grimly. "Our replacement players had a hard time because of timing..."

Simpson did not have any trouble timing his runs, though. Explaining his aggressive methods, he said: "I run to hit the tackler before he hits me. I want to be the punisher, not him."

Possessed by this demoniacal football philosophy Simpson

O. J. Simpson plows over the top against Indiana in the 1968 Rose Bowl game. Simpson gained 128 yards and scored two touchdowns, leading Southern Cal's 14-3 victory.

moved through the 1968 season with a lordly stride. Simpson abandoned conventional padding because he wanted to "feel" football. "Running is a feeling," he explained after one game of his senior year. "I don't want to wear a lot of pads because I want to 'feel' the game, the contact. It helps to be able to feel a tackler hitting you or grabbing at you. You know where he is and what to do."

Simpson was not encumbered by elbow pads nor forearm pads, and instead of the usual hip pads taped a couple of small knee pads to his hips and left his tailbone unprotected. "I feel more loose that way," he noted.

Simpson led USC's opening day victory over Minnesota, a team that had tied for the Big Ten championship the year before, and prompted a euphorious comment from a nationally respected football authority.

"Simpson is better than Red Grange," noted Leo Fischer, sports editor of Chicago's *American*. "I've seen them all. On the basis of his performance against Minnesota, far from the worst defensive team in the country, I think Simpson is the greatest."

But Simpson had taken a brutal beating that game while carrying the ball 39 times and had a badly bruised left thigh to show for it. "Every inch of him hurt," said an observer. And McKay seriously considered withholding Simpson from the Northwestern game the following week. "I almost didn't play him," the Southern Cal coach admitted, "but you (writers) know as well as I do what would have happened if I hadn't." Simpson played with pain, and the Trojans won behind their leading man.

"He's better than (Leroy) Keyes—although we have to meet Keyes and Purdue next week," offered Northwestern end Mark Proskine. (Keyes, of course, was one of the most glorified backs in the nation that year.)

The third game of the 1968 season presented a significant meeting between an irresistible force (Simpson) and an immovable object (Ted "Mad Stork" Hendricks) of Miami. Hendricks' defensive heroics were becoming as famous as the offensive feats of Simpson. His hobby was dismantling automobiles, but Hendricks was just as adept at dismantling ballcarriers. The long-gaited Miami end, whose physical characteristics included huge, flapping arms (hence, "Mad Stork"), was ready for the faceoff with Simpson. And so was Simpson.

The Southern Cal runner had studied films on Hendricks and decided, "He likes to penetrate. He shucks off most blockers, or just pushes 'em away and gets around 'em. He's real strong on the hands and arms. He likes to play cat-and-mouse with the quarterback, too. Force him to pitch, then get the ballcarrier..."

Hendricks buoyed one of the country's best rushing defenses, but it was not good enough to contain one of the best rushing offenses. Simpson slogged and scraped for 163 yards, more than Miami's entire net offense, and scored two touchdowns from close in to help the Trojans win easily over the Hurricanes. When Simpson was not running, Steve Sogge was passing. Simpson was just as effective as a decoy as he was a runner that day. "They lullaby you with Simpson," Miami coach Charlie Tate complained after the game, "and then they hit you with a pass. But it's Simpson's presence that makes everything else work."

Carrying the ball 38 times Simpson had come out of the game with a fresh injury. Already battered from the Minnesota affair, Simpson's left leg was further damaged in the knee. Soreness raged on Simpson's left side from the hip area on down, and he curtailed his practice sessions. But he played—and played well—against Stanford the following Saturday. Against emotionally-charged Stanford players who had "Squeeze O. J." and "O. J. Who?" painted on their helmets, Simpson carried the ball 47 times for 220 yards and included touchdown runs of 3, 46, and 4 in his day's work. Ron Ayala kicked a 34-yard field goal in the fourth quarter to finish off the Indians.

By the time it was over, Simpson had half-forgotten his injuries. "I felt kind of squeamish running early in the game," he explained, "but I felt better as the game wore on." McKay, always ebullient after big victories and hardly ever serious, noted: "I think what probably happened is we ran the injury out of him. If we had only run him 30 times, he'd probably still be hurting."

Against Washington, Southern Cal was flat, but Simpson was stupendous. It resulted in a close Trojan victory, only because of the presence of the princely runner. Simpson could only be stopped with great effort and determination, pointed out Washington coach Jim Owens. "You can't do it with a special defense," he said.

Simpson had a sub-par game against Oregon, a team that continually gave him (and Southern Cal) trouble. The Ducks held Simpson to just 67 yards and one touchdown, but the Trojans won 20-13.

"O. J. doesn't like to play against a quick team like ours," said Oregon's George Dames. "We've watched the films of him, and he likes to come into a hole, look for daylight, and then just shoot up the field. We didn't let him do that."

Simpson concurred: "Oregon is just a real fine defensive team. They're so fast that they even stopped our sweeps. When I would get ready to turn the corner, somebody would come up from behind to throw me down."

Simpson was thrown down plenty the following week by California's strong defenders, but he managed to stay on his feet long enough to have another big day. But after the Trojans' seventh straight victory, Simpson was a walking hospital case with a bruised thigh, a twisted knee, and a sprained ankle. "You name it," he said, "and I've got it. I took more good shots against Cal than in any game I've played since high school."

After some consideration Simpson reflected in a half-hearted joke, "It seems as though I stay sore from game to game. Maybe it's time to retire."

The undefeated Trojans then met undefeated Oregon State in what amounted to a championship game for the Pacific-8 Conference title (the name "Pacific-8" was formally adopted in 1968). Bill "Earthquake" Enyart, in the Heisman Trophy race with Simpson, gave the Beavers a 7-0 lead with a one-yard touchdown plunge. But Sogge ("too short, too slow, too inexperienced," according to one Southern Cal rival) tied the game at 7-7 with a 22-yard touchdown pass to Terry DeKraai in the fourth period. Simpson later contributed 42 yards in a scoring drive capped by Ayala's field goal, and the Trojans had a 10-7 lead.

With less than seven minutes remaining in the game Simpson ran 40 yards for a touchdown to put USC ahead 17-7. As it turned out it was the winning play. Oregon State scored again but fell short by four points. Simpson had tied a USC record in that game, carrying the ball 47 times. He carried the ball 21 times alone in the fourth quarter, when he made 138 of his 238 rushing yards.

The Trojans won a Rose Bowl berth with the victory, and Oregon State coach Dee Andros agreed that Southern Cal deserved to be ranked No. 1 in the country.

In a 28-16 victory over UCLA the following week Simpson carried the ball 40 times for 205 yards, caught three passes for 24 more, and scored three touchdowns. In the process he broke six school records and two National Collegiate Athletic Association marks, the most notable being a new single-season rushing record. (He still had two games to better his own record, of course.)

Simpson's most disappointing game of the year (and the most disappointing for Southern Cal as well) came against Notre Dame on the last day of the regular season. The Fighting Irish held Simpson to only 55 rushing yards, the lowest game total of his USC career, and Joe Theismann was a comparative superman for Notre Dame. After throwing an interception that resulted in a Southern Cal touchdown early in the game, the outstanding sophomore quarterback led Notre Dame to three scores and a 21-7 half-time lead. With Simpson held to 23 yards in the first half the Trojans switched to a pass-oriented attack after intermission and rallied to tie the game, 21-21. It was not enough for either team.

"Deep down in my heart," Theismann said, "I think we should have won it. We had them on the run."

"I'd rather play out there until midnight," noted McKay. "I just don't like a tie."

Simpson: "We started going after them too late. I wish we could have gone into sudden death instead of settling for a tie. I'm disappointed. But a tie is better than losing."

Dropped to No. 2 in the national ratings, Southern Cal prepared to face the nation's new No. 1 team, Ohio State, in the Rose Bowl.

Woody Hayes brought his Ohio State team into the Rose Bowl as ready as any before him. While at Columbus the Buckeyes had trained in their field house with hot blowers to simulate California weather. Once in California, Hayes put the Ohio State players through frenzied practice sessions. He would not let his team overeat, nor enjoy the luscious California scenery. Offensively the Buckeyes drilled with the intention of running into Southern Cal's gut. And that is what they did successfully on Rose Bowl day while beating the Trojans 27-16.

"We knew if they studied us, they'd want to stop us outside first, and they did a good job of it," said Hayes. "But that gave us the inside running and the curl-in passes. They couldn't stop everything."

For a while it looked as though Simpson would close out his college career as a winner. After a scoreless first quarter, Ron Ayala kicked a 21-yard field goal, and Simpson later escaped on a miraculous 80-yard touchdown run to give the Trojans a 10-0 lead. Peversely, though, Simpson's marvelous run gave inspiration to the Buckeyes.

"Now we knew he was for real," said Ohio State tackle Dave Foley. "O. J. put it together for us. He made us go to work."

"You could feel the emotion go down the bench," said another Ohio State lineman, Rufus Mayes. "O. J.'s run was the spark we needed. He lit the fire."

"When O. J. made that run, the offense got together on the sidelines and held a little meeting," noted Ohio State fullback Jim Otis. "We decided that now would be the time. We decided we'd better wake up, or this guy was going to blow us off the field."

Trailing quickly by 10 points Hayes was neither shocked nor depressed. "We'd found out that we could run on 'em," Hayes observed. "And I didn't figure O. J. was going to break another one. I still thought we'd win."

In a matter of less than two minutes the Buckeyes, with their inside running game functioning, scored 10 points and tied the game shortly before the half. Otis went over on a one-yard plunge, and Jim Roman later kicked a field goal. The Buckeyes bubbled with high optimism. "Tying before the half-time gun was a big lift for us," Ohio State quarterback Rex Kern noted. "It gave us the momentum, and it took that away from them."

Roman kicked another field goal late in the third period to put Ohio State into a 13-10 lead, and then the fierce Buckeyes forced a Sogge fumble deep in Southern Cal territory and went in for the killing touchdown. The 1969 Rose Bowl game was over prematurely with Ohio State holding a 20-10 lead at that point. It did not matter that Kern later threw a touchdown pass to Ray Gillian, or that Sogge connected on a disputed touchdown pass to Sam Dickerson in the fourth quarter.

"They never made a mistake," said a deeply depressed USC player. In fact Ohio State did not. While Southern Cal lost the ball three times on fumbles (twice by Simpson), and threw two costly interceptions, Ohio State never lost the ball on fumbles and had no passes stolen.

Fabulous O. J. Simpson on his way to an 80-yard touchdown run against Ohio State in the 1969 Rose Bowl game. But even O. J. could not save the day. Southern Cal was beaten, 27-16.

"When you fumble deep in your own area, you get beat," McKay intoned the obvious. "Yes, they were hitting. It wasn't a game for girl scouts and cookie eaters. O. J. had a fine game, but it detracts when you fumble."

Simpson had produced extraordinary things for Southern Cal that day, although mistake-prone at times. He gained 171 yards rushing and caught eight passes for 85 more. He also returned a kickoff for 20 yards. It was his 80-yard run in the second period, however, that caught everyone's attention. Hayes remarked: "Runners usually cut back on pitchouts. They usually cut behind five players. But he cut behind EIGHT of our players. It was damn near inhuman for a guy to do that."

But if Simpson was prepared for Ohio State, his teammates were not.

"We were simply not ready to play," Sogge insists. "It was our third straight Rose Bowl game. We had not had a Christmas vacation for three years, and you kind of get complacent in a Rose Bowl game. I'm not taking anything away from Ohio State—they were a good team. But we didn't play well, obviously."

Statisticians pointed out that the Rose Bowl game had given Simpson splendid career figures, numbers that boggled the mind. In his combined career at junior college and Southern Cal he had scored 90 touchdowns and gained 5,975 yards running. He would have liked a couple of more touchdowns, of course, against Ohio State.

Fighting back tears after his last game he said soulfully: "It was one of those days. It was a tremendous game, and Ohio State did a good job. But the errors—the errors killed us."

Goodbye O. J., Hello J. J.

More than 100 schools wanted Jimmy Jones, but he only wanted one. "Actually, I made up my mind that I wanted to go to USC about halfway through my senior year in high school," he says. "I always wanted to go to the Rose Bowl."

Jones came to Southern Cal and got his Rose Bowl—and John McKay got his quarterback.

The schoolboy star from Pennsylvania became a college star in California, not only breaking Trojan passing records but grinding them into the dust beyond recognition. In three seasons, 1969 through 1971, Jones moved to the front of the class of all Southern Cal quarterbacks—passing for 4,092 yards and 30 touchdowns in his career. That is more than 1,500 yards and 11 touchdowns better than his closest pursuers in those categories. In addition Jones wound up as Southern Cal's all-time total offense leader (yes, even better than O. J. Simpson) with 4,501 yards. Jones made 409 yards running.

Accomplishments even after his initial few games led one discouraged rival to murmur: "Oh, no. First O. J., now J. J. Why doesn't McKay take all his Js and ...?"

If Simpson was a tragic loss, Jones would help ease the pain. As a sophomore the gifted, black quarterback led Southern Cal to an undefeated, once-tied season and into the Rose Bowl against Michigan. Then he professionally directed the Trojans to victory in that bowl game. All through his first year he had shown coolness under fire, pulling out games at the end with a flair.

"His stock-in-trade became known as the Jimmy Jones Late Show, which was full of surprises and spiced with as much agony as ecstasy," noted sportswriter Jeff Prugh of the *Los Angeles Times*. "The format generally ran like this: Put 'em to sleep for 57 minutes, then give everybody an electro-shock treatment in the final three minutes."

Against Stanford, Jones drove the Trojans 85 yards in the last minute and set up Ron Ayala's dramatic field goal for a 26-24 victory. He passed to Sam Dickerson for late touchdowns that beat Georgia Tech 29-18 and UCLA 14-12. In a 10-3 Rose Bowl victory over Michigan it was Jones who threw a touchdown pass to Bob Chandler.

Ron Ayala kicks a 34-yard field goal at the end to give Southern California a heart-stopping 26-24 victory over Stanford in 1969. Holding the ball is quarterback Jimmy Jones, who moved the Trojans into scoring position in the game's last minute.

At the end of the year Jones had thrown 13 touchdown passes, breaking a Southern Cal single-season mark that had stood for 20 years. In addition he was voted the team's most valuable player.

Already respectful of Jones' powerful throwing arm, rivals were attentive to Jones' remark at the end of his first year. "I know I'll be surer of myself in my junior year," he noted, giving warning. "The fact that I've had a year's experience will give me a lot more confidence."

The Trojans did not rise to the expectations of some in future seasons under Jones, but it was not his fault. He did fulfill his promise to get better.

Before arriving as a polished college performer Jones was carved out of the rough-hewn world of Pennsylvania schoolboy football, the same ground that spawned another quarterback of some fame, Joe Namath. At one point in Jones' career, however, it seemed that it was over before it started. As a sophomore in a Harrisburg high school, he suffered a severe game accident when a rival bowled him over. Five vertebrae in Jones' neck were broken, and he was in traction a week, a body cast for three months, and a neck brace for six weeks more.

When his brace came off, Jones irresistibly came back to football. He began exercising and practicing for his junior year, despite protests by the school doctor. Jones' coach, George Chaump, vehemently argued in Jones' behalf and eventually made a case for his player. He had gathered positive evidence from a divergent group of doctors and presented it before a hastily called meeting of the school board the night before the season's opening game. Jones played that season and the next as well.

In his junior year he passed and ran for 2,300 yards and 20 touchdowns. As a senior it was 2,400 yards and 40 touchdowns. Jones was assaulted by college offers, 112 in all. He said "no, thank you" to 111 of them. He selected Southern Cal because of "USC's record, the chance to live in California, the Rose Bowl, the weather, and the offense." At Southern Cal he immediately went through the grist mill of freshman football. The freshmen played an abbreviated schedule and spent most of their time serving as foils for the varsity. In three freshman games, the entire "season," Jones was good but unspectacular.

Southern Cal's Terry DeKraai eventually caught this ball in his stomach although first letting it slip through his fingers. It happened in the 1969 Washington State game, won by the Trojans 28-7.

Clarence Davis breaks up the middle for a touchdown to help Southern California beat UCLA 14-12 in their 1969 game. Davis: "I do my thing as best I can."

"If he went into a game with more than two or three pass patterns he was damn lucky," noted McKay. "The freshmen here just don't work together as a unit. That's not their job. Their job is to help the varsity get ready each week."

Jones waited impatiently for big-time football, nursing a life-long dream. "Everybody used to tell me blacks couldn't play quarterback," he once remarked before his first varsity game at USC. "They said they were going to switch me to halfback when I got to high school, but that made me more determined to show what I could do at quarterback. There are lots of black guys who can play quarterback but never do. It's just that they never get the chance. There's too many people who have them stereotyped, who think they can't do the job."

If Jones himself was stereotyped, however, it was as a varsity quarterback. Especially after the spring inter-squad game when he completed 19 passes for 392 yards and 5 touchdowns in just 30 minutes.

A sore back threatened to keep Jones out of his opening day assignment against Nebraska, but he would not bow to pain. Seized by muscle spasms three days before the game, Jones was so stiff that he could not bend over. He spent most of his waking hours on a rubbing table with heating pads. It was a throbbing problem for McKay, as well. He could do nothing but

Clarence Davis, "a slower, smaller version of O. J. Simpson."

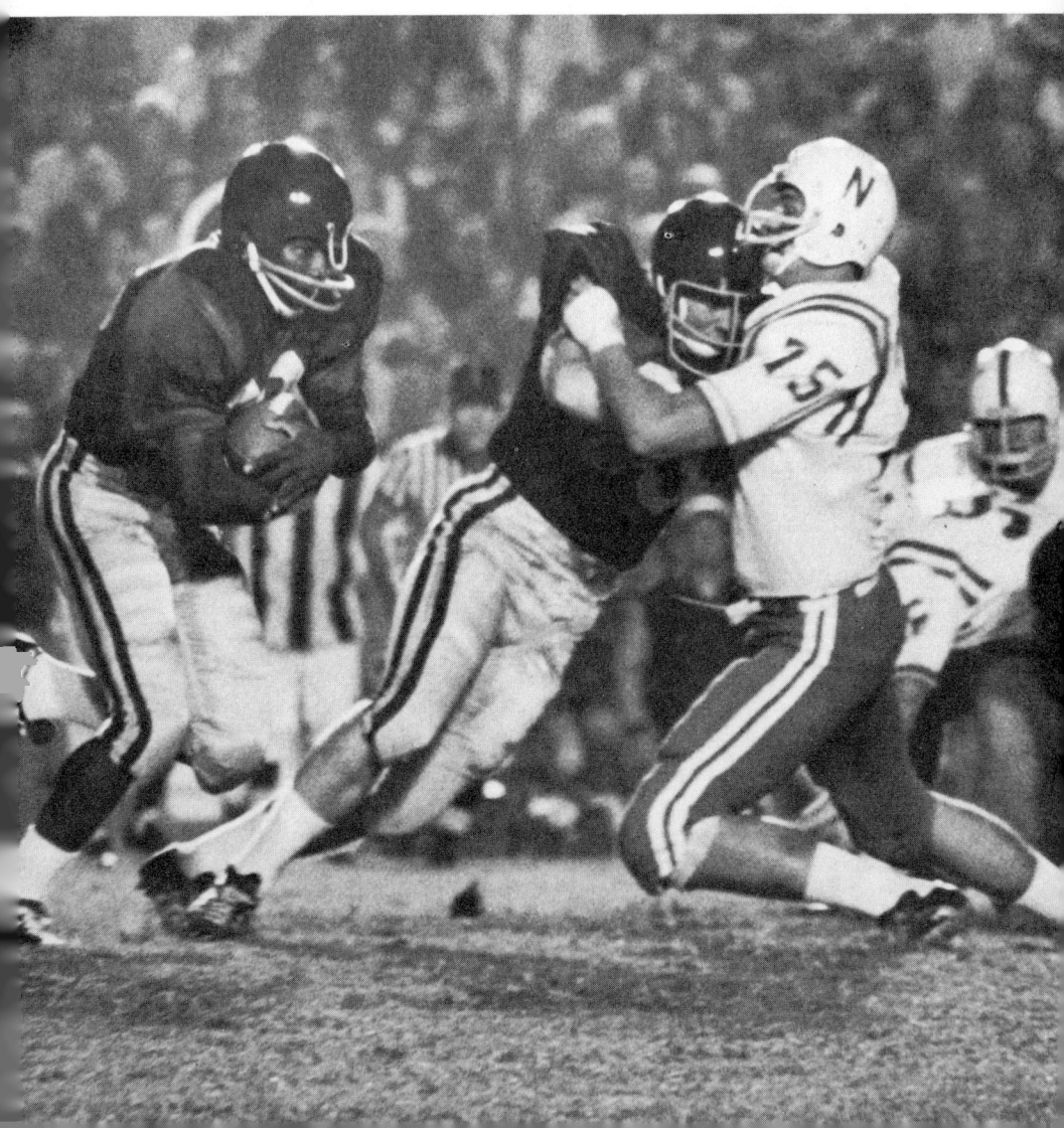

philosophize. "I learned a long time ago that my climbing the walls won't make the pain go away in his back," the coach said.

Two days before the game Jones woke up with some stiffness on one side but told McKay: "I think I can run." The coach responded: "Run tomorrow. More heat today."

Almost up until game time McKay was unsure that Jones should start. "This kid has a great future," McKay said. "We're not going to ruin him for just one game."

Jones warmed up with Sam Dickerson, one of his favorite receivers. Then he ran for 50 yards and then 30 more. "There is just a little stiffness and a little pain, but I can play," Jones told McKay. "Okay," the coach responded. "But no running. Use Clarence more. Just hand off and pass."

"Clarence" was Clarence Davis, a slower, smaller version of Simpson who had replaced O. J. in the Trojan backfield. Davis came to Southern Cal with fabulous marks in junior college where he broke Simpson's national rushing records.

Following McKay's command Jones handed off to his terrific backfield mate. Davis picked up 57 yards in an 80-yard drive, and Mike Berry plunged the last yard for a touchdown. Jones threw passes, but the early ones were just powerful and not precise. Then he began reaching his targets. A 36-yard pass was caught by flanker Bob Chandler at the nine, and he went in for a score to give the Trojans a 14-0 lead. Jones made mistakes, too, sometimes reeling and fumbling under heavy Nebraska rushes. "Sophomores will do that," McKay pointed out. "But I'd still rather have the superior sophomore to the just-average senior." Earlier in the week McKay had noted: "I won't take Jimmy out of a ball game because he's not doing well. If he's thrown an interception or fumbled, I'm not going to panic and take him out."

Jones rewarded McKay for his patience, leading a decisive 31-21 victory over tough Nebraska in his first game. Davis, another sophomore, supplied the running power with 114 yards, and someone duly noted that the figure was 20 yards better than O. J. Simpson did in his first game at Southern Cal.

Happy that it was over, Jones could smile but do little else. His back was as painful as it had been a few days before the game. He hardly could bend. "It felt good early," he said, grimacing, "but then it tightened up. It bothered me the whole game. Every time I passed, something would catch back there. Now it's really sore." Quiet, sometimes painfully shy, Jones responded more animatedly to questions after his successful debut. "I think I could have been better if I was 100 percent," he said. "You know, I think I really am ready to go now."

Blending with Davis and a group of crack defensive players called "The Wild Bunch," Jones cut a swaggering path through Southern Cal's opponents in 1969. The Trojans won 10 games and were tied by Notre Dame during a season that presented a remarkable parallel to 1952. In both seasons Southern Cal met UCLA for a Rose Bowl berth and both times trailed 12-7 in the fourth quarter and came back to win 14-12. In both seasons the

Jimmy Jones carries against Michigan during Southern California's 10-3 Rose Bowl victory in 1970. Jones: "I showed 'em."

Al Cowlings, a member of Southern California's "Wild Bunch," dishes out some rough treatment to Michigan quarterback Don Moorhead in the 1970 Rose Bowl game. Moorhead had just thrown an incomplete pass.

Trojans faced a twice-defeated Big Ten team (Wisconsin in 1952) and won by seven points on a pass from the quarterback to the wing back. Moreover in both seasons Southern Cal had a perfect year stopped at South Bend. (The Trojans lost to Notre Dame in 1952 for their only defeat that year.)

Davis was the perfect complement to Jones. He followed a path similar to that one taken by Simpson. A poor boy raised in Birmingham, Alabama, Davis attended East Los Angeles Junior College and eclipsed Simpson's fabulous rushing records before attending Southern Cal. In his first Trojan season, the 5-foot-11,

190-pounder rushed for 1,351 yards and a writer pointed out, "Had it not been for his predecessors (Simpson and Mike Garrett), he would be famous." Injuries prevented him from fulfilling his full potential as a senior, yet he still had 637 yards in seven games.

"I do my thing as best I can," Davis noted during his halcyon days. "I don't want to be another Garrett or O. J. Football is fun, especially when the big boys block for you. I'm not putting down how tough it is. It's a hard game. It hurts a lot sometimes. But it's the losing game that hurts more often than all the bumps and bruises. Playing is fun and winning is won-

PUTTING OUT THE DOG—Michigan's mascot gets the thumb from a referee in the 1970 Rose Bowl. The little dog wandered on the field during play, but the "12th man" could not help the Wolverines. Southern Cal won, 10-3.

derful."

In so many words "The Wild Bunch" expressed those sentiments exactly. Nicknamed after a Hollywood western which featured killing as the theme, ends Jimmy Gunn and Charlie Weaver, tackles Al Cowlings and Tody Smith, and middle guard Bubba Scott plundered quarterbacks with near-comparative ferocity. Tony Terry and Gary McArthur were alternates in this prideful defensive setup that wrecked many an opponents' game plan and dreams. Whenever teams threatened to score against USC, "Wild Bunch" would ring out repeatedly from the Trojan cheering section. And more often than not this bunch would come to the rescue.

The players themselves enjoyed the recognition that glittered in fanciful nicknames. "It increases our association

Bob Chandler scores the winning touchdown against Michigan after taking a pass from Jimmy Jones in the 1970 Rose Bowl game. Southern Cal beat the Wolverines, 10-3.

with ourselves," said Scott. "It gives us pride," noted McArthur.

Marvin Goux, McKay's guileful assistant and himself a part-time movie villain, instilled a "Wild Bunch" spirit in the group. "The objective of defense is to seek out the ballcarrier and separate him from the ball," Goux said. "Warner Brothers should consider our group for its next western."

Gunn, a starter at defensive end for three years and an all-American along with Cowlings in 1969, felt that "The Wild Bunch" compared favorably with the defenders who helped Southern Cal win the national title in 1967. "The guys then had played more and were more experienced," he pointed out. "We lack experience, but I think we are potentially better."

McKay agreed and carried Gunn's measurement one step further. He called "The Wild Bunch" potentially the best defensive line he ever had at Southern Cal. All had murder in their hearts and mayhem on their minds.

Cowlings, for one, admitted that he was a bully as a kid and had not changed much as a grownup. "Al was famous for his junior high protection agency—pay a quarter or be bullied," noted an associate. Bubba Smith, Tody's older brother of Baltimore Colts fame, once said of the younger Smith: "The only difference between me and Tody is that when I get them down I let them up."

Michigan was not ready for this bloodthirsty group, nor for Jones or Davis, either. Michigan coach Bo Schembechler spent Rose Bowl Day in a Pasadena hospital with a mild heart attack, and it is a good thing he stayed away from the game. He would have gotten sicker watching the Trojans beat his Wolverines.

Michigan middle guard Henry Hill noted after the game that Southern Cal "just punched us around and constantly kept us in bad field position." The Trojans' ability to stack up Michigan's running attack and force the Wolverines into short, harmless passes was half the story of the game. The other half was the passing combination of Jones and Bob Chandler and the running of Davis.

"I showed 'em," said an elated Jones. "I've got two years to go in college, and I think I'll get better."

He did get better in the next two years—but, perversely, Southern Cal got worse.

Going Home

"Gentlemen, I'd like to announce that the Rose Bowl no longer belongs to Radcliffe."—John McKay, 1972.

It was raining most of the week before the UCLA game, but John McKay seemed insouciant about the lack of practice. Puffing on a cigar in his swanky office at Heritage Hall, he said rather airily:

"If I can find the gymnasium in the old building, I'll show you some fantastic athletes. We might be better than we've ever been. At least we've never before had a basketball star at tight end (Charles Young), a shot putter at fullback (Sam Cunningham), a quarter-miler at split end (Edsel Garrison), a flanker who can long jump (Lynn Swann), and a linebacker who can high jump 6-foot-6 (Ray Rodriguez)."

McKay led a visitor to the gym, where Southern Cal's football players were working but not sweating. They laughed and glided through a brief practice, and McKay noted, "If we can play the game indoors in our stockings, I think we're ready."

Such relaxation before the yearly social blast with UCLA was uncharacteristic but understandable. McKay had been winning in 1972. Actually, not merely winning, but winning big.

"The coach must think we're pretty good," reflected Swann, one of the country's best receivers. "Last year he hollered at us a lot. This year he's mellow. When we do something wrong, he just says, 'Way to miss a block, Swann.'"

"When you win," McKay responded, "you don't have to holler so much."

That had not been the case in 1970 and 1971 when McKay's teams had suffered from what was called a "mystery virus" and lost four games each season. Although looked upon as a team of certain Rose Bowl quality, Southern Cal enigmatically proved disappointing. The decline was blamed on injuries, a tough schedule, a sub-par defense, and "the premature daydreams by seniors about fat pro contracts," according to one observer.

McKay hollered plenty then. During one particularly horrendous period of the 1971 season McKay showed obvious disgust and turned his back on the practice field.

"Oh, I tell you, we are yelling a great deal this week," he said mockingly. "We're probably third or fourth in the nation in yelling."

Now came 1972, and an observer noted that the Trojans had "so much talent they look like they could play two or three different sports at once." They actually could. They had guys who could shot-put, wrestle, run the quarter mile, hit baseballs, and shoot basketballs. But they played football the best.

The Trojans opened the year with a resounding 31-10 victory over Arkansas and at once buried the Razorbacks' passionate dreams of a national championship. Quarterback Mike Rae directed three drives for touchdowns, two of them by Rod McNeill. "They kept us off balance all night, run or pass," said Arkansas coach Frank Broyles. "Their offense was as strong physically as any we've faced."

While routing Oregon State 51-6, Southern Cal used all 50 of its players. McNeill, although he could not practice most of the week, scored three touchdowns and made 111 yards. Comparing the Trojans of 1972 to the national championship team of 1967, Oregon State coach Dee Andros noted: "They're much quicker, have much greater overall size, and their quickness just stuns you. They are a bunch of great athletes with one overpowering factor: their aggressiveness on both offense and defense."

Anthony Davis, another in Southern Cal's perennial royal line of running backs, scored two touchdowns in the Trojans'

Sam Cunningham carries the football against Oregon. He could also shot-put.

55-20 victory over Illinois. Swann ripped off a 92-yard touchdown punt return that started the Trojans to a 51-6 rout of Michigan State.

McKay then prepared for Stanford, perhaps the most flagrantly hostile of all USC rivals. McKay had always enjoyed mocking Stanford as the "Radcliffe of the West," alluding to what he considered the school's intellectual snobbery. He wanted to beat the Indians badly, especially since Stanford had beaten Southern Cal the previous two years and gone to the Rose Bowl as well. "They're the worst winners I've come up against," said McKay, talking about the 1970 and 1971 games. "They've shown no class against us. I'd like to beat them 2,000 points."

Just before the game McNeill enlarged on McKay's

outward hostilities: "People tend to think of Stanford players as being more intellectual. I don't place much credence in that. But Stanford felt we were nothing but jocks, and when they could beat us at our own specialty (the last two years) that made them FAR more superior than we were."

Philosophical differences were as apparent as the editorial in Stanford's student newspaper on the day of the game: "Today the Cards host a team that has never been able to keep football in perspective...If they lose, maybe football will die."

McNeill, naturally, disputed that analysis. He insisted that there was a "new awareness" among Southern Cal players and that football was not all that important. "We also enjoy playing chess and reading poetry," he noted.

All the talk was gibberish to McKay, though. He wanted to

Lynn Swann on his way to a 92-yard punt return for a touchdown against Michigan State in 1972. The run started the Trojans to a 51-6 rout of the Spartans.

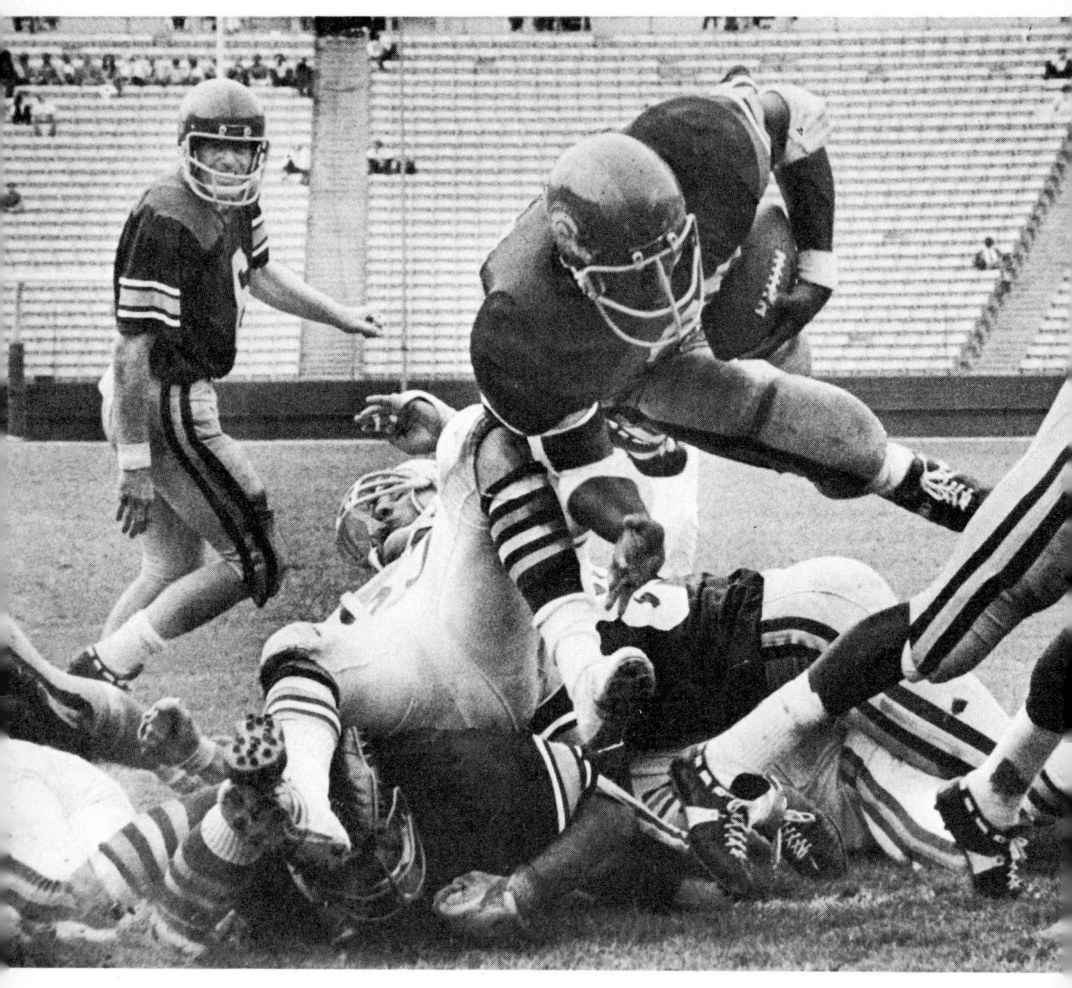

Southern Cal beat California 42-14 in 1972 with the help of this touchdown by Sam "Bam" Cunningham. Quarterback Mike Rae has just sent him over from the one-yard line.

play football. "People talk about philosophies and about being up and down," he said. "But what is going to happen Saturday is that a lot of young bodies are going to collide."

The bodies wearing the Southern Cal uniforms won, 30-21, but the Trojans were not entirely happy. "It was the worst game we've played," said Swann, who caught five passes, one of them for a touchdown. "I still don't think we've paid Stanford what we owed them. Two years ago up here their fans and players made very snide remarks, degrading us and our school. The fans did it again this year. There's a changing attitude among college football players today, and I don't think those remarks help it along. I don't want to hate anybody."

After Davis had scored two touchdowns, Swann's TD catch gave Southern Cal 30 points, but the Trojans were not through trying to score. With 10 seconds left in the game they tried a pass for a needless extra touchdown, and Stanford coach Jack Christiansen observed, "I guess they just wanted to beat the bleep out of us."

Anthony Davis runs to daylight against Oregon in 1972. "I coach him not to get tackled," says John McKay.

Running out of plays with names like Blast Orbit and Student-body Right (tailored for Davis), the Trojans beat California 42-14, Washington 34-7, Oregon 18-0, and Washington State 44-3. Davis was fast becoming a star in his sophomore year, although not starting every game. "I coach him not to get tackled," McKay joked before the game with UCLA.

Against UCLA, Davis was hardly tackled at all. He gained 178 yards in 26 carries and scored on a 23-yard touchdown run through the UCLA middle. And Southern Cal won the game, 24-7, the Pacific-8 championship, and a Rose Bowl berth all in one shot.

Mike Rae drives through UCLA's gut to give Southern California a first down in the 1972 game. After losing to the Trojans 24-7, UCLA coach Pepper Rodgers noted: "I guess USC is the best team I've ever seen, period."

In a state of euphoria Lynn Swann is hoisted aloft by teammates following a victory during the championship season of 1972.

"I don't care what happens the rest of the year because we're going home," said McKay, talking about the Rose Bowl, his "second" home.

Bottom row, left to right: Asst. Coach Dave Levy, Mike Rae, Dave Boulware, Rob Adolph, Pat Haden, Eddie Johnson, Ken Randle, Head Coach John McKay, Artimus Parker, Chris Chaney, John Cantwell, Phil Cantwell, Edesel Garrison, Allen Carter, Asst. Coach Marv Goux. Second row: Asst. Coach Willie Brown, Lynn Swann, Marvin Cobb, J. K. McKay, Charles Hinton, Rod McNeill, Anthony Davis, Ray Washmera, Sam Cunningham, Jim Lucas, Manfred Moore, Danny Reece, Asst. Coach Craig Fertig. Third row: Asst. Coach Wayne Fontes, Steve Fate, Al Pekarcik, Charles Phillips, Kevin Bruce, Ray Rodriguez, Cliff Culbreath, Charles Anthony, Mike Smith, Dave Brown, Bob McCaffrey, Eugene Lawyrk, Asst. Coach Don

1972 CHAMPIONS

Lindsey. Fourth row: Asst. Coach Skip Husbands, Allan Graf, Bob Shaputis, Booker Brown, Mike Ryan, Tom Bohlinger, George Follett, Mike Cordell, Monte Doris, Allen Gallaher, Pete Adams, Steve Riley, Asst. Coach John Robinson. Fifth row: Ronnie Miller, Chris Vella, Glenn Byrd, Richard Wood, Dale Mitchell, Dean Lingenfelter, Ed Powell, Charles Young, George Stewart, Jeff Winams, John Grant, Mike Hancock, Jim Lee. Top row: Asst. Equipment Mgr. Bill Sutton, Equip. Mgr. George Yablonsky, Mgr. Bob Perkiss, Mgr. Brian Hufford, Asst. Trainer Jerry Meins, Asst. Trainer Paul Williams, Head Trainer Jack Ward, Mgr. Bill Bristow, Mgr. Ross Boylan, Asst. Coach Ray George, Asst. Coach Joe Margucci, Head Mgr. Steve Belton.

Pepper Rodgers, the UCLA coach, had a feeling that Southern Cal would do well the rest of the year, though. "I guess USC is the best team I've ever seen, period," he said. "There isn't anything they don't do well on offense or defense, and they know they can do it, and they do it."

Most everyone else in the country thought so, too, and voters continued to support Southern Cal as No. 1 in the wire service polls. Paul Bryant's Alabama team was trying to catch Southern Cal, and McKay took note of it in a characteristic light manner.

"I was talking to Paul on the phone the other day, and I told him I had voted for him in the UPI poll," McKay said, smiling. "I said, 'That's two votes I know you got, but don't blame me for all those other dumb guys voting for us.'"

Even Bryant would have to concede the No. 1 position to the Trojans the following week, though, after they beat Notre Dame 45-23 on a miraculous, six-touchdown performance by the omnipresent Davis. A. D. (as he likes to be called) broke five school records with his extraordinary day, including most touchdowns in a game, most touchdowns in one quarter (3), most points (36), longest scoring kickoff return (97 yards), and most kickoff return yardage in a season (468). In addition Davis accounted for 368 yards overall and went over the 1,000-yard rushing mark for the season with 99 against Notre Dame.

Davis not only had a 97-yard kickoff return for a touchdown in the opening seconds of play but also ran back a 96-yarder to break open a close game in the third period. Those spectacular runs prodded Notre Dame coach Ara Parseghian to the brink of superlatives. "Davis is the greatest I've ever seen on kickoff returns in college," the usually reserved Fighting Irish coach observed.

Parseghian's players had moved within two points of the Trojans, at 25-23, when they kicked off to Davis in the third period. The Southern Cal runner took the ball at his four and went straight up the middle, following his blocking wedge. He darted through a narrow opening and accelerated past most of the Notre Dame tacklers. Then he headed for the left sideline. ("They were big and tough in the middle," Davis noted afterwards.)

One tackler had good position on Davis, but the Southern

Cal runner fooled him. ("I just hold the ball out in front and jack it up and down," Davis later explained, "and whichever way they go, I go the other.")

He made a move as if to go inside, then stepped outside the would-be tackler. A second tackler leaped at Davis from behind, but the runner burst out of his way and was gone. ("I have three accelerations," Davis explained in the locker room. "One when I get the ball, one when I get to the line, and one when I get to the open.")

Davis attached a flair to his touchdown runs by doing a dance in the end zone. Once over the line he slid into the turf like a baseball player stealing second and performed a sort of

Southern California's James Sims (No. 41) and Charles Anthony (No. 55) help tackle an Ohio State runner in the 1973 Rose Bowl game. The Trojans prevailed, 42-17.

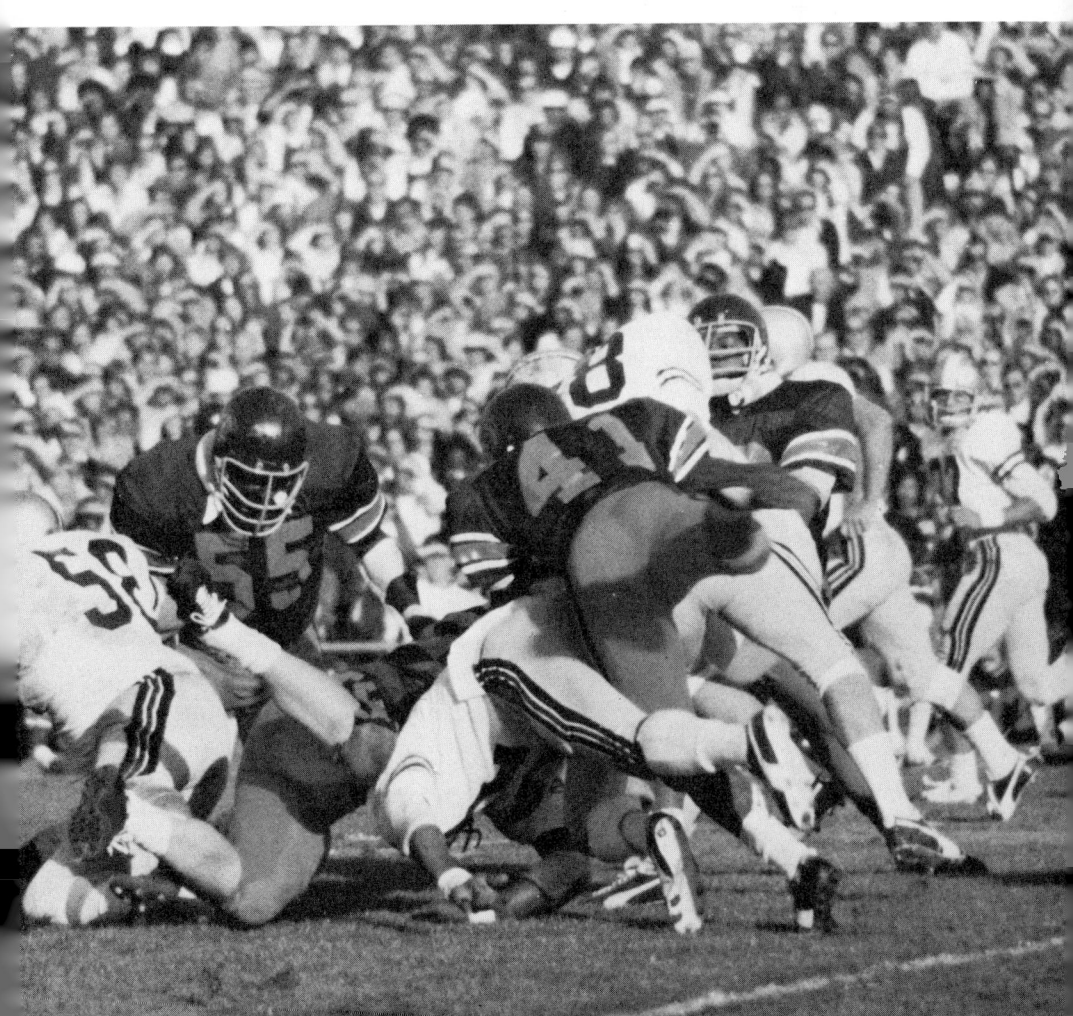

exaggerated Charleston on his knees.

Davis exemplified the speed that gave Southern Cal a dramatic edge over brutish but slow Ohio State in the Rose Bowl. The Buckeyes expected to see something fearful after listening to McKay's comments about his team: "This team has the best people I've ever had. We've played a tough schedule, and nobody has come close to beating us."

While prepared for the supernatural, Ohio State got the superhuman—Sam "Bam" Cunningham. The Southern Cal fullback ripped through the professional-looking Ohio State linemen for four touchdowns, a Rose Bowl record. Davis chalked up 157 yards, Rae passed for 229, Swann caught six

Sam "Bam" Cunningham scores one of his record four touchdowns against Ohio State in the 1973 Rose Bowl game.

passes, and the Trojans ran Ohio State into the Pasadena dust, 42-17.

A flabbergasted Woody Hayes knew his Buckeyes had been beaten by superior beings. "Yes, they are the best college football team I've ever seen," Hayes said.

Aside from the obvious players the big, quick, swaggering Trojans of 1972 had other personnel of many-splendored talents. Before a game with the Trojans a scout once said: "When we line up against USC, every one of our men is going to face the best player he's seen." A national magazine pointed out at one juncture of the season, "This USC squad has convinced a lot of people that it might just be the best team anybody ever coached anywhere." "It has personnel like Kuwait has oil," noted another authoritative magazine.

Charles Young and J. K. McKay, the coach's son, caught Rae's passes along with Swann. Tackle Pete Adams was among a group of sublime blockers who cleared the path for Southern Cal's runners. John Grant played defensive tackle as well as anyone in the country, and for that matter Richard Wood was as good as any linebacker anywhere.

These superb, young warriors won the national championship in a barrage of ballots. The Trojans became the first college football team in history to capture every first place ballot from the voters in the United Press International and Associated Press polls.

Dormant for two years, the sleeping giant had finally awakened.

1973 A. D.

INGLEWOOD, Calif. (AP) — *Anthony Davis, the sophomore sensation of Southern California's national college football champions, "is getting along fine" recovering from an automobile accident that partly severed his left Achilles' tendon, a physician says.*

Davis' sports car hit a light pole Saturday morning after he apparently fell asleep at the wheel, the California Highway Patrol said.

An auto accident stopped Anthony Davis for a while in 1973, but like an enemy football player did not keep him off his feet for long. Driving home from a party in the small hours of a January morning Davis smashed his 1969 Triumph sports car into a light pole. The wounded football hero was rushed to a hospital, suffering from a sliced Achilles' tendon and a punctured knee. A female companion suffered shock. The car was demolished.

After a 90-minute operation, the head of the team that performed surgery on Davis announced: "There is no indication that his career will be hampered...all indications are that he will be able to play baseball by the end of January and football next fall."

Davis was not so sure at first. He remembers lying in his hospital bed with casts on both legs and doubts in his mind. "I thought that all the work I'd done would be wasted," he says. In a brighter moment, though, he expressed renewed hope.

Davis reflects, "I still had the confidence that I'd be back, but that it would just take a little more time."

While the injuries healed, Davis was tormented by innuendo. A man had written him a letter, scolding Davis for setting a poor example for children. "That man," said Davis, "is going to be watching me the next two years. I'm going to make him eat his words."

It took a month before Davis actually knew whether he could move as before. Playing baseball he ran with the old flair and cheerfully announced that he was looking forward to the football season. "Maybe I'll win the Heisman Trophy," he said. A small bump, a badge of his surgery, rose above his left ankle. He felt it and noted, "The soreness here is okay as long as I can run. There's no way they're going to get me out of first-string tailback."

The characteristic swagger was back.

Watching the near-miraculous progress of his star runner, Coach John McKay noted with amusement: "We'll have him doing everything but pump up the footballs."

Confidence and determination had always been Davis' most prominent qualities. As a sophomore in 1972, he did not become a regular until after mid-season, yet scored 19 touchdowns and rushed for 1,191 yards. In the process of an astounding, six-touchdown day against Notre Dame, Davis reflected supreme self-reliance.

McKay remembers that when Notre Dame drew close, Davis stated: "Coach, you sure look worried."

"I said I was," McKay notes. "Then Anthony went out and returned a kickoff for a touchdown. One thing sure about A. D.—he believes in himself. He doesn't have a confidence problem."

Another example of Davis' cool assurance occurred during a practice session. Once watching place-kickers work out, Davis remarked off-handedly to McKay: "I can do that." McKay let him kick, and Davis turned out to have the strongest leg on the team.

Davis was not only the flashiest runner in McKay's backfield during 1972 but also one of the most coachable. "As much as he talks, his voice never seems to get in the way of his hearing," noted an observer. Davis flourished under discipline as a sophomore. Once admonished for his lack of neatness, the only time that McKay lectured him, Davis at once became one of the best dressers on the team. A style-setter, in fact, with a closet of double-knit suits, high-heeled, patent leather shoes, and hats of chic design.

Despite a fabulous sophomore year he never let his confidence build to arrogance. He drove a used car and proudly pointed out that he paid for it by working summers in a museum near the campus. He was proud, also, that he had escaped the dark ages of his youth. Raised in a tough San Fernando neighborhood Davis bears a knife wound on his right elbow as a reminder of earlier days. He was shot at once and ran with hoodlums before running for touchdowns.

Davis became not only a good football player at Southern Cal but a good example for the rest of the team. An urban affairs major, his scholastic grades equaled his marks on a football field. He showed an unselfishness, giving freely of his time to lecture kids on their responsibilities. Meanwhile he never neglected his. He does not smoke or drink. "I don't even like the taste of beer," he says. "I might have a little wine now and then, though." Even girls are not foremost in Davis' mind. Constantly surrounded by good-lookers, Davis is not distracted during the football season. "I tell 'em, 'Don't get in my way, and I won't get in yours.'"

Davis imagines himself as a "thinker...like Coach McKay. I see him out there, always thinking, and that's the way I am. I don't know why." It is said that Davis perhaps thinks too much. Example: "A. D.," as he likes to be called, was trapped for some huge losses against Arkansas in the opening game of the 1973 season, although running for 96 yards in a 17-0 Southern Cal victory. The following Monday morning a crestfallen Davis was in McKay's office asking soulfully: "What happened?" He was told: "You're trying to make every run a 90-yarder. There's nothing wrong with a four-yard gain."

Later analyzing that game Davis remarked: "My style is to scratch and claw for every yard. If two yards are there, I'll take them and hope for more. I get like a psycho on the field, man. I think of something that may have happened to me on the street somewhere, and I make up my mind it's going to be me handing out the punishment. I didn't do that against Arkansas."

Enraptured by the game, John McKay and Anthony Davis are a sideline study in concentration.

Davis was not much happier the week after when he had 71 yards in the Trojans' 23-6 triumph over Georgia Tech. Stripping off his gear he said quietly, "It was frustrating at times when there was no place to go." But McKay was not concerned: "Last year after two games he had a total of only 56 yards. Anthony Davis is the least of my worries."

But Davis had not immediately reached Mt. Olympus, as everyone suspected he would in the 1973 season. Grasping for straws Davis zealots pointed out that perhaps his auto accident had slowed him. But Davis himself put those claims to rest. "The accident," he said, "hasn't cost me any of my speed."

Encountering criticism when he failed to pile up astronomical rushing figures Davis seemed partially at fault. He simply was not running the same way as in 1972. "Coach McKay said I was dancing," Davis explained at one juncture of the 1973 season. "He said I was running for touchdowns instead of first downs, and I took that into consideration. I didn't think so; I just didn't think there was any running room there, and I tried to do the best I could. I looked at the films and saw that maybe I was running for touchdowns a little bit. But it was sort of a combination of my style."

Perhaps the most significant factor was the inexperienced Trojan line. "I didn't have that extra block sometimes," Davis points out. "It's not that everybody wasn't blocking great—but the extra block or two that springs a back. That's been the difference from last year.

"People act as though I've been sitting out the year. People keep asking, 'Where's Anthony Davis? Is he still injured?' Well, I've been here, and I'm healthy and bigger and faster than last year. But we're a young team, and I'm not walking around with an 'S' on my chest. In order for me to do my thing 10 other guys have got to do their thing. By the time I got here people like Charles Young, Pete Adams, Allan Graf, Mike Ryan, Dave Brown, and Sam Cunningham had all been playing three years. And now most of them are in the pros. Man, how do you replace people like those? It takes time."

Davis injured his ankle on the first play of the game with Oklahoma and dismissed the Heisman Trophy from his 1973 plans. "I'm going to have to forget about the Heisman," he said. "To get it you have to be in the right place at the right time.

En route to a 23-6 victory Southern California quarterback Pat Haden side-steps a Georgia Tech tackler in 1973.

Everything has to be going right for you." Davis, however, did come back in the second half to score Southern Cal's touchdown in a 7-7 tie with Oklahoma, considered one of the nation's best teams.

Davis' meager 55-yard total in the Oklahoma game was a disappointment but not as disappointing as the tie was to Southern Cal's supporters. The team had been preseason favorites to repeat as national champions. No less than a perfect record was expected (and usually demanded) on the Trojan campus. The season was further soured when the Trojans were beaten later in the year by Notre Dame 23-14, their first loss in 24 games. Davis scored a touchdown against Notre Dame but only rushed for 55 yards, and a national magazine called the

Trojan runner a "comparative bust" when compared to his sophomore year.

A five-touchdown performance against California put Davis back in the good grace of sportswriters again and seemingly triggered Southern Cal to a happy ending in 1973. The Trojans won all their remaining regular-season games, including a 23-13 decision over UCLA that decided the Rose Bowl representative.

"Aw, well," philosophized UCLA coach Pepper Rodgers, "they've got six all-Americans. Who can play against six all-Americans?"

Actually the Trojans had five—and, uniquely, Davis was not among them. For all the talk about disappointment Davis DID run for more than 1,000 yards in 1973 and DID score 13 touchdowns.

"I wasn't disappointed with the yardage I got this year," Davis noted. "Any time a back can get 1,000 yards with an inexperienced line is good. My goal was to get to the Rose Bowl—I reached that."

Davis' conceptions choked off any disappointment that he might have had for not making all-America with teammates Lynn Swann, Richard Wood, Booker Brown, Artimus Parker, and Steve Riley.

"I don't think all-American means that much because I don't have to prove what I can do," he said. "There were a lot of running backs in the country this year, and the all-Americans were picked on statistics, nothing else. People who pick them don't look at schedules. I think we had the toughest schedule in the nation."

Davis was convinced that it was even tougher after meeting Ohio State in the Rose Bowl. Davis had 74 yards rushing on only 16 carries and threw a touchdown pass, but was overshadowed by a 19-year-old Ohio State quarterback, Cornelius Greene. The Buckeyes bullied the Trojans, 42-21, and Davis and the rest of the Southern Cal players agreed that Ohio State was the best team they had met in 1973.

"The Buckeyes were physical," Davis said after the game. "But that's no surprise, I knew they would be."

The loss was not cause for jumping off the top of Heritage Hall, however. Brighter days are promised if you can believe

McKay.

After a stinging spring practice session in 1974, McKay announced with unsurpressed glee: "We have the best players, and I am the best coach, and we should win."

Translation: "Our defense is better, and our offense is better. Last season we had to replace 19 of 22 starters. This time it will be 8 of 22, and that's the difference." Quite seriously, McKay told reporters, "We have as good a chance as

Ohio State fullback Pete Johnson dives into a mass of bodies in the 1974 Rose Bowl game. Southern Cal defensive back Ted Roberson (No. 47) is among the Trojan defenders.

Ohio State quarterback Cornelius Greene cocks his arm for a pass while Southern Cal's Richard Wood (No. 83) and Charles Anthony (No. 55) close in during the 1974 Rose Bowl game. Greene was able to throw most of the day, and the Buckeyes were able to win, 42-21.

anyone to be No. 1. The defense will be better this year, and we won't allow as many points."

Davis, meanwhile, prepares for new battles. The bittersweet season of 1973 has melted into memory. The automobile injury now is merely a scar of the past. Cloaked in cardinal and gold he runs sublimely as ever, the heels kicking up, the knees jutting high. Bobbing and weaving through muscular linemen Davis is a direct descendant of Trojan royalty. Southern Cal always had princely runners and always will.

The lineage was established way back in one unforgotten time with Morley Drury and upheld through the sweet seasons with such as Gus Shaver, Frank Gifford, Jon Arnett, C. R. Roberts, Mike Garrett, and O. J. Simpson.

Before Davis there were great runners. After Davis there will be, too. Howard Jones started it with the Thundering Herd in the 1920s, and Southern Cal has not stopped running since.

LOS ANGELES MEMORIAL COLISEUM— HOME OF THE TROJANS

By TIM SALINGER

When you are talking about Los Angeles Memorial Coliseum history the University of Southern California and that history are synonymous!

The first football game ever played on the Coliseum gridiron was witnessed by 12,863 people—as USC hosted Pomona College on October 6, 1923.

From that point on it has been a continuous upward climb, as the Cardinal and Gold, in a game with their national rival Notre Dame, jammed 105,236 fans into the huge Coliseum on December 6, 1947 to stand as the all-time record attendance for a college game in Los Angeles.

The largest crowd to ever see a USC-UCLA traditional was also in the fall of 1947, when 102,938 were in attendance just two weeks before the aforementioned record-breaker. There have been two other Trojan-Bruin crowds over 100,000: the turnstiles clicked 102,546 times in 1954 and 100,355 were on hand in 1939.

Obviously, no other stadium in the world or in sports history, for that matter, has the football tradition that belongs to the L.A. Coliseum.

The Coliseum was completed in 1923 and enlarged for the Olympic Games in 1932. After the enlargement for the '32 Olympics, the Coliseum held attendances of 100,000 persons and upwards. The largest crowd to ever attend a Coliseum event was the 134,254 for the last night of the September, 1963 Billy Graham Crusade.

Although the huge saucer is just at the 50-year mark in age it has kept up with "the Jones," so to speak, with over $7 million worth of improvements in the last 27 years alone and many say it is more modern now than many of the brand new super stadia and looks better than it did upon completion of construction.

But it may be the "modern day" Coliseum that will stick more in the mind of the loyal Trojan fan. Since 1964, when theatre-type seating was installed in the great stadium, cutting the seating capacity by over 7,000 to the present 93,791, USC has had some of its greatest moments.

Although the super cross-town clash between USC and UCLA has been on live local TV, it has often been a complete sellout weeks in advance and the games have been equally as dramatic.

In mid-November of 1967 jamming the Coliseum were 90,780 and two years later almost an exact duplicate crowd of 90,771 was on hand for the traditional battle. But the largest crowd to see this titanic after the seating capacity was reduced was 94,085 in 1965.

One of the greatest games ever played in the Coliseum or anywhere, for that matter, was in the 1969 season. Facing certain defeat with but three seconds remaining on the clock and with the gun sounding as the ball was in the air, a Ron Ayala field goal from 34 yards away gave the Trojans a more than thrilling 26-24 victory over Stanford.

Every season USC season ticket sales total nearly 50,000 and with the schedules that the Trojans have lined up for this and future years there is no reason to see any change.

So Coliseum tradition grows and grows with the USC Trojans as an integral part of it!

Appendix

Trojan Football History

The material on the following pages has been compiled over many years by many students of USC athletic history.

HEAD FOOTBALL COACHES

	W	L	T	Pct.
Henry H. Goddard and Frank H. Stuffel, 1888	2	0	0	1.000
Lewis R. Freeman, 1897 (Stanford)	5	1	0	.833
Clair S. Tappaan, 1901 (Syracuse)	0	1	1	.000
John Walker, 1903	4	2	0	.667
Harvey R. Holmes, 1904-07 (Wisc.)	19	5	3	.792
William I. Traeger, 1908 (Stanford)	3	1	1	.700
Dean B. Cromwell, 1909-10, 1916-18 (Occidental)	21	8	6	.686
Ralph Glaze, 1914-15 (Dartmouth)	7	7	0	.500
Elmer C. (Gus) Henderson, 1919-24 (Oberlin)	46	7	0	.868
Howard H. Jones, 1925-40 (Yale)	121	36	13	.750
Justin M. (Sam) Barry, 1941 (Wisconsin)	2	6	1	.278
Newell J. Cravath, 1942-50 (USC)	54	28	8	.644
Jesse T. (Jess) Hill, 1951-56 (USC)	45	17	1	.722
Don R. Clark, 1957-59 (USC)	13	16	1	.450
John McKay, 1960 (Oregon)	109	35	7	.745

ANNUAL TROJAN RECORD IN THE PACIFIC-8

*Indicates tie

1959—1st (3-1-0)*
1960—2nd (3-1-0)
1961—2nd (2-1-0)*
1962—1st (4-0)
1963—2nd (3-1)
1964—1st (3-1)*
1965—2nd (4-1)
1966—1st (4-1)
1967—1st (6-1)
1968—1st (6-0)
1969—1st (6-0)
1970—6th (3-4)*
1971—3rd (2-2-1)*
1972—1st (7-0)
1973—1st (7-0)

ANNUAL WON-LOST RECORD

Year	Team Captain	G	W	L	T	Fin.	Pts.	Opp.
1888	Will Whitcomb	2	2	0	0	....	20	0
1889	No Captain	2	2	0	0	....	66	0
1890	No Varsity	....	....	....	....	....	....	....
1891	Frank Lapham	3	1	2	0	....	48	26
1892	No Varsity	....	....	....	....	....	....	....
1893	No Captain	4	3	1	0	....	56	50
1894	John A. Gray	1	1	0	0	....	12	0
1895	Lee Bradley	2	0	1	1	....	4	14
1896	Fosten Wright	3	0	3	0	....	0	44
1897	Harry Martin	6	5	1	0	....	100	18
1898	Foster Wright	7	5	1	1	....	97	28
1899	Logan Wheatley	6	2	3	1	....	11	33
1900	Harry Woodard	3	1	1	1	....	5	11
1901	Logan Wheatley	1	0	1	0	....	0	6
1902	Daril Caley	5	2	3	0	....	29	44
1903	Daril Caley	6	4	2	0	....	58	27
1904	Jay Bickford	7	6	1	0	....	199	27
1905	Carl Elliott	10	6	3	1	....	211	45
1906	Oliver Best	4	2	0	2	....	36	0
1907	Charley Haigler	6	5	1	0	....	182	20
1908	Stan Burek	5	3	1	1	....	63	18
1909	Hal Paulin	6	3	1	2	....	133	13
1910	Jack Malcolm	8	7	0	1	....	189	24
1911	Rugby	....	....	....	....	....	....	....
1912	Rugby	....	....	....	....	....	....	....
1913	Rugby	....	....	....	....	....	....	....
1914	Tommy Davis	7	4	3	0	....	116	88
1915	Len Livernash	7	3	4	0	....	132	119
1916	Herb Jones	8	5	3	0	....	129	80
1917	Frank Molette	7	4	2	1	....	127	47
1918	Harold Galloway, Keith Hunter	6	2	2	2	....	61	61
1919	John Fox	5	4	1	0	....	87	21
1920	Roy Evans	6	6	0	0	....	171	21
1921	Charley Dean	11	10	1	0	....	362	52
1922	Leo Calland	11	10	1	0	....	236	31
1923	Chet Dolley	8	6	2	0	4T	173	62
1924	John Hawkins	11	9	2	0	5	269	44
1925	Hobbs Adams	13	11	2	0	3T	456	55
1926	Jeff Cravath	10	8	2	0	2	317	52
1927	Morley Drury	10	8	1	1	1T	287	64
1928	Jesse Hibbs	10	9	0	1	1	267	59
1929	Nate Barrager	12	10	2	0	1	492	69
1930	Marshall Duffield	10	8	2	0	2	382	66
1931	Stan Williamson	11	10	1	0	1	363	52
1932	Tay Brown	11	10	0	1	1	201	13
1933	Ford Palmer	12	10	1	1	3	257	30
1934	Julie Bescos	11	4	6	1	8	120	110
1935	Art Dittberner, Cliff Propst	12	5	7	0	8	155	124
1936	Gil Kuhn	9	4	2	3	3	129	65
1937	Chuck Williams	10	4	4	2	6	136	98
1938	Don McNeil	11	9	2	0	1T	172	65
1939	Joe Shell	10	8	0	2	1	181	33
1940	Ed Dempsey	9	3	4	2	7	88	98
1941	Bob de Lauer	9	2	6	1	8	64	134
1942	Don Willer	11	5	5	1	4	184	128
1943	Ralph Heywood	10	8	2	0	1	155	58
1944	Jim Hardy	10	8	0	2	1	240	73
1945	Jim Callanan	11	7	4	0	1	205	150
1946	Doug Essick	10	6	4	0	3	158	106
1947	Don Clark	10	7	2	1	1	193	114
1948	Bob Bastian	10	6	3	1	3	142	87
1949	Jim Bird	9	5	3	1	3T	214	170
1950	Paul McMurtry, Volney Peters	9	2	5	2	7	114	182
1951	Pat Cannamela, Dean Schneider	10	7	3	0	4	224	168
1952	Bob Van Doren, Lou Welsh	11	10	1	0	1	254	47
1953	George Bozanic, Tom Nickoloff	10	6	3	1	3	199	161
1954	Ed Fouch, Lindon Crow	12	8	4	0	2	258	159
1955	George Galli, Marv Goux	10	6	4	0	6	265	158

Year Team Captain	G	W	L	T	Fin.	Pts.	Opp.
1956—Jon Arnett, Ells Kissinger	10	8	2	0	2T	218	126
1957—Jim Conroy, Mike Henry	10	1	9	0	7T	86	204
1958—Ken Antle, Monte Clark	10	4	5	1	3	151	120
1959—Ron Mix, Willie Wood	10	8	2	0	1T	195	90
1960—Mike McKeever, George Van Vliet	10	4	6	0	2	95	152
1961—Britt Williams	10	4	5	1	2T	150	167
1962—Marv Marinovich, Ben Wilson	11	11	0	0	1	261	92
1963—Pete Beathard, Willie Brown	10	7	3	0	2	207	114
1964—Craig Fertig, Bill Fisk	10	7	3	0	1	207	130
1965—Chuck Arrobio, Mike Garrett	10	7	2	1	2	262	92
1966—Nate Shaw, Rod Sherman	11	7	4	0	1	199	128
1967—Tim Rossovich, Adrian Young	11	10	1	0	1	258	87
1968—O. J. Simpson, Steve Sogge	11	9	1	1	1	259	168
1969—Jim Gunn, Bob Jensen	11	10	0	1	1	261	128
1970—Charlie Weaver, Bob Chandler	11	6	4	1	6	343	233
1971—John Vella, Willie Hall	11	6	4	1	4	229	164
1972—Sam Cunningham, John Grant	12	12	0	0	1	467	134
1973—Lynn Swann, Artimus Parker	12	9	2	1	1	322	202

USC's ROSE BOWL RECORD

The Trojans topped the Pacific Coast Conference and lead current Pacific-8 members for both most times played and most wins in the Rose Bowl Game.

The all-time USC record for the New Year's Day classic stands at 13 wins, 6 losses, and 0 ties. The Trojans won their first eight Rose Bowl encounters.

```
1923—USC 14, Penn State 3
1930—USC 47, Pittsburgh 14
1932—USC 21, Tulane 12
1933—USC 35, Pittsburgh 0
1939—USC  7, Duke 3
1940—USC 14, Tennessee 0
1944—USC 29, Washington 0
1945—USC 25, Tennessee 0
1946—Alabama 34, USC 14
1948—Michigan 49, USC 0
1953—USC  7, Wisconsin 0
1955—Ohio State 20, USC 7
1963—USC 42, Wisconsin 37
1967—Purdue 14, USC 13
1968—USC 14, Indiana 3
1969—Ohio State 27, USC 16
1970—USC 10, Michigan 3
1973—USC 42, Ohio State 17
1974—Ohio State 42, USC 21
```

ALL-TIME TROJAN RECORDS

The following is believed to be an accurate record of the outcome of all games of American football played by the USC varsity team. In a few cases where the score has not been verified, it has been omitted, with the outcome of the game indicated by (W), (L) or (T). The name of the head coach for each season is also listed.

1888: H. Goddard & F. Suffel
16 Alliance AC 0
4 Alliance AC 0
—   —
20 (W-2, L-0)   0

1889: No Coach
40 Loyola 0
26 Pasadena 0
—   —
66 (W-2, L-0)   0

1890: No Varsity

1891: No Coach
12 Olive Club 16
34 SC Academy 0
2 Loyola 10
—   —
48 (W-1, L-2)   26

1892: No Varsity

1893: No Coach
14 Chow-Sir Club 2
22 Cal Tech 12
6 Chaffey College 32
14 Cal Tech 4
—   —
56 (W-3, L-1)   50

1894: No Coach
12 Cal Tech 0
—   —
12 (W-1, L-0)   0

1895: No Coach
0 Occidental 10
4 Cal Tech 4
—   —
4 (W-0, L-1, T-1)   14

1896: No Coach
0 Los Angeles AC 22
0 Cal Tech 22
.. Whittier Reform (L)
—   —
0 (W-0, L-3)   44

1897: Lewis Freeman
34 Loyola 0
10 Los Angeles HS 0
38 Chaffey College 0
6 Pomona 0
0 San Diego YMCA 18
12 Ventura 0
—   —
100 (W-5, L-1)   18

1898: No Coach
0 Los Angeles HS 0
17 Pasadena AC 0
0 Los Angeles HS 6
14 Pomona 11
34 7th Regiment 0
27 Phoenix Indians 11
5 Santa Barbara AC 0
—   —
97 (W-5, L-1, T-1)   28

1899: No Coach
11 Norm School 0
0 Santa Ana 11
0 Pomona 12
.. Occidental (T)
.. Occidental (W)
0 Santa Barbara AC 10
—   —
11 (W-2, L-3, T-1)   33

1900: No Coach
5 Occidental 0
0 Los Angeles HS 0
0 Pomona 11
—   —
5 (W-1, L-1, T-1)   11

1901: Clair Tappaan
0 Pomona 6
—   —
0 (W-0, L-1)   6

1902: No Coach
5 Loyola 6
2 Santa Ana 5
16 Pomona 5
6 Santa Ana 0
0 Perris Indians 28
—   —
29 (W-2, L-3)   44

1903: John Walker
5 Cal Tech 0
10 Los Angeles HS 0
0 Occidental 5
12 Loyola 5
31 Orange AC 5
0 Sherman Inst. 12
—   —
58 (W-4, L-2)   27

1904: Harvey Holmes
42 Los Angeles HS 0
35 Cal Tech 0
36 Occidental 4
0 Sherman Inst. 17
60 Whittier Reform 6
Loyola (W-forfeit)
26 SC Prep 0
—   —
199 (W-6, L-1)   27

1905: Harvey Holmes
- 28 Nat'l Guard ... 0
- 12 Harvard School ... 0
- 27 LA Poly HS ... 0
- 75 Whittier Reform ... 0
- 63 Alumni ... 0
- 0 Stanford ... 16
- 0 Occidental ... 10
- 0 Sherman Inst. ... 15
- 0 Loyola ... 0
- 6 Pomona ... 4

211 (W-6, L-3, T-1)   45

1906: Harvey Holmes
- 0 Los Angeles HS ... 0
- 22 Occidental ... 0
- 14 Pomona ... 0
- 0 Sherman Inst. ... 0

36 (W-2, L-0, T-2)   0

1907: Harvey Holmes
- 6 Los Angeles HS ... 0
- 57 Whittier Reform. ... 0
- 51 Santa Ana HS ... 0
- 46 Whittier ... 0
- 16 USS Colorado ... 4
- 6 Los Angeles HS ... 16

182 (W-5, L-1)   20

1908: Bill Traeger
- 0 Los Angeles HS ... 12
- 15 Whittier ... 0
- 28 Arrowhead AC ... 0
- 14 Occidental ... 0
- 6 Pomona ... 6

63 (W-3, L-1, T-1)   18

1909: Dean Cromwell
- 51 Cal Poly ... 0
- 22 Whittier ... 2
- 6 Loyola ... 8
- 51 Orange AC ... 0
- 3 Occidental ... 3
- 0 Pomona ... 0

133 (W-3, L-1, T-2)   13

1910: Dean Cromwell
- 22 Long Beach HS ... 6
- 65 Chaffey HS ... 6
- 9 Cal Tech ... 0
- 32 San Diego HS ... 0
- 35 Redlands ... 0
- 6 Occidental ... 0
- 11 Whittier ... 3
- 9 Pomona ... 9

189 (W-7, L-0, T-1)   24

1911: Rugby

1912: Rugby

1913: Rugby

1914: Ralph Glaze
- 20 Los Angeles AC ... 0
- 41 Redlands ... 0
- 17 Whittier ... 14
- 13 Occidental ... 20
- 13 Redlands ... 6
- 6 Pomona ... 10
- 6 Oregon State ... 38

116 (W-4, L-3)   88

1915: Ralph Glaze
- 21 Los Angeles AC ... 9
- 47 St. Mary's ... 3
- 28 California ... 10
- 0 Oregon ... 34
- 13 Utah ... 20
- 21 California ... 23
- 2 Whittier ... 20

132 (W-3, L-4)   119

1916: Dean Cromwell
- 14 Sherman Inst. ... 0
- 14 Santa Fe AC ... 0
- 12 Utah ... 27
- 0 California ... 27
- 34 Los Angeles AC ... 0
- 28 Pomona ... 3
- 7 Oregon State ... 16
- 20 Arizona ... 7

129 (W-5, L-3)   80

1917: Dean Cromwell
- 31 Arizona ... 6
- 0 St. Mary's ... 7
- 3 21st Inf. ... 0
- 42 Ft. MacArthur ... 0
- 51 Utah ... 0
- 0 Mare Island ... 34
- 0 California ... 0

127 (W-4, L-2, T-1)   47

1918: Dean Cromwell
- 25 Stanford ... 8
- 13 Whittier Reform. ... 13
- 0 Pomona ... 0
- 7 California ... 33
- 6 Occidental ... 7
- 10 Redlands ... 0

61 (W-2, L-2, T-2)   61

1919: Elmer Henderson
- 6 Pomona ... 0
- 27 Occidental ... 0
- 13 California ... 14
- 28 Utah ... 7
- 13 Stanford ... 0

87 (W-4, L-1)   21

1920: Elmer Henderson
- 46 Cal Tech ... 7
- 10 Stanford ... 0
- 48 Occidental ... 7
- 7 Pomona ... 0
- 38 Nevada ... 7
- 21 Oregon ... 0

170 (W-6, L-0)   21

1921: Elmer Henderson
- 62 USS Arizona ... 0
- 35 USS New York ... 0
- 70 Cal Tech ... 0
- 34 Sub Base ... 0
- 42 Occidental ... 0
- 28 Sub Base ... 0
- 35 Pomona ... 7
- 7 California ... 38
- 14 Whittier ... 0
- 7 Oregon State ... 0
- 28 Washington State ... 7

362 (W-10, L-1)   52

1922: Elmer Henderson
20	Alumni	0
20	USS Mississippi	0
54	Pomona	13
15	Arizona	0
6	Nevada	0
0	California	12
46	Occidental	0
6	Stanford	0
14	Idaho	0
41	Washington St.	3
14	Penn St. (RB)	3
236 (W-10, L-1)		**31**

1923: Elmer Henderson
18	Cal Tech	7
23	Pomona	7
33	Nevada	0
0	Washington	22
14	Stanford	7
7	California	13
69	Arizona	6
9	Idaho	0
173 (W-6, L-2)		**62**

1924: Elmer Henderson
78	Cal Tech	6
14	Pomona	0
29	Arizona	0
17	Oregon State	3
21	Nevada	7
0	California	7
10	St. Mary's	14
51	Whittier	0
13	Idaho	0
16	Syracuse	0
20	Missouri	7
269 (W-9, L-2)		**44**

1925: Howard Jones
74	Whittier	0
32	Cal Tech	0
80	Pomona	0
28	Utah	2
9	Stanford	13
56	Arizona	0
51	Idaho	7
29	Santa Clara	9
27	Montana	7
18	Iowa	0
12	Washington St.	17
28	Oregon State	0
12	St. Mary's	0
456 (W-11, L-2)		**55**

1926: Howard Jones
74	Whittier	0
42	Santa Clara	0
16	Washington St.	7
28	Occidental	6
27	California	0
12	Stanford	13
17	Oregon State	7
28	Idaho	6
61	Montana	0
12	Notre Dame	13
317 (W-8, L-2)		**52**

1927: Howard Jones
33	Occidental	0
52	Santa Clara	12
13	Oregon State	12
13	Stanford	13
51	Cal Tech	0
13	California	0
46	Colorado	7
27	Washington St.	0
6	Notre Dame	7
33	Washington	13
287 (W-8, L-1, T-1)		**64**

1928: Howard Jones
40	Utah State	12
19	Oregon State	0
19	St. Mary's	6
0	California	0
19	Occidental	0
10	Stanford	0
78	Arizona	7
27	Washington St.	13
28	Idaho	7
27	Notre Dame	14
267 (W-9, L-0, T-1)		**59**

1929: Howard Jones
76	UCLA	0
21	Oregon State	7
48	Washington	0
64	Occidental	0
7	Stanford	0
7	California	15
66	Nevada	0
12	Notre Dame	13
72	Idaho	0
27	Washington St.	7
45	Carnegie Tech	13
47	Pittsburgh (RB)	14
492 (W-10, L-2)		**69**

1930: Howard Jones
52	UCLA	0
27	Oregon State	7
6	Washington St.	7
65	Utah State	0
41	Stanford	12
33	Denver	13
74	California	0
52	Hawaii	0
32	Washington	0
0	Notre Dame	27
382 (W-8, L-2)		**66**

1931: Howard Jones
7	St. Mary's	13
30	Oregon State	0
38	Washington St.	6
53	Oregon	0
6	California	0
19	Stanford	0
69	Montana	0
16	Notre Dame	14
44	Washington	7
60	Georgia	0
21	Tulane (RB)	12
363 (W-10, L-1)		**52**

1932: Howard Jones
- 35 Utah 0
- 20 Washington St. 0
- 10 Oregon State 0
- 6 Loyola 0
- 13 Stanford 0
- 27 California 7
- 33 Oregon 0
- 9 Washington 6
- 13 Notre Dame 0
- 35 Pittsburgh (RB) 0

201 (W-10, L-0) 13

1933: Howard Jones
- 39 Occidental 0
- 51 Whittier 0
- 18 Loyola 0
- 33 Washington St. 0
- 14 St. Mary's 7
- 0 Oregon State 0
- 6 California 3
- 7 Stanford 13
- 26 Oregon 0
- 19 Notre Dame 0
- 31 Georgia 0
- 13 Washington 7

257 (W-10, L-1, T-1) 30

1934: Howard Jones
- 20 Occidental 0
- 40 Whittier 14
- 6 COP 0
- 0 Washington St. 19
- 6 Pittsburgh 20
- 6 Oregon State 6
- 0 Stanford 16
- 2 California 7
- 33 Oregon 0
- 7 Washington 14
- 0 Notre Dame 14

120 (W-4, L-6, T-1) 110

1935: Howard Jones
- 9 Montana 0
- 19 COP 7
- 0 Illinois 19
- 7 Oregon State 13
- 7 California 21
- 0 Stanford 3
- 20 Washington St. 10
- 13 Notre Dame 20
- 2 Washington 6
- 7 Pittsburgh 12
- 33 Kamehameha 7
- 38 Hawaii 6

155 (W-5, L-7) 124

1936: Howard Jones
- 38 Oregon State 7
- 26 Oregon 0
- 24 Illinois 6
- 0 Washington St. 0
- 14 Stanford 7
- 7 California 13
- 0 Washington 12
- 7 UCLA 7
- 13 Notre Dame 13

129 (W-4, L-2, T-3) 65

1937: Howard Jones
- 40 COP 0
- 0 Washington 7
- 13 Ohio State 12
- 34 Oregon 14
- 6 California 20
- 0 Washington St. 0
- 6 Stanford 7
- 12 Oregon State 12
- 6 Notre Dame 13
- 19 UCLA 13

136 (W-4, L-4, T-2) 98

1938: Howard Jones
- 7 Alabama 19
- 7 Oregon State 0
- 14 Ohio State 7
- 19 Washington State 6
- 13 Stanford 2
- 31 Oregon 7
- 13 California 7
- 6 Washington 7
- 42 UCLA 7
- 13 Notre Dame 0
- 7 Duke (RB) 3

172 (W-9, L-2) 65

1939: Howard Jones
- 7 Oregon 7
- 27 Washington St. 0
- 26 Illinois 0
- 26 California 0
- 19 Oregon State 0
- 33 Stanford 0
- 20 Notre Dame 12
- 9 Washington 7
- 0 UCLA 0
- 14 Tennessee (RB) 0

181 (W-8, L-0, T-2) 33

1940: Howard Jones
- 14 Washington St. 14
- 0 Oregon State 0
- 13 Illinois 7
- 13 Oregon 0
- 7 Stanford 21
- 7 California 20
- 0 Washington 14
- 28 UCLA 12
- 6 Notre Dame 10

88 (W-3, L-4, T-2) 98

1941: Sam Barry
- 13 Oregon State 7
- 0 Ohio State 33
- 6 Oregon 20
- 7 Washington St. 6
- 0 California 14
- 0 Stanford 13
- 18 Notre Dame 20
- 13 Washington 14
- 7 UCLA 7

54 (W-2, L-6, T-1) 134

1942: Jeff Cravath
13 Tulane 27
0 Washington 0
12 Ohio State 28
26 Washington St. 12
6 Stanford 14
21 California 7
40 Oregon 0
0 Notre Dame 13
38 Montana 0
7 UCLA 14
21 St. Mary's PF 13

184 (W-5, L-5, T-1)   128

1943: Jeff Cravath
20 UCLA 0
7 California 0
13 St. Mary's PF 0
34 USF 0
6 COP 0
13 California 0
7 San Diego Navy 10
0 March Field 35
26 UCLA 13
29 Washington (RB) 0

155 (W-8, L-2)   58

1944: Jeff Cravath
13 UCLA 13
18 COP 6
6 California 6
6 St. Mary's PF 0
38 Washington 7
34 St. Mary's 7
28 San Diego Navy 21
32 California 0
40 UCLA 13
25 Tennessee (RB) 0

240 (W-8, L-0, T-2)   73

1945: Jeff Cravath
13 UCLA 6
13 California 2
26 St. Mary's PF 14
6 San Diego Navy 33
52 COP 0
7 Washington 13
0 St. Mary's 26
14 California 0
34 Oregon State 7
26 UCLA 15
14 Alabama (RB) 34

205 (W-7, L-4)   150

1946: Jeff Cravath
13 Washington State 7
0 Ohio State 21
0 Oregon State 6
28 Washington 0
28 Stanford 20
43 Oregon 0
14 California 0
6 UCLA 13
6 Notre Dame 26
20 Tulane 13

158 (W-6, L-4)   106

1947: Jeff Cravath
21 Washington State 0
7 Rice 7
32 Ohio State 0
48 Oregon State 6
39 California 14
19 Washington 0
14 Stanford 0
6 UCLA 0
7 Notre Dame 38
0 Michigan (RB) 49

193 (W-7, L-2, T-1)   114

1948: Jeff Cravath
27 Utah 0
21 Oregon State 6
0 Ohio State 20
7 Rice 0
7 Oregon 8
7 Stanford 6
7 California 13
32 Washington 7
20 UCLA 13
14 Notre Dame 14

142 (W-6, L-3, T-1)   87

1949: Jeff Cravath
42 Navy 20
35 Washington State 7
13 Ohio State 13
10 California 16
40 Oregon 13
40 Washington 28
13 Stanford 34
21 UCLA 7
0 Notre Dame 32

214 (W-5, L-3, T-1)   170

1950: Jeff Cravath
14 Iowa 20
20 Washington State 20
7 California 13
14 Navy 27
30 Oregon 21
7 Stanford 7
13 Washington 28
0 UCLA 39
9 Notre Dame 7

114 (W-2, L-5, T-2)   182

1951: Jess Hill
31 Washington State 21
41 San Diego Navy 7
20 Washington 13
16 Oregon State 14
21 California 14
28 Texas Christian 26
28 Army 6
20 Stanford 27
7 UCLA 21
12 Notre Dame 19

224 (W-7, L-3)   168

1952: Jess Hill
35	Washington State	7
31	Northwestern	0
22	Army	0
20	San Diego Navy	6
28	Oregon State	6
10	California	0
54	Stanford	7
33	Washington	0
14	UCLA	12
0	Notre Dame	9
7	Wisconsin (RB)	0

254 (W-10, L-1)   47

1953: Jess Hill
29	Washington State	13
17	Minnesota	7
27	Indiana	14
13	Washington	13
37	Oregon State	0
32	California	20
7	Oregon	13
23	Stanford	20
0	UCLA	13
14	Notre Dame	48

199 (W-6, L-3, T-1)   161

1954: Jess Hill
39	Washington State	0
27	Pittsburgh	7
12	Northwestern	7
7	Texas Christian	20
24	Oregon	14
29	California	27
34	Oregon State	0
21	Stanford	7
41	Washington	0
0	UCLA	34
17	Notre Dame	23
7	Ohio State (RB)	20

258 (W-8, L-4)   159

1955: Jess Hill
50	Washington State	12
42	Oregon	15
19	Texas	7
0	Washington	7
33	Wisconsin	21
33	California	6
19	Minnesota	25
20	Stanford	28
7	UCLA	17
42	Notre Dame	20

265 (W-6, L-4)   158

1956: Jess Hill
44	Texas	20
21	Oregon State	13
13	Wisconsin	6
35	Washington	7
19	Stanford	27
28	Washington State	12
20	California	7
0	Oregon	7
10	UCLA	7
28	Notre Dame	20

218 (W-8, L-2)   126

1957: Don Clark
0	Oregon State	20
6	Michigan	16
14	Pittsburgh	20
0	California	12
12	Washington State	13
19	Washington	12
7	Stanford	35
7	Oregon	16
9	UCLA	20
12	Notre Dame	40

86 (W-1, L-9)   204

1958: Don Clark
21	Oregon State	0
19	Michigan	20
7	North Carolina	8
0	Oregon	25
12	California	14
13	Notre Dame	20
14	Washington State	6
29	Stanford	6
21	Washington	6
15	UCLA	15

151 (W-4, L-5, T-1)   120

1959: Don Clark
27	Oregon State	6
23	Pittsburgh	0
17	Ohio State	0
22	Washington	15
30	Stanford	28
14	California	7
36	West Virginia	0
17	Baylor	8
3	UCLA	10
6	Notre Dame	16

195 (W-8, L-2)   90

1960: John McKay
0	Oregon State	14
6	Texas Christian	7
0	Ohio State	20
10	Georgia	3
27	California	10
21	Stanford	6
0	Washington	34
14	Baylor	35
17	UCLA	6
0	Notre Dame	17

95 (W-4, L-6)   152

1961: John McKay
7	Georgia Tech	27
21	SMU	16
34	Iowa	35
0	Notre Dame	30
28	California	14
14	Illinois	10
0	Washington	0
30	Stanford	15
9	Pittsburgh	10
7	UCLA	10

150 (W-4, L-5, T-1)   167

1962: John McKay
- 14 Duke 7
- 33 SMU 3
- 7 Iowa 0
- 32 California 6
- 28 Illinois 16
- 14 Washington 0
- 39 Stanford 14
- 13 Navy 6
- 14 UCLA 3
- 25 Notre Dame 0
- 42 Wisconsin (RB) 37

261 (W-11, L-0)   92

1963: John McKay
- 14 Colorado 0
- 12 Oklahoma 17
- 13 Michigan State 10
- 14 Notre Dame 17
- 32 Ohio State 3
- 36 California 6
- 25 Stanford 11
- 7 Washington 22
- 28 Oregon State 22
- 26 UCLA 6

207 (W-7, L-3)   114

1964: John McKay
- 21 Colorado 0
- 40 Oklahoma 14
- 7 Michigan State 17
- 31 Texas A. & M. 7
- 0 Ohio State 17
- 26 California 21
- 13 Washington 14
- 15 Stanford 10
- 34 UCLA 13
- 20 Notre Dame 17

207 (W-7, L-3)   130

1965: John McKay
- 20 Minnesota 20
- 26 Wisconsin 6
- 26 Oregon State 12
- 34 Washington 0
- 14 Stanford 0
- 7 Notre Dame 28
- 35 California 0
- 28 Pittsburgh 0
- 16 UCLA 20
- 56 Wyoming 6

262 (W-7, L-2, T-1)   92

1966: John McKay
- 10 Texas 6
- 38 Wisconsin 3
- 21 Oregon State 0
- 17 Washington 14
- 21 Stanford 7
- 30 Clemson 0
- 7 Miami 10
- 35 California 9
- 7 UCLA 14
- 0 Notre Dame 51
- 13 Purdue (RB) 14

199 (W-7, L-4)   128

1967: John McKay
- 49 Washington State 0
- 17 Texas 13
- 21 Michigan State 17
- 30 Stanford 0
- 24 Notre Dame 7
- 23 Washington 6
- 28 Oregon 6
- 31 California 12
- 0 Oregon State 3
- 21 UCLA 20
- 14 Indiana (RB) 3

258 (W-10, L-1)   87

1968: John McKay
- 29 at Minnesota 20
- 24 at Northwestern 7
- 28 Miami 3
- 27 at Stanford 24
- 14 Washington 7
- 20 at Oregon 13
- 35 California 17
- 17 Oregon State 13
- 28 UCLA 16
- 21 Notre Dame 21
- 16 Ohio State (RB) 27

255 (W-9, L-1, T-1)   168

1969: John McKay
- 31 Nebraska 21
- 48 Northwestern 6
- 31 Oregon State 7
- 26 Stanford 24
- 14 Notre Dame 14
- 29 Georgia Tech 18
- 14 California 9
- 28 Washington State 7
- 16 Washington 7
- 14 UCLA 12
- 10 Michigan (RB) 3

261 (W-10, L-0, T-1)   128

1970: John McKay
- 42 Alabama 21
- 21 Nebraska 21
- 48 Iowa 0
- 45 Oregon State 13
- 14 Stanford 24
- 28 Washington 25
- 7 Oregon 10
- 10 California 13
- 70 Washington State 33
- 20 UCLA 45
- 38 Notre Dame 28

343 (W-6, L-4, T-1)   233

1971: John McKay
- 10 Alabama 17
- 24 Rice 0
- 28 Illinois 0
- 20 Oklahoma 33
- 23 Oregon 28
- 18 Stanford 33
- 28 Notre Dame 14
- 28 California 0
- 30 Washington State 20
- 13 Washington 12
- 7 UCLA 7

229 (W-6, L-4, T-1)   164

1972 John McKay
- 31 Arkansas 10
- 51 Oregon State 6
- 55 Illinois 7
- 51 Michigan State 6
- 30 Stanford 21
- 42 California 14
- 34 Washington 7
- 18 Oregon 0
- 44 Washington State 3
- 24 UCLA 7
- 45 Notre Dame 23
- 42 Ohio State (RB) 17

467 (W-12, L-0)   134

1973 John McKay

17	Arkansas	0	50 California	14
23	Georgia Tech	6	27 Stanford	26
7	Oklahoma	7	42 Washington	19
21	Oregon State	7	23 UCLA	13
46	Washington State	35	21 Ohio State(RB)	42
31	Oregon	10		
14	Notre Dame	23	322 (W-9, L-2, T-1)	202

ALL TIME TEAM RECORDS

Most consecutive games without defeat: 27, 1931 to 1933.
Longest winning streak: 25 games, 1931 to 1933.
Longest losing streak: 5 games, 1957.
Most consecutive games without a win: 8, 1941 to 1942.
Most consecutive games unscored upon: 6, 1943.
Most consecutive games without scoring: 2, 1941 and 1946.
Mos consecutive games without being shut out: 58, 1967 on.
Largest crowd: 123,000, Notre Dame at Soldier Field, Chicago, 1929.

SEASON

Best season: 1972, Won 12, Lost 0, Tied 0 (Scored 467 to 134).
Most points scored: 492 (12 games), 1929.
Fewest points scored: 64 (9 games), 1941.
Most touchdowns: 75, (12 games), 1929.
Fewest touchdowns: 10, (9 games), 1941.
Most extra points: 50 of 52 (11 games), 1921.
Fewest extra points: 4 (9 games), 1941.
Most field goals: 8 (12 games), 1972.
Most yards running: 3954 (12 games), 1929.
Most yards passing: 2222, 1972.
Most yards running and passing: 5269 (12 games), 1929.
Fewest yards running and passing: 1795 (9 games), 1929.
Most passes attempted: 279, (11 games), 1970.
Most passes completed: 141, (11 games), 1970.
Most touchdown passes: 20 (12 games), 1929.
Fewest touchdown passes: 1 (10 games), 1946.
Most interceptions: 31 (11 games), 1952.

SINGLE GAME

Largest margin of victory: 80 points (80-0), Pomona, 1925.
Highest winning score: same as above.
Lowest winning score: 3 points (3-0), 211th Infantry, 1917.
Highest losing score: (35-34), Iowa, 1961.
Most touchdowns: 12, Cal Tech, 1924; Pomona, 1925; Arizona, 1928; UCLA, 1929.
Most touchdowns one quarter: 6, Pomona, 1925; Arizona, 1928.
Most extra points: 10, Cal Tech, 1921.
Most extra points one quarter: 5, Pomona, 1925; Montana, 1931; Wyoming, 1965.
Most field goals: 3, Alabama, 1970.
Most yards running: 753, UCLA, 1929.
Fewest yards running: minus 11, Ohio State, 1941.
Most yards passing: 371, California, 1964.
Fewest yards passing: 0, Washington State, 1921; Cal Tech, 1923; California, 1931; Georgia, 1931; Washington, 1938; UCLA, 1940; Stanford, 1940; Stanford, 1942; College of Pacific, 1945.
Most yards running and passing: 978, Pomona, 1925.
Fewest yards running and passing: 65, Ohio State, 1941.
Fewest yards passing (both teams): 0, USC-California, 1931.
Fewest passes completed (both teams): 0, same as above.
Most passes attempted: 38, Oregon State, 1951.
Fewest passes attempted: 0, College of Pacific, 1945.
Most passes completed: 23, Notre Dame, 1949; Oregon State, 1951.
Fewest passes completed: 0, same as "fewest yards passing" except for Washington State, 1921.
Most touchdown passes: 6, Stanford, 1952.
Most first downs: 43, Pomona, 1925.
Fewest first downs: 1, Notre Dame, 1936; Notre Dame, 1950.

ALL-TIME INDIVIDUAL RECORDS

VARSITY CAREER RUSHING LEADERS

	TCB	YG	NYG	Ave.
1. O. J. Simpson	674	3540	3423	5.08
2. Mike Garrett	612	3314	3221	5.27
3. Clarence Davis	511	2518	2323	4.54
4. Orv Mohler	359	2093	2025	5.63
5. Jon Arnett	336	2019	1898	5.66
6. Gus Shaver	377	1953	1889	5.01
7. Morley Drury	317	1777	1686	5.31
8. Grenny Lansdell	350	1728	1621	4.64
9. Mort Kaer	282	1676	1588	5.65
10. Sam Cunningham	341	1607	1579	4.63
11. Jim Musick	393	1605	1568	3.99
12. Russ Saunders	347	1637	1567	4.51
13. Marsh Duffield	315	1598	1538	4.88
14. Don Williams	320	1498	1408	4.40
15. Howard Elliott	195	1407	1384	7.09
16. Cotton Warburton	325	?	1357	4.17
17. Willie Brown	226	1357	1294	5.73
18. Lou Harris	258	1337	1279	4.95
19. C. R. Roberts	192	1309	1244	6.49
20. Dave Davis	357	?	1196	3.35
21. Anthony Davis	207	1253	1191	5.80
22. Amby Schindler	291	1256	1163	4.02
23. Manual Laraneta	250	1171	1129	4.51
24. Bob Robert	299	1308	1106	5.70
25. Don Doll	227	1129	1067	4.70
26. Al Carmichael	237	1166	1042	4.41
27. Ben Wilson	240	1079	1035	4.31
28. Aramis Dandoy	208	1082	991	4.47
29. Rod McNeill	196	997	955	4.87
30. Ron Heller	219	968	936	4.27
31. Mickey McCardle	210	1065	924	4.40
32. Homer Griffith	270	1020	897	3.74
33. Frank Gifford	234	1084	877	3.74

Most times carried ball: 674, O. J. Simpson, 1967-68.
Most yards gained rushing: 3423, O. J. Simpson, 1967-68.
Highest rushing average: 8.5, Ray Sparling (58 for 491), 1930-32.
Most yards lost rushing: 404, Jim Jones, 1969-70.

VARSITY CAREER PASSING LEADERS

	PA	PC	HI	NYG	Pct.	TD
1. Jim Jones	605	298	25	4092	.493	30
2. Steve Sogge	370	201	17	2542	.543	16
3. Jim Powers	348	186	23	2329	.534	19
4. Mike Rae	323	172	17	2684	.533	16
5. Troy Winslow	276	163	14	2075	.590	17
6. Pete Beathard	330	160	15	2374	.484	18
7. Craig Fertig	290	151	14	2230	.520	16
8. Grenny Lansdell	260	114	12	1247	.438	8
9. Jim Hardy	234	111	18	1536	.474	17
10. Bill Nelsen	238	104	10	1811	.437	5
11. Tom Maudlin	195	89	8	1240	.456	9
12. Mickey McCardle	155	75	13	1106	.484	7
13. Dean Schneider	152	71	4	806	.467	2
14. Wilbur Robertson	135	66	8	632	.489	2
15. George Murphy	126	65	9	684	.516	2
16. Rudy Bukich	130	61	12	771	.469	9
17. Toby Page	113	60	11	699	.530	4
18. Willie Wood	117	55	8	772	.470	7
19. Frank Gifford	111	54	3	521	.487	2

Most passes attempted: 604, Jim Jones, 1969-71.
Most passes completed: 298, Jim Jones 1969-71.
Highest completion percentage: 59%, Troy Winslow, 1964-66.
Most passes had intercepted: 25, Jim Jones, 1969-71.
Most yards gained passing: 4092, Jim Jones, 1969-71.
Most TD passes thrown: 30, Jim Jones, 1969-71.

VARSITY CAREER TOTAL OFFENSE LEADERS

	Plays	Rush	Pass	Total
1. Jim Jones	842	409	4092	4501
2. O. J. Simpson	685	3423	48	3471
3. Mike Garrett	618	3221	48	3269
4. Pete Beathard	551	672	2374	3046
5. Mike Rae	447	321	2684	3005
6. Grenny Lansdell	610	1621	1247	2868
7. Marsh Duffield	422	1538	1178	2716
8. Steve Sogge	481	124	2542	2666
9. Troy Winslow	437	504	2075	2579
10. Jim Powers	480	110	2329	2439
11. Gus Shaver	424	1889	548	2437
12. Orv Mohler	427	2028	351	2379
13. Jon Arnett	407	1898	453	2351

14. Clarence Davis	511	2323	0	2323
15. Craig Fertig	362	63	2230	2295
16. Bill Nelsen	481	478	1811	2289
17. Russ Saunders	420	1567	720	2287
18. Mickey McCardle	365	924	1106	2030

Most rushing and passing plays: 842, Jim Jones, 1969-71.
Most touchdowns rushing and passing: 42, Jim Jones, 1969-71.
Most passes received: 91 Rod Sherman, 1964-66.
Most yards on passes received: 1717, Hal Bedsole, 1961-63.
Most touchdown passes caught: 20, Hal Bedsole, 1961-63.
Most passes intercepted: 13, Manuel Laraneta, 1924-26;
  Jim Hardy, 1942-44; Mike Battle, 1966-68; Bruce Dyer, 1969-71.
Most yards returned intercepted passes: 251, Lindon Crow, 1951-54.
Most punts returned: 99, Mike Battle, 1966-68.
Most yards returned punts: 1025, Johnny Williams, 1949-51.
Highest average yards returned punts: 17.0, Aramis Dandoy,
  (25 for 426), 1951-54.
Most kickoffs returned: 29, Johnny Williams, 1949-51;
  Mike Garrett, 1963-65.
Most yards returned kickoffs: 686, Johnny Williams, 1949-51.
Highest average yards returned kickoffs: 39.0, Anthony Davis (12
  for 468), 1972.
Most punts: 140, Ernie Jones, 1961-63.
Most yards punted: 5490, Ernie Jones, 1961-63.
Most touchdowns scored: 36, Mort Kaer, 1924-26, O. J. Simpson,
  1967-68.
Most extra points kicked: 92, Ron Ayala, 1968-70.
Most field goals kicked: 18, Ron Ayala, 1968-70.
Most points scored: 216, Mort Kaer, 1924-26, O. J. Simpson, 1967-68.

VARSITY CAREER PASS CATCHING LEADERS

	No.	Yards	Avg.	TD
1. Rod Sherman	91	1197	13.15	12
2. Hal Bedsole	82	1717	20.94	20
3. Bob Chandler	80	1112	13.92	8
4. Charles Young	68	1090	16.10	10
5. Willie Brown	65	891	13.40	4
6. Sam Dickerson	63	1245	19.75	13
7. Ron Drake	61	729	11.95	4
8. Lynn Swann	54	848	15.70	5
9. Tom Nicoloff	54	738	13.66	5
10. Jim Lawrence	52	777	14.94	4
11. Gordon Gray	51	788	15.45	7
12. Dave Moton	50	860	17.20	8
13. Fred Hill	47	639	13.59	8
14. Bob Klein	42	482	11.47	5
15. John Thomas	41	581	14.17	6
16. Bob Miller	39	492	12.62	7
17. Don Zimmerman	39	386	10.15	2
18. Edesel Garrison	37	771	20.80	6
19. O. J. Simpson	36	320	8.88	0
20. Mike Garrett	35	389	11.11	4
21. Don Stilwell	34	453	13.32	3
22. Leon Clarke	31	482	15.54	2
23. Terry DeKraai	31	354	11.42	4
24. Earl McCullouch	30	540	18.00	5
25. Marlin McKeever	30	430	14.33	2

VARSITY CAREER PASS INTERCEPTION LEADERS

	No.	Yards	Avg.	TD
1. Bruce Dyer	13	149	11.46	1
2. Mike Battle	13	148	11.46	0
3. Jim Hardy	13	130	10.00	0
4. Manuel Laraneta	13			0
5. Artimus Parker	12	168	14.00	0
6. Lindon Crow	11	251	22.81	1
7. Ron Ayala	11	162	14.72	0
8. Tyrone Hudson	10	194	19.40	1
9. Nate Shaw	10	165	16.50	0
10. Jerry Shaw	10	56	5.60	0
11. Jim Psaltis	9	113	12.55	2
12. John Williams	8	167	20.88	0
13. Don Doll	8	95	11.88	0
14. Willie Brown	8	64	8.00	0
15. George Murphy	8	43	5.37	0
16. Sandy Durko	8	157	19.62	2
17. Ernie Zampese	7	141	20.14	0
18. Adrian Young	7	99	14.15	0
19. Steve Fate	7	84	12.00	0
20. Jim Contratto	7	29	4.14	0

VARSITY CAREER PUNT RETURN LEADERS

		No.	Yards	Avg.	TD
1.	Johnny Williams	92	1025	11.12	0
2.	Mike Battle	99	1014	10.24	3
3.	Jim Sears	42	544	12.92	0
4.	Mike Garrett	44	498	11.31	2
5.	Jon Arnett	28	430	15.35	1
6.	Aramis Dandoy	25	426	17.05	0
7.	Verle Lillywhite	25	418	16.70	0
8.	Lynn Swann	30	410	14.30	1
9.	Mickey McCardle	31	390	12.57	0
10.	Jim Hardy	37	384	10.35	0
11.	Don Doll	25	312	12.48	0
12.	Eddie Saenz	21	290	13.80	0
13.	Tyrone Hudson	41	270	6.68	0
14.	Gordon Gray	17	261	15.35	0
15.	Willie Brown	25	256	10.22	0
16.	Sandy Durko	31	251	8.09	0
17.	Don Buford	22	247	11.21	0

VARSITY CAREER KICKOFF RETURN LEADERS

		No.	Yards	Avg.	TD
1.	Mike Garrett	29	694	23.90	0
2.	Johnny Williams	29	686	23.62	0
3.	Lou Harris	24	630	26.25	1
4.	Jon Arnett	26	628	24.15	0
5.	Willie Brown	22	573	26.04	0
6.	Clarence Davis	16	477	29.98	1
7.	Anthony Davis	12	468	39.00	2
8.	Earl McCullouch	23	449	19.50	0
9.	Jim Lawrence	20	402	19.50	0
10.	Don Buford	16	373	23.30	0
11.	Al Carmichael	20	372	20.10	0
12.	Don Doll	12	369	30.75	0
13.	Lindon Crow	14	362	25.82	0
14.	O. J. Simpson	15	355	23.66	0
15.	Jim Sears	14	350	25.00	0
16.	Aramis Dandoy	12	340	28.33	1
17.	C. R. Roberts	13	322	24.80	0

SINGLE SEASON RUSHING LEADERS

		G	TCB	NYG
1.	O. J. Simpson '68	11	383	1880
2.	O. J. Simpson '67	10	291	1543
3.	Mike Garrett '65	10	267	1440
4.	Clarence Davis '69	11	297	1351
5.	Anthony Davis '72	12	207	1191
6.	Morley Drury '27	9	223	1163
7.	Orv Mohler '30	10	145	983
8.	Russ Saunders '29	11	185	972
9.	Clarence Davis '70	11	214	972
10.	Mike Garrett '64	10	217	948
11.	Gus Shaver '31	11	199	936

Most times carried ball: 383, O. J. Simpson, 1968.
Most yards gained rushing: 1880, O. J. Simpson, 1968.
Highest rushing average: 11.6, Erny Pinckert (17 for 199) 1930.
Most yards lost rushing: 250, Jim Jones, 1969.

SINGLE SEASON PASSING LEADERS

		G	PA	PC	HI	Pct.	NYG	TD
1.	Steve Sogge '68	11	207	122	9	58.9%	1454	9
2.	Jim Jones '70	11	234	121	5	51.8%	1877	10
3.	Mike Rae '72	12	199	114	12	57.3%	1754	5
4.	Craig Fertig '64	10	209	109	10	52.0%	1671	11
5.	Jim Jones '71	11	161	89	10	55.3%	995	7
6.	Jim Jones '69	11	210	88	10	42.0%	1230	13
7.	Jim Powers '59	9	148	87	11	58.8%	1215	12
8.	Troy Winslow '66	10	138	82	5	59.0%	1023	6
9.	Troy Winslow '65	10	127	78	9	61.0%	1019	11
10.	Steve Sogge '67	11	151	75	7	49.7%	1032	7
11.	Pete Beathard '63	10	140	66	7	47.2%	944	5
12.	Jim Hardy '63	10	117	58	9	59.5%	739	10
13.	Pete Beathard '62	11	107	54	1	50.0%	948	10

Most passes attempted: 234, Jim Jones, 1970.
Most passes completed: 122, Steve Sogge, 1968.
Highest percentage of completion: 61%, Troy Winslow, 1965.
Most passes had intercepted: 15, Tom Maudlin, 1958.
Most yards gained passing: 1877, Jim Jones, 1970.
Most touchdown passes thrown: 13, Jim Jones, 1969.

SINGLE SEASON TOTAL OFFENSE LEADERS

	G	Plays	Rush	Pass	Total
1. Mike Rae '72	12	281	247	1754	2001
2. Jim Jones '70	11	292	59	1877	1936
3. O. J. Simpson '68	11	388	1880	15	1895
4. Craig Fertig '64	10	248	24	1671	1695
5. Russ Saunders '29	11	241	972	626	1598
6. O. J. Simpson '67	10	297	1543	22	1576
7. Steve Sogge '68	11	291	49	1454	1503
8. Mike Garrett '65	10	271	1440	42	1482
9. Clarence Davis '69	11	297	1351	0	1351
10. Troy Winslow '65	10	208	319	1019	1338
11. Jim Jones '69	11	302	1230	83	1313
12. Jim Jones '71	11	248	267	995	1262
13. Morley Drury '27	9	223	1165	77	1242
14. Pete Beathard '62	11	207	290	949	1238
15. Grenny Lansdell '39	10	239	742	479	1221

Most touchdowns rushing and passing: 24, Russ Saunders, 1929.
Most passes received: 52, Ron Drake, 1966.
Most yards on passes received: 827, Hal Bedsole, 1962.
Most touchdown passes caught: 11, Hal Bedsole, 1962.
Most passes intercepted: 9, Jim Hardy, 1944, Jim Psaltis, 1952, Bobby Richardson, 1942.
Most yards returned intercepted passes: 129, Ty Hudson, 1969.
Most punts returned: 49, Mike Battle, 1967.
Most yards returned punts: 608, Mike Battle, 1967.
Highest avg. yards returned punts: 18.5, Aramis Dandoy (11 for 204), 1954.
Most kickoffs returned: 15, Johnny Williams, 1951, Jon Arnett, 1955, Mike Garrett, 1963.
Most yards returned kickoffs: 468, Anthony Davis, 1972.
Highest avg. yards returned kickoffs: 39.0, Anthony Davis, (12 for 468), 1972.
Most punts: 63, Ernie Jones, 1962.
Most yards punted: 2498, Ernie Jones, 1962.
Highest punting average: 44.6, Des Koch (22 for 981), 1953.
Most touchdowns scored: 23, O. J. Simpson, 1968.
Most extra points kicked: 49, Mike Rae, 1972.
Most field goals kicked: 8, Mike Rae, 1972.
Most points scored: 138, O. J. Simpson, 1968.

SINGLE GAME

Most points: 36, Anthony Davis, 1972 (Notre Dame).
Most touchdowns: 6, Anthony Davis, 1972 (Notre Dame).
Most extra points: 8, Tim Rossovich, 1965 (Wyoming); Ron Ayala, 1970 (Washington State).
Most field goals: 3, Ron Ayala, 1970 (Alabama).
Most yards running: 251, C. R. Roberts, 1956 (Texas).
Most yards passing: 371, Craig Fertig, 1964 (California).
Most yards running and passing: 348, Craig Fertig, 1964 (California).
Most times carried ball: 47, O. J. Simpson, 1968, (Stanford and Oregon State)
Most passes attempted: 36, Jim Jones, 1970 (Stanford).
Most passes completed: 21, Craig Fertig, 1964 (California); Jim Jones, 1970 (Stanford).
Most touchdown passes thrown: 4, Pete Beathard, 1963 (Wisconsin); (RB); Craig Fertig, 1964 (California); Troy Winslow, 1965 (Wyoming).
Most passes received: 11, Fred Hill, 1964 (Washington).
Most yards on passes caught: 201, Hal Bedsole, 1962 (California).
Most passes intercepted: 4, Adrian Young, 1967 (Notre Dame).

SINGLE PLAY

Longest run (any type): 99 yards, Bud Langley, 1936 (Notre Dame) on 100-yard field; 107 yards, Elwyn Caley, 1902 (Pomona) on 110-yard field.
Longest run from scrimmage: 93 yards, Willie Brown, 1961 (SMU).
Longest kickoff return: 98 yards, Ed Green, 1924 (Cal Tech) on 100-yard field; 107 yards, Elwyn Caley, 1902 (Pomona) on 110-yard field.
Longest kickoff return for touchdown: 97 yards, Anthony Davis, 1972 (Notre Dame) on 100-yard field.
Longest punt return: 93, Ernie Merk, 1955 (Minnesota).
Longest run with intercepted pass: 99 yards, Bud Langley, 1936 (Notre Dame).
Longest run with intercepted fumble: 81 yards, Harold Hammock, 1931 (Georgia).
Longest pass play: 80 yards, Jim Powers to Al Cantor, 1949 (Washington); Jim Contratto to Lindon Crow, 1954 (Washington State).
Longest punt: 85 yards, Ernie Zampese, 1956 (Wisconsin).
Longest field goal: 45 yards, Courtney Decius, 1909 (Occidental).

ALL-TIME USC
ALL-AMERICA SELECTIONS

No.	Year	Name, Position
1	1925	Brice Taylor, G
2	1926	Mort Kaer, B
3	1927	Morley Drury, B
4	1927	Jess Hibbs, T
5	1928	Jess Hibbs, T
6	1928	Don Williams, B
7	1929	Nate Barragar, G
8	1929	Francis Tapapn, E
9	1930	Gar. Arbelbide, E
10	1930	Orv Mohler, B
11	1930	Erny Pinckert, B
12	1931	Johnny Baker, G
13	1931	Erny Pinckert, B
14	1931	Gus Shaver, B
15	1931	Stan Williamson, C
16	1932	Tay Brown, T
17	1932	Aaron Rosenberg, G
18	1932	Ernie Smith, T
19	1933	Aaron Rosenberg, G
20	1933	Irving Warburton, B
21	1938	Harry Smith, G
22	1939	Granny Lansdell, B
23	1939	Harry Smith, G
23	1943	Ralph Heywood, E
25	1944	John Ferraro, T
26	1947	Paul Cleary, E
27	1947	John Ferraro, T
28	1951	Pat Cannamela, LB
29	1951	Frank Gifford, B
30	1952	Jim Sears, DB
31	1952	Elmer Wilhoite, G
32	1955	Jon Arnett, B
33	1959	Ron Mix, T
34	1959	Dan Ficca, T
35	1959	Marlin McKeever, E
36	1959	Mike McKeever, G
37	1960	Marlin McKeever, E
38	1962	Hal Bedsole, E
39	1962	Damon Bame, LB
40	1963	Damon Bame, LB
41	1964	Bill Fisk, G
42	1964	Mike Garrett, B
43	1965	Mike Garrett, B
44	1966	Nate Shaw, DB
45	1966	Ron Yary, T
46	1967	O. J. Simpson, B
47	1967	Ron Yary, T
48	1967	Adrian Young, LB
49	1967	Tim Rossovich, DE
50	1968	O. J. Simpson, B
51	1968	Mike Battle, DB
52	1969	Jimmy Gunn, DE
53	1969	Al Cowlings, DT
54	1969	Sid Smith, T
55	1969	Clarence Davis, B
56	1970	Charles Weaver, DE
57	1970	Marv Montgomery, T
58	1971	John Vella, T
59	1971	Willie Hall, LB
60	1972	Charles Young, TE
61	1972	Richard Wood, LB
62	1972	Sam Cunningham, FB
63	1972	Pete Adams, T
64	1972	John Grant, DT
65	1973	Lynn Swann, FLK
66	1973	Artimus Parker, DB
67	1973	Booker Brown, OT
68	1973	Richard Wood, LB
69	1973	Steve Riley, OT

ALL-TIME USC LETTER WINNERS

A

Abram, Fabian 1955, 56
Acker, Frank 1904, 05
Adams, Gene 1904, 05
Adams, Halley 1923, 24
Adams, Harold 1923, 24, 25
Adams, Holly 1922
Adams, Peter 1970, 71, 72
Adams, William J. 1967
Adelman, Harry 1941, 42
Adolph, Rob 1973
Aguirre, John 1941, 45
Aldridge, Charles 1967
Alekski, Joe 1925, 27
Alexander, Harold 1923
Allan, Roy 1908, 09, 10
Allmon, Richard C. 1967, 68
Almy, J. 1907
Anderson, Charles A. 1960, 61
Anderson, Norman 1922, 23, 24
Anderson, Otto 1922, 23, 24
Anderson, William C.
   1937, 38, 40, 41
Ane, Charles T., Jr. 1951, 52
Anthony, Charles 1971, 72, 73
Anthony, Frank 1927, 28, 29
Antle, Ken Lee 1956, 57, 58
Antles, Russell 1944, 45, 46
Apsit, Marger 1928, 29, 30
Arbelbide, Garrett 1929, 30, 31
Arnest, Henry C. 1961
Arnett, Bob 1957, 58
Arnett, Jon 1954, 55
Arnold, James 1918
Arnold, Paul 1889
Arrobio, Charles Augustus
   1963, 64, 65
Artenian, Mickey 1952, 53
Ashcraft, Walt 1949, 52
Atanasoff, Alex 1937
Audet, Earl 1943
Avery, Ralph 1896, 97
Axe, Fred 1919, 20, 21
Ayala, Victor Ronald 1968, 69, 70

B

Baccitich, John M. 1966
Badgrove, Morris 1924, 25, 26
Bailie, Bert 1904
Bain, Bill 1973
Bain, Marvin J. 1964, 65
Baker, John 1929, 30, 31
Baker, Roy 1922, 23
Baker, Sam
Baldcok, Alvin 1949, 50, 53
Baldridge, Lyle 1925, 26, 28
Baley, Burt 1903, 05
Bame, Damon 1962, 63
Bansavage, Albert A. 1959
Banta, Jack 1938, 39, 40
Barber, Richard A. 1931, 32
Bardin, Oliver 1932, 33
Barnes, Mercer 1949, 50
Barragar, Nathan 1927, 28, 29
Barrager, 1918
Barrett, 1917
Bary, Allan 1952
Barry, Nelson 1930
Barry, Stephen Anthony 1965, 66
Bastian, Bob 1946, 47, 48
Bates, James Edward 1960, 61
Battle, Art 1946, 48, 49
Battle, Michael L. 1966, 67, 68
Bayley, Eugene 1914
Beale, John Paul 1918, 19, 20
Beals, 1917
Beard, Francis 1932, 33, 34
Beathard, Peter 1961, 62, 63
Beattie, Eugene 1926, 27
Beatty, Blanchard 1930, 31
Beatty, Homer 1934, 35, 36
Beck, Eugene 1948, 49, 50
Becker, Henry 1929

Bedsole, Harold J. 1961, 62, 63
Beeson, Bob 1940
Behrendt, Allen 1924, 25, 26
Belko, Max 1934, 35, 36
Bell, Howard 1926
Bell, Joseph A. 1943
Bell, Ricky 1973
Belotti, D. George 1954, 55, 56
Bennett, Frank 1939
Benson, Carl 1939, 40
Berry, Michael H. 1969, 70
Berryman, Richard 1936
Berryman, Robert 1939, 40
Bescos, Julius 1932, 33, 34
Best, Oliver 1904
Bettinger, George 1935
Betz, Bill 1947
Bianchi, Steve 1941
Bickford, John H. 1903, 04, 06
Biggs, Henry 1930, 31, 32
Bird, Jim 1947, 48, 49
Bird, Richard 1919, 20
Black, Rupert 1930
Blair, Horace 1922
Blake, Samuel R. 1916
Blanche, John G. 1966, 68
Blacksmith, Edward L. 1964, 65
Bledsoe, Leo 1941
Bledsoe, Wililam 1940, 41
Bleeker, Melvin 1940, 41, 42
Bockman, 1905
Bohlinger, Tom 1972, 73
Boice, Winchell 1922
Boies, Herbert 1949
Boies, Larry Kenton 1957, 58
Bond, Ward 1928, 29, 30
Bonham, Herschel 1926, 27, 28
Bordier, Warner 1954, 55
Boren, Charles F. 1925, 27, 28
Born, Dennis L. 1957
Bosbyshell, W. 1906
Botelho, Rod 1958
Bott, Clyde 1896, 97
Boulware, Dave 1971, 72, 73
Bowers, William 1950
Bowie, Wilson 1968
Bowman, Charles 1939
Boyle, Johnny 1920, 21, 22
Bozanic, George 1951, 52, 53
Bradford, Joe 1945
Bradley, Joe 1895
Bradley, Otha 1973
Brandt, Harvey T. 1934
Bridewell, Walter 1907
Bright, Kenneth 1932, 33
Brockman, Kenneth 1919
Broderson, Charles
   1898, 1902, 03, 04
Bronson, Richard Alfonso 1957
Brouse, Willard 1931
Brousseau, Raphael 1935, 36, 37
Brown, Booker 1972, 73
Brown, David 1970, 71, 72
Brown, Everett 1928, 29, 30
Brown, F. R. 1906, 08
Brown, George E. 1934
Brown, George L. 1889
Brown, Raymond 1930, 31, 32
Brown, Ronald Lee 1954, 55
Brown, Willie F. 1961, 62, 63
Brownell, Richard L. 1964
Browning, Ward 1932, 33, 34
Brownwood, John R. 1962, 63, 64
Bruce, Kevin 1973
Buckley, Robert 1952, 53
Buford, Don 1957, 58
Bukich, Rudy 1951, 52
Buncom, Frank 1960, 61
Bundra, Mike P. 1959, 60, 61
Bundy, Bill 1939, 40, 41
Bunker, Frank 1907, 09
Burchard, Gerald 1933, 34, 35
Burek, Stanley 1905, 06, 07, 08
Burke, Don 1948

507

Burkette 1916
Burnett, C. W. 1893, 95
Burnside, Donald 1944
Busby, Marvin L. 1934
Busby, Stuart H. 1961
Busch, Ernie 1947
Butcher, Ronald W. 1961, 62
Butterfield, Clarence 1917, 19, 20
Byrd, Glenn 1972
Byrd, MacArthur 1962, 63, 64
Byrd, Louis 1957, 58
—C—
Cahill, Ray 1966
Calabiria, Ronald D. 1954
Caley, Dan 1902, 03
Caley, Elwin 1902, 03
Callanan, George P. 1943
Callanan, Howard 1942
Callanan, James F. 1944, 45, 46
Calland, Leo 1920, 21, 22
Cameron, Don 1923
Cameron, Rodney 1933, 34, 35
Campbell, Gordon 1921, 22, 23
Campbell, Jim 1917
Cannamela, Pat 1950, 51
Cantor, Al 1948
Carmichael, Al 1950, 51, 52
Carmichael, E. W. 1906
Carpenter, Kenneth 1934, 37
Carpenter, Roy 1905, 06
Carten, Red 1893
Carter, Allen 1972, 73
Carter, Kent 1970, 71
Carver, C. E. 1889
Case, Frank 1905
Cashman, Patrick F. 1966, 67
Cassel, Curtis 1920, 21
Chambers, Mahlon 1927, 28, 29
Chandler, Robert D. 1968, 69, 70
Chaney, Chris 1972
Chantilles, Tom 1941
Charles, Ben F. 1959, 60
Chestnut, Bob 1917, 19
Christianson, 1919
Christie, Charles 1896, 97
Chuha, Joe 1957
Clark, 1916, 17
Clark, Don 1945, 46, 47
Clark, Gordon 1931, 32, 33
Clark, Jack 1935
Clark, Jay 1962, 63
Clark, Monte Dale 1956, 57, 58
Clark, Roger A. 1960
Clark, Roger Alan 1961
Clark, Stephen 1905, 06, 07, 08
Clarke, Eugene 1930, 31
Clarke, Leon T. 1953, 54, 55
Clayton, Franklin D. 1952, 53, 54
Cleary, Paul 1945, 46, 47
Clemens, Calvin Jr. 1932, 33, 34
Clemens, Jerry 1919
Cobb, Marvin 1972, 73
Cochran, C. N. 1909
Coffman, Theadore 1923, 24, 25
Cohn, Thomas 1910
Coia, Angelo 1958, 59
Cole, Ralph W. 1921, 24
Colley, Tom 1948
Collins, Pat 1973
Coloneus, 1907, 08, 09
Conde, John 1949, 50, 51
Conforti, Dan
Conroy, James Josep
  1956, 57, 59
Conroy, Jerome G. 1965
Contratto, Jim A. 1953, 54, 55
Cook, Andrew J. 1924, 25
Coones, Ken 1959
Cordell, Mike 1973
Coughlin, Alvie 1932, 33, 34
Courdis, 1919
Covington, Humphrey L. 1968, 69
Cowlings, Allen G. 1968, 69
Cox, Kenneth 1924, 25, 26

Cox, Morgan 1918, 19, 20
Cox, Robert 1951, 52
Coyle, Leslie 1927
Craig, Gerald 1913, 14, 15, 16
Crall, 1907
Cramer, Stanley 1947
Crane, Dennis W. 1967
Cravath, Jeff 1924, 25, 26
Crisp, 1919
Crittenden, Wallace 1944
Critton, 1905
Crow, Lindon 1952, 53, 54
Crowthers, Jim 1941
Cruickshank, Donald 1924, 25, 26
Culbreath, Cliff 1972
Cummings, Ralph 1921, 22, 23
Cunningham, Sam 1970, 71, 72
Curry, Edsel 1943, 46, 47
Curry, Willard 1915, 16
Curtis, Louis Lane 1944
Custin, George 1906
Cutri, Cosimo 1950, 51
—D—
Dahlgren, 1917
Dandol, Aramis M. 1952, 53, 54
Danehe, Richard 1941
DaRe, Mario P. 1952, 53, 54
Davis, Anthony 1972, 73
Davis, Clarence E. 1969, 70
Davis, David 1934, 35, 36
Davis, George 1944, 47, 49
Davis, George 1934
Davis, Joe 1940, 41, 42
Davis, Joe 1973
Davis, Robert 1922
Davis, Thomas 1911, 12, 13, 14
Day, Oliver 1937, 38
Dean, Charles F. 1919, 20, 21
DeArmand, 1917
Debovsky, Philip 1957
Decius, H. 1906, 07, 09
Decker, George 1929, 30
Decker, James Ralph 1953, 54, 56
DeGroote, Clarke 1924, 25, 26
DeHetre, John 1934, 37
DeKraai, Terry L. 1968, 69
Delaney, Gary C. 1960
DeLappe, J. R. 1904
DeLauer, Bob 1939, 40, 41
Del Conte, Kenneth 1960, 61, 62
Demirjian, Ed 1950
Dempsey, Edward 1938, 39, 40
Deranian, Vaughn 1928, 29, 30
Dickerson, Samuel Boyce
  1968, 69, 70
Diehl, Lawrence 1926, 27
Diggs, Shelton 1973
Dill, Dean 1947
Dittberner, Art 1933, 34, 35
Doll, Don 1946, 47, 48
Dolley, Chet 1922, 23, 24
Domis, John 1943
Doris, Monte 1972, 73
Dorsey, Gene 1923, 24, 26
Dougher, Harold 1922
Dougherty, Morton 1902
Douglas, Don 1957, 58
Downs, Bob 1950
Drake, Ronald V. 1966, 67
Dreblow, Milford 1943, 44, 45, 46
Drury, Morley 1925, 26, 27
Duboski, Phillip 1936
Duff, Clinton 1949, 50, 51
Duffield, Marshall 1928, 29, 30
Dunaway, Warren 1934
Dunn, Coye 1936
Dunning, Corwin 1932
DuPuy, Reginald 1922, 23, 24
Durkee, Harvey 1928, 29, 31
Durko, Sandy V. 1968, 69
Duvall, Gordon C. 1953, 54, 55
Dye, George 1929
Dye, John 1931, 32, 33
Dye, William 1933, 34

Dyer, Bruce 1970, 71

—E—
Earle, Raymond 1923, 24, 25
Edelson, Henry 1927, 28, 29
Edgarton, E. O. 1896
Edwards, Hugh 1925
Edwards, Robert 1958, 59
Egan, John G. 1920
Elliott, Carl 1904, 05, 06
Elliott, E. 1893
Elliott, Earl 1904
Elliott, Howard 1925, 26, 27
Elliott, Ian 1941
Elmore, John Jr. 1914
Embree, A. B. 1889, 92
Emmons, Richard 1922
Engle, Roy 1937, 38, 39
Enright, Richard M. 1954, 55
Eriksen, Bob 1971
Erskine, Robert 1931, 32, 33
Essick, Douglas 1941, 42, 46
Evans, R. 1917
Evans, Charles 1969, 70
Evans, John 1943
Evans, Roy 1919, 20, 21
Exley, Landon M. 1952, 53

—F—
Failor, Walt 1970
Fassel, Jim E. 1969
Fate, Steve 1971, 72
Fay, Kenneth 1931, 32, 33
Ferguson, Claude 1902
Ferguson, James T. 1966
Ferrante, Orlando 1953, 54, 55
Ferrarro, John 1943, 44, 46, 47
Fertig, Craig W. 1962, 63, 64
Ficca, Dan 1958, 59, 60
Finneran, Gary 1957, 58, 59
Finney, Hal 1942
Fiorentino, Frank 1956, 57, 58
Fisher, Robert A. 1936, 37, 38
Fisk, Bill 1937, 38, 39
Fisk, William Jr. 1962, 63, 64
Fite, Gary G. 1965
Fletcher, Oliver 1948
Fletcher, Paul 1905, 06
Fletcher, Ronald 1954, 55, 56
Flint, Fay 1902, 03
Flood, Jeff 1973
Floro, Robert S. 1960
Follett, George 1971, 72
Ford, William 1926, 28
Fouch, Edward V. 1952, 53, 54
Fouch, John 1949, 50
Fox, Jack 1926, 27
Fox, John 1915, 16, 19
Freeman, George 1921, 22, 23
Friend, Bill 1924, 25, 26
Fuhrer, Bob 1932, 33, 34
Fuhrman, Seymour 1942
Funk, J. B. 1894

—G—
Gaisford, Bill 1935, 36
Gale, Michael 1961, 62
Galindo, Charles 1925
Gallaher, Allen 1970, 71, 72
Galli, George 1953, 54, 55
Gallowa, Armor 1921
Galloway, Amos 1921, 22
Galloway, Clark 1927, 28, 29
Galloway, Harold 1918, 22
Galvin, Glen 1936, 37, 39
Garlin, Donald 1944, 46, 47, 48
Garrett, Michael Lockett 1963, 64, 65
Garrison, Edesel 1971, 72
Garzoni, Mike 1943, 44, 45, 46
Gaskill, Lynn Dennis 1959, 60, 61
Gaspar, Phil 1937, 38, 39
Gee, Doug 1945
Gelker, Benjamin B. 1943
Geller, Roscoe 1908, 09

Gentry, Byron 1930, 31, 32
George, Ray 1936, 37, 38
Gerpheide, Ben 1923
Gerpheide, Louis 1923
Getz, Bob 1932
Giers, Michael L. 1963, 64
Gifford, Frank 1949, 50, 51
Giguette, Al 1904, 05
Gill, William J. 1934, 35
Givehand, James 1972, 73
Glenn, William 1922
Goller, Winston 1950, 51
Gonta, Stanley L. 1962
Goodenow, Harold 1906, 07, 08
Gordon, Clifford 1920, 21
Gorrell, Ted 1924, 25, 26
Gorrell, Walter T. 1956
Goux, Marvin A. 1952, 54, 55
Gowder, Robert 1927, 28, 29
Gracin, Jerry 1934
Grady, Stephen 1966, 67
Graf, Allan 1970, 71, 72
Grant, John 1970, 71, 72
Gray, Gordon 1943, 44, 46, 47
Gray, John A. 1889, 92, 93
Gray, Ken 1972, 73
Gray, William 1943
Green, Edward 1923, 24
Green, Max 1940
Greene, Paul 1920, 21
Greenwood, Charles D. 1952, 53, 54
Griffith, Charles E. 1954
Griffith, Homer 1930, 31, 32
Grissum, James W. 1968, 70
Gueguett, Dan 1903, 04
Gunn, James 1967, 68, 69
Gurasich, Walt 1956, 57

—H—
Haas, Earl E. 1936
Hachten, Boyd 1948
Haddock, H. 1895
Haden, Pat 1972, 73
Haigler, Charles 1905, 06, 07, 08
Haigler, Chester 1905, 06
Halderman, Richard 1927
Hall, Frank 1954, 55, 56
Hall, Robert H. 1929, 30, 31
Hall, William King 1933, 34
Hall, Willie 1970, 71
Halloway, Clayton 1914, 15
Haluchak, Michael A. 1968, 69, 70
Halvorsen, Ray 1936
Hamilton, Tom 1948
Hamilton, William 1904, 05
Hamilton, Wright 1917
Hammack, Harold 1929, 30, 31
Hancock, Mike 1972, 73
Hanes, Simeon 1914
Hansch, H. J. 1924
Hansen, Owen L. 1935, 36, 37
Hardy, Donald, **1943**, 44, 46
Hardy, James 1942, 43, 44
Harlan, David 1932, 33
Harper, Hueston 1932, 33, 34
Harris, Lou 1970, 71
Harvey, Clarence 1945
Hasen, H. 1902
Haslam, R. 1896
Hatch, William 1908
Hatfield, Harold 1948, 49, 50
Hattig, Bill 1950, 51, 52
Hawkins, John 1922, 23, 24
Hawkins, William 1930
Hawthorne, Addison 1952, 53
Hayes, Jim 1952, 53
Hayes, Luther 1958, 59, 60
Hayhoe, Jerry 1964, 66
Hayhoe, William 1967, 68
Headley, Blake 1944
Heinberg, Sylvester 1945
Heiser, Bert H. 1924, 26, 27
Heller, Ronald M. 1962, 63, 64

Henderson, James 1935, 36
Hendren, Robert 1946, 47, 48
Henry, Michael D. 1956, 57, 58
Hershberger, Lloyd 1924, 25, 26
Hester, Orie 1917, 19, 21
Heywood, Ralph 1941, 42, 43
Hibbs, Gene 1935, 36, 37
Hibbs, Jesse 1926, 27, 28
Hickman, Don 1955, 56, 57
Hicks, Harry 1923
Higgins, Clark 1944
Hill, Arthur 1909, 10
Hill, Frederick G. 1962, 63, 64
Hill, Gary H. 1962, 63, 64
Hill, Hillard 1956, 58
Hill, Jesse T. 1928, 29
Hindley, Lewis 1940
Hinman, C. J. 1893, 96, 97
Hinton, Charles 1971, 72
Hoff, Cecil Wayne 1927, 28, 29
Hoffman, Robert 1937, 38, 39
Hogan, Doug 1973
Holden, Clark 1957, 58, 59
Holland, Bill 1970, 71
Holman, William 1902
Holmes, 1917, 18
Homan, James D. 1965, 66
Hooks, Robert Joseph 1951, 52
Hooks, Roger C. 1954
Hoover, Philip Lynn 1961, 62
Houck, Hudson 1963
Houlgate, Jack W. 1933
Howard, Bill 1957
Howard, William N. 1933, 34, 35
Hubby, Lindsy 1956, 57
Hudson, Tyrone L. 1969, 70
Hughes, Don 1944, 47, 49
Hughes, Jack 1904, 05
Hughes, John 1923
Hull, Michael 1965, 66, 67
Hull, Warren Bruce 1934, 35
Humenuik, Rod 1956, 57, 58
Hummell, Edward 1910
Hunnicut, 1918
Hunt, 1917
Hunt, Loran J. 1961, 62, 63
Hunter, Floyd William III 1965
Hunter, Herbert 1917, 18
Hunter, Keith 1921
Hurst, Joe 1933, 34
Huyck, Harold 1916

—I—

Ickles, Sydney 1908, 09
Ingle, Ray J. 1943
Isaaeson, Robert 1954, 55, 56
Isenhouser, Bill 1919, 20
Isherwood, Ed 1956, 57

—J—

Jacobsmeyer, Walter 1942
James, George 1914
Jamison, Dick 1942
Jaroncyk, William 1966, 67
Jensen, Robert 1930
Jensen, Robert A. 1968, 69
Jesse, John P. 1936, 37, 38
Jessup, Bill 1948, 50
Jeter, Gary 1973
Johnson, C. J. 1904
Johnson, Eddie 1971, 72
Johnson, Gary B. 1960, 61
Johnson, Kendrick 1916
Johnson, Paul Richard 1964, 65
Johnson, Thomas Ansley 1962, 63
Johnston, E. 1918
Johnston, Rex David 1956, 57, 58
Jones, A. E. 1889
Jones, Bob 1939, 40, 41
Jones, Ernie F. 1961, 62, 63
Jones, Herbert 1915
Jones, James 1936, 37, 38

Jones, James A. 1969, 70, 71
Jones, James Randy 1962
Jones, Philo 1895, 96
Jordan, 1917
Jorgenson, Ellwood 1932, 34, 35
Joslin, J. 1917
Joslin, J. Howard 1929, 30, 31
Jurich, Anthony 1929, 32

—K—

Kaer, Morton 1924, 25, 26
Kalinich, Pete 1939
Kaprillian, Michael 1910
Kasten, Donald L. 1958
Keehn, Ludwig 1956
Kellar, Stewart 1909, 10
Keller, Donald W. 1936, 37
Keller, John Theron 1935
Kellogg, 1917
Kelly, Fred 1914, 15, 16
Kemp, Rockwell 1927, 28, 29
Khasigian, Harry 1967, 68, 69
Kidder, Allan 1934, 35
Kincaid, Howard 1920, 21, 22
King, Arthur 1921
King, Eddie Lawrence 1963, 65, 66
King, Oscar 1922
Kirby, Jack 1946, 47, 48
Kirkland, Al 1952
Kirner, Garold B. 1962, 63
Kissinger, Ellsworth H. Jr. 1954, 55, 56
Klein, Robert O. 1966, 67, 68
Klenk, Quenton 1939, 40
Knickrehm, Fred W. 1917
Knoles, Tully 1901, 02
Knutson, Steve 1973
Koch, Desmond D. 1951, 52, 53
Kordich, John 1948
Kovae, Pete 1934
Kraintz, Rudy 1934
Kranz, Douglas 1955, 56
Kreiger, Wm. Karl 1927, 28, 29
Kroll, Darrell 1942
Krueger, Al 1938, 39, 40
Kubas, John C. 1957
Kuhn, Gil 1934, 35, 36
Kurlak, Wayne 1954, 56
Kurle, Alfred 1910
Kuchel, Theodore 1921

—L—

Lary, George 1932, 33, 34
Laisne, Eugene 1927, 28
La Mont, Grant 1925
Lane, R. C. 1904, 05
Langley, Lawrence 1935, 36
Lansdell, Grenville Jr. 1937, 38, 39
Laraneta, Manuel 1924, 25, 26
Lardizabel, Benjamin D. 1945, 46, 47
Larrabee, Duane 1933, 34
La Velle, Leslie 1926, 27
Lavoni, 1905
Lawrence, James D. 1966, 67, 68
Leadingham, John 1918, 19, 20, 21
Leahy, Ed 1920, 21, 22
Learned, 1917
LeDue, William P. 1936
Lee, Bob 1924, 25, 26
Lee, James 1972
Lee, Phillip N. 1964, 65, 66
Lefebvre, Henry 1923, 24, 25
Lehmer, Steven Mark 1967, 68, 69
Leimbach, Chas. V. 1954, 55, 56
Lennox, Walter 1904
Leon, Richard G. 1966
Levingston, Robert W. 1959, 60
Lewis, Mike 1958
Lillywhite, Verl 1945, 46, 47
Lindley, Logan 1918, 19, 20, 21
Lindley, Lowell 1920, 21, 22
Linehan, Tony 1946, 47, 49

Lingenfelter, Dean 1973
Littlejohn, Leroy 1942
Livernash, Leonard
  1911, 12, 13, 14, 15
Lloyd, David 1944, 47, 48
Lloyd, W. F. 1896, 97
Lockett, Frank 1919, 20, 21
Lockwood, John 1964, 65
Lopez, Frank Raymond 1964, 65
Lorch, Karl 1972
Lorentzon, 1907
Loustalot, John **1923**
Love, Robert 1932, 33
Lowell, Russell 1947
Lubisich, Peter 1961, 62, 63
Lucas, Al
Lucas, Lawrence 1914
Lucas, Pete 1917
Lund, Lavalle 1912, 13, 14
Lupo, Thomas Lee 1962, 63, 64
Lynch, Ford 1934, 35, 36

—M—

McArthur, Gary L. 1969
McCaffrey, Bob 1972, 73
McCabe, Hilton 1926, 27, 28
McCall, Donald C. 1965, 66
McCall, Fred 1941, 42, 46, 47
McCardle, Mickey 1942, 43, 46, 47
McCaslin, Lawrence 1926, 27, 28
McConnell, Stephen R. 1968
McCormick, Walt 1945, **46, 47**
McCullouch, Earl R. 1967
McFarland, Don 1954, 55
McGarvin, Tom 1940
McGee, Bob 1950
McGinley, Francis 1931, 32, 34
McGinn, John 1944
McGirr, Mike 1971, 73
McKay, John K. 1972, 73
McGirr, Mike 1971
McKay, John K. 1972
McKeever, Marlin 1958, 59, 60
McKeever, Mike 1958, 59, 60
McKinney, Harry 1944, 45, 46, 47
McMahon, Richard Jr. 1961, 62, 63
McMillan, Walter Dan 1917, 19
McMoore, Robert 1935
McMurty, Paul 1949, 50
McNeil, Don 1936, 37, 38
McNeill, Rod 1970, 72, 73
McNeish, George 1934, 35, 36
McNeish, Robert 1931, 32, 33
MacPhail, Peter 1941, 42, 43
Maddux, James 1955
Magner, Gary David 1965, 66, 67
Malcolm, John 1908, 09, 10
Malette, Frank 1915, 16, 17
Malley, Duane 1941
Mallory, Thomas 1929, 30, 31
Maloney, Al 1930
Manker, Robert 1923
Manlove, Ferdinand 1925
Manning, Dick 1941
Maples, Jim W. 1959, 60, 61
Marderian, Greg 1971, 73
Marinovich, Andrew 1943
Marinovich, Marvin 1959, 61, 62
Marks, Theodore 1915, 16
Marshall, G. 1915
Martin, A. 1897
Martin, G. 1895
Martin, Harry Lee 1893
Martin, William 1948
Marx, Theodore 1915, 16
Marxen, E. 1915
Matthews, Garland 1932, 33, **34**
Matthews, Robert 1933, 34
Mattson, Don W. 1956, 57
Maudlin, Tom 1957, 58
May, Reginald 1965, 66
Mena, Salvador 1938, 39, 40
Merk, Ernest J. 1954, 55
Mietz, Roger 1958, 59, 60
Miller, 1917

Miller, John C. 1953, 54, **55**
Miller, Reed 1902, 03, 04, 05
Miller, Robert Raymond
  1966, 67, 68
Miller, Ronald W. 1951, 52, **53**
Milton, John 1921, 22
Mitchell, Dale 1972, 73
Mitchell, Sheppard 1903
Mix, Ronald J. 1957, 58, 59
Mohler, Orville 1930, 31, **32**
Mollett, Gerald 1959
Moloney, Jerry J. 1950
Monson, Jim 1948
Montgomery, Marvin 1969, 70
Moore, James Dennia 1965, 66
Moore, Manfred 1971, 72, 73
Morgan, Boyd F. 1936, 37, **38**
Morgan, David J. 1959, 60, 61
Morgan, Michael 1970, **71**
Morrill, Charles 1938, 39, 40
Morris, Robert 1944
Morrison, Robert 1932
Mort, C. E. 1894, 95, 96
Mortensen, Jesse 1928, 29
Morton, A. O. 1895
Moser, James 1925, 26, 27
Moses, Don 1927, 28, 29
Mosley, Corlis 1915
Moton, David 1963, 64, 65
Mullins, Gerald B. 1969, 70
Munch, Arlo W. 1934
Murieta, Alfred John
  1886, 87, 88, 89
Murphy, George 1944, 46, 47, **48**
Murray, Philip 1915, 16
Murray, Thomas 1934
Musick, Billie 1941
Musick, Bob 1941, 42, 45
Musick, James 1929, 30, 31
Musick, John Elmore 1944, **45, 46**

—N—

Nason, Craig 1923
Naumu, Johnny 1946
Naumu, Sol 1950
Nave, Sam Doyle 1937, **38, 39**
Neidhardt, David 1929
Neighbors, Sid 1910
Nelsen, William K. 1960, **61, 62**
Newerf, Kenneth 1923
Newman, P. H. 1893, 94, 95
Newman, Wallace 1922, **23, 24**
Nicholson, J. 1905, 06
Nickoloff, Thomas 1951, 52, **53**
Nix, Jack 1948
Nix, Lloyd 1915, 16
Noble, Bill 1941, 42
Noor, Dennis 1936, 37
Nordstrom, Ron 1951
Norene, George 1930, 31
Norris, Neil 1930, 31, 32
Norton, Francis 1928
Norton, Miles A. 1936, 37
Nunis, Dick 1951, 52

—O—

Obbema, Joseph J. 1968
Obradovich, Jim 1973
O'Brovac, Nick 1950
Ochoa, Juan 1905
O'Dell, 1920
Oertley, Bernard 1915
Oertly, George 1917, 18
Oestreich, Newell 1946
Oliver, Ralph 1966, 67
O'Malley, John Patrick 1968
Orcutt, Gary R. 1969
Orsatti, Vic 1925, 26
Ortega, Anthony S. 1956, **57, 58**
Ossowski, Theodore L. 1943
Ostling, Gerald 1933, 34
Oudermeulen, Henry 1924, **25**
Owens, James 1931, **33**

—P—

Packard, David 1932
Packer, Holmes 1919
Packman, 1918
Page, Charles M. 1943
Page, Mike 1957
Page, Toby 1966, 67
Palmer, 1917
Palmer, Ford 1930, 31, 32, 33
Papadakis, John 1970, 71
Pappas, Nick 1935, 36, 37
Parker, Artimus 1971, 72, 73
Parsons, Charles 1903, 04
Parsons, Earle O. 1943
Patapoff, William 1943
Patrick, Douglas 1964, 65
Paulin, Harold 1908, 09, 10
Pavich, Frank R. 1952, 53, 54
Peake, Crawford 1925
Peccianti, Angelo 1936, 38
Pehar, John 1944
Pekarcik, Al 1972
Peoples, Robert 1938, 39, 40
Perrin, Jay 1947
Perry, 1918
Persinger, Gerald D. 1958
Peters, Volney 1948, 50
Peterson, Chuck 1948
Petrill, Larry N. 1965, 66
Petty, Dick W. 1952, 53
Peviani, Bob 1950, 51 52
Phelps, Athur 1923
Phillips, Charles 1972, 73
Phillips, Floyd 1938, 39, 40
Phillips, Victor 1925
Piersen, Mel 1947
Pinckert, Ernest 1929, 30, 31
Pitman, George 1894
Pivaroff, Ivan G. 1960, 61
Plaehn, Alfred 1930, 31, 32
Porter, Don C. 1892
Porter, John 1927, 28
Porter, Vincent 1942
Potter, Gary M. 1962
Poulsen, Alfred 1933
Powell, Edward 1972, 73
Powers, Jim 1947, 48, 49
Powers, W. Russell 1934
Pranevicius, John 1940, 41
Pratt, P. B. 1897
Premo, William 1895
Preston, Ron 1970
Propst, Cliff 1933, 34, 35
Prukop, Al B. 1958, 59, 60
Psaltis, David 1951, 52
Pucci, Edward H. 1951, 52, 53
Pultorak, Steven 1970
Purcell, James 1921, 22, 23
Pye, Ernest Lee 1962, 63, 64
Pythian, Hayden 1922, 23 24

—R—

Radovich, Bill A. 1935, 36, 37
Rae, Michael 1970, 71, 72
Ramey, Theron 1930
Randle, Kenny 1973
Rapp, Vivian 1914, 16
Ratliff, John R. 1961, 62, 63
Ray, Terrel Len 1968
Rayburn, Gordon 1924
Rea, John 1945, 46, 47
Reade, Lynn Del 1962
Reagan, Patrick A. 1956, 57
Reboin, Al 1932, 33, 34
Redding, William C. 1968, 69
Reece, Danny 1973
Reed, Dick 1945
Reed, Robert W. 1936, 37
Renison, William T. 1964
Rhames, Tim 1973
Rice, Carleton 1923
Richman, Denis A. 1964
Riddle, John 1922, 23, 24
Riddle, William Lee 1951, 52, 53

Ridings, Gene 1931, 32, 33
Rightmire, Harold 1918
Riley, Art 1973
Riley, Steve 1972, 73
Rimes, Robert 1902
Ritchey, Bert 1928, 30
Robertson, Ted 1973
Roberts, C. R. 1955, 56, 57
Roberts, Gene 1935
Robertson, Robert 1939, 40, 41
Robertson Wilbur 1949
Robinson, John 1919, 20, 21
Robinson, T. W. 1889, 92
Rodeen, Don 1934, 35
Rodriguez, Ray 1972, 73
Rogers, Don 1948
Rogers, Ed 1934
Rollinson, Bruce 1971
Romer, Marshall 1943, 44, 46
Roquet, Russel 1940
Rorison, James 1934, 35, 36
Rose, Mason, 1935
Rosenberg, Aaron 1931, 32, 33
Rosendahl, Robert A. 1956
Rosin, Benjamin L. 1959, 60, 61
Rossetto, John 1946
Rossovich, Timothy J. 1965, 66, 67
Roundy, Jay 1947, 48, 49
Rubke, Karl J. 1955, 56
Runyon, George O. 1902, 03, 04
Runyon, John 1902, 03, 04
Ruppert, Richard 1970
Rusehhaupt, Theodore 1908
Russell, Lyman H. 1936, 37
Russo, Sam 1923
Ryan, Michael 1970, 71, 72
Ryan, Richard 1927
Ryus, 1899

—S—

Saenz, Edwin M. 1943
Sagouspe, Larry Gene 1962, 63
Sahlberg, Ted 1925
Salata, Paul 1944, 46, 47
Salness, Ty Alwin 1964, 66, 67
Sampson, Ben 1950, 51, 52
Sampson, Vernon G. 1953, 54, 55
Samuels, James W. 1960
Sanbrano, Albert 1950, 51
Sanchez, Armando Raul 1962, 63
Sanders, Robert H. 1934, 35, 36
Sangster, William 1937, 38, 39
Sargent, Hugh 1941
Saunders, Russell 1927, 28, 29
Scarpace, Michael L. 1965, 66, 67
Schabre, Gus 1922
Schaube, Alvin 1926, 27, 28
Scheving, Albert 1925, 26, 27
Schindler, Ambrose 1936, 37, 39
Schmidt, Dennis G. 1962
Schmidt, Henry 1955
Schneider, Dean 1949, 51
Schute, Eugene 1905, 06, 07
Schutte, George 1946, 47, 48
Scott, Daniel Blaine 1966, 67, 68
Scott, Joe 1960
Scott, Walter 1923, 24, 25
Scott, Willard 1967, 68, 69
Sears, James H. 1950, 51, 52
Seitz, William 1928, 29
Seixas, John 1932, 33
Seixas, William 1942
Sellers, Leon 1951, 52, 53
Selph, Ewald 1909
Sentous, Frank 1918
Seymore, Joseph 1902, 03
Shannon, Kenneth 1932, 33
Shatutis, Bob 1973
Shaver, Gaius 1929, 30, 31
Shaw, Gerald 1967, 68, 69
Shaw, Jesse 1928, 29, 30
Shaw, Nathaniel 1964, 65, 66
Shea. Pat 1960, 61
Shell, Joe 1937, 38, 39

Sheppard, 1916
Sherman, Rodney Jarvis
  1964, 65, 66
Sherman, Thomas Bert 1931
Shields, Alan 1959, 60
Shindler, George 1921
Shuey, Edward 1935
Sigler, John 1916
Simpson, Edward 1915, 16, 19
Simpson, Orenthal James (O.J.)
  1967, 68
Sims, James 1972, 73
Single, Forrest 1910
Skiles, John 1970, 71
Skinner, J. 1907
Skvarna, Carl 1960, 61
Slatter, James 1937, 38, 39
Slough, Greg C. 1969, 70
Smedley, Ronald 1961, 62
Smith, Ben 1893
Smith, C. E. 1895
Smith, Charles 1889, 92
Smith, Ernest, 1930, 31, 32
Smith, George 1925
Smith, Harry E. 1937, 38, 39
Smith, Herbert 1917
Smith, J. R. 1892
Smith, James 1918, 19, 20, 21
Smith, James H. Sr.
  1918, 19, 20, 21
Smith, Jeff 1964, 65
Smith, Joe W. 1923, 24
Smith, Lawrence E. 1969, 70
Smith, Mike 1973
Smith, R. 1910
Smith, Robert 1934
Smith, Roy 1954
Smith, S. 1918
Smith, Sidney 1968, 69
Smith, Stanley 1932
Smutz, Huber 1923
Snow, James Carter 1966, 67, 68
Snyder, Ed N. 1937
Snyder, James 1947
Sogge, Steve 1967, 68
Sohn, Ben 1938, 39, 40
Solter, Andrew Ford 1923, 24
Sovers, Glenn 1950
Sparling, Raymond 1930, 31, 32
Spector, Irwin 1953, 54
Speer, 1916
Spraggins, Edward 1934
Sprott, C. W. 1914
Stall, Joseph 1946
Stanley, Ralph 1936, 37, 38
Stare, Jim 1904
Stark, Newton Calvin 1923, 24, 25
Stearn, 1919
Stephens, Barry 1929, 30, 31
Stephenson, Warren W. 1960, 61
Steponovich, Tony Andrew
  1927, 28, 29
Stevens, Lawrence 1931, 32, 33
Stevenson, Edward 1936
Stever, Bill 1924
Stewart, George 1973
Stewart, Melvin 1919
Stillwell, Bob 1947, 48, 49
Stillwell, Don 1950, 51, 52
Stirling, Robert 1970, 71
Stoecker, Howard 1937, 38, 39
Stonebraker, John S. 1938, 39
Stookey, Bryon 1906, 07, 09, 10
Stuart, 1916
Stuart, Melvin 1919
Summer, 1918
Sutherland, James 1934, 35, 36
Svihus, Robert C. 1962, 63, 64
Swann, Lynn 1971, 72, 73
Swanson, Robert S. 1967
Swirles, Frank 1939
Swope, Jess, 1949

—T—

Tancredy, Tom 1949, 50
Tannehill, Ted 1944, 45, 46
Tappaan, Francis 1927, 28, 29
Tatsch, Herbert 1931, 33, 34
Taylor, A. 1917
Taylor, Arthur 1914
Taylor, Brice 1924, 25, 26
Taylor, Michael R. 1966, 67
Taylor, Paul 1941
Templeton, George 1927, 28, 29
Terry, Tony 1969
Teschke, Fred 1911, 12, 13
Theier, Jack 1958, 59, 60
Thiede, Cliff 1929
Thomas, Alonzo 1971
Thomas, Fay 1923, 24
Thomas, John M. 1963, 64, 65
Thomas, Lloyd 1926, 27, 28
Thomas, Max 1926, 27
Thomas, Ronald D. 1940, 41, 42
Thomassin, John 1937, 38, 39
Thompson, A. P. 1893, 94, 95, 97
Thompson, Ed 1904
Thompson, Field 1924, 25, 26
Thompson, Kenneth Frank
  1951, 52, 53
Thompson, P. J. 1892
Thompson, Roderick 1930, 31
Thompson, S. 1923
Thurlow, Leavitt 1934, 35, 36
Thurlow, Leavitt Lee 1962
Tiernan, Phillip 1920, 21, 22
Timberlake, George R. 1952, 53
Timmons, Curt 1971
Tipton, Howard 1930, 31, 32
Tobin, Harold E. 1960, 61
Tolman, Ernie 1947
Tonelli, Amerigo 1936, 37, 38
Toolen, Andy 1919, 20, 21
Townsend, Ken 1918, 19, 20
Trayham, Jerry 1958, 59, 60
Truher, James 1928, 29
Tsagalakis, Sam 1952, 53, 54
Tucker, Sam 1893
Tufs, Ray 1904
Typton, Cyril 1919

—U—

Upton, Gary R. 1965

—V—

Van Doren, Robert 1950, 51, **52**
Van Vliet, George 1958, 59, **60**
Vasicek, Vic 1945
Vella, Chris 1971, 72
Vella, John 1969, 70, 71
Vellone, James C. 1964, 65
Verry, D. Norman 1941, 42, 43
Viltz, Theophile A. 1964, 65
Von Mohr, Frank 1921
Voyne, Don 1957, 58

—W—

Waddell, Don 1945
Walker, James S. 1964, 65
Walker, Tommy 1947
Wall, Fred Willard 1944
Wallace, Carl
  1897, 98, 99, 1900, 01
Wallace, Kenneth 1907, 08, 09, 10
Walton, 1917
Warburton, Irving 1932, 33, 34
Ward, John 1927, 28, 29
Washington, Dave E. 1960
Washmera, Ray 1971, 72, 73
Wayahn, Elmer 1918, 22, 23
Weaver, Charles E. 1969, 70
Webb, James 1932, 33, 34
Webb, John 1904
Weber, Scott 1971
Weber, Tom 1952, 53

Weddle, L. V. 1924
Weeks, Charles I. 1951, 52
Wehba, Ray 1936, 37, **38**
Weiss, Benjamin 1916, 17
Welch, Harry 1951, 52
Wells, Harry L. III 1964
Welsh, Louis 1950, 51, 52
Werner, P. 1915
West, Patrick 1944
Westcott, Clem 1925
Westcott, Jack 1925
Westover, Charles 1905
Westphal, Richard Lee 1954
Wheatley, Pop 1902, 03
Wheeler, Harold 1926
Whitcomb, Ed 1919
White, Jack 1904
White, Kenneth 1921
White, O. 1926
Whitehead, Duane
   1943, 44, 45, 46
Whitlaw, Ben 1892
Whittier, Julian 1929
Wilbur, Robert 1934
Wilcox, Paul 1919
Wilcox, Ralph O. 1928, 29, 30
Wilcox, Thomas 1927, 28, 29
Wilensky, Joe 1934, 35, 36
Wilke, 1916
Wilkins, John A. 1959, 60
Willer, Don 1940, 41, 42
Willhoite, Elmer E. 1951, 52
Williams, Britt 1959, 60, 61
Williams, Carl A. 1897
Williams, Charles A. 1935, **36**, **37**
Williams, Don 1926, 27, **28**
Williams, Hal 1941
Williams, Homer M. 1964
Williams, John 1949, 50, 51
Williamson, Don 1945
Williamson, Frank 1931, **32**, **33**
Williamson, Jack 1932, 33, 34
Williamson, Stanley 1929, **30**, **31**
Willingham, Charles R. 1929
Willis, Jack 1957
Willott, D. Laird 1954, 55, 56
Wilson, Ben I. 1961, 62
Wilson, Charles 1902, 03
Wilson, W. 1916
Winfield, John Irving 1928, **29**, **30**
Winans, Jeff 1972
Wing, Paul 1934, 35
Winslow, Robert E. 1937, **38**, **39**
Winslow, Troy Duane 1965, **66**
Wirching, Carl 1909
Wolf, Joe 1942
Wood, Richard 1972, 73
Wood, Willie 1957, **58**, **59**
Woods, John 1920
Woods, Ray 1940, 41, 42
Woodward, James L.
   1918, 19, 20, 21
Woolen, 1907
Work, Telford 1916
Worsley, Harry 1924, 25
Wotkyns, Haskell Robert
   1932, 33, 34
Wright, Foster C. 1895, 96, 97

—Y—

Yary, Anthony Ronald 1965, 66, 67
Yary, Wayne, R. 1969, 70
Yocum, Sam 1925, 26
Youel, Curtis 1931, 32, 33
Young, Charles 1970, 71, **72**
Young, J. E. 1889, 92
Young, John A. 1968, 69
Young, Matthew (Adrian)
   1965, 66, 67
Youngworth, Pat 1889

—Z—

Zachik, Don 1959, 60
Zampese, Ernest 1955, 56
Ziegler, John 1916
Zimmerman, Daniel 1949, 51